THE AMERICANS
The Colonial Experience

Daniel J. Boorstin has been senior historian of the Smithsonian Institution, Washington, D.C., director of the National Museum of History and Technology and Preston and Sterling Mortin Distinguished Service Professor of American History at the University of Chicago where he taught for twenty-five years. He has won many prestigious prizes for his work, including the Pulitzer Prize in 1974 for *The Democratic Experience*. He was also the Librarian of Congress from 1975 to 1987, during which period public use of the library more than doubled.

Dr Boorstin has spent a good deal of his life viewing America from the outside, first in England where he was a Rhodes scholar at Balliol College, Oxford, winning a coveted 'double-first'. More recently he has been visiting professor of American History at the University of Rome and at Kyoto University, consultant to the Social Science Research Center at the University of Puerto Rico, the first incumbent of the chair of American History at the Sorbonne, and Pitt Professor of American History and Institutions and a Fellow of Trinity College, Cambridge University, which awarded him its Litt.D. degree.

Also by Daniel J. Boorstin

Companion volumes in THE AMERICANS trilogy
The National Experience (Phoenix Press)
The Democratic Experience (Phoenix Press)

Other Works
The Creators (Phoenix Press)
The Discoverers (Phoenix Press)
The Seekers (Phoenix Press)

The Mysterious Science of the Law
The Lost World of Thomas Jefferson
The Genius of American Politics
America and the Image of Europe
The Image: A Guide to Pseudo-Events in America
The Decline of Radicalism
The Sociology of the Absurd
Democracy and its Discontents
The Republic of Technology
The Exploring Spirit
The Republic of Letters
Hidden History
The Chicago History of American Civilization (Ed.; 27 volumes)
An American Primer (Ed)
American Civilization (Ed)

Praise for *The Colonial Experience*

"This is an ambitious book, well-documented throughout, with many stimulating ideas . . . Mr Boorstin is searching for the grandiose motives, probing the words and actions of the colonists for contemporary meaning." Herbert Mitgang, *New York Times*

"Mr Boorstin's focus in this impressive essay in intellectual history is the interplay between ideas and institution. Using this as his perspective, he offers a fresh and arresting reading of the colonial mind." A. Schlesinger, Jr.

"Boorstin's point of view is provocative and controversial. But no one can deny that *The Americans* is a major work, an original contribution in a field which in the last 60 years has abounded in great research and scholarship, a book equally stimulating for the historian and for the general reader." Hans Kohn, *The New Leader*

"A superb panorama of life in America from the first settlements on through the white-hot days of the Revolution . . . an amazingly stimulating and brilliant study of America's past in which its present may be recognized and its future envisioned." Bruce Lancaster, *Saturday Review*

"An important work that is going to be read and talked about for a long time to come" *New York Times*

THE AMERICANS
The Colonial Experience

Daniel J. Boorstin

'It may be said, That in a Sort,
they began the World a New.'
JARED ELIOT

PHOENIX
PRESS

5 UPPER SAINT MARTIN'S LANE
LONDON
WC2H 9EA

For Ruth

A PHOENIX PRESS PAPERBACK

This paperback edition published in 2000
by Phoenix Press,
a division of The Orion Publishing Group Ltd,
Orion House, 5 Upper St Martin's Lane,
London WC2H 9EA

© Copyright, 1958, by Daniel J. Boorstin

A CIP catalogue record for this book
is available from the British Library.

Printed in Great Britain by
Clays Ltd, St Ives plc

ISBN 1 84212 073 5

AN UNKNOWN COAST

*Governor William Bradford, an eyewitness, reported the landing of
the* Mayflower *passengers on the American shore in mid-November 1620:*

"They fell upon their knees and blessed the God of heaven, who had
brought them over the vast and furious ocean, and delivered them from
all the periles and miseries thereof, againe to set their feete on the firme
and stable earth, their proper elemente. . . . Being thus passed the vast
ocean, and a sea of troubles . . . they had now no freinds to wellcome
them, nor inns to entertaine or refresh their weatherbeaten bodys, no
houses or much less townes to repaire too, to seeke for succoure. It is
recorded in scripture as a mercie to the apostle and his shipwraked company, that the barbarians shewed them no smale kindnes in refreshing
them, but these savage barbarians, when they mette with them . . . were
readier to fill their sids full of arrows then otherwise. And for the season
it was winter, and they that know the winters of that cuntrie know them
to be sharp and violent, and subjecte to cruell and feirce stormes,
deangerous to travill to known places, much more to serch an unknown
coast. Besids, what could they see but a hidious and desolate wildernes,
full of wild beasts and willd men? and what multituds ther might be of
them they knew not. Nether could they, as it were, goe up to the tope of
Pisgah, to vew from this willdernes a more goodly cuntrie to feed their
hops; for which way soever they turnd their eys (save upward to the
heavens) they could have litle solace or content in respecte of any outward objects. For summer being done, all things stand upon them with a
wetherbeaten face; and the whole countrie, full of woods and thickets,
represented a wild and savage heiw. If they looked behind them, ther was
the mighty ocean which they had passed, and was now as a maine barr
and goulfe to seperate them from all the civill parts of the world."

*   *   *

*Never had a Promised Land looked more unpromising. But within a
century and a half—even before the American Revolution—this for-
bidding scene had become one of the more "civill" parts of the world.
The large outlines of a new civilization had been drawn. How did it
happen?*

CONTENTS

BOOK ONE

THE VISION AND
THE REALITY

"England purchased for some of her subjects,
who found themselves uneasy at home, a great
estate in a distant country."

ADAM SMITH

AMERICA began as a sobering experience. The colonies were
a disproving ground for utopias. In the following chapters we will
illustrate how dreams made in Europe—the dreams of the zionist,
the perfectionist, the philanthropist, and the transplanter—were
dissipated or transformed by the American reality. A new civilization was being born less out of plans and purposes than out of the
unsettlement which the New World brought to the ways of the Old.

PART ONE

A CITY UPON A HILL

The Puritans of Massachusetts Bay

> "I write the Wonders of the Christian Religion, flying from the depravations of Europe, to the American Strand; and . . . wherewith His Divine Providence hath irradiated an Indian Wilderness."
>
> COTTON MATHER

THE *Arbella,* a ship of three hundred and fifty tons, twenty-eight guns, and a crew of fifty-two, during the spring of 1630 was carrying westward across the Atlantic the future leaders of Massachusetts Bay Colony. The ship had sailed from Cowes in the Isle of Wight, on March 29, and was not to reach America till late June. Among the several ways of passing the time, of cementing the community and of propitiating God, perhaps the most popular was the sermon. The leader of the new community, John Winthrop, while preaching to his fellow-passengers, struck the keynote of American history. "Wee shall be," Winthrop prophesied, "as a Citty upon a Hill, the eies of all people are uppon us; soe that if wee shall deale falsely with our god in this worke wee have undertaken and soe cause him to withdrawe his present help from us, wee shall be made a story and a by-word through the world." No one writing after the fact, three

3

hundred years later, could better have expressed the American sense of destiny. In describing the Puritan experience we will see how this sense of destiny came into being, and what prevented it from becoming fanatical or utopian.

The Puritan beacon for misguided mankind was to be neither a book nor a theory. It was to be the community itself. America had something to teach all men: not by precept but by example, not by what it said but by how it lived. The slightly rude question "What of it?" was thus, from the earliest years, connected with belief in an American destiny.

1

How Orthodoxy Made the
Puritans Practical

NEVER WAS A PEOPLE more sure that it was on the right track. "That which is our greatest comfort, and meanes of defence above all others," Francis Higginson wrote in the earliest days, in *New-Englands Plantation*, "is, that we have here the true Religion and holy Ordinances of Almightie God taught amongst us . . . thus we doubt not but God will be with us, and if God be with us, who can be against us?"

But their orthodoxy had a peculiar character. Compared with Americans of the 18th or the 19th century, the Puritans surely were theology-minded. The doctrines of the Fall of Man, of Sin, of Salvation, Predestination, Election, and Conversion were their meat and drink. Yet what really distinguished them in their day was that they were less interested in theology itself, than in the application of theology to everyday life, and especially to society. From the 17th-century point of view their interest in theology was practical. They were less concerned with perfecting their formulation of the Truth than with making their society in America embody the Truth they already knew. Puritan New England was a noble experiment in applied theology.

The Puritans in the Wilderness—away from Old World centers of learning, far from great university libraries, threatened daily by the thousand and one hardships and perils of a savage America—were poorly situated for elaborating a theology and disputing its fine points. For such an enterprise John Calvin in Switzerland or William Ames in Holland was much better located. But for testing a theology, for seeing whether Zion could be rebuilt if men abandoned the false foundations of the centuries since Jesus—for this New England offered a rare opportunity.

So it was that although the Puritans in the New World made the Calvinist theology their point of departure, they made it precisely that and nothing else. From it they departed at once into the practical life. Down to the middle of the 18th century, there was hardly an important work of speculative theology produced in New England.

It was not that the writing of books was impossible in the New World. Rather, it was that theological speculation was not what interested the new Americans. Instead, there came from the New England presses and from the pens of New England authors who sent their works to England an abundance of sermons, textual commentaries, collections of "providences," statutes, and remarkable works of history. With the possible exception of Roger Williams, who was out of the stream of New England orthodoxy anyway, Massachusetts Bay did not produce a major figure in theology until the days of Jonathan Edwards in the mid-18th century. And by then Puritanism was all but dead.

During the great days of New England Puritanism there was not a single important dispute which was primarily theological. There were, to be sure, crises over who should rule New England, whether John Winthrop or Thomas Dudley or Harry Vane should be governor, whether the power or representation of different classes in the community should be changed, whether the Child Petition should be accepted, whether penalties for crime should be fixed by statute, whether the assistants should have a veto, whether outlying towns should have more representatives in the General Court. Even the disputes with Anne Hutchinson and Roger Williams primarily concerned the qualifications, power, and prestige of the rulers. If, indeed, the Puritans were theology-minded, what they argued about was institutions.

One gets the same impression in looking for evidences of political speculation, for philosophical inquiry into the nature of community and the function of government. Nothing in Puritanism itself was uncongenial to such speculation; Puritans in England at the time were discussing the fine points of their theory: What was the true nature of liberty? When should a true Puritan resist a corrupt civil government? When should diversity be tolerated? And we need not look only to giants like John Milton. The debates among the officers in Cromwell's Puritan Army between 1647 and 1649 reveal how different their intellectual atmosphere was from that of New England. They were not professional intellectuals, but soldiers and men of action; yet even they stopped to argue the theory of revolution and the philosophy of sovereignty.

In England, of course, "Puritanism" was much more complex than it was in Massachusetts Bay Colony. It included representatives of a wide range of doctrines, from presbyterians, independents, and separatists, through levelers and millenarians. Which of these was at the center of English Puritanism was itself a matter of dispute. Within the English Puritan ranks, therefore, there was much lively debate. It was not only criticism from fellow-Puritans that Cromwell and his men had to face. They well knew that any community they built in England would have to find some place for the dozens of sects—from Quakers through Papists —who had made England their home. English Puritan literature in the 17th century sparkled with polemics.

Seventeenth-century America had none of the speculative vigor of English Puritanism. For Massachusetts Bay possessed an orthodoxy. During the classic age of the first generation, at least, it was a community of self-selected conformists. In 1637 the General Court passed an order prohibiting anyone from settling within the colony without first having his orthodoxy approved by the magistrates. Perhaps never again, until the McCarran Act, were our immigrants required to be so aseptic. John Winthrop was bold and clear in defense of the order. Here was a community formed by free consent of its members. Why should they not exclude dangerous men, or men with dangerous thoughts? What right had supporters of a subversive Mr. Wheelwright to claim entrance to the colony? "If we conceive and finde by sadd experience that his opinions are such, as by his own profession cannot stand with externall peace, may we not provide for our peace, by keeping off such as would strengthen him and infect others with such dangerous tenets?"

In the eyes of Puritans this was the peculiar opportunity of New England. Why not for once see what true orthodoxy could accomplish? Why not in one unspoiled corner of the world declare a truce on doubts, on theological bickering? Here at last men could devote their full energy to *applying* Christianity—not to clarifying doctrine but to building Zion. Nathaniel Ward was speaking for Puritan New England when, in his *Simple Cobler of Aggawam* (1647) he declared, "I dare take upon me, to be the Herauld of New-England so farre, as to proclaime to the world, in the name of our Colony, that all Familists, Antinomians, Anabaptists, and other Enthusiasts, shall have free Liberty to keep away from us, and such as will come to be gone as fast as they can, the sooner the better."

The Puritans in New England were surprisingly successful for some years at keeping their community orthodox. In doing so, they also made it sterile of speculative thought. Their principal theological treatises were works by William Ames (who never saw New England) and John Norton's *Orthodox Evangelist,* a rudimentary summary of the works of English divines. In England the presbyterians and independents and levelers within Puritanism were daring each other to extend and clarify their doctrines; but we see little of this in America.

A dissension which in England would have created a new sect within Puritanism, simply produced another colony in New England. The boundless physical space, the surrounding wilderness deprived the New England ministry of the need to develop within its own theology that spaciousness, that room for variation, which came to characterize Puritanism in England. When Anne Hutchinson and her followers caused trouble by their heterodox views and unauthorized evening meetings, she was tried and "excommunicated." The result, as described by Winthrop, was that in March 1638, "she . . . went by land to Providence, and so to the island in the Naragansett Bay, which her husband and the rest of that sect had purchased of the Indians, and prepared with all speed to remove unto." The dissidence of Roger Williams—the only movement within Massachusetts Bay in the 17th century which promised a solid enrichment of theory—led to his banishment in October, 1635. It was only after Williams' return to England and his developing friendship with John Milton that he wrote his controversial books.

In New England the critics, doubters, and dissenters were expelled from the community; in England the Puritans had to find ways of living with them. It was in England, therefore, that a modern theory of toleration began to develop. Milton and his less famous and less reflective contemporaries were willing to debate, as if it were an open question, "whether the magistrate have, or ought to have, any compulsive and restrictive power in matters of religion." Such was the current of European liberal thought in which Roger Williams found himself. But Williams was banished from Massachusetts Bay Colony and became a by-word of heterodoxy and rebellion. He died in poverty, an outcast from that colony. If his little Providence eventually prospered, it was never to be more than a satellite of the powerful orthodox mother-colony.

What actually distinguished that mother-colony in the great age of New England Puritanism was its refusal, for reasons of its own, to develop a theory of toleration. In mid-17th century England we note a growing fear that attempts to suppress error would inevitably suppress truth, a fear that magistrates' power over religion might give them tyranny over conscience. "I know there is but one truth," wrote the author of one of the many English pamphlets on liberty of conscience in 1645, "But this truth cannot be so easily brought forth without this liberty; and a general restraint, though intended but for errors, yet through the unskilfulness of men, may fall upon the truth. And better many errors of some kind suffered than one useful truth be obstructed or destroyed." In contrast, the impregnable view of New England Puritanism was expressed in the words of John Cotton:

> The Apostle directeth, Tit. 3.10 and giveth the Reason, that in funda-mentall and principall points of Doctrine or Worship, the Word of God in such things is so cleare, that hee cannot but bee convinced in Con-science of the dangerous Errour of his way, after once or twice Ad-monition, wisely and faithfully dispensed. And then if any one persist, it is not out of Conscience, but against his Conscience, as the Apostle saith, vers. 11. He is subverted and sinneth, being condemned of Him-selfe, that is, of his owne Conscience. So that if such a Man after such Admonition shall still persist in the Errour of his way, and be there-fore punished; He is not persecuted for Cause of Conscience, but for sinning against his Owne Conscience.

The leaders of Massachusetts Bay Colony enjoyed the luxury, no longer feasible in 17th century England, of a pure and simple orthodoxy.

The failure of New England Puritans to develop a theory of toleration, or even freely to examine the question, was not in all ways a weakness. It made their literature less rich and gave much of their writing a quaint and crabbed sound, but for a time at least, it was a source of strength. Theirs was not a philosophic enterprise; they were, first and foremost, community-builders. The energies which their English contemporaries gave to sharpening the distinctions between "compulsive" and "restric-tive" powers in religion, between "matters essential" and "matters in-different" and to a host of other questions which have never ceased to bother reflective students of political theory, the American Puritans were giving to marking off the boundaries of their new towns, to enforcing their criminal laws, and to fighting the Indian menace. Their very ortho-doxy strengthened their practical bent.

American Puritans were hardly more distracted from their practical tasks by theology and metaphysics than we are today. They transcended theological preoccupation precisely because they had no doubts and allowed no dissent. Had they spent as much of their energy in debating with each other as did their English contemporaries, they might have lacked the singlemindedness needed to overcome the dark, unpredictable perils of a wilderness. They might have merited praise as precursors of modern liberalism, but they might never have helped found a nation.

2

The Sermon as an
American Institution

THE PRACTICAL TEMPER, strengthened by New England orthodoxy and the opportunities of the New World, was not evidenced merely in the absence of theoretical treatises and abstract disputation. The New England sermon gave it vivid expression. During the first decades of settlement, the New England mind found its perfect medium and achieved its spectacular success in the sermon. This success would have been impossible without a firm orthodoxy and a practical emphasis. The Puritans of Massachusetts Bay thus foreshadowed the circumstances which, throughout American history, were to give peculiar prominence to the spoken, as contrasted with the printed, word.

The scarcity of monumental volumes on theoretical questions and the flood of spoken words have been complementary facts about American culture from the very beginning. The public speech, whether sermon, commencement address, or whistle-stop campaign talk is a public affirmation that the listeners share a common discourse and a common body of values. The spoken word is inevitably more topical than the printed word: it attempts to explain the connection between the shared community values and the predicament of man at a particular time and place. It is directed to people whom the speaker confronts, and to their current problems.

In the doctrine of all protestantism there were, of course, special reasons for the importance of preaching. If priestly intermediaries between each soul and God were to be dispensed with, the message of the Gospel had to be brought home to each man. And what better means than the spoken word, in which an eloquent and learned man established the relation of the Word of God to the condition of those before him? Moreover, the 17th century was the great age of English sermons—and not only among Puritans. It was the age of John Donne and Jeremy Taylor, high Anglicans whose preachments were classics of the sermon form. By the mid-17th century, English Puritans had developed so distinctive a style of prose for their sermons that an attentive listener could discover the theology of a minister from the form of his preaching.

In contrast to the involved "metaphysical" style of Lancelot Andrewes and John Donne, the Puritans developed a manner which came to be known, in their own words, as the "plain" style. The rules of this style were codified into preachers' manuals like William Perkins' *Art of Prophecying,* an English handbook found on nearly every book-list in early New England. The mark of the plain style was, of course, plainness. But it was also marked by greater attention to persuasion and the practical consequences of a doctrine than to the elaboration of the theory itself. The Puritan sermon, as Perry Miller explains, was "more like a lawyer's brief than a work of art." Its characteristic plan had three parts: "doctrines," "reasons," and "uses." The "doctrine" was what the preacher discovered by "opening" a Biblical text, which was always the starting point; the "reasons" supported the doctrine; and the "uses" were the application of the doctrine to the lives of the listeners—the "instruction" which came out of the sermon.

Sermons in the plain style were in every way the opposite of highfalutin. "Swelling words of humane wisedome," John Cotton said in 1642, "make mens preaching seeme to Christ (as it were) a blubber-lipt Ministry." That was not the way of Christ, who, rather than give men "a kind of intimation, afar off," had actually spoken "their own in English as we say. . . . He lets fly poynt blanck." The Puritan minister should not quote in foreign languages: "So much Latine is so much flesh in a Sermon."

While the metaphysical preacher depended for effect on intricate literary conceits, the Puritan minister used homely examples. "Gods Altar needs not our pollishings," declared the preface to the Bay Psalm Book (1640), the first book printed in the American colonies. Thus, Thomas Hooker compared the resurrected body to "a great Onyon." Like an onion hung up on the wall, the resurrected body grows "not because any thing is added, but because it spreads itself further; so then there shall be no new body, but the same substance enlarged and increased."

These qualities of the plain style were, as we know, general characteristics of Puritan writing and thinking on both sides of the Atlantic. The Americans had learned their rules from such English textbooks as Perkins, but there were additional reasons for such a style in the New World. As Hooker explained at the beginning of his *Survey of the Summe of Church-Discipline* (1648):

> That the discourse comes forth in such a homely dresse and course
> habit, the Reader must be desired to consider, It comes out of the

wildernesse, where curiosity is not studied. Planters if they can provide cloth to go warm, they leave the cutts and lace to those that study to go fine. . . . plainesse and perspicuity, both for matter and manner of expression, are the things, that I have conscientiously indeavoured in the whole debate: for I have ever thought writings that come abroad, they are not to dazle, but direct the apprehension of the meanest, and I have accounted it the chiefest part of Iudicious learning, to make a hard point easy and familiar in explication.

The simplicity of life in the wilderness, the homogeneity and smallness of the community, and the strength of orthodoxy in the early years, all made the plain style still more plain and virile in America.

In New England, the sermon was far more than a literary form. It was an institution, perhaps the characteristic institution of Puritanism here. It was the ritual application of theology to community-building and to the tasks and trials of everyday life. It was not, as it was inevitably in England, a mere sectarian utterance of a part of the community. It was actually the orthodox manifesto and self-criticism of the community as a whole, a kind of reiterated declaration of independence, a continual re-discovery of purposes.

The pulpit, and not the altar, held the place of honor in the New England meeting-house. So too the sermon itself, the specific application of the Word of God, was the focus of the best minds of New England. What most encouraged Higginson to believe his colony might become an example of the true religion was not the simple rectitude of Puritan doctrine, but "that we have here the true Religion and holy Ordinances of Almightie God taught amongst us: Thankes be to God, we have plentie of Preaching, and diligent Cathechizing."

In England, after the collapse of the Puritan political program in 1660, individual Puritans were thrown back upon themselves. They became introspective: each Puritan sought, as in *Grace Abounding*, to perfect himself, with scant regard to the community. In America, where the Puritans were remote from English domestic politics, they remained free to continue their social enterprise. The history of the New England pulpit is thus an unbroken chronicle of the attempt of leaders in the New World to bring their community steadily closer to the Christian model.

The New England meeting-house, like the synagogue on which it was consciously modeled, was primarily a place of instruction. Here the community learned its duties. Here men found their separate paths to conversion, so they could better build their Zion in the wilderness, a City upon a Hill to which other men might in their turn look for instruction. As the meeting-house was the geographical and social center of the New England town, so the sermon was the central event in the meeting-house.

The sermon was as important a ritual as the occasions on which ancient Mesopotamians learned from their priests the dooms passed in the legislature of their Gods. In New England the ministers were, in their own words, "opening" the texts of the Bible by which they had to live and build their society. The sermons were thoroughly theological and yet thoroughly practical: based on common acceptance of a theology, which left to the minister only the discovery of its "uses" for converting saints and building Zion.

The occasions of the sermon, most of which have been too easily forgotten, bear witness to its central place in the life of early New England. There were two sermons on the Sabbath, and usually a lecture-sermon on Thursday. Attendance was required by law; absence was punishable by fine (an Act of 1646 fixed five shillings for each offense). The laws described the Sabbath-ritual as "the publick ministry of the Word." There was hardly a public event of which the most memorable feature was not the sermon. Most distinctive, perhaps, were the election-day sermons, by which the clergy affected the course of political events and which remained a New England institution through the American Revolution. These explained the meaning of the orthodox theology for the choices before the voters, described the character of a good ruler and the mutual duties of the people and their governors. The artillery sermons, which were delivered on the occasion of the muster of the militia and their election of officers, began in about 1659. In addition, the numerous (19 in Massachusetts Bay in 1639; 50 in 1675-76) Fast and Thanksgiving Days were focused on the sermon, which explained to the people why God was humbling or rewarding them.

Even when the occasion for a sermon was an English tradition, it acquired new significance as a community ritual in New England. The practice of preaching to a condemned man before the gallows, an old English custom, took on new meaning in New England, because of the smallness of the community and the strength of orthodoxy. Even the condemned man himself participated actively.

We have an eye-witness account of what happened before the execution of the murderer James Morgan at Boston in 1686. "Morgan, whose Execution being appointed on the 11th of March, there was that Care taken for his Soul that three Excellent Sermons were preached before him, before his Execution; Two on the Lord's Day, and one just before his Execution." The two Sabbath sermons, each a full hour in length, were by Cotton Mather and Joshua Moody; the sermon at the gallows by Increase Mather. So large an audience gathered to hear Joshua Moody that when they assembled in the New Church of Boston the gallery cracked, and the people were obliged to move to another hall. All the sermons were passionate and eloquent, calling on the criminal to repent while there was yet time and begging the congregation (that is, the whole community) to profit by this example. In the final conversation between Morgan and the minister who walked beside him to the gallows, Morgan answered, "I hope I am sorry for all my sins, but I must especially bewail my neglect of the means of grace. On Sabbath days I us'd to lie at home, or be ill employ'd elsewhere, when I should have been at church. This has undone me!"

Standing before the ladder of the gallows, and looking at the coffin which he was soon to fill, Morgan sought to play his part in the ritual. He seized his last opportunity to give the sermon which only he could give. It was taken down by one of the listeners:

> I pray God that I may be a warning to you all, and that I may be the last that ever shall suffer after this manner. . . . I beg of God, as I am a dying man, and to appear before the Lord within a few minutes, that you take notice of what I say to you. Have a care of drunkenness, and ill company, and mind all good instruction; and don't turn your back upon the word of God, as I have done. When I have been at meeting, I have gone out of the meeting-house to commit sin, and to please the lusts of my flesh. . . . O, that I may make improvement of this little, little time, before I go hence and be no more! O, let all mind what I am saying, now I am going out of this world! O, take warning by me, and beg of God to keep you from this sin, which has been my ruine!

Such a sermon by a condemned man was by no means unique. Cotton Mather filled twenty closely-printed pages of his *Magnalia* with "An History of some Criminals Executed in New-England for Capital Crimes; with some of their dying speeches."

For New England Puritans, the sermon had, of course, additional drawing-power because of the scarcity of other amusements. It offered an occasion to meet distant neighbors, to exchange news and gossip. Without the sermon, the early New Englander would have had few occasions of public drama. He had no newspapers, no theater, no movies, no radio, no television. The lack of these gave the minister a special opportunity to make his preaching fill the attention of his listeners. But the hardships were many. For some years the New England meeting-house had no artificial light and no heat. In the cold autumns and winters, the walls were icy, winds howled, and drafts blew through cracks in the loose clapboard walls. The hands of the earnest listeners were sometimes so numb with cold that they could not take notes. It took decades for the warm but dangerous foot-stove to appear and until the early 19th century there were no open fireplaces. The benches were hard. When pews were finally built (at the private expense of the occupants) they enabled younger listeners to conceal their inattention, or to whisper through the ornamented panels which separated them from neighbors, their frosty breath giving an incriminating clue. To reach these inhospitable meeting-houses, the early New Englander often had to pick his way, sometimes for miles, across landscape without anything that could be dignified as a road. In winter he went plunging through drifts; in the spring and fall he was deep in mud. And for several decades the perils of Indians were added to all the others. All this only underlines the importance of the sermon and the meeting-house in the life of the New England Puritan.

If attendance at the sermon was compulsory, it was expected to be anything but perfunctory. The scarcity of books and the significance of the subject induced many listeners to bring notebooks. A minister, commonly settled in a parish for his lifetime, did not look for a larger or more wealthy congregation. Moreover, his audience was, for that age, remarkably literate and attentive, and he could not hope to amuse or divert them by "book reviews," by concert artists, or outside speakers. All these circumstances served to hold the early New England preacher to a high intellectual standard and encouraged him to make his performances merit their central place.

The New England sermon, then, was the communal ceremony which brought a strong orthodoxy to bear on the minutiae of life—the drowning of a boy while skating on the Charles, an earthquake, a plague of locusts, the arrival of a ship, the election of a magistrate, or the mustering of militia. Theology was an instrument for building Zion in America.

3

Search for a
New England Way

To the Puritans and to many who came here after them, the American destiny was inseparable from the mission of community-building. For hardly a moment in the history of this civilization would men turn from the perfection of their institutions to the improvement of their doctrine. Like many later generations of Americans, the Puritans were more interested in institutions that functioned than in generalities that glittered.

The phrase "The New England Way" was an earlier version, (not entirely different in spirit though vastly different in content) of the modern notion of an American Way of Life. What the Puritans wanted to "purify" in the English church was not its theology but its policy, not its theory but its practice. New Englanders were outspokenly conformist in matters of doctrine. "Be it so that we are in the utmost parts of the Earth;" explained John Norton, "we have onely changed our Climate, not our mindes." Again and again when the leaders of American Puritanism met, they proclaimed their orthodoxy.

This was revealed in the very form of their statements. The basic documents of New England Puritanism were not "creeds" but "platforms." Nearly two centuries before the first American political party produced its "platform" attesting to its greater concern for a program of action than for a frame of thinking, American Puritans had struck off in the same direction. The clearest statement of their religious purposes came out of a meeting of the church elders in Cambridge in 1648. Published under the title, "A Platform of Church Discipline," it came to be known as "The Cambridge Platform." The ministers declared:

> Our Churches here, as (by the grace of Christ) wee beleive & profess the same Doctrine of the trueth of the Gospell, which generally is received in all the reformed Churches of Christ in Europe: so especially, wee desire not to vary from the doctrine of faith, & truth held forth by the churches of our native country. . . . wee, who are by nature, English men, doe desire to hold forth the same doctrine of religion (especially in fundamentalls) which wee see & know to be held by the churches of England, according to the truth of the Gospell.

What disturbed the people of New England, according to John Cotton's preface, was "the unkind, & unbrotherly, & unchristian contentions of our godly brethren, & countrymen, in matters of church-government." To the improvement of church government, the New England clergy pledged its efforts. The text of the "platform," the manifesto of New England congregationalism and its basis for over a half-century, was devoted only to these practical ends.

The orthodoxy of New England churches is a refrain heard again and again in the early synods. "As to matters of Doctrine," the ministers declared in Boston in 1680, "we agree with other Reformed Churches: Nor was it that, but what concerns Worship and Discipline, that caused our Fathers to come into this wilderness, whiles it was a land not sown, that so they might have liberty to practice accordingly." A half-century later, in 1726, Cotton Mather insisted that still the doctrine of the Church of England was more universally held and preached in New England than in *any* nation, that their only "points peculiar" were those of discipline.

The Puritans' emphasis on way of life was so strong that it made any generalized concept of "the church" seem unreal or even dangerous. They became wary of using the word "church" to refer to those who subscribed to a particular body of doctrine, or even to the building in which the congregation met. New Englanders called their place of worship a "meeting-house." It was a dangerous figure of speech, Richard Mather once observed, to call that meeting-house a "church." "There is no just ground from scripture to apply such a trope as church to a house for a public assembly." For years, therefore, when the men of New England spoke of what they had to offer the world, they referred neither to their "creed" nor their "church," but to The New England Way.

Among the chief factors which pushed them in this direction were the special character of their theology, in particular the "federal" idea, and their colonial legal situation. The "federal" theology by which New England Puritans lived was an iceberg of doctrine. Beneath the surface was a dense theological mass, much larger and weightier than what projected above. A full exposition of that hidden base would be nothing less than an anatomy of protestantism. The part which became visible and prominent in New England life was the federal church-way, which came to be known as congregationalism.

The basic fact about congregationalism was its emphasis on the going relationship among men. Each church was not a part of a hierarchy, nor a branch of a perfected institution, but a kind of club composed of individual Christians searching for a godly way of life. The congregational church was a group of going concerns, not a monolithic establishment. When they used the word at all, Puritans usually spoke of the "churches" rather than the "church" of New England. What held them together was no unified administrative structure, but a common quest, a common way of living.

At the heart of the congregational idea was the unifying notion that a proper Christian church was one adapted to the special circumstances of its place and arising out of the continuing agreement of certain particular Christians. What of the *manner* of church-worship? asked the opening chapter of the Cambridge Platform. Its answer was simply that worship "be done in such a manner, as all Circumstances considered, is most expedient for edification: so, as if there bee no errour of man concerning their determination, the determining of them is to be accounted as if it were divine." The size of a congregation was also to be fixed by practical considerations. "The *matter* of the Church in respect of its *quantity* ought not to be of greater number then may ordinarily meet together conveniently in one place: nor ordinarily fewer, then may conveniently carry on Church-work." Each congregation had its own problems, "Vertues of their own, for which others are not praysed: Corruptions of their owne, for which others are not blamed."

A church was formed, then, not by administrative fiat nor by the random gathering of professing Christians, but by the "covenanting" or agreement of a group of "saints," that is, Christians who had had a special "converting experience." The status of minister was not acquired from a seminary or by the laying on of priestly hands. Rather it was a function performed by a godly man in relation to a group of other men. To be a minister at all a man had to be "called" by a group of Christians; when that relation ceased, he was no longer a minister. In the congregational polity, relations among men overshadowed inherited or anointed status: the ways overshadowed the forms.

Not least important in encouraging this point of view was the Puritan use of the Bible. If there was any codification of Puritan beliefs, it was in the Word of God. The Puritans wished to be "guided by one rule, even the Word of the most high." More perhaps than for any other Christians of their age, the Bible was their guide. Through it, they explained in the Cambridge Platform, every man could find the design of life and the shape of the Truth:

> The parts of Government are prescribed in the word, because the Lord Iesus Christ the King and Law-giver of his Church, is no less faithfull in the house of God then was Moses, who from the Lord delivered a form & pattern of Government to the Children of Israel in the old Testament: And the holy Scriptures are now also soe perfect, as they are able to make the man of God perfect & thoroughly furnished unto every good work; and therefore doubtless to the well ordering of the house of God.

But to try to live by the Bible was vastly different from trying to live by the Laws of the Medes and the Persians, by the Athanasian Creed, or even by the Westminster Confession. For the Bible was actually neither a codification nor a credo; it was a narrative. From this simple fact came much of the special character of the Puritan approach to experience. There were, of course, parts of the Bible (like Leviticus and Deuteronomy) which contained an explicit code of laws; the Puritans were attracted to these simply because the commands were so clear. The Ten

Commandments were, of course, in the foreground of their thinking, but the Bible as a whole was the law of their life. For answers to their problems they drew as readily on Exodus, Kings, or Romans, as on the less narrative portions of the Bible. Their peculiar circumstances and their flair for the dramatic led them to see special significance in these narrative passages. The basic reality in their life was the analogy with the Children of Israel. They conceived that by going out into the Wilderness, they were reliving the story of Exodus and not merely obeying an explicit command to go into the wilderness. For them the Bible was less a body of legislation than a set of binding precedents.

The result was that these Puritans were preoccupied with the similarities in pairs of situations: the situation described in a Bible story and that in which they found themselves. "Thou shalt not kill" was accepted without discussion. What interested them, and what became the subject of their debate was whether, and how and why, an episode in the Bible was like one in their own lives. The "great and terrible Earthquake" of June 1, 1638 and the one of January 14, 1639 "which happened much about the time the Lordly Prelates were preparing their injunctions for Scotland" reminded Captain Edward Johnson of how "the Lord himselfe . . . roared from Sion, (as in the dayes of the Prophet Amos)." Almost every page of early New England literature provides an example. "The rule that directeth the choice of supreame governors," wrote John Cotton, "is of like aequitie and weight in all magistrates, that one of their brethren (not a stranger) should be set over them, Deut. 17.15. and Jethroes counsell to Moses was approved of God, that the judges, and officers to be set over the people, should be men fearing God, Exod. 18.21. and Solomon maketh it the joy of a commonwealth, when the righteous are in authority, and their mourning when the wicked rule, Prov. 29.21. Job 34.30."

What the Puritans had developed in America then, was a practical common-law orthodoxy. Their heavy reliance on the Bible, and their preoccupation with platforms, programs of action, and schemes of confederation—rather than with religious dogma—fixed the temper of their society, and foreshadowed American political life for centuries to come.

4

Puritan Conservatism

AMONG THE CIRCUMSTANCES which led the American Puritans to a practical approach to their doctrine, none was more important than the fact that they were colonials. However clear and dogmatic the dictates of their religion, they did not consider themselves free to construct their political institutions of whole cloth. Their fellow-Calvinists in Geneva several decades before had been limited only by their private aspirations and the demands of their dogma. But even in earliest New England one can see the marks of that colonial situation which would decisively affect all American political thought through the era of the Revolution, and which helped shape the moderate, compromising, and traditionalist character of our institutions.

The effects of this colonial situation can be seen, first, in the widely accepted assumption that there were definite limits which the legislators were not free to transgress—this, in a word, was constitutionalism—and, second, in the idea that the primary and normal way of developing civil institutions was by custom and tradition rather than by legislative or administrative fiat. These were rooted less in a deliberate political preference than in the circumstance in which the New England Puritans found themselves.

In the first charter of Massachusetts Bay Colony in 1629, King Charles had authorized the General Court of the colony to make "all Manner of wholesome and reasonable Orders, Lawes, Statutes, and Ordinnces, Direccons, and Instruccons"—but with the provision that they be "not contrairie to the Lawes of this our Realme of England." The colonists, though not lawyers, were of a decidedly legalistic turn of mind; they took this limitation seriously. It was appealed to from all sides, by the ruling clique as well as by the critics and rebels.

The story of the struggle for law in early New England has not yet been fully told. But even what we already know shows that the rulers of this Bible commonwealth were haunted by the skeleton of old English institutions. At every point both rulers and rebels felt bound to assume that an authentic Bible commonwealth could not depart far from the ancient institutions of the mother country. As early as 1635, Winthrop tells us, the deputies were worried that the magistrates "for want of positive laws, in many cases, might proceed according to their discretions." The remedy which they sought, and which they persuaded the General Court to adopt, was plainly on the English pattern: "that some men should be appointed to frame a body of grounds of laws, *in resemblance to a Magna Charta,* which . . . should be received for fundamental laws."

The legislative history of early New England is the story of successive attempts to provide, first, a "Magna Charta" for the inhabitants of Massachusetts Bay Colony and, later, a handy compilation of their laws. The small ruling group of early New England was not eager to embody its institutions in an all-embracing code. Leaders like John Winthrop doubted the wisdom of confining institutions by a pattern of words; they also doubted their authority. They were hardly more worried that their laws should be "scriptural," that is approved by the Bible, than that they should be sufficiently English; and that any changes in English laws should have ample warrant in local needs.

We have been almost blind to this side of early New England life. Dazzled by the light they found in Scripture, we have failed to see the steady illumination they found in old English example. For instance, when historians came upon a little work by John Cotton entitled *Moses His Judicials,* they hastily concluded that since it was Biblical and dogmatic it must have been the Code of Massachusetts Bay. But the evidence shows that his code was never adopted into law, and it may never have been intended to be.

The lawmakers of the colony, to the extent their knowledge allowed and with only minor exceptions, actually followed English example. Their colonial situation made them wary of trying to create institutions according to their own notions, and alert to the need of adapting old institutions to new conditions. They were among the first to take a consciously pragmatic approach to the common law; and it was their colonial situation which gave them the occasion. This spirit was well expressed by John Winthrop in his account of the events of November, 1639:

> The people had long desired a body of laws, and thought their condition very unsafe, while so much power rested in the discretion of magistrates. Divers attempts had been made at former courts [meetings of the legislature], and the matter referred to some of the magistrates and some of the elders; but still it came to no effect; for, being committed to the care of many, whatsoever was done by some, was still disliked or

neglected by others. At last it was referred to Mr. Cotton and Mr. Nathaniel Warde, etc., and each of them framed a model, which were presented to this general court, and by them committed to the governour and deputy and some others to consider of, and so prepare it for the court in the 3d month next. Two great reasons there were, which caused most of the magistrates and some of the elders not to be very forward in this matter. [1.] One was, want of sufficient experience of the nature and disposition of the people, considered with the condition of the country and other circumstances, which made them conceive, that such laws would be fittest for us, which should arise pro re nata upon occasions, etc., and so the laws of England and other states grew, and therefore the fundamental laws of England are called customs, consuetudines. 2. For that it would professedly transgress the limits of our charter, which provide, we shall make no laws repugnant to the laws of England, and that we were assured we must do. But to raise up laws by practice and custom had been no transgression; as in our church discipline, and in matters of marriage, to make a law, that marriages should not be solemnized by ministers, is repugnant to the laws of England; but to bring it to a custom by practice for the magistrates to perform it, is no law made repugnant, etc.

It would be hard to find a better summary of the universal advantages of customary law over the laws of code-makers.

Only a few years later a still more outspoken statement of their legal philosophy appeared. In 1646 Dr. Robert Child and six others presented a petition to the General Court of Massachusetts Bay objecting to many laws of the colony. The petitioners argued that because Massachusetts Bay had made several drastic modifications of English law (for example, in the criteria of church-membership and hence of citizenship), the colony lacked "a setled forme of government according to the lawes of England." But only a thoroughly English government, they said, was "best agreeable to our English tempers."

The reply of the New England magistrates expressed their insistent allegiance to English institutions. They offered a full-dress defense of the Englishness of the government they had set up. Indeed, if a desperate historian wanted to forge a document proving that the colonies accepted English institutions as their standard, he could hardly do better than to compose precisely the declaration which the General Court adopted in reply to the Child petition. "For our government itselfe," the magistrates argued, "it is framed according to our charter, and the fundamental and common lawes of England, and carried on according to the same (takeing the words of eternal truth and righteousness along with them, as that rule by which all kingdomes and jurisdictions must render account of every act and administration, in the last day) with as bare allowance for the disproportion between such an ancient, populous, wealthy kingdome, and so poore an infant thinne colonie, as common reason can afford. And because this will better appeare by compareing particulars, we shall drawe them into a parallel."

The magistrates printed in parallel columns the English institutions with their New England counterparts listed opposite. They began with the Magna Charta: on the left-hand side were its main provisions; on the right-hand side the "Fundamentalls of Massachusetts," that is, the corresponding provisions of colonial law. Next came the leading rules of English common law; arranged opposite were their counterparts in the Massachusetts "Fundamentalls." This exhibit proved more than any argument.

The legislators did confess their weaknesses. They explained that they were mere "novices" in the law, and "therefore such faileings [as] may appeare either in our collection of those lawes, or in comforming our owne to that patterne are to be imputed to our own want of skill. If we had able lawyers amongst us, we might have been more exact." If they had not succeeded in producing an American replica, it was certainly not for any lack of will to do so. But there had not been much time, and they had been poor in professional legal talent. "Rome was not built in a day," the magistrates reminded the Child petitioners. "Let them produce any colonie or commonwealth in the world, where more hath beene done in 16 yeares."

The most important of the early compilations of Massachusetts law was *The Book of the General Lawes and Libertyes* of 1648 which was to be the basis of later legislation and which influenced the laws of other colonies, including Connecticut and New Haven. The preface published by the General Court apologized for the inadequacy of the compilation both as a reproduction of English institutions and as an adaptation to colonial conditions.

> We have not published it as a perfect body of laws sufficient to carry on the Government established for future times, nor could it be expected that we should promise such a thing. For if it be no disparagement to the wisedome of that High Court of Parliament in England that in four hundred years they could not so compile their lawes, and regulate proceedings in Courts of justice &c: but that they had still new work to do of the same kinde almost every Parliament: there can be no just cause to blame a poor Colonie (being unfurnished of Lawyers and Statesmen) that in eighteen years hath produced no more, nor better rules for a good, and setled Government then this Book holds forth: nor have you (our Brethren and Neighbours) any cause, whether you look back upon our Native Country, or take your observation by other States, & Common wealths in Europe) to complaine. . . .

The Puritans of Massachusetts Bay said that they started from "the lawes of God" rather than the laws of Englishmen. Yet in their eyes, the two seemed happily to coincide:

> That distinction which is put between the Lawes of God and the lawes of men, becomes a snare to many as it is mis-applyed in the ordering of their obedience to civil Authoritie; for when the Authoritie is of God and that in way of an Ordinance *Rom. 13.1.* and when the administration of it is according to deductions, and rules gathered from the word of God, and the clear light of nature in civil nations, surely there is no humane law that tendeth to common good (according to those principles) but the same is mediately a law of God, and that in way of an Ordinance which all are to submit unto and that for conscience sake. *Rom. 13.5.*

Their satisfaction was as great as that of Sir William Blackstone a century later and of conservative English lawyers ever since, in discovering that scriptural law and/or natural law happened already to be embodied in the English rules.

Scholarly dispute as to whether early New England law was primarily scriptural or primarily English is beside the point. For early New Englanders these two turned out to be pretty much the same. Very little of their early legal literature attempted to construct new institutions from Biblical materials. They were trying, for the most part, to demonstrate the coincidence between what the scriptures required and what English law had already provided.

We have at least one valuable witness on this matter. Thomas Lechford had had some legal training in England, and although he was in Massachusetts Bay only from 1638 to 1641, those were the crucial years when the Body of Liberties of 1641 was put together. Partly through his own forwardness and partly from the scarcity of legal talent in the colony, he was intimately connected with its legal history. But, because neither his theology nor his method of persuading jurors was orthodox, the magistrates disbarred him and censured him for meddling in church affairs. These and other irritations led him to return to England permanently, where in 1642 he issued a little book, *Plain Dealing: or Newes from New-England.* Its object (stated on the title-page) was to give "A short view of New-Englands present Government, both Ecclesiasticall and Civil, compared with the anciently-received and established Government of England." Lechford—an unsympathetic, if not actually malicious, observer—was distinguished from his contemporaries by some legal knowledge and by personal experience with New England institutions. His book is an informed, though not dispassionate, account of deviations, which he eagerly sought out, of New English from Old English laws.

Lechford's main complaint was, of course, about the churches of Massachusetts Bay. On the one hand, their membership requirements were too strict: it was not enough for a person to be of blameless conduct or to subscribe to the articles of faith. The applicants for church-membership had to satisfy the Elders and then the whole congregation of "the worke of grace upon their soules, or how God hath beene dealing with them about their conversion . . . . that they are true beleevers, that they have beene wounded in their hearts for their originall sinne, and actuall transgressions, and can pitch upon some promise of free grace in the Scripture, for the ground of their faith, and that they finde their hearts drawne to beleeve in Christ Jesus, for their justification and salvation . . . . and that they know competently the summe of Christian faith." This procedure, Lechford observed, was evil—even inhuman—for sometimes a master would be admitted and not his servant, sometimes the servant alone, sometimes a husband and not his wife, sometimes a child and not his parent. The effects of these restrictions were far-reaching since no one could be a "freeman" of the colony unless he had been admitted to the church. And only "freemen" could vote or hold office.

On the other hand Lechford thought the government of New England churches was too democratical, for there were no bishops, and how could a church be well-ordered where in effect every church-member was a bishop? Yet this was precisely what the congregational organization amounted to. "If the people may make Ministers, or any Ministers make others without an Apostolicall Bishop, what confusion will there be? If the whole Church, or every congregation, as our good men think, have the power to the keyes, how many Bishops then shall we have?"

Although the congregational churches of New England never acquired a bishop, even before the end of the 17th century their practical, compromising spirit had led them to modify the strict requirements for church-membership to which Lechford and other English critics objected. By the ingenious doctrine of the "Half-Way Covenant," first officially proposed in the meeting of ministers in 1662, they created a new class of church-membership for those who had not had the intense "converting experience" but who were descended from those who had had the experience. In this way they kept the church-benches filled without abandoning their ideal of a purified church where only "Visible Saints" could be full members.

A careful look at Lechford's criticism of the laws of New England impresses one with how little they deviated from English practice. Even these deviations were easily explained by life in a wilderness colony, and would be removed as soon as the New Englanders could manage it. His first objection was the "want of proceeding duly upon record"—the legal proceedings were carried on orally rather than by exchange of documents. According to Lechford, this tended to make the government arbitrary, depriving the parties and judges of a clear understanding of the issues and making it more difficult to formulate precedents. His second objection, akin to the first, was the prohibition of paid attorneys and advocates. He declared hired lawyers "necessary to assist the poore and unlearned in their causes, and that according to the warrant and intendment of holy Writ, and of right reason. I have knowne by experience, and heard divers have suffered wrong by default of such in New England. . . . But take heede my brethren, despise not learning, nor the worthy Lawyers of either gown, lest you repent too late."

Both these divergences from English practice were due to the lack of trained lawyers. Lechford himself was one of the very few men of legal training in Boston; even judges were commonly untrained in the law. Complex legal documents could not be drawn, nor professional legal counsel given, except by trained lawyers; and, for all practical purposes, such were not to be found in New England.

The magistrates of New England were soon to remove the differences of which Lechford complained. The Body of Liberties of 1641 (Liberty No. 27) provided that if the plaintiff filed a written declaration, the defendant was to have "libertie and time to give in his answer in write-ings, And soe in all further proceedings betwene partie and partie." A law of 1647 which described the evils to which Lechford referred, went still further, requiring such a written declaration to be filed in all civil cases in due time before court opened, so that the defendant would have time to prepare his written answer. But such procedures could not be legislated into being if the community lacked qualified persons to put them into practice. Therefore this requirement was omitted from later compilations of the laws, and it was decades before written "pleadings" (the technical documents which lawyers exchange during a lawsuit) became common. Meanwhile, the absence of written pleadings sometimes gave New England litigants the advantage of having their cases judged on their substance, while English lawyers and judges might quibble over the forms of documents. Increasing commerce and the growing number of men with legal training soon led the legislature of Massachusetts Bay to remove Lechford's other objection: by 1648 it had become legal to employ paid attorneys.

Legal proceedings of the early years give us the impression of a people

without much legal training and with few lawbooks who were trying to
reproduce substantially what they knew "back home." Far from being a
crude and novel system of popular law, or an attempt to create institutions from pure Scripture, what they produced was instead a layman's
version of English legal institutions. The half-remembered and half-
understood technical language of English lawyers was being roughly
applied to American problems. Much remains to be learned of the law
of those days; and the very characteristics we have described (the lack
of written pleadings, for example) handicap the historian. Cases were
not printed; judges did not give reasons for their decisions. Even in the
1670's judicial precedents (English or colonial) or English statutes were
not yet being cited.

But the colonists did use the peculiar technical resources of English
law, even while employing them handily for many novel purposes. In the
records of the decisions of the Suffolk County Courts between 1671 and
1680, about eighty per cent of the civil suits were framed as "actions
on the case." That was one of the classic English "forms of action" which
had had a specific technical meaning, and hence only limited use.
English lawyers had been trained to consider the "action on the case" as a
highly specialized piece of legal artillery, suitable only for shooting at a
particular species of game; American lawyers who lacked the advantages
(and prejudices) of a good professional training were successfully employing it to hit almost any kind of creature in the woods. In this (as in
their casual attitude toward the written pleadings of a case) they were,
from the point of view of a modern lawyer, far in advance of their age.
But for the historian of American institutions this is less important than
two other facts: (1) New Englanders were using this half-understood
technical language of English law to express an English message; the
rights which they protected were fundamentally English legal rights—
what in England would have been protected by an action of "covenant,"
or "debt," or "ejectment," or "trespass." (2) New Englanders, by using
this language after their own fashion, thought they were being English.
They were more conscious of the fact that they were speaking English than
that they were speaking with an American accent.

Whenever the rulers of New England found themselves and their laws
under attack, their first defense was to show how closely their rules adhered to those of England. The General Court of Massachusetts Bay
always argued that the coincidence of New English and Old English laws
was remarkable. When hard pressed they went on to argue that even the
apparent deviations from English law were themselves justified by the
laws of England, under which "the city of London and other corporations

have divers customs and by-laws differing from the common and statute laws of England."

The scarcity of English lawbooks troubled them. The General Court on November 11, 1647 "to the end we may have the bettr light for making and proceeding about laws" ordered the purchase of two copies each of six technical English legal works: Coke on Littleton, The Book of Entries, Coke on Magna Charta, New Terms of the Law, Dalton's Justice of the Peace, and Coke's Reports. The form of early Massachusetts legal documents (deeds, powers of attorney, leases, bonds, partnership agreements, etc.) suggests that they were copied from the same handbooks which guided English lawyers.

If we do not look at the form or language of their law but at its substance, we are again impressed by how few changes were made in New England. The most dramatic and most obvious were in the list of capital crimes. To those crimes punishable by death under the laws of England, the colonists by 1648 had added a number of others, including idolatry (violations of the First Commandment), blasphemy, man-stealing (from Exod. 21.16), adultery with a married woman, perjury with intent to secure the death of another, the cursing of a parent by a child over 16 years of age (Exod. 21.17), the offense of being a "rebellious son" (Deut. 21.20.21), and the third offense of burglary or highway robbery. These were clear cases where the laws of Scripture were allowed to override the laws of England.

But before we attach too much significance to these deviations, we must remember that in the law of capital crimes, both Englishmen and Americans were accustomed to the greatest divergence between practice and theory in those days. In England the merciful fictions of "benefit of clergy" nullified the letter of the law; in New England the practice of public confession perhaps accomplished a similar result. All this, of course, made the New England modifications of the criminal law still less significant. This was a realm where people were accustomed to unenforced rules and where Scriptural orthodoxy could be purchased with the least change in the actual ways of daily life.

5

How Puritans Resisted the
Temptation of Utopia

IF THERE WAS ever a people whose intellectual baggage equipped them for a journey into Utopia it was the New England Puritans. In their Bible they had a blueprint for the Good Society; their costly expedition to America gave them a vested interest in believing it possible to build Zion on this earth. In view of these facts it is remarkable that there was so little of the Utopian in their thinking about society. There are a number of explanations for this. The English law was a powerful and sobering influence: colonists were persuaded by practical interests such as the retention of their charter and the preservation of their land-titles, as well as by their sentimental attachment to the English basis of their legal system. The pessimism, the vivid sense of evil, which was so intimate a part of Calvinism discouraged daydreams. Finally, there was the overwhelming novelty and insecurity of life in the wilderness which made the people more anxious to cling to familiar institutions, and led them to discover a new coincidence between the laws of God and the laws of England (and hence of New England).

The peculiar character of their Biblical orthodoxy nourished a practical and non-Utopian frame of mind. Their political thought did not turn toward delineating The Good Society, precisely because the Bible had already offered the anatomy of Zion. Moreover, the Bible was a narrative and not a speculative work; theirs was at most a common-law utopianism, a utopianism of analogies in situation rather than of dogmas, principles, and abstractions.

Perhaps because their basic theoretical questions had been settled, the Puritans were able to concentrate on human and practical problems. And strangely enough, those problems were a preview of the ones which would continue to trouble American political thought. They were concerned less with the ends of society than with its organization and less with making the community good than with making it effective, with insuring the integrity and self-restraint of its leaders, and with preventing its government from being oppressive.

The problems which worried the Puritans in New England were three. The first was how to select leaders and representatives. From the beginning what had distinguished the Puritans (and had laid them open to attack by Lechford and others) was their strict criterion of church-membership, their fear that if the unconverted could be members of the church they might become its rulers. Their concept of a church was, in its own very limited way, of a kind of ecclesiastical self-government: there were to be no bishops because the "members" of each church were fit to rule themselves. Many of the major disputes of early New England were essentially debates over who were fit rulers and how they should be selected. The early political history of Massachusetts Bay could almost be written as a history of disagreements over this problem. What were to be the relations between the magistrates and the deputies? How many deputies from each town? Many of their sermons and even their "speculative" writings were on this subject.

Their second concern was with the proper limits of political power. This question was never better stated than by John Cotton. "It is therefore most wholsome for Magistrates and Officers in Church and Common-wealth, never to affect more liberty and authority then will do them good, and the People good; for what ever transcendant power is given, will certainly over-run those that give it, and those that receive it: There is a straine in a mans heart that will sometime or other runne out to excesse, unlesse the Lord restraine it, but it is not good to venture it: It is necessary therefore, that all power that is on earth be limited. . . ." The form of the early compilations of their laws shows this preoccupation. The first compilation of Massachusetts law (1641) was known, significantly, as "The Body of Liberties" and managed to state the whole of the legal system in terms of the "liberties" of different members of the community. It began with a paraphrase of Magna Charta, followed by the limitations on judicial proceedings, went on to the "liberties" of freemen, women, children, foreigners, and included those "of the brute creature." Even the law of capital crimes was stated in the form of "liberties," and the church organization was described as "the Liberties the Lord Jesus hath given to the Churches." The preamble to this first Body of Liberties would have been impressive, even had it not come out of the American wilderness:

> The free fruition of such liberties Immunities and priveledges as humanitie, Civilitie, and Christianitie call for as due to every man in his place and proportion without impeachment and Infringement hath ever

bene and ever will be the tranquillitie and Stabilitie of Churches and
Commonwealths. And the deniall or deprivall thereof, the disturbance
if not the ruine of both.

The Puritan's third major problem was, what made for a feasible
federal organization? How should power be distributed between local
and central organs? Congregationalism itself was an attempt to answer
this question with specific institutions, to find a means by which churches
could extend "the free hand of fellowship" to one another without binding
individual churches or individual church-members to particular dogmas
or holding them in advance to the decisions of a central body. The practical issues which did not fall under either of the two earlier questions
came within this class. What power, if any, had the General Court of the
colony over the town of Hingham in its selection of its captain of militia?
This was the occasion when one of the townspeople "professeth he will
die at sword's point, if he might not have the choice of his own officers."
Or, what was the power of the central government to call a church
synod? The deputies of the towns (in a dispute over the character of their
union which foreshadowed the issues of the Revolution and the Civil
War) were willing to consider an invitation to send delegates, but objected
to a command.

All the circumstances of New England life—tradition, theology, and
the problems of the new world—combined to nourish concern with such
practical problems. It is easy to agree with Lechford's grudging compliment that "wiser men then they, going into a wildernesse to set up another
strange government differing from the setled government here, might
have falne into greater errors then they have done."

PART TWO

THE INWARD PLANTATION

The Quakers of Pennsylvania

> "My friends . . . going over to plant, and make
> outward plantations in America, keep your own
> plantations in your hearts, with the spirit and
> power of God, that your own vines and lilies
> be not hurt."
>
> GEORGE FOX

IN 1681, when William Penn received his charter for Pennsylvania from
Charles II, many features of Quakerism seemed to suit it for a New
World mission. The Quakers possessed a set of attitudes which fit later
textbook definitions of American democracy.

Belief in Equality. No Christian sect was more insistent on a belief in
equality. John Woolman complained in a sermon in Maryland (1757)
"that Men having Power too often misapplied it; that though we made
Slaves of the Negroes, and the Turks made Slaves of the Christians, I
believed that Liberty was the natural Right of all Men equally."

Informality. They believed in simplicity and informality in dress and
language, and opposed ceremoniousness of all kinds. We cannot discover
their teachings from any formal creed.

33

Toleration. Believing all men essentially good, the Quakers were less disturbed than most other people by doctrinal differences. William Penn's Frame of Government in 1682 guaranteed religious freedom to all "who confess and acknowledge the one Almighty and Eternal God . . . and hold themselves obliged, in conscience, to live peaceably and justly in civil society." While the Puritans believed the Indians to be cohorts of the devil and had no patience with any people who differed in the slightest from their doctrine, the Quakers were impressed by the extent to which the Indian religion resembled their own. They welcomed men of all sects.

The Quakers lacked neither courage nor energy. It was not so much the actual content of their creed as the uncompromising obstinacy with which they hung on to it, and their attitude toward themselves, that were decisive. The two flaws fatal to the influence of this remarkable people on American culture were, first, an urge toward martyrdom, and a preoccupation with the purity of their own souls; and, second, a rigidity in all their beliefs. The first led their vision away from the community and inward to themselves; the second hardened them against the ordinary accommodations of this world. Neither the martyr nor the doctrinaire could flourish on American soil.

6

The Quest for Martyrdom

To the pilgrims, the Puritans, and the Quakers, America seemed an opportunity to create a society according to plan. Their escape from persecution was perhaps less significant to them than their ascent to rule. America was not merely a way out of prison; it offered a throne in the wilderness. Such swift changes of fortune have always strained the characters of men, and never were changes more dizzying than those which occurred on American soil in the earliest colonial years.

The Puritans, by building institutions in New England, had nourished a worldly human pride which diluted their sense of providence and their faith in the omnipotence of God. The Puritan success was accompanied, if not actually made possible, by the decline of American Puritanism as an uncompromising theology. Quaker success offers a dramatic contrast, for when the opportunities of governing came to them, they preferred to conserve a pure Quaker sect rather than build a great community with a flavor of compromised Quakerism.

English Quakerism had begun as a protest movement. The Quakers believed, in George Fox's classic phrase, "that every man was enlightened by the divine Light of Christ" but that theology, like most other human knowledge, simply obscured men's vision. Fox, the founder of English Quakerism, said in his *Journal*:

> These three,—the physicians, the priests, and the lawyers,—ruled the world out of the wisdom, out of the faith, and out of the equity and law of God; one pretending the cure of the body, another the cure of the soul, and the third the protection of the property of the people. But I saw they were all out of the wisdom, out of the faith, out of the equity and perfect law of God.

In England Quakers remained a minority, raising an accusing and critical voice. In America the earliest Quaker voices had much the same sound. While others saw an opportunity here to pursue their orthodoxy unmolested, the Quakers engaged in a relentless quest for martyrdom. Their spirit was expressed by William Dewsbury, a leading English Quaker who helped ship immigrants to America, when he said that he "as joyfully entered prisons as palaces, and in the prison-house, I sang praises to my God and esteemed the bolts and locks upon me as jewels." From this point of view the earliest Quaker immigrants to the American colonies sought, and found, adornment aplenty. In colonial Rhode Island, where the rulers refused to persecute them, Quakers were unwilling to stay. "We finde that in those places where these people aforesaid, in this coloney, are most of all suffered to declare themselves freely, and are only opposed by arguments in discourse," observed the Rhode Island Court of Trial, "there they least of all desire to come."

The story of earliest Quaker activities in America is puzzling to anyone unacquainted with the mystic spirit and the character of the martyr. It is not merely that these men and women preferred "to die for the whole truth rather than live with a half-truth." One after another of them seemed to lust after hardships, trudging thousands of wilderness miles, risking Indians and wild animals, to find a crown of martyrdom. Never before perhaps have people gone to such trouble or traveled so far for the joys of suffering for their Lord. The courage and persistence shown by 17th-century American Quakers in seeking out the whipping-post or the gallows is equaled only in Cortes' quest for the treasure of the Aztecs or Ponce de León's search for the Fountain of Youth. Never was a reward sought more eagerly than the Quakers sought out their crown of thorns.

The English "Friends" (as the Quakers called themselves) were proud of the abuse willingly suffered by American Quakers at the hands of the New England Puritans. As early as 1659, Humphrey Norton's *New England's Ensigne* made a by-word of their suffering. And George Bishop, also in England, prepared a *Book of Martyrs,* first published in 1661, and later several times reprinted, under the title *New England Judged by the*

Spirit of the Lord. In this thick volume he collected harrowing tales of the punishment of Quaker visitors to Massachusetts Bay.

A few examples will give a hint of the Friends' bizarre and dauntless spirit. In 1658, Sarah Gibbons and Dorothy Waugh left Rhode Island, where they were not being molested, and traveled mostly on foot from Newport to Salem in Massachusetts. Groping through March blizzards and sleeping in the woods, they eventually reached their destination, and they preached undisturbed for about two weeks. Then they "felt moved" to go to Boston, where they received the expected barbaric whipping before being sent packing back to Rhode Island. In the summer of the same year Josiah Coale and Thomas Thurston traveled even farther to suffer for the Truth. They walked from Virginia to New England "through Uncouth Passages, Vast Wildernesses, Uninhabited Countries." The Susquehanna Indians took pity on them, guiding them to New Amsterdam and nursing Thurston when he was critically ill. Like so many others, these two men felt what the Quakers called "the fire and the hammer" in their souls. Finally reaching New England, they preached, first to the Indians and then to the white colonists, until they were committed to prison and driven at last from the colony.

One of the most persistent of the martyrs was Christopher Holder, "valiant apostle of New England Quakerism," who had arrived in 1656 from England to preach the gospel of his sect. In Salem, one Sunday morning in September 1657, he was bold enough to speak a few words after the minister had done. He did not get very far before someone seized him by the hair, and "His Mouth violently stopp'd with a Glove and Handkerchief thrust thereinto with much Fury, by one of your Church-Members And Commissioners." Although he had already been at least once expelled, he and his companion had continued their preaching. They were conveyed to Boston, where the exasperated Governor and Deputy-Governor of the colony inflicted on them a brutal punishment which went even beyond all existing laws. Merely reading the account is strong medicine, but it contributes to our understanding of the price the Quakers sought to pay for their Truth. First the two Quakers were given thirty stripes apiece with a three-cord knotted whip, during which one of the spectators fainted. Then they were confined to a bare cell, without bedding, for three days and nights without food or drink. After that they were imprisoned during nine weeks of the New England winter without any fire. By special order the prisoners were whipped twice each week, the first time with fifteen lashes and each succeeding time by three additional. Having miraculously survived this ordeal, Holder took ship for Barbados, where he spent the remainder of the winter before returning to Rhode Island to preach his gospel without molestation. But this did not satisfy him. In August 1658 he was arrested in Dedham, Massachusetts, and again taken to Boston, where one of his ears was cut off.

The New England Puritan leaders were not sadists. But they too were single-minded men; they had risked everything and traveled three thousand miles for their own opportunity. They wanted to be let alone to pursue their orthodoxy and to build Zion according to their model. What right had the Quakers (or anyone else) to interfere? The Puritans had not sought out the Quakers in order to punish them; the Quakers had come in quest of punishment. Why could not these zealots stay in Rhode Island where they were tolerated, and allow the Puritans to go about their business? Or, as a Puritan minister said in defending the 117 blows with a tarred rope which had brought the Quaker William Brend near to death, he "indeavoured to beat the Gospel ordinances black and blew," and it seemed but just to beat *him* black and blue.

In trying to keep the Quakers away, the governors of Massachusetts Bay were at their wits' end. They showed how little they understood the problem by increasing the legal penalties against intruders. Had they known the Quakers better they might have foreseen that this could only make their colony more attractive to seekers of martyrdom. There was very little popular enthusiasm in Massachusetts Bay for the death penalty against Quakers, but it was enacted in 1658, having passed the House of Deputies by a majority of only one vote.

It was not long before another group of Quakers, inspired by what their own historian called an unquenchable fire, departed from the safety of Rhode Island and arrived in Boston. They were "commissioned" by God; they came to "look your Bloody Laws in the Face." Unflinching before the threat of death, they came prepared. Alice Cowland even brought linen for wrapping the dead bodies of those who were expected to be martyred. One of these unwelcome visitors, William Robinson, wrote in the Boston jail late in 1659:

> In Travelling betwixt Newport in Rhode Island, and Daniel Gold's House, with my dear Brother, Christopher Holder, the Word of the Lord came expressly to me which did fill me immediately with Life and Power, and heavenly love, by which he constrained me and commanded me to pass to the Town of Boston, my life to lay down in His will, for the Accomplishing of his Service, that he had there to perform at the Day appointed. To which heavenly Voice I presently yielded Obedience, not questioning the Lord how He would bring the Thing to pass . . . and willingly was I given up from that time, to this Day, the Will of the Lord to do and perform, what-ever became of my Body. . . . I being a Child, and durst not question the Lord in the least, but rather willing to lay down my Life, than to bring Dishonour to the Lord.

The story of Mary Dyer, who left her husband in Newport to court danger and defy evil in Boston, demonstrates both the uneasiness of the Puritans in crowning the Quaker martyrs and the persistence of the Quakers in earning that crown. Her story, one of the most impressive in all the annals of martyrdom, is worth recounting. Shortly after arriving in Boston in the early fall of 1659, she and her companions (including an eleven-year old girl, Patience Scott) were banished on pain of death. After only a brief stay in Newport, she returned to Boston. "Your end shall be frustrated, that think to restrain them, you call Cursed Quakers, from coming among you, by any Thing you can do to them," she explained, "Yea, verily, he hath a Seed here among you, for whom we have suffered all this while, and yet Suffer." She was tried on October 19, 1659, along with William Robinson and Marmaduke Stephenson, who had shared her mission. The next day, after a sermon cursing them, Governor Endicott pronounced their death sentence. "The Will of the Lord be done," Mary Dyer replied, and as the marshal took her away, she stolidly remarked, "Yea, joyfully shall I go."

A week later the three Quakers were to be executed. Mary Dyer marched to the gallows between the two young men condemned with her, while drums beat loudly to prevent any words they might preach on the way from being heard by the watching crowd. When an official asked Mrs. Dyer if she did not feel shame at walking publicly between two young men, she answered, "It is an Hour of the greatest Joy I can enjoy in this World. No Eye can see, No Ear can hear, No Tongue can speak, No Heart can understand the sweet incomes and refreshings of the Spirit of the Lord which I now enjoy." Still the Puritan officials tried to deprive her of the martyr's ecstasy. The two men were executed, and Mary Dyer was mounted on the gallows, her arms and legs bound and her face covered with a handkerchief as the final preparation for hanging. Then, as if by a sudden decision, she was reprieved from the gallows.

This barbarous proceeding, as we now know, had been planned in advance. During Mary Dyer's trial, the Massachusetts General Court had secretly recorded their judgment that she be banished; but they had also provided that she be present at the execution of the others and be prepared as if for her own hanging. Her reprieve was surely due, in part, to the uneasiness of citizens who still recalled their own sufferings in England.

Mary Dyer's response to this act of grace was thoroughly in character. She refused to accept the reprieve unless the law itself was repealed. But the determined judges sent her off on horseback in the direction of Rhode Island. If they thought they could so easily be rid of Mary Dyer, they were mistaken. "She said," records John Taylor, one of her fellow

Quaker missionaries, "that she must go and desire the repeal of that wicked law against God's people and offer up her life there." On May 21, 1660, less than a year after her banishment from the colony, the irrepressible Mary Dyer returned to Boston and once more heard her sentence of death. But now, insisted Governor Endicott, it was to be executed. Again there were pleas for her life. And again, as she stood on the ladder of the gallows, she was offered her life if she would just leave the colony. But this time she was not to be thwarted. "Nay," she declared, "I cannot. . . . In obedience to the will of the Lord God I came and in his will I abide faithful to death." And she was hanged.

However hard we may find it to understand the motives of the Quakers in their American quest for martyrdom, we must admire their courage. As William Brend wrote:

> I further Testify, in the Fear of the Lord, and witness God, with a Pen of Trembling, That the Noise of the whip on my Back, all the Imprisonments, and Banishing upon pain of Death . . . did no more affright me, through the Strength and Power of God in me, than if they had threatened to have bound a Spider's Web to my Finger.

Even the sympathetic Quaker historian Rufus Jones describes as an "almost excessive Quaker frankness" the spirit which moved Josiah Southwick after his successive whippings to tell his persecutors that "it was no more terrifying unto him, than if ye had taken a Feather and blown it up in the Air, and had said, Take heed it hurteth him not."

7

Trials of Governing:
The Oath

THE MORTAL TEST of Quakers in America was not at the whipping-post or on the gallows. To such ordeals European life had accustomed them, and they endured their suffering with courageous dignity in the New World. As the Quakers suffered they simply strengthened their own faith and the admiration of their spectators. By the middle of the 18th century, there were more Quakers in the Western Hemisphere than in all Britain. More significantly, in America they possessed a community of their own, or at least one in which they held the powers of government. European life had not trained the Quakers to sit in the seats of power; this was to be the novel test provided by America—a test which, in many important ways, they were to fail.

The reasons for their failure teach a great deal about the limitations of their doctrine and about the special requirements of American community life. Before the founding of Pennsylvania, the "tragic collision" with the New England Puritans helped keep Quakerism alive. In the early creative period of Quakerism their leaders were moved by a gospel-sense, by a belief that they had good news for all mankind: they had discovered the World-Church and were trying to show the presence of God in all humanity.

But as the idea of being a "peculiar people" began to dominate them, they became more interested in asserting and perfecting their truth than in diffusing it throughout the world. The very ways which earlier Quakers had used to show contempt for rank and custom gradually became themselves customs as rigid as those they were meant to displace. The Quaker's refusal to remove his hat became as arrogant and purposeless as the non-Quaker's insistence on hat-honor. The drab costume of the Quaker, meant at first to express indifference to outward garments, became a uniform to which the Quaker attached more importance than his neighbors did to their gayer garments. Silence became a "form" of worship, and even the spontaneity of Quaker sermons became compulsory. The same paradox existed in nearly every distinguishing feature of Quaker life, from their use of "thee" and "thou" to their ways of marriage and burial.

While the dogmas of Quakerism grew more fixed and uncompromising, those of Puritanism tended more and more toward compromise. Puritanism—proverbially rigid and dogmatic—expanded and adapted; while Quakerism—traditionally formless, spontaneous, and universal—built a wall around itself. This is the story of one of the greatest lost opportunities in all American history.

In the late 17th century, Quakerism had many qualities which would have suited it to become the dominant American religion. In the Old World it was notorious for its contempt of forms and hierarchies, for its fluidity, and for its antipathy to dogma. But its promise was not to be fulfilled. Its very formlessness, its mysticism, its insistence on personal rectitude and purity were to be its undoing as a community-building religion in America. And because the uncompromising spirit of William Brend, Mary Dyer and their fellow martyrs continued to dominate them, the Society of Friends was doomed to become a minor, however pure, enclave in American civilization.

Some Quaker historians have suggested that it was the "failure" of Quakerism as a religion that accounted for its ultimate ineffectiveness in American life. They have implied that the Society of Friends allowed the letter to kill the spirit of their religion; that because they became untrue to their own teachings they betrayed their cause and failed in their mission to the world. It is certainly clear, as Frederick B. Tolles has shown, that the center of American Quaker life tended to shift "from Meetinghouse to Counting-house" and that numerous Friends left the Society for the more respectable and less demanding ranks of the Presbyterians and Episcopalians. But this is only part of the story. It is more useful to note how the Quakers weakened themselves and their cause not by being false to their teachings, but by being too true to them. The teachings which for George Fox, John Woolman, and other great Quaker prophets expressed a vital spirit were now congealed into absolutes. By the early 18th century, American Quakers were no longer Searchers for the Truth but were its self-righteous Heralds. They were enforcers rather than devotees of the Gospel.

For some years after the founding of the colony in 1682 an informed observer might well have imagined that Quakerism would remain an expanding and creative force in American life. While William Penn was a man of courage and of principle, he was by no means an unworldly or inflexible man and he was anything but doctrinaire in government. The prosperity of the colony in 1739, according to Andrew Hamilton, an eminent Pennsylvania lawyer of the day, was less due to material circumstances than to "the constitution of Mr. Penn."

In the wise preface to his "Frame of Government for Pennsylvania," dated April 25, 1682, Penn actually apologized for specifying any particular form of institutions. Men, he said, were always inclined to arrogate too much knowledge to themselves, especially when they prescribed a specific political form as the cure-all for social ills. There were three reasons why such efforts were misguided:

> *First,* That the age is too nice and difficult for it; there being nothing the wits of men are more busy and divided upon. It is true, they seem to agree to the end, to wit, happiness; but, in the means, they differ, as to divine, so to this human felicity; and the cause is much the same, not always want of light and knowledge, but want of using them rightly. . . .
> *Secondly,* I do not find a model in the world, that time, place, and some

singular emergencies have not necessarily altered; nor is it easy to frame a civil government, that shall serve all places alike.

Thirdly, I know what is said by the several admirers of monarchy, aristocracy and democracy . . . when men discourse on the subject. But I chuse to solve the controversy with this small distinction, and it belongs to all three: Any government is free to the people under it (whatever be the frame) where the laws rule, and the people are a party to those laws, and more than this is tyranny, oligarchy, or confusion.

But, lastly, when all is said, there is hardly one frame of government in the world so ill designed by its first founders, that, in good hands, would not do well enough; and story tells us, the best, in ill ones, can do nothing that is great or good; witness the Jewish and Roman states. Governments, like clocks, go from the motion men give them; and as governments are made and moved by men, so by them they are ruined too. Wherefore governments rather depend upon men, than men upon governments. Let men be good, and the government cannot be bad; if it be ill, they will cure it. But, if men be bad, let the government be never so good, they will endeavour to warp and spoil it to their turn.

The first half-century of Pennsylvania history was strikingly prosperous. "From a wilderness," Richard Townsend observed in 1727, "the Lord, by his good hand of providence, hath made it a fruitful field." Still, during these years there was a great deal of party strife, which had very early led William Penn himself to plead with the colonists that "for the love of God, me, and the poor country" they "be not so Governmentish." But the two principal parties—the democratic and extremist "country party" led by David Lloyd and the conservative party of city merchants led by James Logan—were Quaker. While there were bitter disputes as to which Quaker group should dominate, it was the Quakers who held the reins of government securely.

Almost from the beginning the Quakers realized that their religious doctrines, if construed strictly, would put difficulties in the way of their running a government. It was one thing to live by Quaker principles, quite another to rule by them. Even in the earliest years, they were able to govern only by compromising one principle after another. Not only were they often driven to use fictions and evasions in defending the colony against external enemies, but in the domestic government of the colony also they had to come to terms with the non-Quaker ethic.

The matter of oaths provides an excellent example of how the smallest scruple, if dogmatically held, can produce a creeping paralysis that soon ramifies into all institutions. From the earliest English days of the sect, Quakers had stood against the taking of oaths. In 1656, George Fox had been made to answer to an English court for his "seditious" paper against oath-taking, in which he expressed the classic Quaker position. "Take heed of giving people oaths to swear," Fox warned, "for Christ our Lord and Master saith, 'Swear not at all; but let your communication be yea, yea, and nay, nay: for whatsoever is more than these cometh of evil.'" It was the "light in every man" which gave him the truth and made him testify to it; oaths and swearing were but "idle words" for which men would answer on the Day of Judgment. The only Biblical justification for swearing was in the Old Testament, and those commandments were directed only to the Jews. But what was the word of Jeremiah to count against that of Jesus and James, who had expressly forbidden all swearing? Once committed to this position, the Quakers adhered to it with a scrupulous orthodoxy that amazes our age of figurative interpretation.

To the scriptural and theological arguments the Quakers added others which hardened their orthodoxy into obstinacy. There was the common-sense objection that no oath could turn a liar into a man of truth. "He that makes no conscience of that law that forbids lying," asked Penn, "will he make any conscience of forswearing?" From the notion that oaths were futile, Quakers came to believe that oaths were actually vicious. Somewhat petulantly, they objected that requiring a man to be sworn to provide legal insurance of his truthfulness, somehow implied that he was a liar when not under oath.

By the "Great Law" of 1682 the Quakers in Pennsylvania provided that men give testimony by "solemnly promising to speak the truth, the whole truth and nothing but the truth." They established severe penalties for falsehood to replace those for perjury. In 1685 the provincial council refused to administer an oath to the King's Collector of Customs, despite the fact that he brought with him instructions to be sworn. In England a law of 1689 permitted Quakers to make a simple *affirmation* "in the presence of Almighty God" where others were required to swear; but at the same time the law prohibited Quakers from giving evidence in criminal cases, from serving as jurors or from holding any public office. Nevertheless in Pennsylvania Quakers were actually allowed to go on serving in their Assembly. They ran the government without oaths until 1693, when Penn was deprived of his proprietorship; then they discovered the meaning of the fact that they were not independent of English law.

As the non-Quaker population of Pennsylvania, including many Irish and Germans, increased, they added their objections to those of the English. Could rulers be trusted who refused to swear allegiance to the Crown? Could one believe witnesses or jurors who found subtle reasons for not taking the harmless traditional oaths? Quaker refusal to administer oaths became as controversial as their refusal to take them. The Quaker majority in the Pennsylvania Assembly for some time successfully fought off attempts to disqualify them from office because of their refusal to take or administer oaths; but their efforts at formalizing an "affirmation" as a substitute for the oath were frustrated in England.

In 1703, a number of Quaker members of the governor's council in Pennsylvania were disturbed to learn of a certain order of the English Lords of Trade and Plantations: Quakers might qualify for office by a legally prescribed affirmation in place of an oath, but all other persons required by the laws of England to take an oath or willing to do so, *must* have it administered to them—"otherwise all their proceedings are declared to be null and void." In Pennsylvania this rule created the unwelcome alternatives of chaos or the expulsion of Quakers from office. In some counties, like Chester and Bucks, it became difficult to find enough persons fit to serve as justices who were willing to administer an oath. "Our Friends can no more be concerned in administering an oath than they can take one," members of the council observed, "and in all actions where the case pinches either party, if they can, from any corner of the government, bring in an evidence that demands an oath, the cause must either drop, or a fit number of persons must be there, always to administer it, though only, perhaps, on account of such an evidence." Technicality was piled on technicality. The non-Quakers (knowing that only two members of the provincial council lacked scruples against swearing) insisted that, in order for the government of the colony to proceed, a quorum of at least five members of the council would have to take the oath. Richard Halliwell, one of the non-Quaker party, "insultingly made his boast that they had now laid the government on its back, and left it sprawling, unable to move hand or foot."

To add to the confusion, the oath became an issue within the Quaker community itself. In 1704, David Lloyd, Quaker leader of the antiproprietary party, publicly complained against William Penn that he had not succeeded in securing relief for Quakers from the administering of oaths and that as a result Quakers had been compelled to give up their offices.

Some Quaker office-holders began to compromise, either administering the oath themselves or allowing others to administer it under their authority. Some resigned. Meanwhile, the most influential Quaker voices from across the Atlantic counseled intransigence and purity of principle. Penn himself urged that Quakers in office neither resign nor compromise their opposition to oaths. "I desire you," he wrote from England, "to pluck up that English and Christian courage to not suffer yourselves to be thus treated and put upon. Let those factious fellows do their worst . . . I will bear you out." For many years the oath issue kept the political pot boiling. Penn argued that the charter had granted the Quaker community freedom from oaths; the Attorney-General in London argued that since the law of England required juries to be sworn in capital cases, no colonial charter could change so fundamental a requirement. Others argued that there was ample precedent for affirmations instead of oaths. And so it went, with the Quaker Assembly passing laws on the subject which were sometimes vetoed by the Governor and which, even when approved by him, were repeatedly repealed by the Crown. This was far from an academic question. Since Quakers could not give evidence in court, until some satisfactory provision was made for Quaker scruples there was no security even against murder in a predominantly Quaker community.

Not until 1718 did a law apparently meeting Quaker demands escape repeal by the Crown. This law allowed the affirmation in place of the oath for witnesses and office-holders and established the same penalties for false affirmations as for perjury. But Quaker purists were still not satisfied, for the legal form of affirmation still included the phrase "in the name of Almighty God." James Logan and some others showed a more compromising spirit, "However unfit were that affirmation for Friends in England, yet here, where such a rotten or insensible generation shelter themselves under the name, there is a necessity for a greater security." The six words referring to the Deity had become controversial within the Quaker community; the Yearly Meeting of 1710 had purposely avoided a decision and urged Friends on both sides to show charity. This controversy, which seemed to many but a verbal quibble, was finally settled by the Law of 1725 which omitted from the form of affirmation any reference to God and which secured the approval of the King.

That enactment of 1725 has remained substantially the basis of Pennsylvania law on the subject until the present day. Anyone required to swear an oath could, at his option, take an affirmation instead, but no official could refuse to administer an oath to a person who so preferred. The effect of this rule was to force the most stiff-necked Friends out of judicial and some other offices. The Quaker Yearly Meetings stuck to their principles; some even advised their members not to vote for Quakers for offices in which they might be tempted to violate their principle against administering oaths. A few kept their offices and disobeyed the rules, but generally Quakers refused to accept magistracies. Even in solidly Quaker communities, therefore, some offices were perforce not

filled by men of that religion. And here the matter stood. The best compromise the Quaker rulers of Pennsylvania could manage was one which
permitted anybody but a strict Quaker to be a judge. To the Society of
Friends even this somehow seemed a victory of principle.

But this is not the end of the story. The full moral of the Quaker
experience can be understood only in the light of the price they paid for
preserving their scruple against oaths. Never has there been a better
example of the futility of trying to govern by absolutes, and of the price
in self-deception paid by those who try to do so. Even from their beginning as a sect in England, the Quakers had a strong tradition against the
taking of human life for any reason whatever, whether in war or in peace.
This naturally inclined them against capital punishment, and Pennsylvania's basic Great Law of 1682, shaped and passed under Penn's
personal influence, had made a spectacular departure from English
criminal law on this very point. Instead of the numerous capital crimes
in the England of that day, only treason and murder were punishable by
death in Pennsylvania. So the law remained for over thirty years. But
English opponents of the Quakers used this, like everything else distinctive about them, to label them as dangerous anarchists. The matter was
dramatized in 1715 when Jonathan Hayes, a well-known citizen, was
murdered in Chester County. This happened at the height of the oath
controversy, when Deputy-Governor Charles Gookin had held that the
English requirements applied in Pennsylvania. Because of the predomi-
nance of Quakers in that part of the country, if Hayes's murderers were
to be brought to trial at all, judges, probably witnesses, and some jurors
would have to be Quakers; but since Quakers refused to take the required oaths, no trial was possible and the prisoners suspected of the
crime were released on bail for three years. Meanwhile, Deputy-Governor William Keith came to office, and the case was revived amid
familiar charges that the Quakers' exemption from oaths encouraged
crime. Hayes's murderers were executed before their appeal could be
heard in England, and when the news reached London that British
subjects were being executed in Pennsylvania on the verdict of unsworn
juries, there was an angry outcry. Here was more ammunition for the
anti-Quaker party.

It was just at this time, moreover, that the recurrent threat to exclude
Quakers from office altogether by insisting on the oath came to a head.
The prospect frightened the Quaker Assembly. They were therefore
ready to listen to the Governor's suggestion that, if they gave in on the
question of capital punishment, they might secure a compromise on the
matter of the oath. All that was required was to adopt the criminal laws

of England, which would automatically make many more crimes punishable by death. The Pennsylvania Quakers were persuaded. And so the Act of 1718 which allowed persons to take office without an oath also assimilated the capital laws of Quaker Pennsylvania and those of England. While the evidence for such a bargain is circumstantial, it is overwhelming. As Quaker historians somewhat ambiguously boast, the Act of 1718 was drawn by a Quaker lawyer, was passed by a Quaker Assembly, and was not protested by the Quaker Meetings.

Thus, to remain "pure" in the matter of oaths, the Quakers bargained the lives of all those men and women who might be convicted of any one of a dozen miscellaneous crimes. The episode was not merely a testimony against absolutes as guides to political behavior. It showed how zealous men might sacrifice the welfare and even the lives of their fellowmen to the overweening purity of their own consciences.

8

Trials of Governing: Pacifism

MEN WHO SET too much store by their dogmas and who will not allow themselves to be guided by the give-and-take between ideas and experience are likely to suffer defeat in one way, if not another. The Quakers had set out with at least one more very clear dogma: pacifism. In 1650, George Fox had gone to jail in England rather than take up arms for the Commonwealth against Charles Stuart. He recorded in his *Journal* for 1664 the classic Quaker position which was to be the most important and most continuous of all their beliefs:

> We are peaceable, and seek the peace, good and welfare of all, as in our lives and peaceable carriages is manifested. . . . We are heirs of the gospel of peace, which is the power of God. . . . For Christ said, 'His kingdom was not of this world, if it were his servants would fight.' Therefore he bid Peter, 'put up his sword; for,' said he, 'he that taketh the sword shall perish by the sword.' Here is the faith and patience of

the saints, to bear and suffer all things, knowing vengeance is the Lord's, and he will repay it to them that hurt his people and wrong the innocent; therefore cannot we avenge but suffer for his name's sake. . . . The doctrine of Christ, who never sinned, is to 'love one another,' and those who are in this doctrine hurt no man, in which we are, in Christ, who is our life.

But reciting this doctrine in England, where a Quaker might have to go to jail for it, was different from insisting on it in America, where it might cost the lives of non-Quakers. The Quakers who governed Pennsylvania until the middle of the 18th century held powers of life and death over the community, especially over the backwoods settlers who were menaced by the hostile French and scalp-hungry Indians. The central geographic position of the Quaker colony, the special importance of the Indian groups (the so-called Six Nations, and the Delawares) with whom they had to deal, and the critical necessity for American control of the rivers on the western border—all these magnified the Quaker decisions of peace or war for Pennsylvania into decisions for the British Empire and world politics.

The Quakers discovered that they were less free (for example, to be pacifists) as rulers of a province than when they had been a persecuted minority. "I wish thee could find more to say for our lying so naked and defenceless," James Logan from Philadelphia begged William Penn in England (September 2, 1703), "I always used the best argument I could, and when I pleaded that we were a peaceable people, had wholly renounced war, and the spirit of it; that we were willing to commit ourselves to the protection of God alone. . . .When I pleaded this, I really spoke my sentiments; but this will not answer in English government, nor the methods of this reign. Their answer is, that should we lose our lives only, it would be little to the crown, seeing 'tis our doing, but others are involved with us, and should the enemy make themselves master of the country it would too sensibly touch England in the rest of her colonies."

For many years Pennsylvania Quakers evaded this issue: they were careful that their "Deputy-Governor" (the person holding the executive powers in America on behalf of the Proprietors) be a non-Quaker and therefore a person whose scruples would not conflict with the ordinary business of government. Of over a dozen Deputy-Governors between the founding of the colony and the Quaker abdication in 1756, only one (Thomas Lloyd) was a Quaker. Thus, for a while in Pennsylvania, the Quakers were able to run the government and still keep their own consciences unsoiled.

Sooner or later, however, the Pennsylvania Quakers would have to choose between clear alternatives—both equally unwelcome. Theoretically, but only theoretically, there was a third possibility: if they could have cut themselves off both from England and from the increasing non-Quaker population, they might have been able to conduct their "holy experiment" in all its purity. But this was an unreal possibility. By the mid-18th century the only alternatives were compromise or withdrawal from government.

It would be difficult to find a more tangled story in all American history than that of how the Quakers, in 1756, finally made their choice. A host of conflicting factions and interests were involved. The issue of pacifism was inevitably bound up with the question of taxes, and nothing arouses moral fervor more effectively than finding reasons not to pay taxes. The political conflicts in Pennsylvania were also involved with the struggle against the Proprietors, with the antagonism of the Irish and German settlers toward the English, with the question of currency reform, and with the fight of Presbyterians and Anglicans against Quakers.

Yet, from the Quaker point of view, one could hardly find a story which had a simpler theme. The essential issue was pacifism. If the Quakers had sought to create an environment in which to try their pacifism, they could hardly have done better than invent the circumstances of provincial Pennsylvania. In Europe in the 17th and early 18th century, before the days of a universal manpower draft, the Quaker principle against war could not be severely tested. In all the countries of Western Europe they were a small minority; there could only be a few *causes célèbres*, like the harrying of George Fox during the commonwealth. Not until the Quakers held power in an American province did their problem affect a whole community. Here the question of peace or war faced them directly and repeatedly: in Britain's battle for empire in which they were both a garrison and a valuable stake, and as an aspect of self-defense from the bloody attacks of natives.

Whatever other evils of European life the Quaker immigrants to Pennsylvania had managed to escape, war was surely not one of them. A bare list of the imperial conflicts in America which put colonials on the battle-line might have appalled men with much less distaste for war than the Friends. The half-understood purposes of a government three thousand miles across the ocean involved the Quakers again and again. The colony had been born for less than a decade when, in April 1689, they received word of the English declaration of war against the French, which was the beginning of King William's War. To the English request that the Quakers arm for defense and set up a militia, one of the mem-

bers of their Governor's Council replied that he saw no danger "but from
the Bears & Wolves." As a matter of conscience the Quakers then refused
to take action. Within another dozen years, England was again fighting
France, now together with Spain, in the War of the Spanish Succession,
known in America as Queen Anne's War. Although this war was duly
"proclaimed" in Pennsylvania, the Quaker Assembly repeatedly refused
to enact military laws, with the familiar explanation, "were it not that
the raising money to hire men to fight or kill one another, is matter of
Conscience to us and against our Religious Principles, we should not be
wanting, according to our small abilities, to Contribute to those designs."
Queen Anne's War came to an end in 1713 and for a happy interlude of
twenty-five years the policies of empire did not thrust war upon the
colonies. But this was only an interlude. The period of gravest trial, still
to come, would bring the wars of empire to the front and back doors of
the colony.

The dress rehearsal for the decisive trial of Quakerism began in 1739,
with the outbreak of war with Spain, in the so-called War of Jenkins'
Ear, which became the War of the Austrian Succession, called in the
colonies King George's War. While the earlier "involvement" of the
province in the struggles of the mother country may have seemed merely
technical, the consequences of membership in the British Empire were
now more immediate and more serious. France and Spain, both with
vast interests in America, were at war with England, and hence with
Pennsylvania, whether or not the Quakers wished it so. Colonial wars
were becoming an integral part of European politics. In fact, Spanish
privateers were to be found on the Delaware River. What would the
Quakers in control of the Pennsylvania Assembly do about it?

There followed the familiar struggle between a non-Quaker Governor
who was trying to harmonize the policy of the colony with that of the
Empire, and the die-hard Quakers whose prime concern was to keep
inviolate their pacifist principle. For a while in 1741, the Quakers succeeded in paralyzing the government, withholding the Governor's salary,
and preventing any legislation. They were aided in their policies by many
of the German settlers whom they had alarmed with rumors. The Governor's plan for a militia, they said, would bind settlers to royal governors
in a slavery as brutal as "they were formerly under to their princes in
Germany . . . the expense would impoverish them, and . . . if any other
than Quakers should be chosen upon the assembly they would be dragged
down from their farms and obliged to build forts as a tribute for their
being admitted to settle in the province." This whispering campaign
produced fears of riot and violence within the colony.

Not until 1745 did Governor Thomas finally secure an appropriation for the purposes of the war: a grant of £4,000 for "Bread, Beef, Pork, Flour, Wheat or other Grain" for the garrison at Louisbourg, which was now in the hands of the English. The "other Grain" was apparently intended to be gunpowder. The Quakers had earlier actually aided the defense of the colony but then too only by subterfuge or by appropriations made for unspecified purposes. In 1693 their money was given ostensibly "to feed the hungry and clothe the naked" Indians; in 1701, money was appropriated for a fort, but only "as far as their religious principles would permit"; in 1709, they provided money for an expedition against Nova Scotia, for "although they could not bear arms, their duty was to support the Queen's government by money"; in 1740 the money raised was "for the use of the King, for such purposes as he should direct"—and so it had gone. For the later difficulties some have blamed the tactless Governor, but these may better be explained by the fact that the Quakers "measured their merit by the extent of suffering for conscience sake."

Perhaps the most significant result of the struggle in 1745 was the emergence of a strong compromise party under the leadership of Benjamin Franklin. With a broad popular base, equally opposed to the self-interest of the Proprietors and to the fanaticism of Quaker extremists, Franklin's party would eventually displace the rigid rule of the Quaker minority. In 1747, during the continuing controversy over defense, Franklin published *Plain Truth,* one of his shrewdest political pamphlets. Neither pro- nor anti-Quaker, the pamphlet gave a full, fair and even prophetic picture of the colony and its need for defense. Pennsylvania's fortunate geographic situation at the center of the colonies had explained their repose: "and tho' our Nation is engag'd in a bloody War, with two great and powerful Kingdoms, yet, defended, in a great Degree, from the French on the one Hand, by the Northern Provinces, and from the Spaniards on the other by the Southern, at no small Expence to each, our People have, till lately, slept securely in their Habitations." Pennsylvania, the only British colony which had made no provision for defense, had relied on the length and difficulty of its bay and river to protect it naturally from any enemy.

Franklin argued that this feeling of security was not justified in 1747, even if it had been before, for the colony had become rich enough to repay the effort of plunder. There had been two decades of peace, but "it is a long Peace indeed, as well as a long Lane, that has no Ending," and now the colony must expect the French to show increasing ingenuity and success in stirring up the Indians. "How soon may the Mischief spread to our Frontier Counties? And what may we expect to be the Consequence, but deserting of Plantations, Ruin, Bloodshed, and Confusion!" The seaboard would suffer more of what it had tasted in the preceding summer, when privateers invaded Delaware Bay and plundered plantations near Newcastle. Preparedness was the only answer:

> The Enemy, no doubt, have been told, that the People of Pennsylvania are Quakers, and against all Defence, from a Principle of Conscience; this, tho' true of a Part, and that a small Part only of the Inhabitants, is commonly said of the Whole; and what may make it look probable to Strangers, is, that in Fact, nothing is done by any Part of the People towards their Defence. But to refuse Defending one's self, or one's Country, is so unusual a Thing among Mankind, that possibly they may not believe it, till by Experience they find, they can come higher and higher up our River, seize our Vessels, land and plunder our Plantations and Villages, and retire with their Booty unmolested. Will not this confirm the Report, and give them the greatest Encouragement to strike one bold Stroke for the City, and for the whole Plunder of the River?

It was the plain duty of government to protect the people; no private religious scruple could relieve a legislator of that duty. Franklin urged the Quaker legislators "that if on account of their religious Scruples, they themselves could do no Act for our Defence, yet they might retire; relinquish their Power for a Season, quit the Helm to freer Hands during the present Tempest." The public funds raised from all the people had been spent by the Quakers to secure the enjoyment of their own religion, to oppose anti-Quaker petitions, and to put themselves in a favorable light at the English court. How could they justify their refusal to use these funds for the benefit and defense of all?

The solution, Franklin concluded, was simply for the Quakers to withdraw and allow others to rule and defend the colony. If the Quakers were beyond their rights in sacrificing the whole community for their private religious principles, non-Quakers would be stupid to fail to defend the colony simply because they might save the Quakers along with themselves. Franklin drew up a plan of association to raise money voluntarily for defense, and it was not long before a militia of 10,000 men was organized.

But King George's War was only a rehearsal. The real trial of the Quaker pacifist spirit did not come until large-scale massacres by Indians spread terror along the western border of the colony. That was in the latter part of 1755, when the defeat of the British General Braddock enabled the French to use Fort Duquesne as a base for marauding parties. In addition, the French incited the Delawares to thwart the

Proprietary purchase of western Pennsylvania from the Six Nations by sudden and bloody attacks. The first reaction of the Quakers of eastern Pennsylvania was incredulity: surely their old friends the Delawares *could not* be committing massacres. Showing their usual reluctance to believe ill of their fellowmen, the Quakers insisted that the Indians' grievances must have stemmed from recent unfair treatment by the English themselves.

9

How Quakers Misjudged the Indians

THE POLITICAL SUCCESS, even the very survival of an American colony, often depended on a realistic estimate of the Indian. But the Quakers' view of the Indian was of a piece with their attitude toward war: it was unrealistic, inflexible, and based on false premises about human nature. The problem was never better summarized than in the speech by Teedyuscung, Chief of the Delawares, at a conference with Pennsylvania leaders in July 1756. In his hand he held a belt of wampum, which had lately been given him by the Iroquois: a large square represented the land of the Indians; on one side stood an Englishman and on the other a Frenchman—both ready to seize the land. Chief Teedyuscung pleaded that the Pennsylvanians show their friendship by guaranteeing that no more land would be taken from the Indians. While the Chief's description was an oversimplification he had surely stated the heart of the matter. The increasing, westward-flowing population of the Province was passing like a tidal wave over Indian lands. The troubles of the Indians could no longer be reduced to niceties of protocol, to maxims of fair play, or to clichés of self-reproach. Here was one of those great conflicts in history when a mighty force was meeting a long-unmoved body; either the force had to be stopped or the body had to move.

But the Quakers chose not to see it that way. Their policy in this

crisis of the affairs of Pennsylvania showed a spectacular, if not altogether surprising, failure of practical vision. They seemed as blind to
the long-term problems and interests of the Indians as to the character
of these unfamiliar people with whom they were dealing. In 1748, for
example, the Quaker Assembly had refused to vote money for the
defense of Philadelphia, but appropriated £500 for the Indians, accompanying it by the pious wish that the money be used to "supply them
with necessaries towards acquiring a livelihood and cultivate the friendship between us and not to encourage their entering into a war." How
could Quaker men of the world have failed to guess that Indian lead
and powder would not be used solely to shoot bear and deer? For that
failure of practical judgment Irish and German settlers on the western
border would have to pay dearly. Some years later, in the fall of 1756,
when the Quaker Assembly in Philadelphia heard of the bloodbath in
the west, they at once began to investigate the source of Indian
grievances. Instead of providing for military defense, the Assembly produced a bill for the better regulation of trade with the Indians, authoriz-
ing commissioners who would see that the Indians were fairly treated
and enacting such guarantees as maximum prices on goods sold to them.
Such admirable measures were small comfort to backwoodsmen who saw
their homes in flames, their crops ruined, their wives and children
scalped or captured.

The political conflict between the non-Quaker Deputy-Governor
Robert Hunter Morris and the Quaker Assembly came to the fore.
The Deputy-Governor, in defense of the Proprietors, declared that
Indian grievances against the Proprietors had nothing to do with the
massacres and that the real trouble lay in Quaker pacifism which had
left the province defenseless. On the other side, the Quakers traced all
ills to the wicked policies of the Proprietors. In the middle stood Franklin,
who now had a considerable following among the less orthodox Quakers;
he did not oppose a more just Indian policy, but he demanded immediate measures for military defense. Still the minority of die-hard
Quakers which controlled the Assembly would not budge from its traditional pacifism, though the whole border might burn for it.

The massacres continued; panic gripped western Pennsylvania. Murder
was rampant; whole townships were broken up, their populations driven
from their homes. George Stevenson wrote from York, on November 5,
1755, that the real question there was "whether we shall stand or run?
Most are willing to stand, but have no Arms nor Ammunition." The
government gave no answer to appeals. "People from Cumberland are
going thro this Town hourly in Droves and the Neighbouring Inhabits

are flocking into this Town Defenseless as it is." While settlers on the border suffered the murderous blows of the tomahawk, those further east had the burden of supporting growing numbers of refugees.

It is hardly surprising that the patience of the people of Pennsylvania had worn thin. Toward the end of November 1755, about three hundred desperate Germans from the west arrived in Philadelphia to demand action of the Assembly. They succeeded in frightening the Assembly into a show of compliance and, through the Provincial Agent, petitioned the English Privy Council to remedy their defenseless condition. These months saw a growing and unprecedented division of sentiment within the Quaker community itself. The Philadelphia Yearly Meeting in September still evaded the issue by refusing to take a position on the large military appropriation needed for defense. Many would have agreed with Israel Pemberton that the events of the summer and fall of 1755 had "produc'd a greater & more fatal change both with respect to the state of our affairs in general & among us as a Society than seventy preceding years."

By July 1756, the French commandant at Fort Duquesne reported with satisfaction that he had "succeeded in ruining the three adjacent provinces, Pennsylvania, Maryland, and Virginia, driving off the inhabitants, and totally destroying the settlements over a tract of country thirty leagues wide reckoning from the line of Fort Cumberland. . . . The Indian villages are full of prisoners of every age and sex. The enemy has lost far more since the battle than on the day of his defeat."

But still the Quakers had not been shocked into discovering the weaknesses of their idealized Indians. They seemed indifferent to the fact that the Indian leaders with whom they dealt were sometimes half-demented with drink. For example, the wildly contradictory demands of their good friend Teedyuscung, while the Quakers were purporting to represent him in late July 1756, were made while he was under the influence of liquor. But somehow, whether from optimism, pity, or blindness, the Quakers were not prepared to take this fact into account.

The needs of the London Government and the policies of Virginia and Maryland identified Pennsylvanians in the eyes of the Indians with British expansion, and with land-grabbing enterprises like the Ohio Company, however much the people of Pennsylvania might deplore it. Indian politics were no simple matter: a gesture of friendship to one tribe might be taken as a declaration of war by that tribe's enemies. By choosing an alliance in 1742 with the Iroquois, for example, Pennsylvania had willy-nilly become involved in the troubles between the Iroquois and the Delawares and thus sowed seeds of trouble to be reaped thirteen years later. When, in 1756, the Quakers were present at negotiations with Teedyuscung, Chief of the Delawares, they pressed their non-Quaker Governor to conclude a peace treaty, but Governor Morris had the good sense to see that such a separate peace would probably incense the powerful Iroquois. This was all an intricate and delicate business not to be settled by moral slogans or abstract principles.

Some initiative by the Quakers was urgent if they were not to lose all popular support at a time when the colony was panicked by Indian violence. They chose to take this initiative entirely outside the government, even in competition with it, when, in July of 1756, they formed the "Friendly Association for Regaining and Preserving Peace with the Indians by Pacific Measures." Through this non-governmental association the Quakers intended to deal with the Indians and to pacify them without sacrifice of principles. Despite their noble intentions, the Quakers' activities among the Indians in those desperate times can hardly be called anything but meddling. The Governors of Pennsylvania, however tactless or ineffective, did at least see quite accurately the character of the Indian problem. The Friendly Association succeeded only in further confusing matters, in leading the Indians to distrust those rulers of Pennsylvania with whom they would finally have to deal, and in postponing any arrangement satisfactory to the new settlers of Pennsylvania.

On one occasion during the slippery negotiations of 1756, the Quakers persuaded the Delaware Indians to designate Israel Pemberton, a Quaker leader, as the representative with whom the Governor of Pennsylvania would have to deal in all Indian affairs. This ambiguous confidence pleased the Quakers, but they had only the vaguest notion of whom or what they were representing. Actually they were in no position to serve either the Indians or the people of Pennsylvania. They simply complicated the Governor's problem and led him to threaten that he would treat them as enemies of the King if they did not cease their tampering.

The Quaker preoccupation with their principles blinded them to the most obvious facts. In April 1751, for example, the Quaker Assembly, refusing the offer of the Proprietors of the Province to help build a fort, showed their usual complacency. "As we have always found that sincere, upright Dealing with the Indians, a friendly Treatment of them on all Occasions, and particularly in relieving their Necessities at proper Times by suitable Presents, have been the best Means of securing their Friendship, we could wish our Proprietaries had rather thought fit to join with us in the Expence of those presents, the Effects of which have at all Times so manifestly advanced their Interests with the Security of our Frontier

Settlements." Even after the storm broke on the frontier and after the western inhabitants of Pennsylvania had begun to reap the fiery harvest of a half-century of Quaker generosity and non-resistance to the Indians, many Quakers remained blind to the practical moral of it all. One of the most fantastic examples of this blindness is found in the journal of Daniel Stanton, one of the numerous itinerant Quaker zealots who carried the messages of the Philadelphia Yearly Meeting to remote parts of America. To him the relatively small number of Quakers massacred by the Indians during the frontier attacks of 1755-56 was a testimony of God's approval of the Quaker policy. He could not deny that the Indians had been "an heavy rod of chastisement on this land; yet remarkable it was, that through the protection of Almighty, which was as the shadow of a mighty rock in a wearied land, few called by our name were ill used during all this calamity." A more valid explanation of Quaker luck, though less flattering to their self-righteousness, was that almost all the Quakers were then living in the eastern portion of the province, separated by two hundred miles of mountainous and river-traced terrain from the "barbarous and cruel enemy."

Franklin was not impressed by the fact that the Quakers on the eastern seaboard had, by good luck or God's grace or whatever other means, still escaped the fury of the Indians. He was more concerned, in August 1756, to see "our frontier people continually butchered," and he lamented the delays in fighting back. "In short," Franklin concluded with characteristic directness, "I do not believe we shall ever have a firm peace with the Indians, till we have well drubbed them."

10

The Withdrawal

BY THE SPRING of 1756, even the die-hard Quakers in Pennsylvania were beginning to wonder whether they could long continue to hold both the reins of government and the principles of their religion. As early as 1702, James Logan reported to William Penn that governing was "ill-fitted to their principles," and events of the first half of the 18th century confirmed the accusation now repeated by their enemies that "to govern is absolutely repugnant to the avowed principles of Quakerism."

At the moment of crisis, the conflict was no longer simply between a Quaker oligarchy in Pennsylvania and a hard-headed imperial government in London. In Pennsylvania three parties contested. Benjamin Franklin's popular party included broad-minded Quakers among others and was opposed equally to religious absolutes and oligarchic rule. They proposed a militia bill making all men subject to military duty (commutable by a fine) with officers democratically elected by the soldiers. Quakers would not have to bear arms, but they would be required to help pay for defense. Against Franklin's party were the Quaker extremists, led by such unbending pacifists as Israel Pemberton, who had refused to pay any tax to be used for any military purpose. Against both of them stood the Proprietors and their Governor, who were unwilling that the Proprietors bear the Quakers' share of the costs. They feared the democratic method of electing militia-officers, but had no sympathy for pacifism.

Despite the growing opposition, the increasing non-Quaker population of the Province, and the exasperation of successive Governors, the Quakers were still in control at the beginning of 1756. In that year the Quakers, probably comprising less than one-fourth the population, held twenty-eight of the thirty-six seats in the Pennsylvania Assembly. Of that number, the die-hards were the most influential and active.

As news of the border massacres reached London, agitation against Quaker rule was redoubled; the English government again threatened some decisive measure, such as permanent disqualification of Quakers from holding office in Pennsylvania. Opinion on both sides of the ocean seemed to support such a measure. Dr. John Fothergill, a weighty member of the London Yearly Meeting, summarized the Proprietary case against the Quakers:

> The point upon which all rested, was you are unfit for government. You accept our publick trust, which at the same time you acknowledge you cannot discharge. You owe the people protection, & yet withhold them from protecting themselves. Will not all the blood that is spilt lye at your doors? and can we, say they, sit still and see the province in danger of being given up to a merciless enemy without endeavoring its rescue.

Several practical considerations became important: fear of the law disqualifying Quakers, hope that some blame for the Indian massacres might be shifted to other shoulders by putting the government in non-Quaker hands, and a desire to keep open the possibility of return to power at a later time. All these combined with the desire to preserve inviolate the principle of pacifism.

London Quakers urged the Quakers of Pennsylvania to abdicate quickly while there was still time to hand to others some of the blame for bloodshed. They busied themselves on the backstairs of the government in London, and finally negotiated a bargain with Lord Granville, President of the Privy Council: if he would see that the Quakers were not disqualified from officeholding, they would see that the Friends in Pennsylvania withdrew from the Provincial Assembly. Dr. John Fothergill in London wrote to Israel Pemberton explaining the need for withdrawal, and the Philadelphia Yearly Meeting wrote back their pledge that everything would be done to induce Quakers not to hold office in time of war. But this pledge did not satisfy the London Friends, who promptly sent over two of their number, John Hunt and Christopher Wilson, to see that the promise was fulfilled, and to try to heal the breaches within the Quaker community in Pennsylvania.

In late spring of 1756, when the Governor and Council declared war against the Delaware and Shawnee Indians, matters came to a head. On June 4, 1756, six leading Quakers in the Assembly offered their resignations. They complacently disavowed "any Design of involving the House in unnecessary Trouble" but, they declared, "as many of our Constituents seem of Opinion that the present Situation of Public Affairs call upon us for Services in a military Way, which, from a Conviction of Judgment, after mature Deliberation, we cannot comply with, we conclude it most conducive to the Peace of our own Minds, and the Reputation of our religious Profession, to permit in our Resolutions of resigning our Seats, which we accordingly now do; and request these our Reasons may be entered on the Minutes of the House." Quaker rule in the Pennsylvania government, after a stormy three-quarters of a century, thus came to an end—not by defeat but by abdication.

London Quakers breathed a sigh of relief. In the colony men of all persuasions were glad to be disburdened of doctrinaire principles. Franklin reported with audible pleasure that "all the stiff rump, except one that would be suspected of opposing the service from religious motives, have voluntarily quitted the Assembly; and 'tis proposed to chuse Churchman [Anglicans] in their places." These changes would finally "promise us some fair weather which I have long sigh'd for."

Franklin might well have been pleased; it was his party that profited most from the withdrawal. In the special election to replace the strict Quakers, six reliable Franklin men were chosen. And in October came the regular elections for the thirty-six members of the Assembly. The emissaries from the London Yearly Meeting did not arrive in time to persuade the Quakers not to vote for Quakers or, preferably, not to vote at all. In the final count, despite a temporary coalition of Franklin and the Proprietary party (who cordially hated each other) sixteen Quaker Assemblymen were elected. This was, of course, a measure of the reluctance of Quakers to acquiesce in the decision made for them by Israel Pemberton and other intransigents. Soon after the votes were counted, Hunt and Wilson, the English Quaker emissaries, added their voices to Pemberton's. Each of the elected Quakers was called individually before the Quaker Meeting for Sufferings to persuade him to resign. Four did so, leaving twelve professed Quaker Assemblymen of whom, as both Quakers and their enemies were pleased to discover, only eight were in good standing in the Society of Friends.

Even though people continued to speak of the "Quaker Assembly" at least until 1776, this was only because many of the members still preferred to take an affirmation or were related somehow to earlier Quakers. In fact, the dramatic withdrawal of 1756 was much more than a gesture; it was an abdication of political power by the Philadelphia Yearly Meeting, the highest authority of Quakers in Pennsylvania. Some pseudo- and semi-Quakers continued to seek and to hold political power in the Assembly, but these were disavowed by the orthodox. Strict Quakers made it plain that they were neither represented by these backsliders nor responsible for their decisions. The die-hards went on "labouring" among all good Friends to keep them from standing for the Assembly or voting for any Quakers who stood. There were already hints that some of these Quaker leaders looked to the day when the end of war in the colony would enable them to resume power.

That day was never to come, for the reins of government cannot be picked up and laid aside at will. The Quaker abdication, with its avowal of the inconsistency between their principles and the responsibilities of government, was perhaps the greatest evidence of practical sense they were ever to give. But their secret hope of returning to power with the peace of the 1760's showed their fundamental failure to understand society and its problems.

Whatever chance there may have been for such a political comeback was smashed by the American Revolution: the Quaker principle against war was also a principle against revolution. "The setting up and putting down Kings and governments," their Yearly Meeting had declared nearly a century before, "is God's peculiar prerogative, for causes best known to himself." As the Quakers had tried to remain neutral in the plots and counterplots of troubled England during the 17th century, so they sought neutrality during the days of the American Revolution. Again they were less concerned with complex questions of government than with whether any law violated their private Quaker consciences. As the Revolution approached, the Yearly Meeting asked of every Monthly Meeting, "Are Friends careful not to defraud the King of his Dues?" Some of the more far-sighted Friends in England, aware that the cause of liberty in England was bound up with the success of the American cause, urged the American Friends not to obstruct it. But the Americans looked to their consciences, were scrupulously subservient to all non-military requirements of the English government, and were, on the whole, equally uncooperative with the British and the American armies. They refused to pay taxes and fines levied by the American government, and were, understandably, labeled as Tories. To the charge of fanaticism hung on them in 1756 was now added the greater odium of treason.

After the Quakers withdrew from government in 1756 they gave much of their great energy to the purification of their own sect. By 1777 the Yearly Meeting called for "a reformation." If they could not rule the Province, they must at least not cease to be a "peculiar people." Some of the Quarterly Meetings, like that at Chester, sought "a revival of ancient simplicity in plainness of apparel, household furniture, the education of youth, and a due and wakeful attendance of our religious meetings." They sought, for example, to remove and abolish gravestones, as simply another of the vanities of this world. They attempted to increase the religious influence in their education. They began more intensively "to labour for a Reformation in Respect to the Distiling and Use of Spirituous Liquors amongst Friends and the Polluting Practice of keeping Taverns, Beerhouses, etc.," and they were beginning to report "a number of Friends having Used Spirituous Liquors very Sparingly in the time of our late Harvest and others have with great satisfaction used none at all." They intensified their effort to secure the freedom of all slaves held by Quakers. In a word, they undertook to build a wall around the Society of Friends against all alien influences, opposing even attendance at the religious services of other sects. There is no denying that their abdication of political power led them to look more closely into their own hearts and to preserve more strictly the tenets of their sect.

Fortunately for the Society of Friends, and for the Province of Pennsylvania, the Quakers did not withdraw entirely from communal concerns. Some of them became prosperous merchants and enterprising men of science. The humanitarian currents within Pennsylvania Quakerism grew stronger as the political currents weakened. During the 18th century they gave increasingly of themselves in the growing movement against slavery and the slave-trade, in the building of hospitals, and in the humanizing of prisons and insane-asylums. Many surviving institutions, like the Philadelphia Lying-In Hospital, are monuments to the effectiveness of Quakers in one small area of the practical world. But that very success, which was a measure of what the Quakers no longer gave to politics, was a fitting, if ironical, criterion of the unfitness of their dogmas for the larger tasks of building a new society in a new world.

11

The Curse of Perfectionism

IN THE PERSPECTIVE of European history, the Quaker withdrawal is simply another example of the failure of a religious sect to hold control of a government. In the perspective of American history it is a good deal more: it illustrates the special trials of dogmas in America, marked in this instance by the peculiar contradictions within the Quaker teachings themselves. Quaker experience in Pennsylvania can be described in terms of three tendencies which will help us understand what caused the Quakers to fail in government and what helped them continue, despite heavy trials, to be dedicated Quakers.

Self-Purity and Perfectionism. Although Penn had originally set himself the task of a holy experiment, of building a community on Friendly foundations, leading Quakers of Pennsylvania showed an unremitting preoccupation, sometimes close to obsession, with the purity of their own souls. On more than one occasion, we have seen, the Quakers in power seemed more anxious for their own principles than for the welfare, or even the survival, of the Province itself. Before expressing unqualified admiration for such steadfastness, we might well examine its implications for the survival of a sturdy Quakerism and for the daily lives of those many others who, according to the Quakers themselves, had a right to live and prosper in America. Somehow, whenever tested, the Quakers chose the solution which kept themselves pure, even though others might have to pay the price. To avoid taking oaths, Quakers sacrificed the humanity of criminal laws. While die-hard Quakers kept free of the taint of militarism and preserved inviolate their testimony against war, hundreds of innocent women and children were being massacred by Indians in western Pennsylvania. And so it went. Numerous Quaker preachers who came from England to harden the obstinacy of the Friends of Pennsylvania exhorted them to "walk in white" at any cost. Even in the wilderness they must be "as a lily amongst thorns."

Repeatedly they were urged to "mind their own business as Friends do everywhere else." For a Quaker to mind his own business meant for him to pursue the purity of his principles. This turning inward brought blindness to the facts of life about him—to the character of Indians, to the threat on the western borderlands, to the self-interest of other men. His resignation to the will of God made him indifferent to the stream of everyday life.

"Let's do our duty," William Penn had urged as early as 1701, "and leave the rest with God." Battles should be fought not by men but by God; governments should be raised up and torn down by Him alone. Men like Franklin, "who can have no Confidence that God will protect those that neglect the use of rational Means for their Security," might be continually faced with moral problems. But Quakers thought all such problems could be settled in advance. John Woolman and his fellow Quaker Saints, striving "for a perfect Resignation . . . a Belief, that whatever the Lord might be pleased to allot for me, would work for Good," induced men to furbish their own souls while the community shifted for itself. Yet neither self-purity nor resignation to God's unaided will could build a wall against fighting enemies. Nor construct a community in the wilderness.

Cosmopolitanism. One of the distinctive features of the Pennsylvania experiment was that American Quakers were subject to constant persuasion, surveillance, and scrutiny from afar. The powerful rulers of the London Yearly Meeting were remote from the perils, opportunities, and challenges of America; yet their influence was a check on what might have been the normal adaptation of Quaker doctrines to life in America.

The Society of Friends had become a kind of international conspiracy for Peace and for primitive Christian perfection. Some years after the Revolution, Thomas Jefferson called them "a religious sect . . . acting with one mind, and that directed by the mother society in England. Dispersed, as the Jews, they still form, as those do, one nation, foreign to the land they live in. They are Protestant Jesuits, implicitly devoted to the will of their superior, and forgetting all duties to their country in the execution of the policy of their order." Emissaries from the London Yearly Meeting tried to shape Pennsylvania policy in the interests of the international Quaker community. Only occasionally and by chance, as when they urged the Pennsylvania Quakers to widen their use of capital punishment in order to avoid the oath, did that interest happen to lead to compromise. More often, they pushed American Friends toward rigid orthodoxy. In the tense days of 1756, Dr. John Fothergill from London and the two emissaries, John Hunt and Christopher Wilson, added their voices to those of American extremists; they urged Quakers to withdraw from government so they might preserve their pacifist principles inviolate. In this, the interest of the English Quaker community was dominant.

Pressure from England was not merely occasional. A constant flow of itinerant ministers carried the "refreshing" currents of world Quakerism even into the smaller villages and the back country. In the period of less than a century between the founding of Pennsylvania and the outbreak of the American Revolution, well over a hundred Quaker men and women ministers came from abroad, mostly from England. The leading historian of colonial Quakerism, Frederick B. Tolles, has described how an "Atlantic Community" of the Society of Friends emerged during this period. After 1670 the eyes of English Quakers were turned westward. Traveling preachers built and preserved that transoceanic community and, in George Keith's words, "kept the Quakers so strong in countenance." The fact that they were often preaching to the converted did not mean that they retailed flabby platitudes. They preached strong medicine. The spirit of the earlier Quaker martyrs lived on in them. Their cheerfulness was as remarkable as their courage. One of them, Samuel Fothergill, the brother of Dr. John Fothergill, wrote his wife in 1755:

> I have now travelled 2550 miles, upon the continent of America; of which, one horse has carried me 1750; he is an excellent creature, and providentially put into my hands by a friend near Philadelphia. He cost me about five pounds sterling; he travels with great ease and safety, and sometimes, like his master, with hard fare, and sometimes none at all, but we both jog on contentedly.

But, contented or not, these ministers had set themselves a grim task: to be Jeremiahs in the wilderness, recalling American Quakers to their mission as a peculiar people.

Their dominant theme was a warning against the temptations of prosperity and a plea for the primitive virtues of the Society of Friends. Some, like Thomas Chalkley, who came over from England in 1698, stayed on; a member of the Philadelphia Monthly Meeting for over forty years, he never lost the spirit of the missionary, the zealot, and the prophet. He recorded in his journal for 1724:

> I was concerned at that Meeting at Philadelphia to let the People know, That as God had blessed the People of that City, and the Province, with spiritual and temporal Blessings, and made the Land naturally fruitful, to the Inriching many of the Inhabitants, he now expected Fruits from them of Piety and Virtue; and that if there was not a stricter walking with God in Christ Jesus, they might expect his divine Hand, which had visited them with Favours from Heaven above, and from the Earth beneath, would visit them with a Rod in it, and that he had already given them some gentle Strokes therewith.

Such Jeremiads were of course familiar enough to Puritan New England, and might have had little effect in Pennsylvania had they not been coupled there with a menacing insistence on certain otherworldly dogmas. Prominent among them was, of course, the principle of pacifism. As early as 1739, with King George's War in the offing, Chalkley traveled about the province urging Friends to hold themselves aloof. Visiting ministers from England, like William Reckitt who first came in 1756, went about reproaching the people of Pennsylvania for worrying over defense of the colony "in which several had been meddling and concerning themselves." So the Pure Truth was replenished from abroad and the people were saved from the curse of prudence.

The plea for universalism had the simultaneous effects of strengthening Quakerism and of weakening its influence in American society. For Friends in Pennsylvania, the close tie to England was a tie to orthodoxy, an anchor against the winds and currents of the New World. Isaac Norris, the Philadelphia Quaker, preened himself and criticized the provincialism of New England Christianity. "Your New England ministers, so called," he wrote in 1700, "seem to have much zeal for religion, but have a peculiar talent in the application and practice; and by looking no farther than their own narrow limits, do not consider the universality of God's love to the creation." Yet without that very talent for "application and practice" no ministry could incorporate its teachings into the social mind.

Insularity. As the Quakers of Philadelphia deferred to the London Yearly Meeting, they insulated themselves from their neighbors, whom they had to understand if they were to rule the broad province of Pennsylvania. To the Quakers, their obstinacy doubtless seemed a purity of principle and their rigidity a steadfastness in belief. But some of their more perceptive contemporaries saw the perils hidden in these virtues. William Penn himself wrote in exasperation from England in 1705:

There is an excess of vanity that is apt to creep in upon the people in power in America, who, having got out of the crowd in which they were lost here, upon every little eminency there, think nothing taller than themselves but the trees, and as if there were no after superior judgment to which they should be accountable; so that I have sometimes thought that if there was a law to oblige the people in power, in their respective colonies, to take turns in coming over for England, that they might lose themselves again amongst the crowds of so much more considerable people at the custom-house, exchange, and Westminster Hall, they would exceedingly amend in their conduct at their return, and be much more discreet and tractable, and fit for government. In the mean time, pray help to prevent them not to destroy themselves.

During those great crises which put their principles to the test, strict Pennsylvania Quakers looked down their noses at neighbors who had lost the character of a peculiar people, and had become "as salt which hath lost its savour." Policies which Benjamin Franklin opposed because they set Quakers apart were, for that very reason, favored by men like the visiting missionary Samuel Fothergill. He hoped that the passing of the hated militia tax would separate the sheep from the goats, the true believers from the hypocrites, and so be a "winnowing of the people." To Fothergill and his like, resignation from government seemed not a flight from responsibility but a symbol of the desire to "live in peace and quietness, minding their own business as Friends do everywhere else."

This insularity of the Pennsylvania Quakers took several forms. In the first place, it was geographical. For a number of reasons they were not swept along in the westward current which carried wave after wave of Irish, Scotch-Irish, and Germans across the Allegheny Mountains to the outposts of western Pennsylvania. From the beginning they settled and prospered for the most part either in Philadelphia and its environs or in one of the three "Quaker" counties of Philadelphia, Chester, and Bucks, tightly clustered on the eastern seaboard. Quakers did not settle in western Pennsylvania until about 1770, a fact which gave substance to the charge that Quakers grew fat in the warm metropolis while others risked everything. More serious, it kept them from sharing the common and characteristic experience of the people of their province in their age. Had they gone along with the Irish and Germans to live in the back country, the Pennsylvania Friends might better have comprehended the attitudes of western settlers toward the Indians, and they might have found reasons to be less unbending in their pacifist orthodoxy.

Even their belief in religious toleration, which had been embodied in Penn's first Frame of Government and continued as a principle, helped put the Quakers in a minority and, eventually, in an isolated position.

While most Quakers remained in their original eastern settlements, a motley flood of Lutherans, Presbyterians, Methodists, and even Catholics, poured in around them. Within less than a half-century after founding Pennsylvania, Quakers could only describe themselves (in Penn's prophetic phrase) as "Dissenters in our own country."

Quaker discipline required Friends to set themselves apart. Intermarriage with non-Quakers was frowned on or prohibited; a young Friend would be officially warned against the charms of the particular non-Friend whom he had been courting. The Quaker Meetings, ostensibly for reasons of peace and good fellowship, required their members to submit disputes to arbitration by the Meeting itself rather than use the regular courts of law. They even organized the "Friendly Association" which they set up to deal with the Indians outside the government. In these ways they put themselves outside the law, confined by ghetto walls built by their principles and cemented by the purity of their consciences.

It is possible that Quakers might have broken down these walls and become more infused by a worldly spirit, had they tried to proselytize. But concern for their own purity overshadowed their desire to improve their community. The Quakers who traveled to Massachusetts Bay went not so much to make converts, as to give their bodies in testimony to their Truth. Perhaps no sect of equal size has had so many "missionaries," yet none has sought fewer converts. Quaker missionaries, whether from abroad or from within the province, were for the most part missionaries to the Quakers. Instead of urging the Truth upon their unenlightened neighbors, energetic Quaker missionaries visited one Quaker Meeting after another hoping to save the Society of Friends from trifling faults.

Their self-righteousness and their rigidity are symbolized by an anecdote which John Churchman relates. During his ministerial wanderings in the 1750's he came to know a thoughtful and studious barber whose shop he patronized. On one occasion the barber proudly showed his visitor a difficult work in algebra which he had been studying on his own. "I said it might be useful to some," Churchman answered sanctimoniously, "but that I could take up grubbing, or follow the plough, without studying algebra; as he might also shave a man, &c. without it. Besides I found it a more profitable and delightful study, to be quietly employed in learning the law of the Lord written in mine own heart, so that I might walk before him acceptably." In such a situation, a Puritan might have admired the barber's industry, have expressed interest in his subject, and finally perhaps have noted that God himself was the greatest of all algebraists. The intellectual and dogmatic character of Puritanism had shown the enquiring Puritan a path to God from every little fact. But the Quaker was preoccupied with his rites of self-purification. With the obstinacy of the mystic he refused to admit the existence of the enemy's cudgel, even though his own or another's head be broken by it. The close alliance with English Quakerism and the insularity of American Quakerism preserved his dogma from the most corrosive of all tests, the acid of everyday experience.

Finally, the Quakers made a dogma of the absence of dogma. It was a primary article of their creed that a true Christian could have no creed. This deprived the Quaker of that theological security which had enabled the Puritan gradually to adapt Calvinism to American life. The Quaker was haunted by fear that every compromise was a defeat, that to modify anything might be to lose everything. Because his doctrine was suffused with the haze of mystical enthusiasm, he could not discern clearly which were the foundations and buttresses of his cathedral and which the ornamental gargoyles.

PART THREE

VICTIMS OF PHILANTHROPY

The Settlers of Georgia

> "It is a melancholy thing to see how zeal for a good thing abates when the novelty is over, and when there is no pecuniary reward attending the service."
>
> EARL OF EGMONT

SOMETHING about the fabled lushness and tropical wealth of Georgia inspired both extravagance and rigidity in the plans of those who wished to develop it. The supposed prodigality of the land seduced men to believe that they could cut the colony to their own pattern. These early planners combined a haziness about the facts of life in Georgia with a precision in their schemes for that life. What cosmopolitanism and self-purity did to Pennsylvania, paternalism and philanthropy did to Georgia. How and why Georgia became the victim of its benefactors, and what that story tells us of the character of American life, is the subject of the following chapters.

12

The Altruism of an
Unheroic Age

THE VIRTUES, like the vices, of any age bear its peculiar flavor. The swashbuckling grandeur of the projects of Sir Walter Raleigh and Sir Francis Drake expressed the aspirations and daring of Elizabethan England. The clarity, simplicity, and doggedness of the purposes of William Bradford and John Winthrop were that special combination of grand end and commonplace means which characterized the England of Oliver Cromwell. Similarly the altruism of the founders of the Georgia colony in 1732 was a touchstone of the limited aspiration of the England of that day.

In England, the middle decades of the 18th century were distinctly unheroic. It was an age more concerned about living within its spiritual and intellectual means than with seeking unfamiliar horizons. Its aesthetic ideals were sobriety and good sense; never were people more content that their reach should not exceed their grasp. They were as thoroughly reconciled to the narrow limits of life as was Alexander Pope to the confinement of the heroic couplet. It was an age which chose David Hume for its arbiter of Truth, Dr. Samuel Johnson for its arbiter of Beauty, and *Pamela* and *Tom Jones* for its epics. There was probably never an age with more limited possibilities nor one which so thoroughly exploited them. There has probably never been an age with a more narrow imagination, nor one which used its imagination more robustly.

In English domestic politics, the second quarter of the century was corrupt and pettifogging. If Sir Robert Walpole was effective as England's "first Prime Minister" it was as much because of his readiness to persuade with pensions, peerages, and ecclesiastical sinecures, as because of his other political talents. The prevalent cynicism was expressed in the facetious rumor on the death of the Queen in 1737 that there had been prepared a third place in the royal burial vault—"designed by his Majesty for Sir Robert Walpole; so that when both the latter die there will lie together, King, Queen and Knave." The machinery of parliamentary politics worked by corrupt bargains, patronage, and influence.

The philanthropy of the age was directed toward the removal of poverty, especially those forms of poverty and of vice which were an eyesore to a gentleman walking the streets of London or which added to the cost, danger, and stench of life in the great city. One of the largest English philanthropic enterprises was the so-called Charitable Corporation, incorporated in 1707 with a capital of £30,000, which it increased to £600,000 through small loans to the poor and to small tradesmen. In 1731 it was discovered that the cashier and storekeeper had made themselves beneficiaries of the Charitable Corporation by absconding with £570,000 of its capital. The resulting debate in the House of Commons was somewhat restrained by the fact that relatives of members of the House were among the culprits.

In such an atmosphere of selfishness and cynicism, some poets and social critics looked hopefully westward. Contemporary Europe seemed almost a perfect contrasting background for any grand gesture of truly disinterested philanthropy. Bishop Berkeley, himself promoter of a Bermuda project, wrote in 1726:

> There shall be sung another golden age,
>   The rise of Empire and of arts,
> The good and great inspiring epic rage
>   The wisest heads and noblest hearts.
> Not such as Europe breeds in her decay,
>   Such as she bred when fresh and young,
> When heavenly flame did animate her clay,
>   By future poets shall be sung.
> Westward the course of Empire takes its way,
>   The four first acts already past,
> A fifth shall close the drama with the day,
>   The world's great effort is the last.

We cannot find it hard to understand, then, why the proposal in 1730
to establish a colony to be called Georgia between the Altamaha and the
Savannah Rivers, south of the Carolinas, made such a welcome impression on the English mind: Georgia, alone of all the continental American
colonies, was sponsored by men who promised to make no profit from
the undertaking. The rare example of a vast enterprise with a thoroughly
altruistic motive became the subject of much poetry and self-congratula-
tion.

General James Oglethorpe was in many ways an appealing figure, and
enthusiasts were ready to invest him with the heroic qualities for which
the age was starved. No sensitive observer could fail to note the contrast
between the selfless zeal of the Trustees of Georgia and the cynical spirit
of many leading figures in English public life. "They have, for the benefit
of mankind," we read in a promotional pamphlet reputedly written by
Oglethorpe himself, "given up that ease and indolence to which they were
entitled by their fortunes and the too prevalent custom of their native
country." It would be hard to find another venture of 18th-century
colonizing and empire-building whose leaders were more disinterested or
more free of sordid motives. Nevertheless, although the motives of the
founders of the colony were altrustic, they were still distinctly this-
worldly. Their altruism bore the birthmark of the age: it was practical,
limited, and without any of the theological fantasy or grandiloquence
which had flavored the older colonies. The fulfillment of the colony
would properly be measured by its strength and prosperity.

Almost from the beginning, plans for a colony south of the Carolinas
had been embellished with extravagant hopes for that "Most delightful
Country of the Universe." In 1717, even before Oglethorpe, Sir Robert
Montgomery had published a blueprint for such a colony. The prospec-
tive investor was assured "That Nature has not bless'd the World with
any Tract, which can be preferable to it, that Paradise with all her
Virgin Beauties, may be modestly suppos'd at most but equal to its Native
Excellencies." The promotional literature for Georgia fifteen years later
seemed to qualify its extravagances only to make them more credible.
The author of *A New and Accurate Account of the Provinces of South
Carolina and Georgia* (1733) promised a climate matchlessly temperate,
a land where "all things will undoubtedly thrive . . . that are to be found
in the happiest places under the same latitude." The woods were easily
cleared, and the oranges, lemons, apples, pears, peaches, and apricots
were "so delicious that whoever tastes them will despise the insipid
watery taste of those we have in England"—and yet so abundant that
men fed them to the hogs. Wild game, fowl, and fish easily supplied a
bounteous table. "Such an air and soil can only be fitly described by a

poetical pen, because there is but little danger of exceeding the truth."

The reader who comes to the history of Georgia, after seeing the dogmatic clarity with which the New England Puritans built their "city upon a hill" or the mystic grandeur which enveloped the Pennsylvania Quakers' hope for a community of peace and brotherhood, cannot fail to be interested, and puzzled, by the curious combination of sentimental vagueness and detailed concreteness of the aspirations for Georgia. Founders of other colonies tried to follow large blueprints of the Truth; the promoters of Georgia started with detailed, almost petty, specifications.

There is a remarkably intimate record of the motives of the founders in the diary of Lord Percival, first Earl of Egmont, who, with Oglethorpe, was among the leading spirits. His private journal displays the prosaic patchwork of motives which stirred English life in the Age of Walpole: the incongruous combination of corruption, sycophancy, virtue, hardheadedness, honor, and philanthropy. On one page he reveals his strenuous effort to wangle an Irish earldom for himself so that his children might marry into families of solid wealth; on another he worries over the spiritlessness of religion in his day. At one time he describes his own attempt to buy an official post in the East India Company for a cousin; at another he denounces the unprincipled behavior of his Prime Minister. On one page he maliciously gossips about the amours of the Prince of Wales, on another he reveals his own efforts to gain the favor of the Prince. Never did an age display a more engaging ambidexterity.

Out of the mouth of Egmont came the authentic aspiration of the day: at once vague, secular, common-sensical, and practical. "Ah, Madam," he told the Queen, " 'tis for persons in high station, who have the means in their hands to do good." This aspiration needed no particular theology to support it. Sensible Englishmen, exasperated by the wild fanaticism which had turned England upside down in the Age of Cromwell, were glad to see reformers fenced about with moderation and common sense. In the lexicon of the Age of Walpole, to do good was to do certain very specific things. And whatever one might have criticized in the project for Georgia, one could hardly deny that it was detailed, concrete, and intelligible to a man of good sense.

General Oglethorpe was an imperious and tough-minded military man of good will, endowed with a zest for action and a strong body that carried him into his 90th year. Yet he possessed, in Boswell's phrase, an "uncommon vivacity of mind and variety of knowledge" which earned him a place in Dr. Johnson's circle of dinner-companions beside Edmund Burke and Sir Joshua Reynolds. Johnson warmly admired Oglethorpe; no man's life, he said, could be more interesting, and he even offered to write the General's biography. Many admired Oglethorpe's combination of an active temperament with what Alexander Pope called a "strong benevolence of soul"—a benevolence without the severity of a Cromwell, the passion of a Bunyan or the subtlety of a Milton. Such a virtue commended itself to an unheroic age.

The promises and the weaknesses of the Georgia venture were symbolized in its two leaders: Lord Percival, the wealthy aristocrat, interested in doing good for his fellow Englishmen and in strengthening his nation, insofar as this could be accomplished from an upholstered chair in a town-house, on the floor of Parliament or in a coffee-house, or from the lordly ease of his Irish estates; and General Oglethorpe, the man of action, clear and specific in his purposes, arbitrary and impatient, and unbending with the doctrinaire rigidity of the completely "practical" man. Together Percival and Oglethorpe expressed the combination of vagueness and concreteness which was the virtue and the fault of 18th-century humanitarianism. Their enterprise was to suffer because of the haziness of their purpose of doing good; it was also to suffer because of the excessively detailed specifications of the particular good deeds they were bent on doing. Compared with the Puritans or Quakers, they were clearly men of this world, neither befuddled by theological dogma nor distracted by mystic enthusiasm. Actually their crucial mistake was in having made specific plans too far in advance and too far from the scene of the experiment—plans which they sanctified as though they were principles.

Of the twenty-one trustees named in the Georgia Charter of 1732, all had been active earlier in purely charitable ventures. Ten of them had been members of the House of Commons committee on the state of the jails (1729); some were interested in the Parliamentary committee to relieve imprisoned debtors; all had been associates of Dr. Thomas Bray in his enterprise to convert Negroes in the British Plantations, and some were active supporters of the protestant missionary societies of the day. But as the project for the new colony moved from dream into reality, its prudential aspect became more and more important.

A strong colony of English families on the river Savannah (which marked the southern boundary of Carolina) would protect the borderlands from Indian, Spanish, and French invasions; and improvement of these lands would enrich Great Britain. How this was to be accomplished was agreed upon in advance by Oglethorpe and other respectable associates of Lord Percival:

> It is proposed the families there settled shall plant hemp and flax to be sent unmanufactured to England, whereby in time much ready money will be saved in this Kingdom, which now goes out to other countries

for the purchase of these goods, and they will also be able to supply us with a great deal of good timber. 'Tis possible too they may raise white mulberry trees and send us good raw silk. But at the worst they will be able to live there, and defend that country from the insults of their neighbours, and London will be eased of maintaining a number of families which being let out of gaol have at present no visible way to subsist.

Oglethorpe himself never neglected to emphasize the practical purpose of the enterprise. In his now-classic statement of purposes (in a letter to Bishop Berkeley in May, 1731), he boasted the motives of "charity and humanity," but he also declared that to this undertaking Englishmen would "owe the preserving of their people, the increasing the consumption of their manufactures, and the strengthening their American dominions. Mankind will be obliged to it, for the enlarging civility, cultivating wild countries, and founding of colonies, the posterity of whom may in all probability be powerful and learned nations." The official statement of purpose in the preamble to the Royal Charter of the colony (June 9, 1732) recorded His Majesty's desire to relieve the plight of his poor subjects "through misfortune and want of employment, reduced to great necessity," by offering them the opportunity to support themselves comfortably in a new land. To settle the regions south of Carolina would at the same time "increase the trade, navigation, and wealth of these our realms." These purposes were repeated with monotonous regularity on the floor of the House of Commons when the Trustees of Georgia made their periodic appeals for money.

The promotional literature of the Trustees sometimes seems crudely calculating. In *A New and Accurate Account of the Provinces of South Carolina and Georgia,* written perhaps by Oglethorpe, "the benefits which may arise to Great Britain by peopling this fruitful continent" were reduced to simple arithmetic. "A man who is equal in ability, only to the fourth part of a laborer, (and many such there are,) we will suppose to earn four-pence per diem, five pounds per annum, in London; his wife and a child of above seven years old four-pence per diem more: upon a fair supposition (because it is the common cause) he has another child too young to earn any thing. These live but wretchedly at an expense of twenty pounds per annum, to defray which they earn ten pounds; so that they are a loss to the rich and industrious part of the nation of ten pounds per annum." In Georgia this same family could raise rice and corn and tend cattle, earning from the prodigal fertility of the soil not less than sixty pounds per annum. The moral was obvious. How improvident to lay out ten pounds every year to support a family on charity when barely twice that amount spent transporting them to Georgia would make them permanently self-supporting and an asset to the British economy! "England will grow rich by sending her Poor Abroad."

Roman precedent appealed to these empire-builders. "The Roman state discharged not only its ungovernable distressed multitude, but also its emeriti, its soldiers, which had served long and well in war, into colonies upon the frontiers of their empire. It was by this policy that they elbowed all the nations round them." From the Georgia outpost the British people could also expand. Despite their occasional protests to the contrary, their ancient model was surely not Jesus but Caesar.

The Trustees and Common Council of Georgia went to great trouble in selecting settlers. Although one of their stated purposes had been to provide refuge for foreign Protestants, they distrusted "enthusiasts who take it in their head that everything which comes uppermost is the immediate impulse of the spirit of God." They agreed to send over the Protestants who had been persecuted by the Archbishop of Salzburg, only after they were satisfied of their industry and sobriety. Whenever possible they interviewed a prospective emigrant. They were careful not to encourage the emigration of men who were already earning their own livings (and so were already useful in Great Britain); they chose from needy applicants only those likely to strengthen a frontier outpost. Again and again the Trustees rejected applicants whose only fault was that they "could get their bread at home." They did not forget that Parliament was supporting their project (by a sum which eventually amounted to over £130,000) in the hope, as one member put it, that they would "carry off the numbers of poor children and other poor that pester the streets of London."

While unwilling to enrich the prosperous, the Trustees were equally wary of subsidizing the vicious. They wished, in Oglethorpe's phrase, to help "such as were most distressed, virtuous and industrious." They investigated the moral character of applicants and the circumstances which accounted for their distress. They even advertised the names of prospective emigrants in London newspapers a fortnight before departure so that creditors and deserted wives might have ample warning. Very few, perhaps not over a dozen, imprisoned debtors were brought to Georgia. Even these were chosen because they showed promise of becoming sturdy colonists.

13

London Blueprint for
Georgia Utopia

WHEN Sir Robert Montgomery in 1717 offered his romantic plan for a Margravate of Azilia, he insisted that the disappointments of all earlier colonies in that land "of natural Sweetness and Beauties" had been the result only of "a want of due Precaution in their Forms of Settling." "Men once got together, 'tis as easy to dispose them regularly, and with due Regard to Order, Beauty, and the Comforts of Society, as to leave them to the Folly of fixing at Random, and destroying their Interest by indulging their Humour." In the area which was to become Georgia, Montgomery therefore proposed a geometric scheme of settlement delineated in a drawing accompanying his pamphlet.

No plan could have been neater, more concrete, or more fantastic. Each district was to be laid out as a precise square, in each quarter of which was centered a square park for cattle to graze in. The remainder of the district was divided into numerous smaller squares. "The 116 Squares, Each of which has a House in the Middle, are, Every one a Mile on Each Side, or 640 Acres in a Square, bating only for the High Ways, which divide them; These are the Estates, belonging to the Gentry of the District, who, being so confin'd to an Equality in Land, will be profitably Emulous of out doing Each other in Improvement, since that is the only way, left them to grow richer than their Neighbours." The Governor-in-Chief was to be placed exactly in the center of a system of radiating paths and clearings: "By these means the labouring People (being so dispos'd, as to be always watchful of an Enemies Approach) are themselves within the Eye of those, set over them, and All together under the Inspection of their Principal." Montgomery looked forward to the time when the whole colony would be covered by such checkerboard villages. Never had anyone better mapped the geography of a pipe-dream.

The plans of Oglethorpe and the Trustees of Georgia differed from the earlier scheme of Montgomery not in spirit, but in execution. Conviction that they were doing good for the settlers, for the neighboring colonies, and for all Great Britain hardened their obstinacy against the facts of life in Georgia.

The basic error of the Trustees, from which many other evils flowed, was the rigidity of their rules for the ownership, use, sale, and inheritance of Georgia's primary resource—land. By preventing the free accumulation, exchange, and exploitation of the land they stultified the life of the colony.

What could most profitably be grown in that remote part of the New World? How many acres did a man need for subsistence? The Trustees knew the answer to neither of these questions—nor, for that matter, to any of the other elementary problems of land-use or natural resources in their colony. Their sin was not so much that they were ignorant (although they might have done more to acquaint themselves with the facts), but that they acted as if they *did* know, and by their laws imposed their ignorance upon the settlers. Had they been more willing to learn the lessons of the New World, their enterprise might have had a different end.

The Trustees' plan would have served just as well for a colony on the borders of Timbuktoo. In any border colony, they reasoned, the population should be prepared for defense. On each parcel of land, therefore, an able-bodied man should reside. Since there should be no gaps through which an enemy might penetrate, each man should possess only a small parcel of land. Since everyone should be industrious, the parcels should not be so large that any owner might live in indolence off the labor of others on his land. To prevent speculation or emigration, land should not be salable.

Guided by these specifications, the Trustees devised a system of land tenure which they imposed on the colony. They limited the size of individual holdings to no more than 500 acres. Each family going "on the charity" received a grant of 50 acres which was neither salable nor divisible. Land, held by a tenure which the lawyers of the day called "tail male," could not be willed; it could be inherited only by a male heir. If the deceased tenant had only daughters, or if a son did not want to work the land himself, the land reverted to the Trustees.

The Trustees sitting in London saw the Negro as a menace to their scheme. "It was thought the white man, by having a negro slave, would be less disposed to labor himself; and that his whole time must be employed in keeping the negro to work, and in watching against any danger he or his family might apprehend from the slave, and that the planter's wife and children would by the death, or even the absence of the planter, be at the mercy of the negro." The Londoners thought the possession of Negroes would promote absentee ownership, and that, in time of war, the Negroes would be the logical allies of any invaders threatening the security of the colony. Moreover, the Trustees reasoned, "the produces designed to be raised on the colony would not require such labor as to make negroes necessary for carrying them on." To prohibit slavery and to forbid the importation of Negroes was therefore integral to the whole design.

The paternal interest of the London Trustees led them beyond land and labor to morals. To preserve the colonists against luxury and indolence, they sought to protect them against strong drink. Soldier-settlers had to be sober to defend the border. The problem of drunkenness, which was still far from solved in London, seemed easily soluble in a new colony. The Trustees aimed to dispose of it by their Act of 1735, which declared that "no Rum, Brandies, Spirits or Strong Waters" could be brought into Georgia, that kegs of such liquors found in the colony should be publicly destroyed, and that sale of liquor should be punished as a crime.

The fantastic neatness of the Trustees' scheme for the strength and virtue of the colonists was equaled only by their plans for Georgia's place in the economy of Great Britain. According to the mercantilist theory expounded by the propagandists for Georgia, "It is at all times our interest to naturalize as much as we can the products of other countries; especially such as we purchase of foreigners with ready money, or otherwise to our disadvantage. . . . Because by so doing we not only gain a new provision for our poor, and an increase of our people by increasing their employment, but by raising such materials ourselves, our manufactures come cheaper to us, whereby we are enabled to cope with other nations in foreign markets, and at the same time prevent our home consumption of them being a luxury too prejudicial to us." Luckily for the logic of their scheme—but not for the future of their enterprise—one product, silk, seemed perfectly suited to become Georgia's staple product. In such pamphlets as *Reasons for establishing the Colony of Georgia, with regard to the Trade of Great Britain* (London, 1773), the friends of Georgia developed the economic argument. The annual cost of Italian, French, Dutch, Indian and Chinese silks imported into Great Britain, they pointed out, amounted to £500,000. This large sum of foreign exchange or bullion could be saved by simply raising enough silk in Georgia. Such a silk industry, furthermore, would provide employment for at least 20,000 people in the colony during the four months of the silk season and for at least 20,000 more in England the year round. Italian competition, they argued, could be easily defeated because in Georgia land could be had for the asking and the precious mulberry leaves grew wild. They even hoped to export silk from Great Britain and eventually capture the European market.

What evidence had nourished these hopes? There was the tradition, which had gained all the authenticity of legend, that in Georgia mulberry trees grew wild and in great abundance. The promoters had not yet discovered that it was the black mulberry (with leaves too harsh for silkworms) which flourished in their colony rather than the white mulberry. As early as 1609 adventurers to Virginia listing the "most excellent fruites by planting in Virginia" had reported "silke-worms, and plenty of mulberie-trees, whereby ladies, gentlewomen and little children (being set in the way to do it) may bee all imploied with pleasure, making silke comparable to that of Persia, Turkey, or any other." Much publicity had been given to the fact that in 1660 the coronation robe of Charles II was woven of Virginia silk. "The air, as it is healthy for man, (the latitude about thirty-two,)" the promoters of Georgia argued, "is also proper for the silk worms." Sir Thomas Lombe, who had won fame by smuggling himself into an Italian silk mill in 1718 and taking the secrets to England, was probably the foremost English authority on the manufacture of silk. Engaged as adviser to the Trustees, he wrote a strong testimonial—as rich in enthusiasm as it was poor in first-hand knowledge —to the possibilities of silk-culture in Georgia.

From such threads of legend, hope, and half-truth, the Trustees wove their illusions. The forty-odd thousand persons to be engaged in silk-production would include many not otherwise employable. "Nor need they be the strongest, or most industrious part of mankind; it must be a weak hand indeed that cannot earn bread where silk-worms and white mulberry trees are so plenty. Most of the poor in Great Britain, who are maintained by charity, are capable of this, though not of harder labor."

The Trustees fastened these illusions on the unfortunate settlers of Georgia. Not only did they encourage silk-culture by a guaranteed inflated price and by bounties and prizes for the product delivered in England, but they even wrote into land-grants provisions requiring each grantee, in order to validate his claim, to plant at least 50 white mulberry trees on every 50 acres; every grantee of 500 acres had to plant 2000 trees within twenty years. When the laws against holding Negroes were revised, each planter was required to possess one female Negro well-trained in silk-culture to every four male Negroes. When at long last the

Trustees provided a representative assembly, they required that to serve in it an inhabitant must have planted at least 100 white mulberry trees on each 50 acres of his land.

Had the Trustees succeeded in building Georgia according to their blueprint, it would have been a neat, antiseptic, efficient, and thoroughly dull community. Its people would have been settled along the border on equal plots of land, each defended by an able-bodied man fit for the militia. A sober, unenvious, industrious population would have worked with uniform zeal while, of course, they would lack ambition to accumulate more land, to move to better land, or to rise in the social scale. Such a cheerful and diligent people would be immune to fatigue, boredom, or despair, and hence would not need strong drink. There would be no merchants from neighboring colonies to sell Negroes, rum, or superior land. The people, possessed of equable temperaments in an equable climate, would employ their women, their children, and their aged in the care and feeding of silkworms, because silk was, after all, so valuable to the economy of the empire. The Georgians were to be ignorant of or indifferent to the profits of other enterprises.

The only flaw in this scheme was that it had to be carried out by real people at some real place on earth. And there never was a people or a place suited to this purpose—least of all the unhappy refugees from 18th-century London who had been transported to the pine-barrens of Georgia.

14

A Charity Colony

LONDON PHILANTHROPISTS were trying to make Georgia fulfill a European dream. They were less interested in what was possible in America than in what had been impossible in Europe. Their ideals for the new colony were the Englishman's picture of what such a colony ought to be: protector of the frontier, refuge for the unfortunate and unemployed of London, and source of valued semi-tropical products. In a sense, of course, the dreams of New England Puritans and Pennsylvania Quakers were also woven from European experience, but they possessed a theological generality.

No features of English society in the 18th century were more valued than security and dependence. Security came from the assurance of living in a network of familiar and predictable relationships. Squire Allworthy and Squire Western in Fielding's *Tom Jones* were symbols of the security which the English middle class could enjoy for itself and could, incidentally, confer on its dependent classes. The substantial squire who was a justice-of-the-peace, a pillar of respectability, a doer of good, a protector of the weak, and a defender of the national interest was no mere fiction. The obverse of the security he symbolized was dependence. It was the dependence of the honest peasant on his squire, of the squire on the noble lord, of the rector on his bishop, of the writer on his patron, and even the dependence of the noble Lord Egmont on Sir Robert Walpole and the Crown as the fountains of honor and profit. These and a thousand other dependencies gave English life the security and comfort it held for many. Such a system required, of course, the willingness of each party to accept the role assigned him by others. Nothing perhaps was more characteristic of English life, nor did anything more sharply distinguish it from life in the New World, than this set of well-assured relationships. Except for the people dislocated by enclosures or by early industrialism and for occasional vagrants, each man knew what was expected of him; and by doing that he could count on living respectably for his station in life.

For men who had been caught in this ancient web, much of the appeal of America was escape. Franklin, advising prospective immigrants to America, did not lure them with the paternal bounty of a just employer— rather with the fluidity and the promise of life here. It was precisely this openness which fired Crèvecoeur's enthusiasm later in the century: in America the servile European could begin to have his will of the world —always at some risk of course—but that was what made him an American. The flavor of American life was compounded of risk, spontaneity, independence, initiative, drift, mobility, and opportunity. Even the American ideal of equality could not be imposed from above.

But the Georgia settlers suffered from the fact that they were in the hands of benefactors. While investors seek profits, benefactors pursue an abstract purpose. Investors are not unduly inquisitive about the conduct of their enterprises if they yield fair returns. But the benefactor's dividend is in doing good in his own special way. The Trustees of Georgia were no exception.

The philanthropic motive of the founders was written into the very charter of the colony, which provided that no Trustee could hold any office, own any land, or gain any profit under it. Whatever the Trustees did was supposed to be solely for the benefit of the settlers or of Great Britain. Despite the storms of protest that battered the Georgia Trusteeship, no credible evidence was ever offered that any of the Trustees had, even in spirit, violated the terms of his trust.

The Trustees themselves contributed heavily to the support of the colony. Oglethorpe, as he on one occasion declared, had "not only ventured his life and health" and reputation but within five years of the founding had laid out £3000 of his own money; by 1744 he had advanced, mostly for military purposes, over £90,000, all of which Parliament later repaid by unanimous vote. The people of England made numerous contributions in small sums without expecting to be repaid. Lord Egmont notes in his diary that one evening in June 1733, "an unknown hand sent me by a porter £30 for the poor of Georgia." All over England sermons were delivered appealing for contributions. Again and again the Trustees were approached by people like Sir Edward Debouverie, whose father had left a general bequest of £500 for charitable uses, who gave the whole sum plus a similar amount of his own. The £18,000 raised by private subscription in the first eight years expressed the friendly interest of hundreds of parishioners who had been stirred to put their few shillings into collection-plates.

But much more was needed. Private charity could not support so vast an enterprise. The philanthropic purposes of the venture, together with its importance to imperial defense, repeatedly led members of Parliament to support Georgia by direct parliamentary grants—in sums which before the Trusteeship had expired totaled over £130,000. Never before —except for purely military purposes—had the British Government supported any of its colonies with public funds.

Crucial consequences flowed from these subsidies. Since Georgia's public expenses were covered by the gifts of charitable individuals or by governmental appropriations from England, there was no need for the colonists to pay taxes; and hence no representative assembly was needed to levy taxes. For many years there was no foundation for self-government in Georgia. The settlers of the colony, who would otherwise presumably have been confined to a London jail or have wandered the streets without employment, were public beneficiaries. As wards of the community, they were without any right to complain.

London philanthropists had carefully provided for the needs of the colonists as they saw them. We have some notion of the extent of that care from the "Rules for the year 1735," as recorded by Francis Moore, who was the keeper of the stores:

> The Trustees intend this year to lay out a county, and build a new town in Georgia.
>
> They will give to such persons as they send upon the charity, To every man, a watch-coat; a musket and bayonet; a hatchet; a hammer; a handsaw; a shod shovel or spade; a broad hoe; a narrow hoe; a gimlet; a drawing knife; an iron pot, and a pair of pot-hooks; a frying pan; and a public grindstone to each ward or village. Each working man will have for his maintenance in the colony for one year (to be delivered in such proportions, and at such times as the Trust shall think proper) 312 lbs. of beef or pork; 104 lbs. of rice; 104 lbs. of Indian corn or peas; 104 lbs. of flour; 1 pint of strong beer a day to a man when he works and not otherwise; 52 quarts of molasses for brewing beer; 16 lbs. of cheese; 12 lbs. of butter; 8 oz. of spice; 12 lbs. of sugar; 4 gallons of vinegar; 24 lbs. salt; 12 quarts of lamp oil, and 1 lb. spun cotton; 12 lbs. of soap.
>
> To the mothers, wives, sisters or children of such men for one year, that is to say, to every person of the age of 12 years and upwards, the following allowance, (to be delivered as before,) 260 lbs. of beef or pork; 104 lbs. of rice; 104 lbs. of Indian corn or peas; 104 lbs. of flour; 52 quarts of molasses for brewing beer; 16 lbs. of cheese; 12 lbs. of butter; 8 oz. of spice; 12 lbs. of sugar; 4 gallons of vinegar; 24 lbs. of salt; 6 quarts of lamp oil; half lb. of spun cotton; 12 lbs. of soap.
>
> For every person above the age of seven, and under the age of twelve, half the said allowance, being esteemed half a head.
>
> And for every person above the age of two, and under the age of seven, one third of said allowance, being esteemed one third of a head.
>
> The trustees pay their passage from England to Georgia; and in the voyage they will have in every week four beef days, two pork days, and one fish day. . . .

Such provisions for the emigrants to Georgia have more the ring of a well-run jail or of a mercenary army than of a colony of free men seeking their fortune in a new world.

The minutes of the Trustees and their Common Council (the governing body of Georgia which met in London) reek with paternalism. Thomas Causton, official storekeeper of the colony, had reportedly declared in public that the colonists "had neither lands, rights or possessions; that the trustees gave and that the trustees could freely take away." If an officer had been brave beyond the call of duty, Oglethorpe appealed to the Trustees to reward him because "no Society can subsist without rewarding those Who do well, and punishing those Who do ill." If there was to be a schoolmaster or a midwife at Savannah, the Trustees in

London had to include compensation in the year's budget. The Trustees appropriated a saucepan as solemnly as they did the material for making bodices for twenty-six of the women from Salzburg. In a word, the Trustees had taken upon themselves control of the daily lives of people whom they barely knew, living in a land they themselves had never seen.

"The Board will always do what is right," declared the Trustees unanimously at a meeting in July 1735, "and the people should have confidence in us." This arrogance, or at best, condescension, in the rulers bred dependence and discontent in the ruled. Georgia settlers complained of their food, shelter, and equipment, and awaited, or demanded, remedies from the good fathers in distant London. After the first year of guaranteed subsistence, settlers who found the going rough demanded another year's security. The Trustees had little choice but to comply. The efforts of the Trustees to keep the colonists happy and well-supplied postponed the day of their independence.

As early as 1739, Lord Percival saw financial trouble ahead if the paternalistic policy were continued. While the sponsors found themselves more and more deeply involved, the colonists were neither prosperous nor hopeful. In Georgia these needy English city-folk suffered not only from their common weaknesses of character, but from lack of the special skills of the backwoodsman. Before long the Trustees had to concede that the poor "who had been useless in England, were inclined to be useless in Georgia likewise."

15

Death of a Welfare Project

EVEN IF the Trustees had found colonists who believed that "the Board will always do what is right," they would have failed, for they would have set up a docile principality instead of an enterprising colony.

The colonists were also cursed by the universal ills of bureaucracy: pettiness, arbitrariness, corruption. The rations promised to settlers "on the charity" were kept in storehouses and were dispensed by men who could not resist using some supplies for their own purposes. There was, for example, the case of Thomas Causton, whom Oglethorpe had left as bailiff and storekeeper of the colony in 1734. Having the power to give or to deny supplies, he became one of the most hated men in Georgia. No one in Causton's unenviable position could have satisfied both his London employers and his Georgia wards, and it was not long before he was the butt of assorted accusations: bad beef, short rations, profiteering, and bribery. Most of these accusations seem to have been well-founded, but because Causton, as deputy of the London Trustees, possessed the power of government he could prevent his own punishment.

The most basic, most ill-conceived, and most disastrous of the Trustees' plans concerned the land. Fifty acres of Georgia pine-barren proved insufficient to support a family. Yet the work of clearing the trees and of planting the crops was more than enough to occupy an able-bodied man assisted only by his family. Whether a people more ascetic, more industrious, or more heroic might have managed is beside the point, for the Trustees had set themselves the task of colonizing a particular kind of person.

Their rigid provisions for manning the frontier had incidentally removed much of the incentive to increase the productivity of the colony. A settler who had no male heir or whose son did not want to farm the land would discover after years of labor that he was not allowed to sell his property. Why should he improve his property for the benefit of the Trustees? Since settlers were supposed to be soldiers in "Frontier Garrisons," each exchange of land was a matter of governmental policy, to be approved in London only after proof that it served the public interest. The records of the London meetings are full of quibbles over the transfer of fifty-acre parcels.

The Trustees came to discover that they had assumed a responsibility they could neither fulfill nor abandon. Each enforcement of their system seemed to make every later exception more unfair. In 1738, for example, the people of the little Georgia town of Hampstead, complaining that their land was pine-barren, petitioned for something better in exchange. The matter was considered by the Trustees in Oglethorpe's house in London:

> He said he knew the land at Hampstead perfectly well, and it was indeed most of it pine barren, but with pains might be rendered very fruitful as other pine land had been rendered by others; that if these people were humoured in this, there would not be a man in the Colony but would desire to remove to better land, who yet have at present no

thoughts of it. That the disorder this would occasion in the Colony is unexpressible. That we ought to consider that if these men were allowed to remove to new land, they would expect a new allowance of provision for a year, which we are not in a condition to give, and the same would be expected by others.

The disgruntled colonists thus found themselves shackled to plots of unfertile land. Since the law prevented their adding to these parcels, or selling or exchanging them, the only alternative was flight.

Although settlers accepted the need for a limit on the amount of land to be held by any individual—"as it is preventive of those unreasonable, and even impolitic monopolies of land, which have greatly retarded the strength and improvement of other places"—this was far different from an enforced equality. Where, they asked, was the incentive for the industrious if not in the opportunity to better his condition? "There being many lazy fellows in the number," a Captain Pury reported to the Trustees in 1733 on arrival from Georgia, "and others not able to work, those who work stoutly think it unreasonable the other should enjoy the fruits of their labour, and when the land is cleared, have an equal share and chance when lots are cast for determining each person's division."

When clamor from Georgia increased, Oglethorpe tried to convince the other Trustees that complaints came only from the shiftless and the self-seeking, the "disaffected" who had been stirred up by land-speculators from South Carolina. It was not until 1738 that the Trustees began a series of modifications in Georgia's land-policy, regarding each as if it were a sacrifice of principle. In 1738, the Trustees permitted females to inherit land in Georgia; the next year tenants without natural heirs were allowed to will their lands; in 1740 leases were allowed and fewer improvements were required; and in the following year the maximum holding was increased from 500 to 2000 acres. Recognizing differences in the quality of parcels, the Trustees gradually allowed a freer exchange of pine-barren for more fertile land, and granted an additional fifty acres to those who had fenced and cultivated their original grants. Quit rents were first reduced, and later abolished. It was not until 1750, when the Trustees were about to give up their charter, that tenure of land in the colony was increased to an absolute inheritance. Now finally a Georgian could buy, sell, lease, exchange, or will his land like that in any of the other American colonies. But Oglethorpe remained sullen and resistant, arguing that only the strict regulation of the land had preserved the colony from invasion.

Oglethorpe was right in believing that the whole system would have to be abandoned if any part of it were given up. All the illusions had been woven together; they would unravel at the same time. For example, as soon as the size of the individual land-holding was increased, many arguments against the use of Negro laborers were destroyed and strong new arguments created in favor of allowing their importation. Larger holdings required more and cheaper labor. Year after year, colonists in northern Georgia, prodded by Carolina Negro-merchants, protested to London that lack of Negroes caused the colony's stagnation and discontent. In London in March 1748, the Trustees resolved "never to permit the Introduction of Negroes into the Colony of Georgia, as the Danger which must arise from them in a Frontier Town is so evident; And as the People, Who continue to clamour for Negroes declare that the Colony can never succeed without the use of them, it is evident they don't intend by their own Industry to contribute to its Success, and must therefore rather hinder than promote it." They advised any who could not succeed without Negroes to go elsewhere. It was only two years later, in 1750, that the Trustees retreated fully; explaining that conditions in the colony had changed, they threw open the door to a slave economy.

In their plans for Georgia's morals, the Trustees had no more success. It was one thing to pass a well-phrased Act "for Suppressing the odious and loathsome Sin of Drunkenness" but quite another to enforce it on a population sparsely spread over hills and swamps. One correspondent reminded the Trustees that poverty, distress and frustrated hopes always drove men to drink "to keep up their Courage." Even in England most people had nothing to choose but either to be "quite Forlorn without hopes or Mad with Liquor. Now to bring them [the Georgia settlers] to a proper medium would be to give them Sound & Strong reasons to hope for better times & by degrees to humor them with proper Notions Such as are the most usefull to them."

There were also sober objections to prohibiting traffic in rum. Because timber was the most likely export of the colony, and its logical market was the sugar islands of the British West Indies which could send back little but rum in return, prohibiting the importation of rum was in effect cutting off trade with the West Indies. This deprived the empire of needed lumber and deprived the Georgians of profitable commerce. There was also the "medical" argument: "the experience of all the inhabitants of America, will prove the necessity of qualifying water with some spirit, (and it is very certain, that no province in America yields water that such a qualification is more necessary to than Carolina and Georgia) and the usefulness of this experiment has been sufficiently evident to all the inhabitants of Georgia who could procure it, and use it with moderation." Finally, there was the universal argument against unenforceable laws:

bootleggers claimed profits which might have gone into the pockets of respectable citizens and "as it is the nature of mankind in general, and of the common sort in particular, more eagerly to desire, and more immoderately to use those things which are most restrained from them; such was the case with respect to rum in Georgia." The enterprising Carolina rum-runners proved more decisive than any argument.

The Trustees, over Oglethorpe's loud objections, finally beat an ungraceful retreat. In 1742, while still keeping the Act against rum on their books, they ordered their agent to cease enforcing it. Later that year they repealed prohibition, but they still allowed only rum imported from another British colony in exchange for native Georgia products.

Of all items in the plan for Georgia, the last to die was the project for raising silk. "Till the silk becomes a commodity," a colonial official reported in 1740, "the only trade of the colony will be lumber and fresh meat to carry to the islands." The Trustees did, from time to time, look into the production of wine, but silk—perhaps simply because they knew less about it—possessed their imagination. However intractable were the London poor to the schemes of the Trustees, the silkworms proved even more so. The fiat of London philanthropists made not the slightest impression on them. The chronicle of the Georgia silk industry was one of futile bickerings and unfulfilled hopes.

It was not surprising that raising a new and fragile product like silk proved difficult in the American wilderness. Tending the worms and winding the threads was a skilled and delicate business, but this was hardly less delicate than dealing with the temperamental Piedmontese on whom the Trustees depended for training the settlers in the art of silk culture. The first debacle involved a Nicholas Amatis who with several other Piedmontese was sent over soon after the founding of the colony. The simplest facts were hard to come by in London. Some informants reported that Amatis' assistants had broken the silk machinery, spoiled the seed, destroyed the mulberry-trees and escaped into Carolina; others, that Amatis himself just before he died had burnt all the worms and machines because the magistrates had denied him a Catholic priest in his last illness. On Amatis' death, instruction in silk-culture fell into the hands of Jacques Camuse and his wife, who was supposed to teach Georgians the art of silk-winding. But Mrs. Camuse was afraid to teach the ladies of the colony too well, lest her own services become superfluous.

Meanwhile the Trustees in London were exaggerating the significance of their small success. From the beginning the promoters had spent a disproportionate amount of their effort in securing favorable publicity, and they actually became victims of their own propaganda. They made a great to-do over the gown "of Georgia silk" they presented to Queen Caroline, and which she declared the finest silk she ever saw. Yet Georgia silk came only irregularly and in small quantities. As late as 1740 the Trustees heard that Mrs. Camuse had taught the people so little that, if she died, the whole art of silk culture would be lost to Georgia. The only substantial progress was made, under the greatest difficulties, among the Salzburghers who were extraordinarily industrious, persistent, and independent and who had developed some local enthusiasm for silk-culture. Of the 6301 pounds of silk cocoons produced in the whole of Georgia in 1751, all but three hundred pounds came either from Whitefield's orphanage or from the Salzburghers at Ebenezer. And in 1741 malcontents spread the rumor in England that the silken gown presented to Queen Caroline had contained few if any Georgia threads.

In May 1742 nearly half the silkworms in Savannah died, proving that Georgia's climate was not suited to raising silkworms. If any part of Georgia was proper for silk-culture, it would have been inland where the climate was less variable, but this was some distance from the areas first settled. Moreover, strong economic forces worked against the silk-culture of Georgia.

Economical production of silk, as the experience of other parts of the world had demonstrated, required laborers who were both highly skilled and extremely cheap—neither of which could be said of the inhabitants of the new colony. Silk-laborers were hard to find because an ordinary Georgia laborer, who could earn two shillings a day at other work, could expect no more than one shilling from working at silk. In the major silk-growing areas of the world, peasants were receiving no more than threepence a day.

Despite all this, the Trustees remained blind and incorrigible in their optimism; they still hoped to create a mulberry aristocracy. In their law of March 19, 1750 they declared that, after June 4, 1751, no one could be a representative in the Georgia Assembly who did not have at least one hundred mulberry trees planted and properly fenced upon every fifty acres of his land; and, after June 4, 1753, no one could be a deputy who did not have at least one female in his family instructing in the art of reeling silk and who did not produce at least fifteen pounds of silk upon every fifty acres he owned. When finally in 1751 the Trustees declared their intention to give up the government of Georgia and return the colony to the Crown, they listed among the reasons not the unfitness of Georgia for the culture of silk, but their lack of enough money "to give any Encouragements for the Produce of Raw Silk." One Parliamentary opponent of the Georgia project recommended that the best cure for Georgia illusions was to require its inhabitants to drink only their own wine and to be clothed only in their own silk. But illusions die hard, and the brighter they are the longer they take adying. The production of silk in Georgia dwindled on through the days of the Revolution, when the Georgia Assembly transformed the old silk factory into a ball-room and house of worship for which it was used until it was consumed by fire a half-century later.

The government of Georgia failed too because the Trustees had burdened themselves with powers which no one could wisely exercise from London. They produced a bizarre combination of anarchy and tyranny. The worst confusion and the most irritating abuses appeared in the courts. Legislation could be made in London, but only in the Georgia courts was it applied to particular individuals. While purporting to enforce the laws of England, the Trustees had confused and combined the jurisdiction of different English courts and had entrusted their administration to amateur judges who ruled by prejudice and favoritism. Oglethorpe himself, whatever his other virtues, hardly possessed a judicial temperament; and his deputies took their cue from him. Where, the colonists wailed, were their vaunted liberties as British subjects?

Complaint increased: pamphlets, petitions, and protests followed with annoying frequency. Even the Trustees' own agent had to admit that these protests, against every one of the major rules as well as against the spirit of the government, spoke the mind of a substantial part of the population.

As problems multiplied and public enthusiasm in England declined, the interest of the Trustees, who after all were only volunteers, also dwindled. Oglethorpe's own devotion to the venture was hardly increased when in 1744 he was court-martialed (though fully acquitted) for alleged irregularities in his administration of the Army in Georgia. His relations with the other Trustees became uncomfortable, and he attended no meeting after early 1749. In 1742 Egmont resigned from the governing body, partly because of ill-health and partly because of the declining public support. "It is a melancholy thing," he had shrewdly observed some years before, "to see how zeal for a good thing abates when the novelty is over, and when there is no pecuniary reward attending the service. Had the Government given us salaries but of £200 a year, few of our members would have been absent."

The Trustees handed their charter back to the Crown and surrendered their interest in Georgia on June 25, 1752, even before its twenty-one year term had expired. A project which had been lavishly supported by individual charity and public philanthropy, had come to a dismal end.

It is uncertain just how much of the population had deserted Georgia for the freer opportunities of Carolina and the other colonies by the middle of the century. The claim of the malcontents ten years before, that only one-sixth of the original inhabitants were left, was probably an exaggeration. But many had left, and there was more than romance or malice in the notion that Georgia was on the way to becoming a deserted colony.

"The poor inhabitants of Georgia," unhappy settlers lamented, "are scattered over the face of the earth; her plantations a wild; her towns a desert; her villages in rubbish; her improvements a by-word, and her liberties a jest; an object of pity to friends, and of insult, contempt and ridicule to enemies." By the time of the Revolution, Georgia—the darling of philanthropists, the spoiled child of charitable London—was the least prosperous and least populous of the colonies.

16

The Perils of Altruism

IF THE FOUNDERS of the colony of Georgia lacked the grand vision which inspired the Massachusetts Puritans or the mystic enthusiasm of the Pennsylvania Quakers, they did possess a precise prosaic frame within which they hoped to build a colony. Their difficulties came, not from lack of a plan, but from too much of one. Their problems and their opportunities arose neither from the dogmatic clarity of their principles nor from the consuming intensity of their conviction nor even from any vagueness in their notion of what they were about. Their essential weakness was a frame of mind which stifled the spontaneity and experimental spirit which were the real spiritual wealth of America. However noble the impulses of Percival, Oglethorpe, and some of their associates, these impulses found expression in niggling prudential gestures. Had their aspiration been larger and more abstract—or had it been more self-seeking—there might have been elbow-room for the possibilities opened by life in the New World.

But philanthropists, like martyrs, missionaries, and apostles of the

Good, have never been noted for their experimental spirit; they are philanthropists precisely because they know what is good and how to accomplish it. By nature they are inclined to be too clear and too dogmatic about any situation. So, indeed, were the Trustees of Georgia. The discontented settlers properly complained that what an American colony needed was a willingness to experiment: "At first it was a trial, now it is an experiment; and certainly no man or society need be ashamed to own, that from unforeseen emergencies their hypothesis did misgive; and no person of judgment would censure for want of success where the proposal was probable; but all the world would exclaim against that person or society who, through mistaken notions of honor or positiveness of temper, would persist in pushing an experiment contrary to all probability, to the ruin of the adventurers."

This part of the Georgia story holds more than the lessons of irony and defeat. For the clue to the failure of the Trusteeship is a clue to the success of other forms of community in America. The Georgia project was not abandoned because its settlers had found America unpromising but, on the contrary, because what its settlers wanted was opportunity—with all its risks—and what they were given was a plan. The opportunities of the New World could not be encompassed by any plan, however selfless or noble, devised by the Old World imagination. The dream to be fulfilled here was more exotic than 18th-century London could believe. American possibilities were not the same as European impossibilities; they had a character all their own. Even to dream fruitfully of the life here, it was necessary to compound the English dream with the American experience.

PART FOUR

TRANSPLANTERS

The Virginians

> "Thus, in the beginning, all the world was America, and more so than it is now. . . ."
>
> JOHN LOCKE

> "In the beginning, All America was Virginia."
>
> WILLIAM BYRD

VIRGINIA is a different story. Here we see no grandiose scheme, no attempt to rule by an idea, but an earthy effort to transplant institutions. If other colonies sought escape from English vices, Virginians wished to fulfill English virtues. Let other colonies dazzle the world with a City upon a Hill, inspire by a commonwealth of brotherly love, or encourage with a vast humanitarian experiment. The model in Virginians' heads was compounded of the actual features of a going community: the England, especially the rural England, of the 17th and 18th century. If Virginia was to be in any way better than England, it was not because Virginians pursued ideals which Englishmen did not have; rather that here were novel opportunities to realize the English ideals. A middle-class Englishman was to find space in Virginia to become a new kind of English country gentleman. An unpredictable alchemy transformed the ways of the English manor-house into the habits of a New World republic. Squire Westerns and Horace Walpoles underwent an Atlantic sea-change which made them into Edmund Pendletons, Thomas Jeffersons, and George Washingtons. What made them American was not what they sought but what they accomplished.

17

English Gentlemen,
American Style

In ENGLAND in the later 17th century the ambition of a prosperous tradesman was to become a country gentleman. To retire from a place behind the shop-counter or from a seat at the clerk's desk to a spacious manor house in the midst of broad acres—this was the daydream of the rising middle class. It was the counterpart in that age, of the 20th-century businessman's dream of a costly suburban estate, membership in the country-club, and winters in Florida. But it was more than that; becoming a country gentleman in those days meant joining the governing class. To acquire a manor house meant also to become a justice of the peace, a power over the local pulpit, a patron and father-confessor to the local peasantry, an overseer of the poor, and perhaps sooner or later a member of Parliament, a knight, a baronet—even conceivably a member of the House of Lords.

The country house was thus the rising Englishman's way station to heaven. Although it offered good living, it was no wallow of luxury or indolence. And in the wholesome English folklore the burden of government and public responsibility rested on those who sat comfortably in the seats of gentlemen. "In the greatest fortune," observed Richard

Brathwait in his *English Gentleman* (1630), a handbook which substantial Virginians consulted, "there is the least liberty." "He sinnes doubly, that sinnes exemplarily: whence is meant, that such, whose very persons should bee examples or patterns of vigilancy, providence and industry, must not sleepe out their time under the fruitlesse shadow of Security. Men in great place (saith one) are thrice servants; servants of the Soveraigne, or state; servants of Fame; and servants of Businesse. So as they have no freedome, neither in their persons, nor in their actions, nor in their times." The ideal of the English gentleman, then, while surely not ascetic, was decidedly moral and public. Rising English tradesmen who aspired to become gentlemen were aiming, not only at a life of ease, but at a realm of larger and more dignified responsibilities.

In the earliest years of colonial Virginia the opportunity to rise into the ranks of the gentry was not uncommon. Until nearly 1700, white immigrants were probably better off in Virginia than they had been in England. Scarcity of labor made wages higher; in 1623, George Sandys complained that the Virginian expected, in addition to his food, a pound of tobacco every day. With tobacco valued at a shilling a pound, the Virginian earned in a day what his English counterpart earned in a week. And there was the promise of rising in the world. After only a few years of service, youths who had come as mere apprentices, according to the author of *A Perfect Description of Virginia* (1649), could expect "Land given them, and Cattel to set them up." The records of land transfers studied by Thomas Jefferson Wertenbaker show that in Virginia in the later 17th century there was a numerous "yeomanry"—men who owned between 20 and 500 acres. At the upper end of the social scale, the man who had come with moderate capital also probably had a better chance of enlarging it; moreover, his money could buy more social status in Virginia than in England. The system of granting land by "headrights," under which anyone could receive 50 acres of land for every person he transported to the colony, made it simple enough to buy an entourage of dependents.

To sit in a seat of power in a new country like 17th-century Virginia, it was not yet necessary to nudge someone else out. If one could not lead an already-existing community, one could start a new one. Many Virginia families were founded by tradesmen or artisans, men of extraordinary talents, prosperity, or good luck, who acquired broad acres and soon could afford the style of life appropriate to a country gentleman. The standards of gentility, if self-consciously modeled on those of England, were necessarily vaguer and less rigid. This fluidity of social classes was shown in many ways. For a while every free white man could vote for members of the House of Burgesses; there was no property qualification. The carping author of *Virginia's Cure* (London, 1662) objected that wise legislation seldom passed the Virginia House of Burgesses, because a majority of them "are usually such as went over Servants thither, and though by time and industry, they may have attained competent Estates; yet by reason of their poor and mean education they are unskilful in judging of a good Estate either of Church or Common-wealth, or of the means of procuring it." So long as white indentured servants remained the principal source of labor, that is, until around 1700, there was no racial barrier against the rise of fortunate or industrious workmen. Those were the halcyon days of "democracy" in Virginia.

But they did not last long. Near the end of the 17th century, a host of circumstances dissipated that fantasy-world where any man might become a gentleman. "There is little or no incouragement for men of any tolerable parts to come hither," Governor Francis Nicholson noted in his report to the Council of Trade and Plantations on Dec. 2, 1701. "Formerly there was good convenient land to be taken up, and there were widows had pretty good fortunes, which were incouragements for men of parts to come. But now all or most of these good lands are taken up, and if there be any widows or maids of any fortune, the Natives for the most parts get them; for they begin to have a sort of aversion to others, calling them strangers."

Virginia society was beginning to be frozen. By 1670, the legislature, following the English example, established a property qualification: voters included only "such as by their estates real or personal, have interest enough to tye them to the endeavor of the public good." As time passed, the suffrage was further restricted to exclude leaseholders and life-tenants; after 1699 one could not vote unless he was a "freeholder," that is, one who owned land outright. One hundred unsettled acres or 25 acres with a house and plantation came to be required for a voice in choosing burgesses. Suffrage in Virginia had become substantially the same as that in England.

It was not only that the most fertile lands and the richest widows had been taken up or were no longer available to casual immigrants. The character of the laboring class had begun to change. By 1680 Negro slaves were being imported in increasing numbers; the six thousand brought in during the first nine years of the 18th century probably exceeded the entire importation of the previous century. Negro slaves were displacing white indentured servants as the dominant labor-supply, and slavery in Virginia grew at an accelerating pace during the early 18th century, for slavery made the large plantation more profitable. The increasing difficulties of the small planter discouraged immigration of white servants, and the decrease of white servants in turn made the colony more dependent on Negro slaves.

Toward the end of the 17th century every decade saw the situation of the small planter grow less promising. After 1660 the stricter enforcement of the Navigation Acts, designed to tighten the Empire's mercantilist fabric, narrowed the margin of colonial profit and created new problems for planters of all classes. The small man found himself constantly in debt. A short-lived rebellion led by Nathaniel Bacon in Virginia in 1676 was at least partly due to these sufferings. Bacon himself declared small farmers to be indebted beyond "the power of labor or industry" to save them. Until around 1660 it was customary for an indentured servant to remain in the colony at the end of his term of service to acquire a piece of land, and to look hopefully up the social ladder. When land for this purpose became scarce, the General Court of the colony had even from time to time (as in 1627) specially provided certain parcels. But in the last decades of the century, liberated servants looked to the greener fields which some of the other colonies were offering.

In the early 18th century Virginia had become for most of the poorer white immigrants nothing but a port-of-entry—southward to the wilderness-frontier of North Carolina, westward over the mountains, or northward to Delaware, Maryland, and western Pennsylvania. This exodus of the poorer white colonists, who might have formed a solid yeomanry after the English pattern, worried Virginians but they could not agree on its causes. Before the end of the 17th century, the English Board of Trade instructed Governor Nicholson to see how it could be stopped. Over the next decades the Board and the Governor debated how to keep a future yeomanry from leaving Virginia. Governor Nicholson complained that the main cause of emigration was the special encouragement offered by colonies like Pennsylvania to craftsmen to set themselves up in the woolen manufacture and in other skilled trades. "The members of the Council and others . . . in the Government," explained Edward Randolph in 1696, "have from time to time procured grants of very large Tracts of land, so that there has not for many years been any waste land to be taken up by those who bring with them servants, or by such Servants, who have served their time faithfully with their Masters, but it is taken up and ingrossed beforehand." In 1728, Governor Gooch denied this explanation by showing that Spotsylvania County, where large grants were the rule, was more heavily populated than Brunswick, where there had been many small grants.

While observers disagreed over the causes, the effect was unmistakable: Virginia had become an aristocracy. By the beginning of the 18th century, according to Wertenbaker, not more than five per cent of the newcomers were becoming landowners. Most of the families which were to rule Virginia later in the century—the Fitzhughs, Byrds, Carters, Wormeleys, Lees, Randolphs, Harrisons, Digges, Nelsons, and others—had already laid the foundations of their fortunes in vast land grants acquired before 1700. The "best" families tended to intermarry and by mid-century probably not more than a hundred families controlled the wealth and government of the colony.

Virginia had arrived at a society strangely resembling that of the English countryside, but the resemblance was less in content than in form. It was as if the landed families of Virginia had brought with them the text of a drama long played on the English stage which now would be played on the American. A bizarre, and in some respects inept, set of players was taking the old English parts: The English Country Gentleman—Lord Effingham Blank or Squire Brown of Ancient Acres—was now played by The American Planter; The English Peasant, by The Negro Slave; The Steward, by The White Overseer. We recognize the parts by certain conspicuous signs. The Virginia (like the English) Country Gentleman rode in a coach, ate off silver inscribed with his family coat of arms which had been approved by the College of Heralds in London, sat on the bench as justice of the peace, served as vestryman of the local Anglican church, read the books of a gentleman, and even flavored his conversation or his letters with an occasional literary allusion in a classic language. The uncouth Negro slave, only a generation or two from the African jungle, was taught to play the role of peasant.

The contrast with the British West Indies, where so many other circumstances were similar, is dramatic and revealing. There, absenteeism prevailed, and the plantation owner, following the Spanish pattern, expected to establish colonies of slaves, housed in barracks and daily driven to the fields, like the Indians in the Spanish *encomiendas*. But the Virginian, with the model of the English country gentleman before him, had to cast his slaves in another role to make his own role probable. "He expected to live on his estate himself," John S. Bassett reminds us, "and he wanted to group his slaves around him where he would know them, physic them, give them in marriage, and in his good-natured way train and swear at each one individually." The successful Virginia planter came to live a life far different from that of the indolent West Indian planter; he worked long hours and was close in his supervision. The planter's wife acquired new, and hardly ornamental, tasks.

The new Virginia pattern was surprisingly old English, especially in the relationship of social classes. At first, the American situation had opened up some of the privileges and pastimes of English gentlemen. For example, the keeping of a deer-park was a centuries-old symbol of gentility: to hunt deer and to prosecute poachers were prerogatives of an upper class. But in the wilderness of seventeenth-century Virginia, deer were not confined to the lordly estates of gentlemen. Promotional brochures, like *A New Description of Virginia* (1649) and *A True Relation of Virginia and Maryland* (1669), advertised that native deer and elk were found in wild abundance. "One sees at times many hundreds together," William Byrd boasted as late as 1737, "They are, however, not quite as large as the European ones, but on the other hand, much better flavor, and big and fat all the year long." Symbolically, few facts were more important than that America had made the very idea of poaching obsolete.

If the Virginia gentry had been deprived of ancient insignia like the deer-park, they were not slow to devise others more American. Horse-racing, for example, though not yet the Sport of Kings, was already confined to gentlemen. In 1674, the York County Court ordered:

> James Bullocke, a Taylor, having made a race for his mare to runn w'th a horse belonging to Mr. Mathew Slader for twoe thousand pounds of tobacco and caske, it being contrary to Law for a Labourer to make a race, being a sport only for Gentlemen, is fined for the same one hundred pounds of tobacco and caske.

When Governor Sir Francis Nicholson declared an annual field day in 1691 and offered prizes, he limited contestants to "the better sort of Virginians only."

There appeared other evidences of more rigid social classes. Even the Negroes, who in the later 17th century had been "servants" (not necessarily for life) were gradually forced into the life-long status of slavery. The universal manhood suffrage of the mid-17th century was restricted, step by step, until by 1700 voting requirements in Virginia were virtually the same as those in the mother country.

18

From Country Squire to
Planter Capitalist

IN ENGLAND people had long believed in the mystique of the gentleman. "A gentleman I could never make him," King James I had replied
to his nurse who requested that he make her son a gentleman, "though I
could make him a lord." In Virginia, as we have seen, an aura also surrounded the gentleman, but an aristocratic family could more easily be
manufactured with money. Colonial Virginia thus foreshadowed the
wholesome crudity of the American attitude toward aristocracy. Whenever coats of arms can be bought for ready cash, people are bound to be
skeptical of all charters of nobility. The obvious salability of social
position in America has helped dissipate the mystique of the European
hereditary aristocracy. If the poor see their "betters" pay cash for their
titles, how can they believe the myth of a charter sealed by God?

The spirit of business enterprise was kept alive in Virginia even among
the congealing aristocracy. Leading Virginia families like the Ludwells,
Spencers, Steggs, Byrds, Carys, and Chews, to mention only a few, were
but recently descended from merchants. For several reasons a successful
planter was likely to remain something of a merchant, constantly seeking
new investments for his capital. First, there were the characteristics of
Virginia's tobacco-agriculture. Since Virginians did not replenish the
nitrogen and potash which growing tobacco sucked from the soil, it was
only on virgin land that tobacco could flourish; the second crop was usually the best. After the fourth season land was customarily abandoned to
corn and wheat, before finally being turned back to wild pine, sorrel,
and sedge. Under this system a prudent planter dared not put more than
a small portion—say, ten per cent—of his acreage in tobacco at any
one time. Foresight required that he continually add to his land-holdings
since every year he was, in the Virginia phrase, "using it up." Soon the
term "tobacco land" became synonymous with "new land." The "sour
land" or "old fields" which had presumably yielded all their profit pro-

vided the sites for schools and churches in tidewater Virginia. A prudent planter thus had to be a land speculator, alert to opportunity, ready to make new purchases. The landholdings of the principal families were constantly increasing and often shifting location. The most ancient plantation houses—like those of the Carters, Randolphs, and Byrds—remained fixed and became wellsprings of family tradition, but the lands from which these families drew their wealth were capital equipment to be discarded or exchanged when they no longer yielded a fair return. Under these circumstances, large planters discovered special advantages in an enslaved labor-force which could be moved about the countryside as one or another piece of land promised greater profit. This wasteful system was not an unmixed evil, at least from the point of view of the civic institutions of Virginia, for it subjected the wealthy planter class—who were also the political leaders—to an unrelenting test of alertness and enterprise.

The second factor which stimulated a mercantile and enterprising spirit among the planters and which had shaped the character of the plantation system itself was the lack of large towns. "The inhabitants do not live close together," noted the French traveler Francis L. Michel in 1702, "and the country is not settled in villages, because every twenty or thirty years new ground must be broken." This was not the only reason. The simple facts of geography were equally important. Tidewater Virginia, extending southeastward toward the Chesapeake Bay, was a rich lowland which was cut into fingers by several deep and navigable rivers: the Potomac, the Rappahannock, the York, and the James. Each finger was in turn reticulated by a veinwork of smaller rivers, many of which were large enough to carry traffic toward the ocean. These were the circulatory channels of economic life. Up came ships carrying Negro slaves from Africa and the West Indies, clothing and household furnishings from London; down went ships laden with hogsheads of tobacco from the vast plantations of the Lees, the Carters, and the Byrds.

From a commercial point of view, then, cities were superfluous. Each of the larger planters had his private dock. The tobacco grower could load his hogsheads directly from his own dockside onto the ship which went to his agent in London; his imports could be landed at his private port-of-entry. For this reason Virginia had no commercial capital, no Boston or Philadelphia, during the colonial period; her commerce dwelt in these scores of private depots scattered along the riversides. "No Country in the World can be more curiously watered," observed John Clayton in his Letter to the Royal Society in 1688. "But this Conveniency, that in future Times may make her like the Netherlands, the richest Place in

all America, at the present I look on the greatest Impediment to the
Advance of the Country, as it is the greatest Obstacle to Trade and Commerce. For the great Number of Rivers, and the Thinness of the Inhabitants, distract and disperse a Trade. So that all Ships in general gather
each their Loading up and down an hundred Miles distant; and the best
of Trade that can be driven is only a sort of Scotch Peddling; for they
must carry all Sorts of Truck that trade thither, having one Commodity
to pass off another. This (i.e.) the Number of Rivers, is one of the chief
Reasons why they have no Towns." Why, asked the authors of *The Present State of Virginia* a few years later, should the planter-merchant, comfortably seated in the country with his customers all about him, wish to
change his life or invite the competition of town merchants?

In an age when land transportation was rudimentary, in a new country
where roads barely existed, the Virginia planters and those who bought
at their docks seemed favored by nature. "Most Houses are built near
some Landing-Place," the Rev. Hugh Jones noted in 1724, "any Thing
may be delivered to a Gentleman there from London, Bristol, &c. with
less Trouble and Cost, than to one living five Miles in the Country in
England; for you pay no Freight for Goods from London, and but little
from Bristol; only the Party to whom the Goods belong, is in Gratitude
engaged to freight Tobacco upon the Ship consigned to her Owners in
England."

The critics of Virginia frequently complained that the low state of
culture, religion, and commerce was due to this lack of towns. Because
the work of English furniture-makers was so cheaply carried to Virginia
plantations in the holds of ships coming for bulky hogsheads of tobacco,
native craftsmen were discouraged. The very ease of river transportation
actually provincialized the thinking of many planters. "At the first settlement of the Country," Governor Spotswood reported in 1710, "people
seated themselves along the banks of the great Rivers and knew very
little of the inland parts beyond the bounds of their own private plantations, being kept in awe by the Indians from vent'ring farther; neither had
they any correspondence than only by Water." To promote "cohabitation" in towns would, critics said, produce the higher forms of civilization.
Some proposed legislation, tax-benefits for town-dwellers, and other en-
ticements, but all these failed and geography had its way. Until late in the
18th century, the commercial life of Virginia—and, with it, the commercial virtues—remained diffused among the larger planters. Because there
were no towns, the Virginia country gentleman, more than his English
counterpart, had to acquire the town talents: a spirit of enterprise, a
capacity for sharp-dealing, and a townsman's eye for profit and loss.

Tobacco, unlike the crops of many English country gentlemen, was not part of a traditional subsistence economy; it was a commercial crop, raised for profit. The planters' investments in slaves, land, and equipment were supported by large cash loans. The account-books of George Washington and many others tell this story with discouraging vividness. Virginia was, as some complained, "a colony founded on smoke," and Jefferson, like others before him, pleaded for a more diversified economy. But the plantation system, exemplified in the West Indies and Virginia, was, according to some historians, the first great experiment in large-scale commercial agriculture since the Roman Empire.

The English country gentleman was traditionally interested in the details of his farm. Even so great a lord as the eighth Duke of Devonshire (several decades later) experienced "the proudest moment of his life" when his pig won first prize at Skipton Fair. The large Virginia planter could not be satisfied by prizes at a local fair. His tobacco had entered the exacting competition of the world market, and he had to keep a sharp eye on the cost of a hundred different tasks. When M. Durand de Dauphiné visited Rosegill, the magnificent Wormeley estate in 1686, he thought he was entering "a rather large village." Life on a large plantation was far from that in a simple agrarian economy. There were hundreds of slaves, white craftsmen, overseers, stewards, and traders who were producing tobacco as a money-crop, raising food, and manufacturing tools, farm instruments, and clothing for their own use and for sale in local and foreign markets to which they were sometimes carried in the planter's own ships. A Virginia plantation was an 18th-century version of a modern "company town" rather than a romantic rural village. The plantation-owner needed both business acumen and a large store of practical knowledge to run his little world of agriculture, trade, and manufacturing. Breadth and versatility, so impressive in men like William Byrd and Thomas Jefferson, were common to the larger and more successful Virginia planters of the 18th century: they were interested in natural history, had a respectable knowledge of medical remedies and mechanics, were at home in meteorology, and felt obliged to know the law. How devious it is to explain these plantation necessities as if they were inspired by the distant example and abstract teachings of the European Enlightenment! They were nothing more than an index to the problems of a Virginia planter.

If all these influences produced a breed of men with some characteristic New World virtues, the product was none the less aristocratic. While the Virginia gentleman felt more incentive to enterprise, was less fearful of soiling his hands in trade, was more capitalistic in his frame of mind, had a sharper eye for the cash-balance sheet, and was more versatile in his intellectual interests, he was still a member of a small privileged class. Foundations of this class had been solidly laid before the opening of the 18th century. Col. Robert Quarry reported back to the Lords of Trade in 1704 that on each of Virginia's four great rivers there lived between ten and thirty men "who by trade and industry had gotten very competent estates." By mid-century the number of such men had increased, and there were some upstarts, like the Jeffersons and Washingtons among them. But the very process which had multiplied the larger planters had decimated the smaller ones. The social gulf between a substantial gentleman planter and everybody else was probably never wider in Virginia than around the year 1750.

That heyday of the tobacco aristocracy in Virginia—the middle decades of the 18th century—was the youth of nearly all the leaders of Revolutionary Virginia and of those who were to become the "Virginia Dynasty" in the young Federal government. Washington was born in 1732; Monroe, the last of the group, in 1758. The biographies and letters of these men reveal a closely intermarried social "four-hundred." When Governor Alexander Spotswood reported to the Secretary of State on March 9, 1713 that he had finally filled three vacancies in the Governor's Council with three suitable men "of good parts, loyal and honest principles, and of plentiful Estates," he complained that but for these three he could find none qualified. All others already held places of profit under the government "or elce. . . . are related to one particular Family [the Burwells] to which the greatest part of the present Council are already nearly allyed." In the list of ninety-one men appointed to the Governor's Council from 1680 till the American Revolution, there appear only fifty-seven different family names, nine names providing nearly a third, and fourteen others about another third. Five Councilors were called Page; three each went by the name of Burwell, Byrd, Carter, Custis, Harrison, Lee, Ludwell, or Wormeley. A member of the Council would be likely to hold more than one office. "The Multitude of Places held by the Council," some complained, "occasions great Confusion, especially in such things wherein the Places are incompatible: As when their Collectors Office obliges them to inform their Judges Office against an unfree Bottom: Or when their Honours, as Counsellors, sit upon and pass their own Accounts, as Collectors." This monopoly of offices was not confined to the Governor's Council; in local communities, the same substantial planter was likely to be vestryman, justice of the peace, commander of the militia, and delegate to the House of Burgesses.

The few surviving letters of Thomas Jefferson's youth (written between 1760 and 1764), which tell us nearly all we know about him firsthand before the age of twenty-one, read much like the Society Page: the names in his social pageant are almost without exception those of the "best" Virginia families. The Rebecca Burwell who was his first romantic love came of that very family which ruled the Governor's Council fifty years before. "Dear Will," he wrote to young Fleming, "I have thought of the cleverest plan of life that can be imagined. You exchange your land for Edgehill, or I mine for Fairfeilds, you marry S[ucke]y P[otte]r, I marry R[ebecc]a B[urwel]l, [join] and get a pole chair and a pair of keen horses, practise the law in the same courts, and drive about to all the dances in the country together. How do you like it?" Through the letters of this young socialite run the names of Page, Mann, Carter, Nelson, Lee, Bland, and Yates, none of which could have been excluded from a Virginia Social Register.

No wall separates this world of the 1760's and 50's and 40's from 1776. No mutation of ideas distinguishes the thinking of the late years from those of the middle years of the century. On the contrary, the more we learn of Virginia life the more continuity we see between the ways of the Revolutionary generations and those of their fathers and grand-fathers. The more we begin to see the local lineage of their ideas, the less we need seek a cosmopolitan philosophic ancestry or try to explain them as ideas which lack a local habitation but are supposed to have been "in the air" all over the world. The motives of the Revolution will dissolve into the commonplace. The philosophers of the European Enlightenment who have been hauled into the court of historians as putative fathers of the Revolution may then seem as irrelevant as the guilty cousin who suddenly appears in the last scene of a bad mystery play. The motives and patterns of action which were to reach a climax in the Revolution were already taking form a century before in the daily life of Virginia.

19

Government by Gentry

IT WOULD BE A great mistake to assume that the cozy, aristocratic character of Virginia society had nothing to do with its civic virtues. Only a perverse hindsight has made the political institutions of colonial

Virginia a leveling democracy in embryo. When George Washington feared for the preservation of self-government and the rights of Englishmen, it was the political customs of mid-18th century Virginia that he must have had in mind, for he knew no others. Those customs were the representative institutions of a Virginia-bred aristocracy, whose peculiarly aristocratic virtues nourished American representative government at its roots. And those roots reached back to Virginia's Golden Day.

Never did a governing class take its political duties more seriously: power carried with it the duty to govern. Thus, while Virginia had a restrictive suffrage throughout the colonial period, it also had a law of compulsory voting. In a few other colonies occasional statutes punished the qualified voter who did not appear at the polls, and it is uncertain how strenuously the Virginia law was enforced, but the continuous course of such legislation in Virginia from the early days till after the Revolution testifies to the persistent belief that government was a duty. If the ordinary voter was required to cast his ballot, men of greater substance were expected to carry heavier burdens. When Jefferson, under particularly unhappy circumstances in 1781, yearned for "the independance of private life," he was describing the relief for which many men of prominent Virginia families must have longed.

Just as the owner of a large plantation had thrust on him tasks of management which he could not escape—he had to lay out orchards, decide on the time to plant and to cut the tobacco, find raw materials for shoes and clothing, and look after the health of the slaves—so he had political duties which he could not shirk. The successful planter developed perforce the habit of command. He came to manage the affairs of the colony with the same self-assurance he showed in managing his private estate. If the plantation was a little colony in itself, which had to be governed with tact, authority, and prudence, the colony of Virginia was in turn ruled like a large plantation. The major dignities and decisions rested on those who held the largest stake.

The roster of the House of Burgesses is a list of leading planters. The upward political path from the seat of the vestryman or justice of the peace to the Governor's Council was guarded all along the way by the local gentry. Seeking a political career without their approval was hopeless. And the House of Burgesses, which increased in power during the colonial period until it dominated the Governor and Council, was hardly more than the political workshop of a ruling aristocracy. Here were made the major decisions about the price and quality of tobacco, taxation, education, Indian relations, and religion. It was here that men were trained and scrutinized before advancement to higher office. Freeholders elected the Burgesses, but only the Burgesses themselves had the power to advance Virginians to higher honors, and the Burgesses conscientiously sifted upper-class Virginians for the tasks of government. Although there were less than a hundred seats in the House of Burgesses in the mid-18th century, nearly all prominent Virginians of the century had served an apprenticeship in the House.

Members disagreed much less than we might suppose, and their discussions little resembled the debate of a modern legislature. Although outspoken conflict marked the years of the Stamp Act, the politics of the House did not harden into party lines. Virginians were not prepared for the idea of political parties in the early years of the new government. As the 18th century wore on, the ruling Burgesses seemed to become more harmonious and singleminded, willing to recognize leadership among men of quite different political complexions. Thus when the House, sitting as the Virginia Convention of 1774, chose its delegates to the first Continental Congress, it elected Peyton Randolph, Richard Bland, and Edmund Pendleton, who had been conservatives in the recent Stamp Act controversy, as well as their opponents, Richard Henry Lee and Patrick Henry.

Perhaps never in recent times has a ruling group taken a more proprietary attitude towards public office. During the years of the Revolution and the first decades of independence, the Burgesses selected (almost exclusively from their own membership) the Virginia governors, councilmembers, judges, military officers, and delegates to Federal conventions. Their personal knowledge of each member of the Virginia ruling class qualified them to distribute public dignities and burdens with an impressive, if not quite infallible, wisdom.

This snugness of the ruling Virginians did, of course, have its less attractive side, which was displayed in the notorious Robinson Affair. No modern journalist could have concocted anything more sensational than these sober facts. When John Robinson, Speaker of the House of Burgesses and Treasurer of the colony, died, Purdie's *Virginia Gazette* (May 16, 1766) with unintended irony declared it "a calamity to be lamented by the unfortunate and indigent who were wont to be relieved and cherished by his humanity and liberality." The embarrassing dimensions of Robinson's generosity, though long suspected, were not confirmed until the administrators of his estate began to cast up their accounts. They then discovered that Robinson, while Treasurer of the colony, had drawn on the public funds to the extent of £100,761:7:5, which he had lent out to scores of his friends. These amounts varied from £14,921 lent to William Byrd III (who had failed to inherit his an-

cestors' business acumen and was unlucky at cards to boot), Lewis Burwell's £6274, Carter Braxton's £3848, and Archibald Cary's £3975,
down to Richard Henry Lee's £12 and Patrick Henry's £11. Members
of the Governor's Council owed Robinson nearly £16,000; those of the
House of Burgesses over £37,000. Edmund Pendleton, administrator of
the estate, who spent twelve of the best years of his life trying to settle it,
had himself been favored with £1020. As the accounts of the estate un-
folded, it appeared that there was hardly a Virginia family of prominence
that had not been helped in distress by Robinson's generosity with the
public funds. This vast network of indebtedness explains the reluctance of
the Burgesses over so many years to separate the offices of Speaker and
Treasurer or to make a thorough audit of the colony's accounts. The
affable Robinson had made the public treasury a relief chest for the ruling
clique.

Two peculiar facts about this affair give us valuable clues to the morals
and customs of the rulers of Virginia. First, Robinson had never used any
of the funds for his personal benefit—except insofar as he was benefited
by the gratitude of his friends. Second, when the facts were revealed the
leading Burgesses hardly reproached Robinson for misappropriating public money; they came near praising him for his excess of virtue. When
Robert Carter Nicholas (Robinson's successor as Treasurer) hinted at
some impropriety, he was denounced for the suggestion; he found it
politic to deny the innuendo and declared the loans "more owing to a
mistaken kind of Humanity and Compassion for Persons in Distress."
Governor Fauquier expressed the general sentiment when, after hearing
Pendleton's report on the Robinson estate, he said, "Such was the Sensi-
bility of his too benevolent Heart." Whatever we may think of Robinson
himself, his career revealed a community where public power belonged
to a privileged few.

This power did carry with it corresponding and sometimes burdensome
duties. Almost from the beginning the House of Burgesses strictly required all members to be present at the opening of each session. A
Burgess who failed to attend the convening of the House was, according
to an Act of 1659-60 and repealed reënactments, fined three hundred
pounds of tobacco for every twenty-four hours of unexcused absence. At
the opening sitting, the Speaker would read letters from members explaining their absence, and their reasons would be approved or rejected.
It was not unknown—as in the case of James Bray in 1691—for the
House to be so offended by an explanation that the Speaker issued a
warrant for the member's arrest, holding him in custody until he offered
suitable apology. Special tasks, such as the election of the Speaker, made

attendance at the opening session important, but the House was only slightly indulgent toward Burgesses who missed any regular session. Before the end of the 17th century the fine of two shillings and sixpence was increased to one hogshead of tobacco for each absence from a sitting. When, during the session of 1684, five members failed to answer a roll-call and were found to have gone home without consent of the House, a resolution ordered the sheriffs of their counties to collect from each negligent Burgess a fine of one thousand pounds of tobacco. They were not readmitted to the House until they had apologized.

The House of Burgesses very early (in 1666) disclaimed the right to relieve any duly elected member of his duty of attending, even when his constituents formally requested it. This doctrine survived the 18th century to plague the unhappy Jefferson in May 1782 when, just after his retirement under a cloud of censure as Governor of Virginia, the people of Albemarle County elected him delegate to the House. Weary of office and smarting from the public ingratitude, Jefferson wished to decline the office. When he sent his refusal to John Tyler, Speaker of the House, the ominous reply informed him that "the Constitution in the Opinion of the Members will not warrant the acceptance of your resignation." Tyler warned Jefferson "that good and able Men had better govern than be govern'd, since 'tis possible, indeed highly probable, that if the able and good withdraw themselves from Society, the venal and ignorant will succeed." Finally Jefferson was urged "to give attendance without incuring the Censure of being siezed."

The Virginia Burgesses were, of course, "elected." Their election, if less corrupt and more open to talent, much resembled the English "election" of members of Parliament in the same period. It was nothing like a free-for-all in which any ambitious young man could seek his political fortune; the election was a process in which freeholders made their choice from among the gentlemen. Technically the qualifications for a Burgess were no greater than those for a voter, but in practice the candidates for the House were members of the gentry.

Elections took place in an intimate atmosphere which emphasized both the munificence of the candidates and the power of the freeholders, a strange combination of protocol and conviviality. Campaign oratory seems to have counted for very little; only an unusually pompous and obtuse gentleman would orate to neighbors who had known him since childhood. Seldom was there a public debate on the "issues," but even the best known candidate could not hope for success unless he had taken the trouble to mingle with his constituents. Convention forbade a candidate's soliciting votes, or even voting for himself, and there was no party organization. A candidate was, however, expected to use indirect (usually gastronomic) means of persuasion; no one could hope for election without "treating" the voters. Large quantities of rum punch, ginger cakes, and barbecued beef or pork persuaded prudent voters that their candidate possessed the liberality and the substance to represent them properly in the Assembly. Such entertainment was expensive. Samuel Overton of Hanover County estimated his cost for two elections at £75; George Washington's expenditures when he stood for Burgess were never less than £25 and on one occasion about £50. Such a sum was several times what it would have cost a man to buy the house and land required to qualify him as a voter. A Virginia statute did, of course, prohibit anyone "directly or indirectly" giving "money, meat, drink . . . present, gift, reward, or entertainment. . . . in order to be elected, or for being elected to serve in the General Assembly," but this law seems to have been seldom enforced. A general reputation for hospitality was actually the best defense against suspicions of bribery at election time.

Voting took place in the county courthouse or, in good weather, on the courthouse green. It differed from a modern American election mainly in the publicity given to every voter's choice and in the resulting opportunity for gratitude or resentment between the candidate and his constituents. By an almost unbroken custom, candidates were expected to be present at the voting-place. At a table sat the sheriff, the candidates, and the clerks (including one for each candidate). The voters came up one at a time to announce their choices, which were recorded publicly like a box-score. Since anyone present could always see the latest count, a candidate could at the last minute send supporters to bring in additional needed votes. As each voter declared his preference, shouts of approval would come from one side and hoots from another, while the betting-odds changed and new wagers were laid. The favored candidate would rise, bow, and express thanks to the voter: "Mr. Buchanan, I shall treasure that vote in my memory. It will be regarded as a feather in my cap forever." This personal acknowledgment of the voter's confidence was so customary that in the rare case when the candidate could not be present he delegated a friend to make his obeisances for him. When George Washington's command of the Frederick militia kept him at Fort Cumberland during the 1758 election, his friend James Wood, the most influential man in the county, sat at the poll and thanked each voter individually for his compliment to the absent colonel. A less common method of voting was by a show of hands, acclamation, or some other informal expression.

The control of the gentry over elections was by no means confined to their ability to earn the favorable opinion of the voters. For the gentry chose the sheriff from among themselves, and the sheriff managed the elections. He decided whether any individual was qualified to vote; he set the date of the election; he fixed the hour for opening and closing the polls; there was no appeal from his decisions except to the House of Burgesses, which was always reluctant to override local officials.

"Gentlemen freeholders," the sheriff would finally proclaim from the courthouse door, "come into court and give your votes or the poll will be closed." Sometimes the election would be ended by two o'clock in the afternoon, but if the sheriff found that many voters had been kept away "by rain or rise of watercourses," he might prolong the election into another day. What modern candidate would not envy the Virginia gentleman his power to keep the polls open until the winning votes had been rounded up!

Virginia law permitted a gentleman freeholder to vote in every county where he possessed the property qualification. If he was qualified in three counties he could vote for three sets of Burgesses. Since a man could represent in the House of Burgesses any district where he could vote, this further widened the political opportunities of the larger planters. They could choose to run where their chances seemed best. Many great Virginians, including George Washington, Patrick Henry, John Marshall, and Benjamin Harrison, used their extensive and dispersed landholdings to advance their political fortunes.

20

A Republic of Neighbors

THE ARISTOCRATIC CHARACTER of Virginia republicanism helps explain why Virginians like Jefferson and Washington had more confidence in representative government than had many of their thoughtful contemporaries from other parts of the country. John Adams, Alexander Hamilton, and Gouverneur Morris came from colonies where "the people" were a volatile city crowd: "a great beast." For Virginians a "republican" government was an intricately balanced traditional arrangement.

If a modern historian had invented an allegory to tell this story he could hardly have done better than *The Candidates; or, the Humours of a Virginia Election,* a comedy in three acts written by Robert Munford of Mecklenburg in 1770. This little play is perhaps the first to express the American talent for making sport of politics. In it a small group of voters plays an affable and passive, but by no means foolish, role. Everyone, including the candidates, is confident that these voters can judge human quality and that they will see through a designing, ambitious, or dishonest candidate.

> *Wou'dbe.* Well, I've felt the pulse of all the leading men, and find they beat still for Worthy, and myself. Strutabout and Smallhopes fawn and cringe in so abject a manner, for the few votes they get, that I'm in hopes they'll be soon heartily despised.
>
> > The prudent candidate who hopes to rise,
> > Ne'er deigns to hide it, in a mean disguise.
> > Will, to his place, with moderation slide,
> > And win his way, or not resist the tide.
> > The fool, aspiring to bright honour's post,
> > In noise, in shouts, and tumults oft, is lost.

The gentlemen freeholders naturally come to despise Strutabout and Smallhopes and the wealthy toper Sir John Tody, while they learn to respect Wou'dbe and Worthy.

> *Worthy.* I have little inclination to the service; you know my aversion to public life, Wou'dbe, and how little I have ever courted the people for the troublesome office they have hitherto imposed upon me.
>
> *Wou'dbe.* I believe you enjoy as much domestic happiness as any person, and that your aversion to a public life proceeds from the pleasure you find at home. But, sir, it surely is the duty of every man who has abilities to serve his country, to take up the burden, and bear it with patience.

The well-oiled machinery of aristocracy, far from thwarting the will of the people, simply saves the people from mistakes: the sheriff is always there to close the polls at the appropriate moment. The sensible neighbors finally elect the two able candidates by acclamation. This is happy evidence, Wou'dbe rejoices, of "a spirit of independence becoming Virginians."

These customs of the Virginia countryside bred a similar independence among the Burgesses themselves. Everything that made Virginia's elections aristocratic—the tendency to inherit posts in the House of Burgesses, the self-assurance and security of the large planters—encouraged Burgesses to be reasonable and independent in their judgment. Once in the legislature they seldom glanced over their shoulders for the smile or frown of their constituency, a habit which often makes a modern representative the fragile mirror of those who elect him.

It was generally accepted in Virginia in those days that the ruling planters of good family had a prescriptive right to become ruling Burgesses, always, of course, provided they had earned the good opinion of their less substantial neighbors. "There is a greater distinction supported between the different classes of life here," observed John F. D. Smyth as late as the Revolution, "than perhaps in any of the rest of the colonies; nor does the spirit of equality, and levelling principle, which pervades the greatest part of America, prevail to such an extent in Virginia." The large planter, busy with his own affairs, was deterred from standing for Burgess less by the risk of defeat than by the certainty of victory.

This security of social position bred a wholesome vigor of judgment which made the Virginia House of Burgesses a place for deliberation and discussion rarely found among modern legislatures. Burgesses came close to Edmund Burke's ideal of the representative who owed allegiance not to the whim of his constituency but only to his private judgment. The voters in colonial Virginia had just enough power to prevent the irresponsibility of their representatives, but not enough to secure their servility. This was a delicate balance, but it had a great deal to do with the effectiveness of the legislature. In Munford's *Candidates* the virtuous Wou'dbe scrupulously avoided promising to do whatever the people wished, since the people would not have chosen him unless they had preferred his judgment to theirs. The most famous example of this Burkean independence comes from a later day: in 1788, in the Virginia Convention called to ratify the new Federal Constitution, at least eight delegates voted for the new government against the wishes of their electors.

The contrast between the atmosphere in the Virginia Burgesses and in a modern state legislature is only partly explained by the talents of the representatives. The seriousness, wisdom, honesty, and eloquence in the deliberations of the Burgesses during the crucial years of the Stamp Act—the "most bloody" debates which Jefferson, then a student at the College, heard from the door of the chamber—was not due only

to the greatness of the men and the issues. These men were not satisfied
to be spokesmen of their voters' whims. Their speeches were serious and
sometimes subtle arguments directed to fellow-legislators. Their debate
lacked that meandering and miscellaneous, if amusing, irrelevance of the
modern Congressional Record and its local counterparts. In those days
it was still customary for a legislator (at least in Virginia) to give more
time to the deliberations of his House than to answering mail from his
constituents, to making "news" in legislative committees, or to seeking jobs for faithful supporters. American folklore has only a little exaggerated: the Virginia House of Burgesses was a meeting of gods on
Olympus compared to a modern state legislature.

These men were talking to each other; none of them was much impressed by the flowery phrase. With the conspicuous exception of a
few like Patrick Henry, Virginia's representatives talked in sober and
conversational style; there has seldom been an age of representative
government when the power to orate was less important. Within the
intimacy of the House of Burgesses, which any visitor to Colonial
Williamsburg can sense today, persuasive argument was of first importance; demagoguery was useless. Jefferson was not an eloquent
speaker, a fact which led him later to send his annual messages to
Congress rather than deliver them in person; Washington and Madison
were hardly better. And the leading figures in the Burgesses in the 18th
century—men like Richard Bland, Peyton Randolph, and John Robinson
—were all ungraceful speakers. The House of Burgesses (like its English
counterpart, the House of Commons) was an exclusive club where
gentlemen seriously discussed public problems.

Virginia was governed by its men of property. There was no family
of substance without members in the Governor's Council, the House of
Burgesses, the county court or other governing bodies; and there was
no governing body of the colony that was not dominated by the men of
substance. These men presumably, and usually in fact, possessed the
best knowledge of the large economic and political problems of the community: the price of tobacco and the cost of producing it, the quality
of essential imports, the location of indispensable markets, the character
of necessary shipping, the routes of primary roads, the places of the
most useful ferries.

Land—land to use, to waste, to divide among one's children—was
the foundation of all the governing families and the fortunes of Virginia.
The power to give or to deny land, those vast virgin tracts expected to
appreciate most in the next decades, rested in the hands of the government, especially in the House of Burgesses and the Governor's Council.

The Burgesses also possessed important routine powers over already-settled land, powers which in England were held by the courts. In England if a landholder inherited entailed land which he wanted to deal with as full owner, he followed certain complicated but routine court procedures which ingenious lawyers had developed. Not so in Virginia. There any heir who wanted to get rid of such restrictions had to secure in his own name, and for that particular piece of land, a private Act of the House of Burgesses. Between 1711 and 1774 a total of one hundred and twenty-five such Acts were passed; nearly three-fourths of them for members of such leading families as the Armisteads, Beverleys, Braxtons, Burwells, Carters, Dandridges, Eppes, Pages, Tazewells, Wormeleys, Washingtons, and Yeates. All these, either in their own person or through relatives, would have been represented in the House which acted on their petition. Such private Acts of the House were a necessity for the substantial planter: without them he was not free to deal with his land, to move his labor force, or to dispose of worn-out parcels in order to acquire lands farther west.

Still more important was the power of the Burgesses and the Governor's Council over that treasure-house of the West to which they held the legal keys. There was nothing secret or underhanded about any of this. Under the prevailing system of soil-exhaustion, with fluctuating tobacco prices and the exorbitant demands of London merchants, simple prudence had made tobacco planters into land speculators. George Washington, though shrewd and ambitious, was no gambler, but he seized opportunities to enlarge his holdings. He saw that a westward-pushing population would raise the value of the fertile piedmont; it was important to be alert and acquire good land early. In June 1767 Washington advised his friend, the unfortunate Captain John Posey who had been sinking deeper and deeper into debt, to "look to Frederick, and see what fortunes were made by the Hites and the first takers up of those lands: Nay, how the greatest estates we have in this Colony were made. Was it not by taking up and purchasing at very low rates the rich back lands which were thought nothing of in those days, but are now the most valuable lands that we possess?" In the middle years of the century, after his stint with Braddock and before his Revolutionary command, Washington like many of his fellow Virginia aristocrats, was in Douglas Freeman's accurate phrase, a "land hunter."

To satisfy land-hunger in Virginia one needed not only a strong body but a shrewd political sense. The pathway to landed wealth lay, not only through uncharted tracts in the wilderness, but also through the corridors of government buildings in Williamsburg. This was the "inside track," well-worn by leading Virginians, to the fertile expanses of the unsettled south and west. There was hardly a fortune in Virginia which had not been sought out in this fashion. When William Byrd was appointed by the government to survey the dividing line between Virginia and North Carolina in 1728, he saw the wealth of the fertile bottom-land and christened it the "Land of Eden." He seized the morally dubious opportunity to buy 20,000 acres from the North Carolina commissioners to whom it had been given for their services. In 1742, he secured the again "lucky" chance to patent another 105,000 acres, which he had hoped to get free but for which he actually paid the bargain price of £525. At his death this man owned 179,440 acres of the richest land in the colony —the fruit of his "public services" as much as of his business enterprise.

In none of the "public business" which engaged Washington's interest during his early years in the House of Burgesses was he more active than in trying to secure parcels of land for himself and his fellow-veterans of 1754. Governor Dinwiddie's emergency Proclamation of February 1754 had supposedly rewarded these veterans with "200,000 acres of his majesty's lands on the Ohio," but it was Washington's activity—which included the promotion of bills in the House of Burgesses, letters to the Governor, and addresses to the Governor's Council—that eighteen years later secured the actual allotment of thousands of acres. Washington took the initiative in securing the grant, in locating the land, and in allotting the acreage among different claimants in proportion to rank. His own reward was 24,100 acres. Of this 18,500 was his personal allotment, which he himself apportioned, and 5600 came from allotments of others which his special position had enabled him to buy cheap. He also had the advantage of knowing first-hand precisely the land which would be divided; and hence he could be sure that the tracts rewarding his patriotism were not unworthy of him. Under the circumstances Washington had no reason to feel that he had unduly favored himself. "I might add without much arrogance," he wrote, "that if it had not been for my unremitted attention to every favorable circumstance, not a single acre of land would ever have been obtained." With no more immodesty Washington might have claimed credit for the thousands of acres which he and other leading Virginians were to secure through the Great Dismal Swamp Company and the Mississippi Company; in every case the help of government agencies was essential.

The weaknesses of representative government in Virginia's Golden Age were on the side of realism, practicality, and a too nice equivalence of economic and political power. These were the mistakes of men of affairs rather than of visionaries, reformers, or revolutionaries. While

Virginians of great landed wealth could grow wealthier, white men at the bottom of the ladder sometimes found it impossible to reach the next-to-the-bottom rung, and the Negro had no chance to rise above servitude. It was, however, also true that their aristocracy showed as high a talent for government as that of any other community before or since. And once a man was on his way up the ladder, there was little to stop him.

How irrelevant to look to the bookish prospectuses of English or French political theorists—of Locke, Montesquieu, or Rousseau—to explain Virginia's political enthusiasms! Americans who knew the reality did not need the dream. Virginians who would fight to preserve representative government and would offer "their Lives, their Fortunes, and their sacred Honor" on the altar of the British Constitution had not produced a single important treatise on political theory. Knowing what representative government was, why should they speculate about what it ought to be? The great Virginians were in the closest touch with the world of conflicting interests. They possessed a sense of full-bodied economic and political reality, but no particular genius for the abstractions of closet-philosophy. This was to prove one of their greatest strengths.

Why should Burgesses disparage the common people—or declaim in favor of government by "the rich and the well-born"? They actually lived where the people acquiesced in government by the rich and well-born; and where the rich and well-born did not overbear the people. Those Virginians who came to show an uncritical faith in the will of the people had founded it on a solid but narrow experience: their experience of rural neighbors who trusted the political talents of their extraordinarily able aristocracy. Business, the opportunity to get rich and to get poor, had vitalized and added mobility to that aristocracy. One could move into it and, if incompetent, one would almost surely drop out of it, or at least be denied the avenue to political power.

During the 18th century there was little evidence of dissatisfaction with the way of government described here. Since the people acquiesced, the ruling Burgesses had no reason to think ill of their way of life. Although there were some minor political and economic reforms in Virginia during the latter half of the century, these were all very much within the established framework of Virginia's Golden Age. In the eyes of the more influential (and even the more Revolutionary) Virginians, the American Revolution was itself an attempt to preserve the moderate ways of that age.

As the ruling Virginians admired the ideal of the English gentleman, the genteel canon they most scrupulously followed was Moderation. Unlike some of their English gentlemen-contemporaries, they did not despise trade or labor, nor did they admire an idle aristocracy. Nor, unlike some later Jacksonian Americans or European leveling democrats, did they particularly idealize the horny-handed laborer. In Brathwait's *English Gentleman,* Virginians could read that Moderation had a threefold aspect, and must be exercised equally in matters of Mind, Body, and Fortune. "Moderation," they learned, was "a vertue so necessary, and well deserving the acquaintance of a Gentleman, (who is to be imagined as one new come to his lands, and therefore stands in great need of so discreet an Attendant) as there is no one vertue better sorting ranke." This ancient virtue, needed for governing a community, was no less desirable in those matters of religion, over which Europeans had tortured one another for centuries.

21

"Practical Godliness":
An Episcopal Church Without Bishops

VIRGINIA was not founded by religious refugees, and the religion of earliest Virginia was not utopian or "purified." The going religion of England was to become part of the life of English gentlemen in America. No fact was more decisive in the history of Virginia and, through Virginians, in shaping the American character. In 1724, the Rev. Hugh Jones, who personally knew the colony, remarked:

> If New England be called a Receptacle of Dissenters, and an Amsterdam of Religion, Pennsylvania the Nursery of Quakers, Maryland the Retirement of Roman Catholicks, North Carolina the Refuge of Run-aways, and South Carolina the Delight of Buccaneers and Pyrates, Virginia may be justly esteemed the happy Retreat of true Britons and true Churchmen for the most Part; neither soaring too high nor drooping too low, consequently should merit the greater Esteem and Encouragement.

The sectarians of New England, Pennsylvania, and Maryland believed that the "purity" of their religion required them to protest against the institutions of the mother country. But even before the others had set up their protesting communities, the Virginians had begun to transplant English religious life to American shores. Although small secessionist movements had troubled English religious life from the Middle Ages, the Roman Catholics were the only major religious group outside the Established Church in England at the time Virginia was founded in 1607. The Church of England, instead of being only one among numerous religious sects, in Virginia was a catholic church, practically coextensive with the community. Many things changed in Virginia between its founding and the later 18th century, but Virginia's religion somehow retained this catholic quality. Theirs was not a violent passion inspiring men to rebuild Zion or to make a City of Brotherly Love, but a quietly pervasive sentiment which suffused the institutions of the colony with a mild aura of divine sanction. The fabric of Virginia society was held together by ancient and durable threads of religion.

"Let others take what courses they please in the bringing up of their posterity," Robert Carter wrote (July 14, 1720) from Rappahannock to the London agent supervising the education of his sons, "I resolve the principles of our holy religion shall be instilled into mine betimes; as I am of the Church of England way, so I desire they should be. But the high-flown up top notions and the great stress that is laid upon ceremonies, any farther than decency and conformity, are what I cannot come into the reason of. Practical godliness is the substance—these are but the shell." In mid-18th-century Virginia this moderate spirit was expressed as much in warm but quiet devotion to the ways of the Established Church as in immunity to the more dramatic appeal of extremists. There were few dissenters of any denomination.

How had this moderation come into being in Virginia? The first explanation was historical. The English Establishment had arisen from a compromise and, in Lord Macaulay's phrase, continued to hold "a middle position between the Churches of Rome and Geneva." This mediating spirit qualified Anglicanism to be the State religion of a liberal society and helps explain its extraordinary vitality. In those days, even in England the emphasis of Anglicanism was traditionally on institutions rather than on doctrines. The catholic character of the church in Virginia simply increased that emphasis.

In Massachusetts Bay, Puritanism became more practical and less interested in dogma than it had been in England. The Puritans in England had been, doctrinally speaking, in a state of siege, but in New England they were free to practice their way of life. Challenged by few theoretical opponents, they showed less interest in sharpening their theological rapiers. The responsibilities of governing New England also dulled the edge of dogma so that by the late 17th century they had begun those prudent compromises which would produce 18th-century Congregationalism and 19th-century Unitarianism.

Anglicanism in Virginia, for similar reasons, was destined to be even more practical and compromising than it had been in England. Virginia was more barren of theological treatises than New England had been, and Virginians devoted their energies to the institutions of Anglicanism, to the problems of the parish, the vestry, the church-wardens, the assisting of government, the enforcement of morality, and provision for the poor. The practical character which Puritan New England paradoxically achieved by its doctrinal orthodoxy, Anglican Virginia arrived at by its catholicity and its traditionalism.

This practical religious spirit appears, for example, in the planters' libraries, which contained many books about religion. In the library of Edmund Berkeley, a fairly typical planter-aristocrat who died in 1718, of one hundred and thirteen titles, the largest group (thirty-two) dealt with religion. So too in the libraries of William Fitzhugh, Ralph Wormeley II, Richard Lee II, Robert Carter, and William Byrd II, to mention only a few. In these collections, works of theological controversy were extremely rare; religious books consisted mainly of such Anglican guides as Richard Alestree's *The Whole Duty of Man,* or Clement Ellis' *The Gentile Sinner; or, England's Brave Gentleman.* Even the occasional book of religious controversy was likely not to be theological but institutional, concerned with the organization and government of churches.

Although the Church of England, in becoming the Church of Virginia, had not altered its theology one iota, it had undergone a sea-change in institutions. While the ocean insulated Virginia Anglicans from the controversies of the metropolis, wilderness-spaces made a new thing of the English church. The Anglican has commonly been called the "Episcopal" church because it is a church of bishops; but in colonial Virginia there would be no bishops. Anglicanism, in contrast to the dissenting churches, was proverbially a church of hierarchy; but in Virginia congregations became notoriously independent and self-governing. There is surely no better example of the talent of Virginians for adapting English institutions, for bending the outward form without breaking the inner spirit. This transformation was accomplished in two ways: first, by nullifying the power of English bishops in the colony, and second, by diffusing the episcopal power into the local vestries. The Virginia Church did not in fact become truly "episcopal"—that is, it did not acquire a bishop—until 1783, after the separation from England.

During the colonial period the question of whether Virginia should have a bishop had agitated people on both sides of the water. It was generally assumed, although the legal origins were obscure, that the control of the colonial church lay in the hands of the Bishop of London, but the more prudent Bishops refused to assert a control they felt they could not enforce. "For a Bishop to live at one end of the world, and his Church at the other," Bishop Thomas Sherlock (Bishop of London, 1748-1761) wrote, "must make the office very uncomfortable to the Bishop, and in a great measure useless to the people." As a result of legal ambiguities, political ambitions, and hysterical fears, colonial Virginia never had its own bishop; in 1771, the House of Burgesses of Episcopalian Virginia took the same stand against bishops that had been taken by Puritan Massachusetts. The sole tie between the colony and the Mother Church throughout the colonial period was a vaguely empowered official called a Commissary.

Without a bishop in Virginia, every candidate for the Anglican clergy had to go to England to be ordained. "The people of the Country," Bishop Sherlock complained in 1751, "are discouraged from bringing up their Children for the Ministry, because of the hazard and expence of sending them to England to take orders where, they often get the small pox, a distemper fatal to the Natives of those Countrys." English clergymen, arguing for colonial bishops, painted the unhappy plight of young Virginians aspiring to the ministry. "And if they have the fortune to arrive safe, being here without friends, and without acquaintances, they have the sad business to undergo, of presenting themselves unknown to persons unknown, without any recommendation or introduction, except certain papers in their pocket. Are there not circumstances in this case, sufficient to deter every ordinary courage, and to damp the most adventurous spirit?" In 1767, an American writer noted, the trip could not cost less than £100, and, of the fifty-two candidates who had recently gone to England for ordaining, only forty-two had returned in safety.

These hazards and expenses of travel enabled Virginia Anglicans to build an *American* church, very different from the English church which they purported to imitate. Without manifestoes, without treatises to defend their position or new dogmas to buttress it, without sounding theological trumpets—and all under the respectable Anglican cloak— Virginians developed their novel institutions. Long before the Revolution, Virginia possessed a congregationalism all its own. It differed from the congregationalism of New England partly because it lacked any explicit theological defense. The ancient hierarchical pile of the Church of England was a defensive façade behind which Virginians built their own modest, self-governing structure. They were so unobtrusive and so successful that the full significance of what they were doing remained long hidden. If they could maintain an "episcopal" church without bishops, what other improvising miracles could they not perform?

Before the middle of the 18th century, the Church of Virginia had acquired a fixed character: it was a group of independent parishes, governed in temporal matters by the House of Burgesses and in doctrinal matters by no central authority at all. So far as we know, there was no regular gathering of clergymen and hence no authentic voice of dogma. Under these circumstances the supervision of the clergy and the definition of religious practices fell into the hands of the leading lay members of the parish, who of course believed it was in the best possible hands.

In England an Anglican minister held his post from the bishop; once "inducted" he had a kind of property in his parish. He held it regardless of, sometimes in spite of, the will of the parishioners, and could be removed only by a trial before his bishop. The result was the notorious twin evils of English parish life in the 18th century: "pluralism" or the holding of numerous parishes by a single clergyman; and "absenteeism" or the holding of a parish where the clergyman did not reside, and in some cases had never visited. The unfortunate English parishioner was powerless.

The Virginia remedy was nothing more complicated than the power of each parish through its vestry to choose its own minister and to retain him only so long as he satisfied them. The Anglican laymen of Virginia had not acquired this power by legislation; they simply took advantage of a legal technicality which they quietly transformed into a major institution. Technically, a minister in Virginia came into full possesson of his parish and into legal control of the "glebe" (farmland owned by the parish to help support the minister) only after he had been "presented" by the vestry to the Governor and Council and then "inducted" into the living. After induction he had a kind of property in the position; but until that time he held his post at the will of the parish. Practical Virginians, bent on getting their money's worth from their tithes, developed the simple practice of not "presenting" or "inducting" their ministers. Thus the ministers were kept on year-to-year contracts, "which they call by a Name coarse enough," Hartwell, Blair, and Chilton reported with disgust in their *Present State of Virginia* in 1697, "viz. Hiring of the Ministers; so that they seldom present any Ministers, that they may by that Means keep them in more Subjection and Dependence." Thirty years later, the Rev. Hugh Jones still worried over "such Vestry-

Men, who erroneously think themselves the Masters of their Parson, and aver, that since they compacted but from Year to Year with him as some have done, they may turn off this their Servant when they will."

But most fears for the Virginia clergy were ill-founded. In 1724 Virginia clergymen had, on the average, served the same parish for twenty years. Yet, of the twenty-eight replying to the Bishop of London's questionnaire in that year, twenty-three had never been "inducted" into their parishes and so, technically, were still on year-to-year tenure.

In England the pauper curate, filling a pulpit for a wealthy absentee who lived comfortably on a distant estate, received treatment befitting his squalor and servility: he ate with the butler and the lady's maid. But in Virginia even the lower clergy had the status of gentlemen. "Any young ministers that intend to marry," Commissary Blair cheerfully reported, "after some proof that they are sober good men, need not fear but that they may match to very good advantage with the Gentlemens daughters of the Countrey." It would be pleasant to report that the Anglican clergy of Virginia were all men of learning and high morals; the fact is that we know too little about the character of individual ministers. But we have no reason to doubt that the Anglican ministers in Virginia parishes were on the whole a conscientious and hard-working lot. In 1759, the Rev. Andrew Burnaby noted that Virginia's sixty-odd clergymen were "men in general of sober and exemplary lives." They were not much inferior to the ministers of other days and were decidedly superior to their English contemporaries.

But the clergyman's life was suffused with the special aroma of the colony, the aroma of tobacco. If there was some exaggeration in saying that the colony had been "founded on smoke," there was much less exaggeration in the remark that in Virginia "the Establishment is indeed Tobacco." In one sense at least, this was literally true, since almost from the beginning the compensation of clergymen had been defined and paid in tobacco. After 1695, the annual salary of a clergyman was fixed by law at 16,000 pounds of tobacco. Since the tobacco in which a minister was paid was that of his particular parish, the money value of his wage depended very much on the quality of that crop. "Some Parishes," the Rev. Hugh Jones lamented, "are long vacant upon Account of the badness of the Tobacco." The minister who found himself in a parish which raised the cruder "Oronoko" type considered himself unfortunate compared with his colleague who preached to parishioners who grew the milder, broader-leaved (and higher-priced) tobacco called "Sweet Scented." When Commissary Blair wrote back to the Bishop of London in 1724 requesting more clergymen for Virginia, he compared the vacancies in "five sweet scented Parishes" with "about double that number of Oranoco ones vacant." The old Virginia parable is still useful for an ambitious clergyman: "The best way to get sweet-scented Tobacco is to use sweet-scented Words."

Virtually the only occasion when ecclesiastical matters became a pressing political issue in colonial Virginia was the so-called "Parson's Cause" (1763). Then Patrick Henry, at the age of 27, first gained popular notice and began his public career. No question of theology or even of church-government was involved, but simply whether, in a period of high tobacco prices, vestries should be permitted to pay their clergymen in the money-values of an earlier age of cheap two-penny tobacco.

"The public or political character of the Virginians," the Rev. Andrew Burnaby sharply reported in 1759, "corresponds with their private one: they are haughty and jealous of their liberties, impatient of restraint, and can scarcely bear the thought of being controuled by any superior power." By the end of the 17th century the practice had become established for the people of the parish, through their vestrymen, to select their own minister. It was actually supported by an opinion of English Attorney General Sir Edward Northey in 1703, but never reached clear judicial decision. After Commissary Blair's bold defense of the principle against Governor Spotswood in 1719, it was never again seriously challenged in colonial Virginia: the parishes went on selecting their own ministers, and employing them on a yearly basis. Thus the battles of the American Revolution, as Bishop Meade has observed, had already been fought in Virginia vestries for a hundred and fifty years. "*Taxation and representation* were only other words for *support and election of ministers*. The principle was the same."

"Self-government" in 18th-century Virginia—in religious no less than in civil matters—was, of course, self-government by the ruling planters on behalf of their servants and neighbors. The parish was their elementary school in the political arts. By law the members of the vestry, not over twelve in number, were supposed to be elected by the parishioners. Since no regular intervals were legally fixed for these elections, however, the ruling planters developed the convenient custom of allowing vestrymen to continue in office indefinitely, until death or resignation. When vacancies occurred, the vestry itself named new members. This self-perpetuating power was important, and the ruling planters were reluctant to give it up. The "rebellious" session of the Virginia Assembly which met under the domination of Nathaniel Bacon in 1676 enacted numerous "reforms," many of which survived; but later Assemblies refused to reënact the requirement that vestrymen be elected every three years. Throughout the 18th century vestries remained self-perpetuating. It was not until 1784, when Anglicanism was no longer established in Virginia, that regular elections of the vestry were required. During this long period, the only appeal from the decisions of the vestrymen was to the General Court or the Assembly of the colony.

On the whole, these self-elected representatives of the parish did their job well. They met at least twice a year, normally at the home of one of their members. The power to choose the minister and to continue or terminate his employment rested with them. Qualified by education, morals, and property, they appear to have exercised their powers with wisdom and restraint. If Virginia was remarkably free of the absenteeism, pluralism, docility, and corruption which cursed English parishes, if Virginia parishes refused as ministers those from England "who could roare in a tavern and babble in the pulpit," the credit was the vestry's.

The parish, through the vestrymen or their deputies, the church-wardens, wielded some of the powers of a modern sheriff, of a district attorney, and of a grand jury. Among other things, vestrymen had the duty of presenting to the court persons guilty of such moral offenses as drunkenness, blasphemy, profanity, defamation, sabbath-breaking, staying away from divine services, fornication, and adultery. The vestry levied parish taxes, assessed property for their payment, and defined the boundaries of landed property. Once in every four years, under the supervision of the county court, the vestrymen appointed two persons to "procession" the land, that is, to examine and renew old landmarks and to record the bounds in the parish books.

The parish, acting through its churchwardens, was the main social welfare agency. It was the vestry's general duty to call attention to cases of extreme poverty and in the absence of an almshouse to provide for the "poor and impotent" by boarding them at public expense in the homes of willing citizens. The vestry tried to save the parish the support of bastards by binding out the mother, compelling the father to give bond, and indenturing the children till the age of thirty. In the western counties it was the vestry that looked after children orphaned by marauding Indians. Between 1748 and 1752 Augusta Parish, in the Valley where the Indian menace was greatest, found new homes for forty-seven orphans. The people of Norfolk, who saw their town burned on New Year's Day of 1776, had their vestries to thank for relieving their suffering. In the late 17th century it was not unusual for the parish tax-levy to equal three or four times the amount of all other taxes. Just before the Revolution, Truro and Fairfax, the two parishes into which Fairfax County was divided, each had larger budgets than the county government.

No prominent citizen could decently withdraw from churchly institutions, for church duties and civic duties were one. Justices of the county courts were commonly also vestrymen: George Washington, George Mason, and George William Fairfax, all justices of Fairfax County, were all vestrymen of Truro Parish; four of the nine vestrymen of Wicomico Parish who met on Nov. 10, 1757, were justices—and so it went. The officers of the militia, who had to be recommended to the Governor by the county justices, were apt to be these very same men. In 1785 after the Church had been disestablished in Virginia, many powers of the vestry were transferred to the county court, but the leading planters still did the parish jobs in their capacity as county justices.

It would have been strange had not the political and social leaders of Virginia been leading Anglicans. Of the more than a hundred members of the Virginia constitutional convention of 1776, only three were not vestrymen. Two-thirds of all the signers of the Declaration of Independence were members of the Established Church; six were sons or grandsons of its clergymen. During the Revolution the movement toward resistance and independence flourished in the Virginia vestries. When, after the colonial legislature had been dissolved and the county courts abolished, each county was required to elect a small committee of safety to act as a de facto government, an Anglican clergyman was elected a member, in many cases president, of that committee in a third of the counties. It is hard to name a leader of the Revolution, including such men as George Washington, James Madison, Edmund Pendleton, and Patrick Henry, who were not securely within the fold of the Church. The fact that there were also outspoken Loyalists like the Rev. Jonathan Boucher who were loyal Anglicans does not alter the case. For in Virginia a quiet devotion to the English Church—both as a bulwark of things ancient and English and as a local expression of the passion for independence—nourished that very reverence for the British constitution and for the traditional rights of Englishmen which inspired the Revolution.

There is no paradox then in the facts that the leaders of Virginia were almost to a man good Anglicans and that these same Virginians led the Revolution. It has been all too easy to imagine that the "English" church in Virginia, like the British government over the colonies, was shaken by a rationalist, anti-clerical, and anti-traditionalist earthquake with its epicenter somewhere in Europe. Such a view does not square with the facts.

22

"Practical Godliness":
Toleration Without a Theory

THE VAST EXTENT of the Virginia parishes naturally affected the quality of their religious experience. By 1740 a small parish measured about twenty miles in length and possessed a scattered population of about seven or eight hundred white persons gathered in about a hundred and fifty families. A larger parish might be sixty miles long, or even more if it extended southwestward toward the dim border between Virginia and North Carolina. Churches were ten or more miles apart. "Their large extent," the Rev. Alexander Forbes (whose own parish was sixty miles long and eleven miles wide) complained in 1724, "is not only the cause of the omission of Holy days; but very often I have found that labor to be fruitless, which I have imployed in room of their observation; for sometimes after I have travell'd Fifty Miles to Preach at a Private House, the Weather happening to prove bad, on the day of our meeting, so that very few or none have met; or else being hindred by Rivers & Swamps rendered impassable with much rain, I have returned with doing of nothing to their benefit or mine own satisfaction." As a quantitative measure of religious zeal, he added that while parishioners were faithful enough to go five or six miles to church, ten or fifteen miles were simply too much for them. The large numbers of recently arrived Africans or unassimilated white indentured servants made cautious planters reluctant to leave their plantations unattended by an adult male of the family.

The lack of any central church authority to enforce uniformity of ritual, and the scarcity of church "ornaments," bred an informality alien to the spirit of the English Church. "After the minister had made an end," a Sunday visitor to a tidewater church noted in 1715, "every one of the men pulled out his pipe, and smoked a pipe of tobacco." We do not know for sure how many, like those later parishioners of neighboring Carolina who so annoyed the Rev. Charles Woodmason, actually brought their dogs to church. But we do know that in some places there was no font for baptizing; in others no surplice for the minister; elsewhere it became common for people to take communion in their seats instead of kneeling before the altar. "Every Minister," the Rev. Hugh Jones wrote, "is a kind of Independent in his own Parish, in Respect of some little particular Circumstances and Customs." Many rituals of the church came to be performed at home.

> The Parishes being of great Extent . . . many dead Corpses cannot be conveyed to the Church to be buried: So that it is customary to bury in Gardens or Orchards, where whole Families lye interred together, in a Spot generally handsomly enclosed, planted with Evergreens, and the Graves kept decently: Hence likewise arises the Occasion of preaching Funeral Sermons in Houses, where at Funerals are assembled a great Congregation of Neighbours and Friends; and if you insist upon having the Sermon and Ceremony at Church, they'll say they will be without it, unless performed after their usual Custom. In Houses also there is Occasion, from Humour, Custom sometimes, from Necessity most frequently, to baptize Children and church Women, otherwise some would go without it. In Houses also they most commonly marry, without Regard to the Time of the Day or Season of the Year.

The vast American spaces were accomplishing in Virginia what in England had required decades of theological controversy. In their own peculiar way, and even without intending it, Virginians were "purifying" the English church of its atmosphere of hierarchy and of excessive reliance on ritual. And were not these the very defects which Massachusetts Puritans had strenuously and stridently attacked?

While space "purified," it also diffused the religious spirit. The more we learn of the spirit of the Church of Virginia, the more natural it seems that Virginia should have become a haven of toleration in the 18th century, and even that Virginia should have been among the first of the colonies with established churches to disestablish them. In Virginia this process began in 1776; while in Connecticut, Church and State remained united until 1818 and in Massachusetts until 1833. We need not look abroad to violent winds of doctrine to explain the moderation of Virginians.

The key to toleration in Virginia was the practical compromising spirit which built the Church of England in its English home and gave it new vitality when transplanted. It was Edmund Pendleton, devoted supporter of the Established Church, and others like him who organized the government and held Virginia together during the anarchic days of the Revolution. Pendleton, as Philip Mazzei, the traveling Florentine,

orded, was popularly known by the nickname of "Moderation."
Irginians were not passionate about religious dogma, for the simple
.eason that they often knew nothing about it. George Washington, though
an active vestryman, probably could not have told the difference between
the Church of Virginia and any other, except that the Established
Church stood for moderation in all things and was the bulwark of
decency in his community.

Virginians had founded their community, not as religious refugees
held together by a common fanaticism, but as admirers of the English
way of life who hoped to preserve its virtues on this side of the water.
Their desire to increase their population and their lack of interest in
theology made them generally lax in enforcing laws against dissenters.
They were tolerant even of Papists and Quakers so long as they kept
the peace. William Fitzhugh, himself a devoted Anglican, lived happily
beside George Brent, a Catholic; he even developed a scheme for importing Catholics to a settlement of their own. Yet he also sought to
attract French Huguenots. Many other leading Virginia Anglicans tried
to make their colony a haven for all decent Christians. A Quaker, John
Pleasants, despite the letter of the law, was elected to the House of
Burgesses, and only because he refused to take the oath of office did he
vacate his seat. When King James II in 1687 issued his edict suspending
the laws against non-conformists (both Protestant and Roman Catholic),
the news was received with such enthusiasm in Virginia that it occasioned
the beating of drums and the firing of guns! The Council prepared an
address of thanks. The Burgesses approved, and a Roman Catholic was
duly elected a member from Stafford County. Against the Quakers, who
had shown their usual unwillingness to help defend the community, and
whose itinerant ways made them a source of information for the
colony's French and Indian enemies, Virginians remained ready to use
force. But they distinguished even among Quakers; when Thomas Story
early in the 18th century won their confidence, they permitted him to
wander at will preaching heterodoxy.

Men who wished to strengthen their colony with a solid citizenry—
of English non-conformists, of Scots, Irish, Huguenots, Germans, and
Dutch—could not split theological hairs. "With regard to the affair of
Mr. Davis the Presbyterian," the English Board of Trade wisely advised
the Council of Virginia in 1750, "A Toleration and a free exercise of
Religion is so valuable a branch of true Liberty, and so essential to the
improving and enriching of a Trading Nation, it should ever be held
Sacred to his Majesty's Colonies." From time to time, of course, they had
to restrain religious troublemakers who menaced the peace or security of

the colony. Virginians forbade the coming of Puritans in 1640 and the assembly of Quakers in 1662; a hundred years later (1770) they imprisoned wild Baptist preachers. But these were emergency measures which expressed no general spirit of persecution.

Before the middle of the 18th century, dissenting sects—Presbyterians, Baptists, and even Quakers—had acquired a recognized place in the life of the colony. "If there are among you any dissenters from this Church with consciences truly scrupulous," Gooch declared in his inaugural address as Lieutenant-Governor in 1728, "I shall think an indulgence to them to be so consistent with the genius of the Christian Religion that it can never be inconsistent with the interest of the Church of England." The laws against Quakers seem to have been enforced not to insure religious orthodoxy but rather to prevent violence or to guard against their helping the colony's military enemies under their guise of itinerant preaching. In 1721, the court of King George County dismissed charges against persons presented for not going to the Anglican parish church, because the defendants called themselves Presbyterians. In 1724, Hanover parish in that same county actually erected a chapel for a group of dissenters and provided a salary for their minister, instead of requiring them to attend the parish chapel. By 1744, the colony embodied its attitude in law: the Act of that year, while still requiring all to attend church regularly, permitted any Virginian to satisfy the law by attending the church of his choice.

When the militant, sometimes called "New Light," Presbyterians invaded Virginia in the 1740's, the Rev. Patrick Henry (uncle of the famous Patrick, and Anglican minister of the parish of St. Paul's, Hanover) described their ways:

> They thunder out in awful words, and new coin'd phrases, what they call the terrors of the law, cursing & scolding, calling the old people, Grey-headed Devils, and all promiscuously, Damn'd double damn'd, whose [souls] are in hell though they are alive on earth, Lumps of hell-fire, incarnate Devils, 1000 times worse than Devils &c and all the while the Preacher exalts his voice puts himself into a violent agitation, stamping and beating his Desk unmercifully until the weaker sort of his hearers being scar'd, cry out, fall down & work like people in convulsion fits, to the amazement of spectators, and if a few only are thus brought down, the Preacher gets into a violent passion again, Calling out Will no more of you come to Christ? thundering out as before, till he has brought a quantum sufficit of his congregation to this condition, and these things are extoll'd by the Preachers as the mighty power of God's grace in their hearts, and . . . they who don't are often condemn'd by the lump as hardened wretches.

Ministers like these, he warned, would stop at nothing. "Enthusiastick Preachers," who said that they were "as sure of going to Heaven at last, as if they were there already," could inspire criminals with the confidence that no crime prevented salvation. Despite this threat to public order, the Rev. Henry did not give up hope of domesticating the New Lights. He even allowed one of their leaders, George Whitefield, to preach from his pulpit—on condition that the Book of Common Prayer be read before the sermon!

The Virginians can hardly be blamed if they trembled at revivalist antics. Was it tyrannical simply to require erratic preachers to register the places of their preaching? Many refused even to do this. The *cause célèbre* during this wild evangelical campaign was the "case" of the Rev. Samuel Davies, whom the authorities had willingly licensed as the minister of seven meeting-houses in five different counties in 1748. But they refused to license him as minister of any more congregations. Did he, they wondered, envisage a new kind of itinerant absenteeism, or a network of religious agitators presided over by some super-pastor to keep them stirred up?

The so-called Separate Baptists invaded Virginia around 1767. The Regular Baptists had lived in peace in Virginia for a decade and were undisturbed by the law; in fact there was no record in Virginia of a Baptist suffering any punishment for his religion until the later Baptist itinerants came into the colony. In this new group, many were lay preachers who were ineligible for licensing: the others, who were ordained by their denomination, refused to obey the simple requirement that they register for licenses as ministers, and that they list their "preaching-points" and meeting-houses. The nearly fifty Separate Baptist preachers who were sent to jail between 1768 and 1776 were imprisoned not on ecclesiastical charges, but for "disturbing the peace" or refusing to give bond to keep the peace in the future.

"I apprehend the Gospel of Christ will justify no other than mild and gentle arguments," Col. William Green, Culpepper County justice of the peace and a vestryman, wrote on Feb. 7, 1767, to the Baptist minister who was preaching in his parish. "And whoever proceeds further, however fond he may be of his own Opinions, and whether he be Churchman or Anabaptist, or by whatever Name or title he may be called has not, I humbly conceive a True Christian Spirit in him." His explanation might well have been the manifesto of Virginia's "Practical godliness":

> For my part, I think I Could Live in Love & Peace, with a good Man of any of the various Sects Christians; Nor do I perceive any necessity for differing or quarreling with a Man, because he may not Think exactly as I do. I might as well quarrel with him for not being of the same

Size or Complexion with myself. For the different Operations of the
Mind are not to be accounted for. . . . God is no Respector of persons;
therefore it is a high Presumption and Folly, for us to pretend to confine
God's Mercies to any particular Nation, or Sect.

Only a few months later, Col. John Blair of Williamsburg, a member of
the Governor's Council, urged forbearance on his fellow Anglicans
because, he said, these very Baptists had done some good: they had
reformed some sinners, had brought some to repentance, and, by censur-
ing idlers, had made them provide for their families.

In Quaker Pennsylvania, Franklin also rejoiced in the happy diversity
of doctrine by which different gods led men in diverse ways to decent and
productive lives. But Virginians had become accustomed to another way
of thinking. Their first thought was to include all within their church: to
transform the Church of Englishmen into the Church of Virginians.
Their church was not a fellowship of visible saints, nor a society of the
pure of conscience, nor even a communion of possessors of the True
Dogma. It was a loose practical affiliation of those whose Christianity,
in different and inarticulate ways, helped them to be good Englishmen
and decent Virginians. It was a convenient umbrella for all men of good
will.

The drama of the Rev. Patrick Henry lending his Anglican pulpit
to the heterodox George Whitefield was reënacted in a thousand different
ways. When confronted by the movers and ranters of the so-called Great
Awakening, the Virginians' first instinct was to draw them into the
Church of Virginia, to learn from them whatever was good, and to infect
them with a contagious respectability and decorum. From neighboring
Maryland, whose established Church was substantially indistinguishable
from that of Virginia, the Rev. Hugh Jones reported in 1741 that within
the Church he found "enthusiasm, deism, and libertism."

In a country without a bishop, or without even a church assembly, who
would enforce orthodoxy? The religious doctrine of many of the leading
Virginians, including George Washington, Thomas Jefferson, Patrick
Henry, and James Madison, was nondescript. This did not mean that
they were unorthodox Anglicans; no one knew for sure what one had
to believe to be a good member of the Church of Virginia. They were
members of a catholic church: "catholic" not in the sense that it possessed a dogma for all men (for its dogma was vague and inarticulate),
but in the sense that all, excepting only fanatics and agitators, could live
within it while holding their own private dogmas. This was, indeed, a
foreshadowing of the interdenominationalism of 20th-century American
religious life.

In England the higher clergy of the 18th century wrote books of great intellectual distinction. One of the most impoverished eras in the spiritual life of the church was one of the richest in philosophic works by churchmen; Bishop Berkeley, Bishop Butler, and Bishop Hoadley modernized theology for the battles of a new age. But as each defined his ideas and clarified his distinctions he separated himself from his neighbors. Virginia was barren of such products, not only because it had no bishops, but also because such distinctions did not interest its leaders. The very "weaknesses" of intellectual life in Virginia thus helped save the community from theological division.

The College of William & Mary was established by charter in 1693 "for the breeding of good Ministers," and its first president was Commissary James Blair, technical head of the Church of Virginia. The orthodox Anglican clergy came to think of the college as "an advantageous and laudable Nursery and strong Bulwark against the contagious dissentions in Virginia," but it never acquired that clerical or theological orientation which some of its English founders looked for. Instead it became a bulwark of the moderate, catholic, and secular culture which was the life of Virginia in the 18th century. Thirty years after the founding of the College, the Rev. Hugh Jones prescribed the ingredients of successful clergymen in Virginia:

> They likewise should be Persons that have read and seen something more of the World, than what is requisite for an English Parish; they must be such as can converse and know more than bare Philosophy and speculative Ethicks, and have studied Men and Business in some measure as well as Books; they may act like Gentlemen, and be facetious and good-humour'd, without too much Freedom and Licentiousness; they may be good Scholars without becoming Cynicks, as they may be good Christians without appearing Stoicks. They should be such as will give up a small Matter rather than create Disturbance and Mischief. . . .

But from the fact that Virginia was barren of religious acrimony we must not conclude that she was barren of religious sentiment. Among the leaders of Virginia, religion itself nourished tolerance and an unwillingness to contend over the dots on theological I's. The catholic and compromising spirit of their Anglican church had made toleration a religious institution in Virginia long before its Act for Religious Freedom. Luckily, Virginia—appropriately called "The Old Dominion"—had become a community before the hundred-and-one dissenting sects had separated from the Church of England, before the 17th century had made England a jungle of religious monstrosities. And even in the 17th century she remained happily remote from the cut-throat enthusiasms and fanatic fervor of the Age of the Puritans. In Virginia, moreover, there was ample time to consolidate this catholic spirit of the Established Church.

"Persecution, religious pride, the love of contradiction," Crèvecoeur observed in late 18th-century America, "are the food of what the world commonly calls religion. These motives have ceased here; zeal in Europe is confined; here it evaporates in the great distance it has to travel; there it is a grain of powder inclosed, here it burns away in the open air, and consumes without effect." Moderation has too often been confused with lukewarmness. Since it is easier to measure the *odium theologicum* than the love of God, the ages and nations in which men are readiest to kill for religion acquire the reputation of being the most religious.

That liberal spirit in religion which we properly honor, and whose American patron saints were the great Virginians, need not be explained by any desire to displace tradition by something new and "enlightened." Without clericalism there cannot be anti-clericalism. The identification of the great Virginians with French "atheism" and "rationalism" was mostly accomplished long after the fact, by theological enthusiasts like Timothy Dwight who could not imagine a decent society surviving doctrinal diversity. But the life of Virginia had given the lie to library distinctions. Just as the faith of many Virginians in republican government stemmed from their happy experience with gentlemen freeholders in a planting aristocracy, so men raised under the broad Virginia Church could not be horrified by diversity of religious belief. They had seen diversity in their own well-ordered community.

23

Citizens of Virginia

NOTHING could be more misleading than to think of Virginians as "Citizens of the World." In common with American leaders since their day, they preferred to start from their own problems. Their point of departure was their location in time and space.

If George Washington seems colorless to us today it is partly because our latter-day democratic prejudices have blinded us to the colors of his Virginia. It is hard to bring ourselves to believe that the great Virginia fathers of the Republic were nourished in the soil of aristocracy, slavery, and an established church. Modern American democracy, we are told, must have had its roots in some 18th-century "democracy"; so we have looked for its seeds in the New England Town Meeting (supposed to be a microcosm of democracy) rather than in the Virginia tobacco aristocracy. But the ways of history are obscure and even self-contradictory. May not the proudly independent spirit of the Virginia planting aristocrats have been rooted in their vast plantations, in their sense of aristocratic responsibility? May not the value they placed on their individual liberties have been increased by the sharp contrast with the slavery they saw about them? May not their aristocratic habit of mind—their "habit of command" and their belief that they could make judgments on behalf of their community—have helped make them leaders of an American Revolution? Perhaps revolutions are always led by people who build, in Justice Holmes' phrase, "upon an aristocratic assumption that you know what is good for them better than they—which no doubt you do." Perhaps a reliable toleration has its roots in the quiet catholicity of a not-too-passionate established church, rather than in the explicit liberalism of rationalists and anti-religionists.

The Virginians had indeed inoculated themselves against all strong viruses; they, least of all people, sought to grasp the truths—whether of religion, of government, or of society—suddenly and as a whole. Their empirical, and even their reforming, spirit was grown in the tobacco-soil of Virginia, and not in the corrosive absolutes which poured out of Europe in their century. Traditionalism—their loyalty to the working ways of ancient England—rooted them in time; localism—their loyalty to the habits of their parish and county and to their friends and neighbors—rooted them in space. The strength of both these sentiments (and, to be precise, we should call them sentiments rather than philosophies) accounts for much of what they made of Virginia, and of what Virginia in the critical early years of the Republic gave to America. The strength of their traditionalism was before long to be expressed in the American Revolution in defense of the rights of Englishmen. The strength of their localism was expressed in the autonomy of the parish and in the federal spirit, in the Constitution and in the devotion to States' rights. The fact that their tradition was loosely stated—their model was the life of the English country gentleman—made their tie to tradition no less real. There was no part of life which an ideal so vague and so real did not touch. Their narrower, more legal traditionalism was also to have its day: in the Revolution, when they would be required to state in precise legal language how their rights as Englishmen had been violated. But the traditionalism of Virginia in the Golden Age was lived out with a quiet and pervasive intensity. Their very strength as transplanters came from their willingness to transform as they transplanted, to flavor the distant past with the local present.

Their localism has been given far too little attention and too little credit. In these days, when States' rights are out of fashion, we are too often told that a man's preoccupation with the habits of the place where he lives can only drag the national progress. We are fortunate that 18th-century Virginians thought differently. Their concern with the special requirements of their own particular place on earth not only flavored their political life and expectations; it gave all their thinking the aroma of the specific and kept all their social ideals within finite bounds. It was the seed of Federalism, without which the nation could not have lived and liberal institutions could not have flourished. When Jefferson listed for his tombstone the three achievements for which he wished to be remembered, only one, the Declaration of Independence, reached beyond the bounds of Virginia; the other two—the Virginia statute for religious freedom and the University of Virginia—were strictly local.

If we run the gamut of Virginia life in the 18th century we see one fact after another which tied the leader of the community to his particular place, even more intimately than in contemporary England. The river-avenues and the difficulties of land communication tended to keep commercial life close to the plantation houses, on their private wharves. The same was true of the cultural life: the centers of literary culture, including the best libraries, remained scattered over the colony in widely-separated mansion houses. Children of the substantial planters did not go to school in a metropolitan center but in a local "old-field" school house, or else studied with a private tutor under the family roof.

Although Williamsburg remained the political center, it never became a metropolis; and the lack of cities left the parish meeting-houses, the county court-houses and the rural residences as the natural foci of social gatherings and community interest. From the days of the author of *Virginia's Cure* (1662), who complained that their "scattering Habitations" were the root of a dangerous independence and a deviation from rigid Anglicanism, we read pleas "that the only way of remedy for Virginia's disease . . . must be by procuring Towns to be built, and inhabited in their several Counties." Again and again well-meaning cosmopolites sought to lift Virginia to a respectably English level of literary culture and religious orthodoxy by forcing the building of towns. This pressure created the so-called "Cohabitation" Controversy between those who hoped for an urban Virginia as enlightened and cultivated as Mother England and those who were satisfied that Virginia should become enlightened and cultivated in her own way. The Cohabitation Act of 1680 sought to conjure up towns by act of the legislature, but that Act and its successors (including even the Act of October 1705, which exempted town-dwellers from three-fourths of their taxes) succeeded in producing towns only on paper. The local spirit and the pressures of geography and tobacco-culture, reënforced by such institutions as the county court and the vestry, were simply too strong. Why, planters sensibly asked, should they found towns to drain commerce from their wharves and power from their local courts and churches?

Not the least significant consequence of this thriving localism was a wholesome identification of self-interest with political activity. A man who entered politics in Virginia was doing so not only because he had large property and family interests to be protected, but because he was personally involved in every aspect of life in a particular place and he therefore wished to be a voice for that place. When Jefferson wrote to his nephew, young Peter Carr, in August 1785, he advised that personal ambition should be a prudent admixture of self-interest and public concern. "Every day you lose, will retard a day your entrance on that public stage whereon you may begin to be useful to yourself. . . . When your mind shall be well improved with science, nothing will be necessary to place you in the highest points of view, but to pursue the interests of your country, the interests of your friends, and your own interests, also with the purest integrity, the most chaste honour." In those years, and for long after, when Jefferson said "my country" he meant Virginia. This identification of the public man with the interests of his particular place led Virginians to find the counsels of politics not in the peremptory commands of absolutes but in a balancing of local interests. Localism, like traditionalism, was an enemy of political dogma.

Their success in developing an institutional frame of mind—the suppleness of spirit for which they were to be preëminent—would have been impossible without certain providential coincidences. In the late seventeenth and eighteenth century, men of common sense could imagine transplanting many features of English country life to Virginia. Yet conditions were not so similar that a transfer of English ways was easy and mechanical. If Virginia had been less like England, the 18th-century attempt to reconstruct these English institutions in the New World might have been absurd and romantic. If Virginia had been more like England, emulation of things English might have become mere mimicry and living English institutions might have become American fossils. No intelligent Virginian could hope to reënact the drama of English life word-for-word, yet none could fail to feel that the Virginia drama would be in the same tradition, with similar actors, similar dialogue, and a similar moral.

The caricature of the English colonial administrator, dining formally in his dinner-jacket in his straw-hut in the jungle, is precisely the incongruity which Virginia country gentlemen managed to avoid. Many of the settlers of Jamaica and Barbados in the 18th century also hoped to build their little Englands, but the exotic flora and fauna, the enervating tropical climate, and myriad other differences put anything resembling English life outside the bounds of a sane imagination. Before long those who could not tolerate an alien way of life returned to temperate England. They left the Caribbean islands to resident-managers and to the few expatriate English plantation owners who preferred a frankly exotic way of life with its special privileges of luxuriance, indolence, despotism, and irresponsibility. In contrast to all this, the climate and landscape permitted Virginians to live in reasonable facsimiles of English country houses and to transplant English institutions. Yet they avoided the temptation of making imitation a dogma or building by a blueprint of English life.

Tobacco was the leading institution of Virginia; willingness to be ruled by it was both the strength and the weakness of the Virginians. While embracing the landscape, they were sometimes seduced by it. The promoters of Georgia were obstinately determined that the exotic silkworm must grow in their colony, but the leading men of Virginia, finding that tobacco grew well on their land, allowed it to dominate their life.

The supreme irony in the story of Virginia was the last act in the colonial drama. That act occurred in the Revolution itself, in the framing of the Federal Constitution and in the rule of the Virginia Dynasty (Washington-Jefferson-Madison-Monroe) within the Federal government. The leaders of that age were the last flower of the aristocracy of mid-18th century Virginia, not the first flower of a national spirit. The Revolution which the Virginia aristocracy did so much to make and "win" was in fact the suicide of the Virginia aristocracy. The turmoil of the War, the destruction wrought in Virginia by British troops, the disestablishment of the Church, the disruption of commerce, and the decline of tobacco-culture all spelled the decline of the aristocracy and its institutions.

The Federal Constitution was a national road on which there was no return. The leadership of Virginians in Federal life continued only so long as the national government was an aristocratic camaraderie like that of Virginia. When the United States ceased to be a greater Virginia, Virginians ceased to govern the United States. The virtues of 18th-century Virginia, when writ large, would seem to be vices. Localism would become sectionalism; the special interests of where a man lived would come to seem petty and disruptive.

BOOK TWO

VIEWPOINTS
AND INSTITUTIONS

"We are, I think, in the right Road of Improvement, for we are making Experiments."

BENJAMIN FRANKLIN

"They are more inclinable to read Men by Business and Conversation, than to dive into Books, and are for the most Part only desirous of learning what is absolutely necessary, in the shortest and best Method."

HUGH JONES

THEY saw new perspectives and found new viewpoints in their new place. There was no American system of thought, but there were signs of American ways of thinking. As the community-plans drawn in Europe were changed in each colony, ways common to the colonies began to appear. The following chapters will illustrate these ways of thinking about knowledge and education, about the learned occupations, about law, medicine, and science. New things were seen from the New World, not because Americans had sharper vision but because their vision was less obstructed by the piled-up wealth of the past.

PART FIVE
AN AMERICAN FRAME
OF MIND

"We hold these truths to be self-evident . . ."

The Declaration of Independence

24

Wanted: A Philosophy
of the Unexpected

BY THE EARLY 17th century, Europe had accumulated a rich but cumbersome cultural baggage. Systems of thought, established institutions, professional traditions, dogmatically-defined bodies of knowledge regarded as all that was worth knowing—these cluttered the landscape of England and of Europe. The bare earth was almost nowhere visible.

Systems always breed more systems; when new liberating movements arose in England and on the continent during the 17th and 18th centuries, they took the familiar European form of anti-systems. Thus, "the Enlightenment," which claimed to free men from superstition and from the dogma of old authority and petrified thought, itself acquired much of the rigidity and authoritarianism of what it set out to combat. The European Enlightenment was in fact little more than the confinement of the mind in a prison of 17th- and 18th-century design. The new "rationalism"—which Europeans boasted was their new freedom—was the old human dogmatic servitude. What Carl Becker described as "The Heavenly City of the 18th-Century Philosophers" was a mirage of freedom. The best European minds of that age labored to build the new-model walls in which they were to be confined. Liberation could not be conceived in any other way in Europe.

149

Life in America was to give new meaning to the very idea of liberation. For Americans, cultural novelty and intellectual freedom were not to mean merely the exchange of one set of idols for another; they meant removal into the open air.

The most fertile novelty of the New World was not its climate, its plants, its animals, or its minerals, but its new concept of knowledge. The wealth of the new-found land could enable men to live well by Old World standards, but the realization that knowledge itself might be different from what men had before believed—this opened up realms never before dreamed of. Men in the New World found unsuspected possibilities in life everywhere. No American invention has influenced the world so powerfully as the concept of knowledge which sprang from the American experience. To understand that discovery we must look to the earliest colonial days.

When has a culture owed so little to its few "great" minds or its few hereditarily fortunate men and women? One of the contrasts between the culture of Europe and that of the United States is that the older culture traditionally depended on the monumental accomplishments of the few, while the newer culture—diffused, elusive, process-oriented—depended more on the novel, accreting ways of the many.

In most past societies—certainly in the aristocratic societies of western Europe—rulers and priests had been the "explaining" classes. They were the acknowledged possessors of the ways of knowing, the secret keys to the ancestral treasurehouse of mystery and of knowledge. The Protestant Reformation, with its dogma of the universal priesthood of all believers, did, of course, discourage reverence toward a special class of "knowers," but there soon arose a "protestant" priesthood (in the Geneva of Calvin or the London of Archbishop Laud) which, in its turn, denied freedom of discovery to the laity or to heretics. The common people could show their good sense only by acting according to ways approved by their "betters."

American life quickly proved uncongenial to any special class of "knowers." Men here were more interested in the elaboration of experience than in the elaboration of "truth"; the novelties of a New World led them to suspect that elaborate verification might itself mislead. As William James explained at the close of the 19th century, technically completed verifications are seldom needed in experience. In America, he said, "the possession of truth, so far from being . . . an end in itself, is only a preliminary means toward other vital satisfactions." Sometimes consciously, sometimes through the force of circumstance, Americans listened to the dictates of "self-evidence." Before long this appeal to self-evidence became a distinctive popular epistemology—a substitute for philosophy or a philosophy for non-academic thinkers.

The more encumbered a society is with ancient culture and institutions, the more likely is its most profound and well-organized thought to diverge from its way of acting. One of the ways in which American experience liberated the New World was by freeing men from the notion that every grand institution needed a grand foundation of systematic thought: that successful government had to be supported by profound political theory, that moving religion had to be supported by subtle theology—in a word, that the best living had to have behind it the most sophisticated thinking. This mood was to explain the superficially contradictory strains of the practical and the traditional in the American mind— the openness to novel ways that worked and the readiness to accept ancient and traditional laws—for both common sense and common law were time-proven and unreflective ways of settling problems.

In America what seemed to be needed was not so much a new variant of European "schools" of philosophy as a philosophy of the unexpected. Too much of the best-elaborated thinking of the European mind added up to proof that America and its novelties were impossible. A less aristocratic and more mobile New World required a way of interpreting experience that would be ready for the outlandish and would be equally available to everyone everywhere.

"Common sense" was, of course, an old and thoroughly respectable notion in western European civilization. Some Scottish thinkers in the 18th century—they were not without their influence in America and one actually had become the favorite philosopher of George III—elaborated a special "philosophy" of common sense. In America, however, the more influential appeal to self-evidence did not take any such academic form; it was a philosophy which had no philosophers. It had to be so, for it was a way of thinking pervaded by doubt that the professional thinker could think better than others.

The appeal to self-evidence did not displace more academic and more dogmatic modes of thinking among all Americans, but American life nourished it until it became a prevailing mode. It was not the system of a few great American Thinkers, but the mood of Americans thinking. It rested on two sentiments. The first was a belief that the reasons men give for their actions are much less important than the actions themselves, that it is better to act well for wrong or unknown reasons than to treasure a systematized "truth" with ambiguous conclusions, that deep reflection does not necessarily produce the most effective action. The second was a belief that the novelties of experience must be freely admitted into men's thought. Why strain the New World through the philosophical sieves of the Old? If philosophy denied the innuendoes of experience, the philosophy—not the experience—must be rejected. Therefore, a man's mind was wholesome not when it possessed the most refined implements for dissecting and ordering all knowledge, but when it was most sensitive to the unpredicted whisperings of environment. It was less important that the mind be elegantly furnished than that it be open and unencumbered.

25.

The Appeal to Self-Evidence

"WE HOLD these truths to be self-evident," the second sentence of the Declaration of Independence proclaims. In deriving the essential social truths from their "self-evidence"—rather than from their being "sacred & undeniable" as the original draft had read—the Declaration was building on distinctly American ground.

The roots of the appeal to self-evidence were described by the Rev. Hugh Jones as early as 1724 in his character of the Virginians:

> Thus they have good natural Notions, and will soon learn Arts and Sciences; but are generally diverted by Business or Inclination from profound Study, and prying into the Depth of Things; being ripe for Management of their Affairs, before they have laid so good a Foundation of Learning, and had such Instructions, and acquired such Accomplishments, as might be instilled into such good natural Capacities. Nevertheless thro' their quick Apprehension, they have a Sufficiency of Knowledge, and Fluency of Tongue, tho' their Learning for the most Part be but superficial.
>
> They are more inclinable to read Men by Business and Conversation, than to dive into Books, and are for the most Part only desirous of learning what is absolutely necessary, in the shortest and best Method.

The matured statement of this point of view is found in Franklin and Jefferson, the most eloquent spokesmen of an American and anti-aristocratic way of thinking about thinking. On more than one occasion

Franklin refused to engage in learned controversy. "Disputes," he retorted to European critics of his ideas on electricity, "are apt to sour one's temper, and disturb one's quiet." If his observations were correct, he said, they would readily be confirmed by other men's experience; if not, they ought to be rejected. He expressed the gist of his belief in self-evidence to an English correspondent in his 1786 report on American progress in government. "We are, I think, in the right Road of Improvement, for we are making Experiments. I do not oppose all that seem wrong, for the Multitude are more effectually set right by Experience, than kept from going wrong by Reasoning with them." This is much the same as Jefferson's notion (in his draft preamble to the Virginia Bill for Establishing Religious Freedom) "that the opinions and belief of men depend not on their own will, but follow involuntarily the evidence proposed to their minds."

The founders of European liberal thought declared that in any public battle between truth and error, truth would eventually prevail. Theirs was only another declaration of faith in philosophers, in the magical ability of enlightened and profound minds to grasp the truths of contending systems, in the philosophers' capacity to devise systems corresponding to the actual shapes and laws of nature. Theirs was simply another aristocratic faith, but now the aristocracy were philosophers and scientists. Progress was identified with what Sir Francis Bacon called "The Advancement of Learning": the talented and privileged few played the leading role. The classic French statement, the Marquis de Condorcet's *Sketch for a Historical Picture of the Progress of the Human Mind* (1795), made the deepest philosophers—Descartes, Newton, and Leibnitz—the heroes in the battle to liberate the human mind. Their improved metaphysics had enabled men to break out of the political and religious prisons built by centuries of kings and priests. This was the work of "men of genius, the eternal benefactors of the human race."

Such an explanation was alien to America. Even John Adams, who thought human *in*equality was the wellspring of history, was outraged. "What a pity," Adams exclaimed in irony, "that this man of genius cannot be king and priest for the whole human race!" And Adams added in 1811:

> The philosophers of France were too rash and hasty. They were as artful as selfish and as hypocritical as the priests and politicians of Babylon, Persia, Egypt, India, Greece, Rome, Turkey, Germany, Wales, Scotland, Ireland, France, Spain, Italy or England. They understood not what they were about. They miscalculated their forces and resources: and were consequently overwhelmed in destruction with all their theories.

The precipitation and temerity of philosophers has, I fear, retarded the progress of improvement and amelioration in the condition of mankind for at least an hundred years.

The public mind was improving in knowledge and the public heart in humanity, equity, and benevolence; the fragments of feudality, the inquisition, the rack, the cruelty of punishments, Negro slavery were giving way, etc. But the philosophers must arrive at perfection per saltum. Ten times more furious than Jack in the Tale of a Tub, they rent and tore the whole garment to pieces and left not one whole thread in it. They have been compelled to resort to Napoleon, and Gibbon himself became an advocate for the Inquisition. What an amiable and glorious Equality, Fraternity, and Liberty they have now established in Europe!

Adams' distrust of the ruthless demands of genius and his preference for the slower, more sober advances of the public mind expressed a deep current in American feeling: the difference between Washington and Napoleon; between Roosevelt, Truman, and Eisenhower on the one hand and garret-spawned European illuminati like Lenin, Mussolini, and Hitler.

In America what would liberate men was not the opportunity to combat ancient and erroneous philosophic systems by modern ones, but the opportunity to bring all philosophy into the skeptical and earthy arena of daily life. No philosophy would be too sacred for such a test. Americans saw less value in the full-dress intellectual tournaments of learned academies, in the passionate arguments of artists and prophets on the Left Banks of the world, than in the free competition of the marketplace. Such competition was hardly yet known to Europe, and it might never be known there in its crude American form. When Justice Oliver Wendell Holmes wrote in 1919 that "the best test of truth is the power of the thought to get itself accepted in the competition of the market," he was not appealing from the individual philosopher to the guild of philosophers. Rather he was appealing from professional thinkers to the bulk of Americans.

In the 18th century, if not earlier, American experience had already begun to give this flavor to our thinking. "If what is thus published be good," Franklin wrote in the *Pennsylvania Gazette* on July 24, 1740 defending the freedom of printers, "Mankind has the Benefit of it: If it be bad . . . the more 'tis made publick, the more its Weakness is expos'd and the greater Disgrace falls upon the author, whoever he be." So too, Jefferson in urging freedom of speech, press, and religion, argued less from the desirability that every mind be enlightened by modern philosophers than from the desirability of allowing each mind its free and direct response to its unique experience. "Your own reason is the only oracle given you by heaven," advised Jefferson "and you are answerable, not for the rightness, but uprightness of the decision." The basic American questions were to be settled in the arena of experience rather than of controversy or of learning. The straight short path by which Americans arrived at their conclusions can be illustrated by their idea of progress.

By the 18th century many European thinkers had arrived at the idea of progress by devious and painful intellectual paths. There was the speculative philosophical path explored by Francis Bacon and Descartes; there was the speculative historical path explored by Fontenelle, Condorcet, and Gibbon. Some thinkers argued from the essential character of man or the laws of nature; others extended their historical vision back to the Romans, to Socrates, or even to primitive tribes. Some dissected man, society, and the universe to find the elements of inevitable progress; others took their bearings from distant points in time to trace their lines to the present and into the future.

All these were the reflections of learned men. In England progress seemed the slow and undramatic product of a long relatively peaceful past. In France progress seemed a hope which could be fully justified only by the future. But in America one needed to be neither historian nor prophet: progress seemed confirmed by daily experience.

From the beginning, people in provincial America noted that in the New World progress was self-evident. "Let them produce any colonie or commonwealth in the world," we have heard the magistrates of Massachusetts Bay reply to the Child petitioners (1646), "where more hath beene done in 16 yeares." When, about a century later, Burnaby visited Philadelphia, he exclaimed that where only eighty years before had been a "wild and uncultivated desert, inhabited by nothing but ravenous beasts, and a savage people," there was now a flourishing city. "Can the mind have a greater pleasure than in contemplating the rise and progress of cities and kingdoms? Than in perceiving a rich and opulent state arising out of a small settlement or colony? This pleasure everyone must feel who considers Pennsylvania." American history could be summarized in the phrase which appeared on more than one title page: "The Progressive Improvements . . . of the British Settlements in North America."

The American situation made it natural to identify progress with growth and expansion. The very survival and vitality of the American colonies was itself a proof of progress. Franklin drew his conclusions about progress in America from what anybody could notice: a growing population in the continental American emptiness. There could be no greater mistake, Franklin explained in his *Observations concerning the*

Increase of Mankind, Peopling of Countries, etc. (1755), than to generalize about the growth of population from the experience of the Old World: "nor will Tables form'd on Observations made on full-settled old Countries, as Europe, suit new Countries, as America." It would be futile to try to restrict American manufactures or to seek to confine the American population. "For People increase in Proportion to the Number of Marriages, and that is greater in Proportion to the Ease and Convenience of supporting a Family. When families can be easily supported, more Persons marry, and earlier in Life." Plentiful land and the ease of getting on in America would induce people to marry early and to have more children: here the population would surely double every twenty years. "But notwithstanding this Increase, so vast is the Territory of North America, that it will require many Ages to settle it fully; and, till it is fully settled, Labour will never be cheap here, where no Man continues long a Labourer for others, but gets a Plantation of his own, no Man continues long a Journeyman to a Trade, but goes among those new Settlers, and sets up for himself, &c. Hence Labour is no cheaper now in Pennsylvania, than it was 30 Years ago, tho' so many Thousand labouring People have been imported." While the high cost of labor here would prevent the colonies from competing with the mother country in manufactures, their increasing population would yearly enlarge the American market for British goods.

> There is, in short, no Bound to the prolific Nature of Plants or Animals, but what is made by their crowding and interfering with each other's means of Subsistence. . . . Thus there are suppos'd to be now upwards of One Million English Souls in North-America, (tho' 'tis thought scarce 80,000 have been brought over Sea,) and yet perhaps there is not one the fewer in Britain, but rather many more, on Account of the Employment the Colonies afford to Manufacturers at Home. This Million doubling, suppose but once in 25 Years, will, in another Century, be more than the People of England, and the greatest Number of Englishmen will be on this Side of the Water. What an Accession of Power to the British Empire by Sea as well as Land! What Increase of Trade and Navigation! What Numbers of Ships and Seamen!

Franklin saw that already American facts were destroying European theories. For example, the theory of "mercantilism" by which England and her rivals justified their contest for empire had been shaped by the facts of a crowded Europe. Behind mercantilism lay the assumption that the wealth of the world was a pie and that a bigger slice for one country meant a smaller slice for all the others. In the ever-expanding New World, all this seemed doctrinaire. Why should America follow the pattern of Europe? Why should an increase of people here menace the wealth of England? On the contrary, as Franklin observed, to enlarge the American colonies would decrease the probable competition from American manufactures while increasing the market for English products.

> Manufactures are founded in poverty. It is the multitude of poor without land in a country, and who must work for others at low wages or starve, that enables undertakers to carry on a manufacture, and afford it cheap enough to prevent the importation of the same kind from abroad, and to bear the expence of its own exportation.
>
> But no man who can have a piece of land of his own, sufficient by his labour to subsist his family in plenty, is poor enough to be a manufacturer, and work for a master. Hence while there is land enough in America for our people, there can never be manufactures to any amount or value. It is a striking observation of a very able pen, that the natural livelyhood of the thin inhabitants of a forest country is hunting; that of a greater number, pasturage; that of a middling population, agriculture; and that of the greatest, manufactures; which last must subsist the bulk of the people in a full country, or they must be subsisted by charity, or perish. The extended population, therefore, that is most advantageous to Great Britain, will be best effected, because only effectually secured by the possession of Canada.

In his *Interest of Great Britain considered with regard to her Colonies and the acquisitions of Canada and Guadaloupe* (with the collaboration of Richard Jackson, 1760), Franklin applied this reasoning to British policy in North America after her victory over the French. The question then being debated in pamphlets and on the floor of Parliament was whether the British should drive the French from North America by annexing Canada or should instead take the sugar island of Guadeloupe. Orthodox mercantilists argued that the frigid, unsettled wilderness of Canada, adding a long boundary to be protected while yielding only a scanty fur-trade, would become a heavy burden on Mother-England; and that to remove the French from North America would dangerously increase the independence of the Americans. But Franklin saw the question differently; according to him, growth, expansion, and multiplication were the law of American life. All ancient analogies between the human body and the body politic were faulty because there were actually no natural limits on the growth of a body politic. The American market, by consuming English manufactures, would provide more employment for English labor, and would eventually increase tenfold the population of the mother-island. The influence of Franklin's pamphlet is hard to measure, especially since a number of powerful Englishmen (including the great Pitt himself) already shared his views, but the British did acquire Canada and not Guadeloupe by the Peace of Paris in 1763, and so they removed the French menace from the continental American colonies.

This way of thinking had actually provided fresh American arguments for expansion of the Empire. It also expressed a novel and naïve approach to the idea of progress itself. The 18th-century expansion of the American colonies might not have carried so forceful a lesson had not Franklin and others prepared Americans in a way of naïveté, in a readiness to argue from what seemed self-evident.

The same could be said for other American ideas of the provincial age which at first sight looked like the conclusions of the European "Enlightenment" philosophers. After a second look these American doctrines often prove to be "self-evident" conclusions from the facts of American life. For example, the versatile interests of a French *philosophe* expressed his belief in the sovereign unity of reason and his encyclopedic interests affirmed a theoretic "rationalism." But the versatility of a Virginia planter owed more to the actual diversity of his responsibilities—for the government, crops, medicine, religion, and everything else in his little plantation world. Again, while in France the essential equality of mankind had to be laboriously demonstrated by research and speculation (for example in Rousseau's "Essay on the Origin of Inequality"), in America the idea of equality had a self-evident meaning all its own. Of course, American facts would also limit American ideals; where the "facts of life" in America seemed to deny equality (as in the case of the Negro or the Indian), many good Americans felt strong doubts.

From the beginning, Americans formed a habit of accepting for the most part only those ideas which seemed already to have proved themselves in experience. They used things as they were as a measure of how things ought to be; in America the "is" became the yardstick of the "ought." Was not the New World a living denial of the old sharp distinction between the world as it was and the world as it might be or ought to be?

26

Knowledge Comes Naturally

IN OUR DAY it has become common for remote parts of the world
to be explored, mapped, botanized, and described before they are
densely settled by migrants. The explorer, the geographer, and the naturalist now go first; the settler follows. The stock of novelty is thus used
up—or appropriated by specialized scientists—even before a settled
culture begins to develop. For some time now, for example, we have had
more varied, more voluminous, and more precise knowledge about
Africa, Inner Mongolia, and the Arctic than provincial Americans possessed about any but a narrow strip along the Atlantic seaboard.

The haze which covered the New World in that age probably covers
no part of the world today; America was one of the last places where
European settlers would come in large numbers *before* the explorers,
geographers, and professional naturalists. With little more than hearsay
and advertising to guide them, early Americans had many of the joys
and tasks, the surprises and disappointments of explorers though they
lived the lives of permanent settlers. This was a crucial fact; it would
brighten their thinking about the world around them; it would affect
their ideal of man; it would liberate them from many of the metaphysical
and dogmatic problems which plagued the more introspective, library-
oriented man of Europe; it would entice their eyes and minds to varied,
shifting, unpredictable shapes of the world around them—shapes on
which every man, sometimes the first viewer, was his own authority. The
time had come for the overcultivated man of Europe to rediscover the
earth on which he walked.

Perhaps never before in a civilized country had physical and intellectual expansion been so clearly synonymous. To enlarge the country
and to populate it automatically enlarged man's knowledge of the world.
The crowning symbol of this American identity was the Lewis and
Clark Expedition (1804-1806), conceived and fitted out by Jefferson
for the most mixed intellectual-political reasons. Even from the earliest
records of Captain John Smith, William Bradford, or John Winthrop,

the enlarging of knowledge of America was simultaneous with the enlarging of the new American community. We sometimes forget how gradual was the "discovery" of America: it was a by-product of the *occupation* of the continent. To act, to move on, to explore meant also to push back the frontiers of knowledge; this inevitably gave a practical and dynamic character to the very idea of knowledge. To learn and to act became one.

The continent itself was a great reservoir of the unknown, and it remained so until well into the 19th century. It was not only that a new species of plant or animal might be encountered near a rural doorway; many of the simplest facts of geography were yet to be described. Anyone who reads Jedidiah Morse's pioneer one-volume *American Geography* (1789) sees vast unknown areas which challenged the leading American geographers of that day. The first extensive and systematic geography of America was produced by an industrious German scholar, Christoph Daniel Ebeling (1741-1817), whose seven-volume *Erdbeschreibung und Geschichte von Amerika: Die Vereinten Staaten von Nordamerika* (1793-1816) collected and sifted bits of knowledge from a hundred different sources. Americans were too busy exploring their land to write elaborate books about it. While the provincial age produced many regional surveys like Belknap's *History of New Hampshire,* Williams' *History of Vermont,* and Jefferson's *Notes on Virginia,* and useful handbooks like Morse's, American interest was directed to the uses of the land rather than to a full schematic description of it. Even before Ebeling's multivolume work, the most important contributions to the writing of American geography had not been made by Americans. "So imperfect are all the accounts of America hitherto published, even by those who once exclusively possessed the best means of information," Morse explained in his Preface, "that from them very little knowledge of this country can be acquired. Europeans have been the sole writers of American Geography, and have too often suffered fancy to supply the place of facts, and thus have led their readers into errors, while they professed to aim at removing their ignorance."

Although the eastern seaboard was known in some detail, knowledge of the area across the Appalachians was full of conjecture. Some of these vagaries had political consequences. Jefferson's plan for future Western states makes no sense on a correct modern map; it must be understood in the light of the conjectural geography of the West which was current in his day. Morse's New Map of North America "from the latest and best Authorities" (1794) placed the southern tip of the Rocky Mountains northwest of Lake Superior! It designated "Head of the Misouri unknown" and omitted the Columbia River and anything like the Sierra

Nevada Mountains. Morse frankly confessed ignorance of the geography of all North America except the Atlantic seaboard: of the bays, sounds, straits, and islands of the continent "(except those in the United States . . .) we know little more than their names."

The heart of the continent was so uncharted that hypotheses about it were commonly used to explain peculiarities of the climate of the settled seaboard. The impenetrable forests, which were supposed to cover the interior parts of the continent (presumably keeping the land from being heated by the sun), explained the relatively cold climate of America. On the seaboard where the land had been deforested and where the sea-winds could reach inland, the winter climate was said to have become progressively milder since the earliest settlements.

New "facts" of natural history, both real and imaginary, were the very substance of the earliest promotional tracts designed to bring settlers to America or to sell them land here. The authors of these brochures were no more cautious or prone to understatement than the advertising copy-writers in any other age. The writers of travel-books were always tempted to turn up, or if necessary to invent, exotic novelties. Few went so far as the Turkish writer Ibrahim Effendi who in 1729 described the delightful "Wakwak" tree whose fruit was ripe and attractive women, but many others exercised their imagination in describing bizarre plants and the Eldoradan wonders of the water and climate.

Much of the authentic knowledge of the New World was the by-product of travels undertaken for some specific practical purpose. When William Byrd in 1728 served on the commission to survey the boundary between Virginia and North Carolina, he kept a journal, the "History of the Dividing Line," which deserves to be a more widely-read classic of the truly New World literature. In his naïve and colloquial fashion, Byrd not only described the actual problems of surveying an American wilderness. He collected all the miscellaneous remarkable details of life around him: the superstitious Indian fear "to provoke the Guardian of the Forrest, by cooking the Beasts of the Field and the Birds of the Air together in one vessell"; how Indian men on horseback "rode more awkwardly than any Dutch Sailor, and the Ladies bestrode their Palfreys a la mode de France, but were so bashful about it, that there was no persuading them to Mount till they were quite out of our Sight"; the habits of the wild turkey; the qualities of rattlesnake root as an antidote against snakebite; the virtues of the American wild grape; the habits and edibility of the bear; and the surprisingly sweet flavor of polecat meat.

A hundred other practical missions produced thousands of oddments about the New World: from official surveyors like Byrd, Peter Jefferson (father of Thomas), and Charles Mason and Jeremiah Dixon who spent five years (1763-68) surveying the ominous line which bears their name; from private speculators like George Washington, bent on discovering and claiming the best land; from itinerant ministers like the Anglican Charles Woodmason, the Quaker Thomas Chalkley, or the Wesley brothers, each determined to save souls in his own particular way; and from merchants like the fanciful bookseller James Dunton. From remote Fort Pitt, one of its British officers Henry Bouquet on Feb. 3, 1762 sent John Bartram in Philadelphia a parcel of specimens. "I thought it might be agreeable to you to know what nature produces, in those wildernesses. ... I should be much obliged to you, to send me, at your leisure, a catalogue of trees and plants, peculiar to this country, which are not natural to the soil of Europe; as I propose to send a collection to a friend, when we have more peaceable times."

All knowledge in America seemed to come in small, miscellaneous parcels. The almost overwhelming temptation was simply to gather up these parcels as one came upon them, not worrying too much whether they were marketable in the familiar European categories. While Americans collected the novelties, the more academic and bookish Europeans systematized them. European, and especially English, gardeners and naturalists helped make Americans aware of the wealth around them. John Bartram, the self-educated Philadelphian who probably discovered more plants than any other American and founded the first Botanic Garden in America, owed his start in botanical collecting and the funds for his extensive travels to Peter Collinson, London botanist and dealer in nursery-goods who distributed American imports to English gardeners. But Bartram was, as a contemporary described him, "more collector than student" and, though "a Wonderful Natural Genius," possessed a scanty knowledge of botanical principles. The significance of his seeds and plants for systematic botany was discovered by English naturalists like Sir Hans Sloane and Mark Catesby, by the Dutch botanist Johann Friedrich Gronovius, and by the great Swede Carl Linnaeus. Bartram's aptness for collecting new items and his inability to systematize them symbolized tendencies in American thought.

Perhaps the other most famous American botanist of this type was John Clayton, the clerk of Gloucester County, Virginia, whose specimens provided the raw materials for Gronovius' famous treatise *Flora Virginica* (1739-43), which was extensively used by Linnaeus himself. It was thoroughly in character that *Flora Virginica,* the leading methodical treatise on American botany in the colonial age, should have been the work of European scholarship.

During the provincial age the most conspicuous American effort to contribute to systematic science was made by the energetic and brashly speculative Cadwallader Colden. Born in Scotland, Colden had secured a master's degree at Edinburgh and a medical education in London. He came to the colonies in 1710. From 1718 until his retirement from public life in 1750 he held a number of public offices in New York—surveyor-general, member of the Governor's Council, and eventually Lieutenant-Governor. For most of his life he carried on these jobs through deputies and, while supported at public expense, devoted himself to the scientific pursuits in which he was determined to attain immortality. Of a systematic turn of mind, he was very early attracted by Linnaeus' classification. Although Colden thought and wrote a great deal about a mythical "natural" botanic system and liked to speculate on the most general scientific problems, these thoughts brought little notice or recognition; it was his collection and description of American botanic novelties that brought him international fame. His *Plantae Coldenghamiae,* a list of plants found in the neighborhood of his New York farm, was probably the closest approach to a systematic botany by an American hand during the provincial age. It was never fully printed in America.

The atomizing influence of the American environment seemed contagious. When in 1748 Peter Kalm, a learned Swedish professor, came here at the expense of the Royal Academy of Sciences at Stockholm to survey plants and trees of possible use in Sweden, he too was seduced by the fascinating miscellany of America. Though he added some new species, and even genera, of American plants, his principal product was nothing systematic. His *Travels in North America* included such assorted items as the brevity of Canadian women's skirts, the wastefulness of American farmers' methods, and the habits of black ants.

Buffon and Linnaeus encouraged Americans to explore and discover their New World: European interests coincided with American opportunities. But the Americans, well located to provide raw materials for European systematizers, seldom served their knowledge up *à l'Europe.* Sometimes the very existence of so many systematizers in contemporary Europe seemed to make Americans feel that they themselves did not need to seek large generalizations. Anyway, they lacked the leisure; they were far from ancient libraries and centers of learning, and their new world beckoned with many varieties of "unthought-of phaenomena." In Europe, discovering something new in the natural world required the concentration of a philosopher, the researches of a scholar, or the industry of an encyclopedist. In America it took effort to avoid novelty.

27

The Natural-History Emphasis

TO MAKE DISCOVERIES the American needed neither boldness nor imagination. In ancient populous England, nearly every new fact or experience was gained by effort, talent, or courage. Not so in America, where novelty seemed to force itself on even the most indifferent and insensitive eye.

Was the American to be blamed, then, if he believed too readily that new knowledge came from just looking sharply at the world, and from acting in it? How could he fail to be less willing than his Asiatic or European contemporary to seek knowledge from contemplation and from study? As the Marquis de Chastellux observed in 1782:

> The more the sciences approach perfection, the more rare do discoveries become; but America has the same advantage in the learned world, as in that which constitutes our residence. The extent of her empire submits to her observation a large portion of heaven and earth. What observations may not be made between Penobscot and Savannah? between the lakes and the ocean? Natural history and astronomy are her peculiar appendages, and the first of these sciences at least, is susceptible of great improvement.

One of the most valuable, and certainly one of the most distinctively American, contributions to knowledge was to be the recording of the experiences and scenes of daily life. This was natural history.

In England in the later 17th century, Robert Boyle, Sir Isaac Newton, and others in the flourishing Royal Society charted new laws of physics. But such additions to knowledge, far from being mere bits of new information, were sophisticated generalizations. It was precisely in this realm that the stirring discoveries were made in England during the American colonial period. The physical sciences were, of course, confirmed by experience and observation; but in their atmosphere, in their emphasis, even in their purpose they differed from *natural history,* which was the realm of the New World's promise.

The difference between natural history and the physical sciences suggests the difference between New World and Old World concepts of
knowledge in the colonial period. To describe 18th-century Americans
and Europeans simply as "scientists" or as "children of the Enlightenment" obscures what is most interesting. At least two large features
distinguish the world of physical science from the world in which American "scientists" were busiest and most successful in the colonial era.
First, the physical scientist must come to his experience ready to organize
it by a theory. In contrast, men have often contributed to natural history
merely by keeping a notebook of miscellaneous items which have caught
their attention; such are Gilbert White's *Natural History of Selborne*,
Charles Darwin's *Voyage of the Beagle*, and the natural-history classics
of colonial America, Peter Kalm's *Travels*, Mark Catesby's *Natural History of Carolina, Florida and the Bahama Islands*, and Jefferson's *Notes
on Virginia*. No such notebook would be useful to a physicist. Second,
the physical scientist—the physicist or chemist—does not deal with the
subject-matters and classifications of everyday life. He speaks of entropy,
of gravity, of chemical substances, of hydrogen, oxygen, etc. This is in
contrast to the natural historian, who is almost always close to the
popular vocabulary; he speaks of water, earth, rain, and air.

It is a commonplace in the history of colonial American science that,
while great advances were made here in natural history, few epochal
contributions were made to the physical sciences. This character of
American thought has too often been described as nothing more than its
immaturity: the stultifying consequence of colonial life, of American
remoteness from ancient centers of learning, of lack of leisure and of
books, and of the urgencies of settling a new country. But such an explanation hides from us some of the continuous features of American
culture, for the distinctively American bias in science is rooted in the
colonial age. "This Country opens to the philosophic view," Charles
Thomson wrote to Jefferson on March 9, 1782, "an extensive, rich and
unexplored field. It abounds in roots, plants, trees and minerals, to the
virtues and uses of which we are yet strangers."

* * *

Knowledge *of* the New World gathered *in* the New World was inevitably ill-assorted; men noted first whatever came first to their attention. What they saw always depended on the luck of the traveler and
the fortunes of the seasons. John Josselyn enthusiastically retailed the
marvelous things he had seen and heard in New England on June 26,
1639—the tales "of a young Lyon (not long before) kill'd at Piscataway

by an Indian; of a Sea-Serpent or Snake, that lay quoiled up like a Cable upon a Rock at Cape-Ann: a Boat passing by with English aboard, and two Indians, they would have shot the Serpent but the Indians disswaded them, saying, that if he were not kill'd out-right, they would be all in danger of their lives . . . of a Triton or Mereman which he saw in Casco-bay . . . who laying his hands upon the side of the Canow, had one of them chopt off with a Hatchet by Mr. Mittin, which was in all respects like the hand of a man, the Triton presently sunk, dying the water with his purple blood, and was no more seen." No wonder Josselyn concluded "that there are many stranger things in the world, than are to be seen between London and Stanes."

After reading Josselyn's and other accounts of observant travelers, how can one believe that a "descriptive" approach to knowledge confines the imagination? The Goddess of Miscellany reigned even in such early promotional tracts as Francis Higginson's *New-Englands Plantation* (1630), which described how God had arranged the Earth, Water, Air, and Fire in America to be most favorable to human life. William Wood's *New Englands Prospect* (1634) enumerated in poetic disarray:

> The kingly Lyon, and the strong arm'd Beare,
> The large lim'd Mooses, with the tripping Deare,
> Quill-darting Porcupines and Rackcoones be,
> Castell'd in the hollow of an aged tree;
> The skipping Squerrell, Rabbet, purblinde Hare,
> Immured in the selfe same Castle are,
> Lest red eyd Ferrets, wily Foxes should
> Them undermine, if rampird but with mould.
> The grim fac't Ounce, and ravenous howling Woolfe,
> Whose meagre paunch suckes like a swallowing gulfe.
> Blacke glistering Otters, and rich coated Bever,
> The Civet scented Musquash smelling ever.

A century later, variegated New World novelties filled William Byrd's *History of the Dividing Line* (1728), and Jefferson's most important literary product apart from the Declaration of Independence, his *Notes on .Virginia* (1784), was an omnium-gatherum of information about minerals, plants, animals, institutions, and men. This flood of impressions pouring out of America to interest stay-at-home Englishmen was the main stream of new knowledge from the New World. America was shaping the very concept of knowledge.

The modern reader can still pick up a copy of Mark Catesby's *Natural History of Carolina, Florida and the Bahama Islands* (1731-43), the writings of John Bartram and William Bartram, Alexander Wilson's

American Ornithology (1808-14), or Audubon's casual writings, and read them with enjoyment and profit. Writers of most works on natural history—even of ostensibly "systematic" accounts of flowers, trees, birds, or mammals—described objects within the scope of common men. Despite an occasional Latin name or learned reference, their works made sense to any person with eyes, ears, and some curiosity. The drawings had some of the universal intelligibility of the 20th-century picture-magazine. Such books of travel and natural history required no theoretical training; they did not depend on abstruse definitions or on a structure of philosophy or argument. They were a warehouse of "facts" stored more or less at random, as the discoverer had come upon them. There was no single or necessary order of material; one did not need to progress from definitions and premises through conclusions. They were thus as different as possible from such classic works of "explanatory" science as Newton's *Principia*. Moreover, while few men could understand Newton, much less themselves contribute to physics, any alert American might add to natural history by noticing a plant, some habit of the opossum or deer, or a custom of the Indians.

* * *

We have too long been told that a "unified" scheme of knowledge is required to give meaning and unity to society; that men have a greater sense of sharing values and of working to a common end if they are united by a grand overarching system of thought; that somehow an articulate and systematic philosophy is likely to provide such a system of shared meaning. The stock example is, of course, the Middle Ages when such theologians as Thomas Aquinas and Duns Scotus constructed monuments of speculative philosophy. It has become an unexamined commonplace that a more unified philosophy will produce a more unified society, that ours would be a better and more meaningful world if we in America possessed such systematic and "unifying" thought.

But is this really true? It may have seemed so in earlier societies where the frame of meaning was supposed to be accessible only to a priestly or ruling class. Could it remain so in a modern literate society where most people would be expected to understand the purposes of the community? One cannot unify such a society by mere *concepts,* however refined and subtle, however vivid to a few philosophers or theologians. "The attempt to bridge the chasm between multiplicity and unity is the oldest problem of philosophy, religion, and science," observed Henry Adams in *Mont-Saint-Michel and Chartres* (1905), "but the flimsiest bridge of all is the human concept, unless somewhere, within or beyond it, an energy not individual is hidden; and in that case the old question instantly reappears: What is that energy?" To say that a society can or ought to be "unified" by some total philosophic system—whether a *Summa Theologica,* a Calvin's *Institutes,* or a Marx's *Capital*—is to commit oneself to an aristocratic concept of knowledge: let the élite know the theories and values of the society; they will know and preserve for all the rest.

When life thus draws its meaning from a system of philosophy, when philosophy becomes the device for unifying knowledge, knowledge itself becomes a monopoly. To understand a system, one must begin at the beginning; one must acquire the prerequisites, which are often in a learned or foreign language; and one must build from definitions, axioms, and propositions, to corollaries and conclusions.

But the kind of new knowledge which life in America made possible, precisely because it was factual and miscellaneous, required no preliminary training. One could plunge in anywhere. Knowledge of the New World—its climate, geography, plants, animals, savages, and diseases— was accessible to everyone. The crude carving on the bark of a tree recording that here Daniel Boone "CillED A. Bar" or the casual report of the course of a river were pieces of natural history. The American did not need to begin with explicit premises or with precise definitions and propositions; he began with the first novelty that came to his attention. If "knowledge" was miscellaneous, men could educate themselves with the random materials of experience. They could become "self-made" men, because they could start anytime anyplace. John Bartram and Benjamin Franklin were paragons of this kind of learning, and there were many others who "improved" their experience to become models of learning in the American mold. The ideal of knowledge which came from natural history was admirably suited to a mobile society. Its paths did not run only through the academy, the monastery, or the university; they opened everywhere and to every man.

PART SIX

EDUCATING THE

COMMUNITY

"A certain Person among the Greeks being a
Candidate for some Office in the State, it was
objected against him, That he was no Scholar.
True, saith he, according to your Notion of
Learning I am not; but I know how to make a
poor City rich, and a small City great."

JARED ELIOT

28

The Community Enters
the University

IN EUROPE a "liberal" education, which would supposedly liberate
a man from the narrow bounds of his time and place, was the property
of an exclusive few. The traditional hallmark of liberal education insofar
as there was any in 18th-century England—the "Bachelor of Arts" degree
—was under Parliamentary authority awarded only by Oxford and Cambridge. This ancient clerical-aristocratic monopoly had, of course, preserved the learned tradition and produced many of the finest fruits of
European thought. But the universities had been hothouses where only
certain kinds of thinking could flourish. Their ancient walls had been
doubly confining: they insulated the inmates from the general community, while they separated people outside from the community's
bookish wisdom.

True, there were signs of change in England in the 17th and 18th
centuries. During the 17th century, especially after the Act of Uniformity
(1662) had required all clergymen, college fellows, and schoolmasters
to accept everything in the Book of Common Prayer, noncomformists
set up their so-called "dissenting academies" to train a ministry of their

own and to offer higher education to the children of dissenters. Much of English intellectual life then centered in associations like the Royal Society of London or was carried on by gentlemen in their country houses. All this tended to secularize and to broaden the currents of English thought. Still, at least until the early 19th century, the citadel of English learning remained in Oxford and Cambridge. Even if Gibbon's familiar picture of an Oxford "steeped in port and prejudice" is a caricature, lethargy did fall upon the universities during the 18th century. But because of their ancient tradition, their endowments, their monopoly of degree-giving, their great and freely growing stock of books (under the licensing acts each of the two Universities received a copy of every book licensed in England), their power to publish (for much of the 17th and 18th centuries they were among the few printing agencies authorized outside London), and their control of avenues of political and ecclesiastical preferment, they were hard to dislodge from their dominion over English higher learning. The "democratizing" of English higher learning in the earlier 19th century did not occur through growth of the "dissenting academies" into universities; it came about mostly through liberalizing the religious tests for admission to Oxford or Cambridge, and through accepting more scholarship students. Even today Oxford and Cambridge link aristocracy and learning in English life.

But many facts, from the very beginning, shaped American life and diffused our collegiate education. Here we will observe only two.

First: The American legal vagueness and the blurring of distinctions between college and university helped break educational monopolies.

Although the origins of Oxford and Cambridge were shrouded in medieval mists, their control over higher learning in England came largely from their clear legal monopoly. Legally speaking, they were undeniably the only English Universities. Oxford in 1571 and Cambridge in 1573 had received charters of incorporation and held for all England the exclusive powers to grant degrees; their monopoly was complete until, after a struggle, the unorthodox London University was founded in 1827.

In England the distinction between "college" and "university" was always more or less sharp and significant: a *college* was primarily a place of residence or of instruction, largely self-governing, but without the power to give examinations or grant degrees; a *university* was a degree-granting institution of learning, usually offering instruction in one of the higher subjects of Law, Medicine, or Theology in addition to the

Seven Liberal Arts and Philosophy, and possessing special legal authority (first in the form of a papal bull, later of a Royal or Parliamentary charter). Until the early 19th century, then, there were many English "colleges" but only two "universities," Oxford and Cambridge. Efforts to found additional degree-granting institutions were repeatedly defeated. For example, Gresham College, founded in 1548, possessed seven professorships and eventually became a great center of learning in the form of the Royal Society of London; but it never became a university. The "dissenting academies," which produced such figures as Daniel Defoe, Bishop Joseph Butler, Joseph Priestley, and Thomas Malthus, survived in the form of secondary schools ("public" schools) or theological institutions, but did not acquire the power to grant degrees.

The significance of all this for English life and learning, while complicated and not easy to define, was nevertheless persistent and pervasive. At least since the Age of Queen Elizabeth I, the universities have possessed a social prestige which has remained undiminished, or has perhaps even increased, with their academic decay. By the 18th century the lethargy of Oxford and Cambridge—like the collegiate rowdyism of American colleges in the early 20th century—had become a standing joke. "From the toil of reading, or thinking, or writing, they had absolved their conscience," wrote the great Edward Gibbon of the fellows of Magdalen College, Oxford, about 1752. "Their conversation stagnated in a round of college business, Tory politics, personal anecdotes, and private scandal: their dull and deep potations excused the brisk intemperance of youth." Few professors performed their proper functions. Between 1725 and 1773, no Regius Professor of Modern History at Cambridge delivered a lecture, although one did achieve notice when he killed himself by falling from his horse in a drunk. But the social amenities were not neglected: Oxford and Cambridge remained fashionable resorts for noblemen's sons, who sometimes came with their own tutors, servants, and hunting dogs.

Despite all this, the great and ancient universities were far from dead. Sir Isaac Newton, Edmund Halley (of Halley's Comet), Sir William Blackstone, and Edward Gibbon, among others, were nourished there. Oxford and Cambridge continued to be the museum and the citadel of the nation's high-culture.

How different was provincial America! Neither the virtues nor the vices of these antique monopolies could be transplanted across the Atlantic. The time-honored English distinction between "college" and "university," like so many other Old World distinctions, became confused and even ceased to have meaning in America. For one thing, the legal powers of the different colonial governments, especially their powers to create corporations and to establish monopolies, were varied, fluid, and uncertain. Nothing was more fertile than this vagueness of the American legal situation.

According to English law in the colonial period, a group of individuals ordinarily could not act as a legal unit, own property, sue and be sued, nor survive the death of individual members. They could not act as a "corporation" unless they had been granted these privileges by their government. Lord Coke declared the orthodox English doctrine: "None but the King alone can create or make a corporation." This was the legal theory. There were a few special exceptions (corporations "by prescription" or "at the common law," and the Bishop of Durham's power to create corporations in his "county palatine"), but the general power to create a corporation remained one of the most closely hedged prerogatives of government, and many an enterprise hung on the willingness of Crown or Parliament to grant the artificial immortality of a corporate charter.

Who, if anyone, in the American colonies, possessed this important power to create corporations? This proved to be a question with many answers. There were several kinds of colonies—"charter," "royal," and "proprietary"—each with a different legal character. The proprietary charters (of Maine, for example) generally contained a "Bishop of Durham clause" giving the English Bishop's peculiar regal powers to the proprietor. But the *explicit* delegation to a colonial agency of the right to incorporate was seldom found, and this area became a happy hunting ground for legal metaphysicians. Add to this the many uncertainties over the relative legal powers of colonial governors versus colonial legislatures and of all the colonial governments as against the powers in London. On this uncharted legal terrain many disorderly, inconsistent, and unpredictable institutions sprouted.

The first American college was set up in a typically American legal haze. The founding of Harvard is now generally dated from 1636, when the General Court of Massachusetts appropriated four hundred pounds "towards a schoale or college," but its legal structure and the extent of its authority could hardly have been vaguer. Harvard actually granted its first degrees in 1642, although by that time the college had received from nobody the legal authority to grant a degree; it had not even been legally incorporated. When the college finally received a charter from the Massachusetts General Court in 1650, there was still no mention of degrees, perhaps because of uncertainty over the General Court's own authority to confer the degree-granting power. The boldest act of Henry

Dunster, the first vigorous President of Harvard College (1640-1654), was to confer any degrees at all. As Samuel Eliot Morison explains, this was "almost a declaration of independence from King Charles." Even the legislative charter of 1650 seemed so insecure legally that when Increase Mather was in England after the Revolution of 1688 he tried, though unsuccessfully, to secure a special Crown charter. The legal foundations of Harvard, the origins of its authority to grant degrees, and the question of whether, and in what legal sense, if at all, it is properly a "college" or a "university"—all these have remained uncertain and unresolved into the 20th century. From the beginning, the President and Fellows exploited this uncertainty, and exercised any convenient powers.

Yale came into being at a time when the legal foundations of Harvard, which had already been prospering and granting degrees for nearly sixty years, seemed most shaky. Harvard's special legal problems had been compounded, of course, by the insecurity of the charter of Massachusetts Bay Colony; obviously no secure legal rights could be derived from a colonial government which itself might be unlegal. Who could hope to satisfy the General Court, the Governor, and the changing English government, while respecting ancient forms of English law and duly regarding colonial convenience? There was the further slippery question of whether a colony which overstepped its legal authority, say by incorporating a college or university when it actually possessed no such power, might not be violating its own charter. Such a violation might invite unfriendly English politicians to challenge the legal existence of the whole colony. During these years neither Massachusetts Bay nor Connecticut lacked enemies back home who would have been delighted to seize such an opportunity. "Not knowing what to doe for fear of overdoing . . . ," explained Judge Samuel Sewall and Isaac Addington in 1701 concerning the Act which they drafted to found Yale, "We on purpose, gave the Academie as low a Name as we could that it might better stand in wind and wether; nor daring to incorporat it, lest it should be served with a Writt of Quo-Warranto." With prudent modesty and ambiguity they decided to call their institution "a collegiate school." Not until nearly half a century later (1745), after Yale had awarded dozens of degrees, was it formally incorporated.

The history of colonial colleges is one of the most remarkable instances of the triumph of legal practice over theory and of the needs of the community over the abstruse distinctions of professional lawyers. Before the outbreak of the Revolution, at least nine colonial institutions which would survive into the 20th century were already granting degrees.

In all of England at this time there were still only *two* degree-granting institutions, Oxford and Cambridge, whose ancient monopoly was
still secured by the neatly-wrought distinctions of lawyers. The oldest
American colleges—Harvard, William & Mary, and Yale—all must
today find the origin of their legal degree-granting power in what
lawyers call "prescription," that is, in the simple fact that they have
been granting degrees for a very long time without being successfully
challenged. If the sharp English distinction between a properly-incor-
porated, degree-granting monopoly called a "university" and all other
types of institutions had been successfully transplanted here; if a single
royal university had been founded for all the American colonies; or if
the power to grant degrees had been clearly and explicitly forbidden in
all the colonies, the history of American higher education—and possibly
of much else in American culture—might have been very different.

Second: Outside control drew the college into the community.

In 17th-century Europe, and certainly in England, the universities and
their colleges were centers for a proud and eminent group of learned
men. The medieval clerical tradition had left them a form of academic
self-government which remains the pattern in much of Europe to this
day. The scholars who gathered round the university, controlling its
books, its buildings, its endowments, and its sinecures, were jealous of
their powers. To them the universities seemed very much their own.
Whatever may have been the effect of all this on "academic freedom,"
one plain result was to make universities independent of the community
and to isolate the university and the community from each other. This is
still expressed in the English antithesis between "town" and "gown."

The Protestant spirit which pervaded the American colonies was of
course congenial to the growth of "lay" (that is non-academic) control.
Medieval universities had been ecclesiastical agencies, and their "self-
government" had followed simply from the autonomy of the clergy. The
Protestant Reformation had given laymen a share in governing their
churches; another way of breaking the power of a priestly class was to
admit laymen into the government of universities. "Since the Reformation from Popery," an American author wrote in 1755, "the Notion of
the Sanctity of Colleges and other Popish Religious Houses has been
exploded. . . . The Intention herein was not to destroy the Colleges or
the Universities, and rob the Muses, but to rescue them from Popish
Abuses. . . . in forming new Universities, and Colleges, the British
Nation has perhaps made them a little more pompous, in Compliance
with Customs introduced . . . in Popish Times; which Customs being of

long Standing they chose to suffer to continue in them. But the Protestant Princes, and Republicks, and States, in whose Territories there was no University before, had no Regard to any Popish Usages or Customs in erecting Colleges, and Universities, and only endowed them with such Privileges and Powers, and Officers, as were properly School Privileges, Powers and Officers." In old England, despite Protestantism, university faculties remained entrenched behind their medieval walls. In America there were no such walls.

As we look back on the story now, it seems clear that "lay" control of American colleges owed less to anyone's wisdom or foresight than to sheer necessity and to America's nakedness of institutions. While European universities in the 17th and 18th centuries had inherited rich lands, buildings, endowments, governmental appropriations, and intangible resources, the first American colleges were, as Hofstadter and Metzger point out, brand new "artifacts." They were founded by small communities; lay boards of control helped marshal their limited resources and kept the college in touch with the whole community, without whose support there would have been no college at all.

In Europe the universities had historically been a kind of guild of men of clerical learning. No such guild could exist here for the simple reason that there was no considerable body of learned men. Control of the new institutions inevitably fell to representatives of the community at large. The learned, eminent, or at least aged men who led the faculties of European universities could plausibly claim the power to govern themselves. But at Harvard—where in 1650, President Henry Dunster had just turned forty, his treasurer was twenty-six, and the average age of his "faculty" (then mostly a transient body of students preparing for the ministry) was about twenty-four—the staff of the college could hardly expect to receive deference or power from the surrounding community.

Thus there emerged during the colonial period that pattern of outside control which would permanently characterize American colleges. In the early government of Harvard and of William & Mary there were some signs of the growth of a system of dual control under which the faculty would rule subject to veto by an outside body. But in neither place did such a system last. As early as 1650, Harvard was plainly under the control, not of professors, but of magistrates and ministers, and so it remained. By the mid-18th century, when William & Mary College was flourishing, the gentry had clearly prevailed over the academics.

The prototype of American college government was actually established at Yale and at Princeton, where representatives of the community were organized in a single board of trustees which legally owned and effectively controlled the institution. These trustees were not members of the faculty; they were ministers, magistrates, lawyers, physicians, or merchants. American colleges would not be self-governing guilds of the learned.

Outside control incidentally produced another institution: the American college president. Under the ancient European system where the fellows of a college or the faculty of a university governed themselves and were supported by ancient endowment or clerical livings, there had been no place for such an officer. But the American system of college government by outsiders created a new need. The trustees were often absentees, with neither the time nor the inclination to govern; the college teachers who were on the spot were often youthful and transient. Into this power vacuum came the college president. He alone represented both the faculty and the public, for he was a member of the governing board who resided at the college. Technically an employee of the trustees, he was usually the best informed of them and so became their leader. As the principal member of the faculty he came to speak for them too. Upon his promotional ability depended the reputation or even the very existence of the institution. He combined the academic and the man of business; he was supposed to apply learning to current affairs and to use business judgment for the world of learning. With no counterpart in the Old World, he was the living symbol of the breakdown of the cloistered walls.

29

Higher Education in Place
of Higher Learning

IN AMERICA the college became a place concerned more with the diffusion than with the advancement or perpetuation of learning. "University" education in America became, for all practical purposes, undergraduate education. No one of the causes of the dispersion of higher education was unique to America, but all of them together added up to an overwhelming force against legal monopoly and geographic concentration.

Religious sectarianism and variety. Each of the three earliest colleges —Harvard, William & Mary, and Yale—was founded to support the established church of its particular colony; and these were the only colleges until 1745. Not until the mid-18th century—after the Great Awakening had aroused religious enthusiasms and sharpened sectarian antagonism, and when prosperity gave people money enough to send their sons to college and to build college buildings—did the rash of colonial colleges appear. This was what President Ezra Stiles of Yale called "the College Enthusiasm." While in England the admirable dissenting academies did not even secure the power to grant degrees, in America the school of every sect arrogated the dignity of an ancient European university. By the time of the Revolution nearly every major Christian sect had an institution of its own: New-Side Presbyterians founded Princeton; revivalist Baptists founded Brown; Dutch Reformed revivalists founded Rutgers; a Congregational minister transformed an Indian missionary school into Dartmouth; and Anglicans and Presbyterians worked together in the founding of King's College (later Columbia) and the College of Philadelphia (later the University of Pennsylvania).

Each college founded by a sect was another good reason for every other sect to found its own college in order to save more Americans from the untruths of its competitors. And all these sectarian colleges were so many good reasons for secularists to found their own in order to rescue youth from all benighting dogma. Here was an accelerating movement. Once begun it was not easily stopped; it was only delayed by hard times during the Revolution. Between 1746 and 1769, twice as many colleges were founded in the colonies as in the previous hundred years; between 1769 and 1789 twice as many again as in the preceding twenty years. And so it went. The movement gathered momentum, and seems hardly yet to have stopped.

Such competition, incidentally, had a liberalizing effect. While the founding sect in each case could hope to dominate, it dared not monopolize its own institution. Under American conditions the sharpening religious antagonisms of the second half of the 18th century actually produced *inter*denominational boards of control. While the college president usually came from the dominant sect, it was commonly necessary to conciliate hostile sects by including their representatives among the trustees. King's College, which was an Anglican institution, possessed on its first governing board ministers of four other denominations;

Brown's board, although dominated by Baptists, included a substantial number of Congregationalists, Anglicans, and Quakers. Of the twenty-four trustees of the University of Pennsylvania (which had grown out of a nonsectarian academy), six trustees represented all the principal denominations, including the Roman Catholic.

Among these many new institutions there arose a lively competition for students, because there were few places in sparsely populated America where any single sect could furnish the whole student body of a college. Perforce no American college during the colonial period imposed a religious test on its entering students. Thus, a nonsectarianism, which was not the product of an abstract theory of toleration, became an ideal of American higher education. It was typically expressed by Ezra Stiles who had become President of Yale in 1778 when the college was still suffering from the narrow-minded orthodoxy of the obstinate Thomas Clap (Rector and President, 1740-1766). Stiles's tolerance helped revive the college. He, of course, admitted his own conscientious preference for congregationalism, but by that he dared not be governed.

> There is so much pure Christianity among all sects of Protestants, that I cheerfully embrace all in my charity. There is so much defect in all that we all need forbearance and mutual condescension. I don't intend to spend my days in the fires of party; at the most I shall resist all claims and endeavors for supremacy or precedency of any sect; for the rest I shall promote peace, harmony, and benevolence.

Provincial America had already begun to find safety in diversity. Only a decade later the authors of *The Federalist* (No. 51) observed with prophetic wisdom that "In a free government the security for civil rights must be the same as that for religious rights. It consists in the one case in the multiplicity of interests, and in the other in the multiplicity of sects." The proliferation of sects and the growth of religious enthusiasm in 18th-century America had produced an unpredicted and unplanned (often an undesired) religious tolerance. Where every sect lacked power to coerce, they all wisely "chose" to persuade.

Geographic distance and local pride. The great geographic distances which dissipated religious passion also dissipated the intellectual passion which might have been focused in one or two centers of higher learning. There never has been an effective American movement for a national university. The numerous and diverse American colleges, separated by vast distances, never formed a self-conscious community of learned men. Even efforts to adopt uniform standards of college admission or to form a general association of colleges were feeble and unsuccessful until the 19th century. Organizations like the Phi Beta Kappa Society (founded in 1776), which aimed at an intercollegiate community of educated men, exerted slight influence. American colleges were emphatically institutions of the local community. Harvard, William & Mary, and Yale were designed by and for their particular provinces; their support came from their own localities.

The primary aim of the American college was not to increase the continental stock of cultivated men, but rather to supply its particular region with knowledgeable ministers, lawyers, doctors, merchants, and political leaders. While the university centers of traditional English learning were detached from the great political and commercial center of London, the early American colleges tended to be at the center of each colony's affairs. The location of William & Mary at Williamsburg (and the comparable locations of Brown, Yale, and the University of Pennsylvania) where students like Jefferson could drop in during their spare time to hear the debates of the House of Burgesses, linked learning and public life. It symbolized both the easy intercourse between American higher learning and the community as a whole and the identification of leading men with the special problems of their particular regions.

In England, the leading families sent their sons away to the few best "public" schools, and afterwards these young gentlemen were gathered— if only for hunting and wassailing—at Oxford and Cambridge. Anyone who could afford it thus went to a distant, "national" institution. "If he returned to work in his native place he was no longer quite a native of it," G. Kitson Clark has explained, "he spoke a different language from most of its inhabitants, had bonds of friendship which drew his mind away from its borders, and above all had not had with his fellow townsmen that close association in youth which is perhaps the closest neighbourly bond there is. Perhaps this helped to impede the development of that vigorous provincial life which England needed and still needs, and, worse than that, it helped to create a caste, to emphasize a horizontal social division, at a time of growing wealth and growing social tensions when a horizontal division was particularly dangerous." In America the basis of higher education was territorial; this distinction was important, for the diffusion of American higher education nourished the local roots of a federal union. Mere proximity and the lower cost of attending college near home seem to have been deciding factors in the choice of a college by many pre-Revolutionary students in America.

Americans came to believe that no community was complete without its own college. The famous provisions for an educational land-fund in the Land Ordinance of 1785 and in the Northwest Ordinance of 1787, which later became the bases for state universities, probably had some such motive. Real estate developers in the early 19th century included plans for colleges in their schemes to attract settlers to new towns.

Social and geographic mobility: the competition for students. These insecure new institutions were competing for reputation, for financial support, and—most important of all—for students. The Colleges of New Jersey and of Rhode Island (later to be Princeton and Brown), which charged the lowest fees, and Dartmouth, where some students could work for their expenses, rapidly increased their enrollment. The College of Philadelphia and King's College, sometimes called "the gentlemen's colleges," drew the fewest students from afar and had the smallest student bodies.

Nearly all the modern techniques of student recruiting, except the football scholarship, were used before the end of the colonial era. There were many examples of the puffing brochure and of alumni acting as recruiting agents. Along with these came lower standards of admission and graduation and "popular" courses to attract the students whose tuition fees were desperately needed. "Except in one neighbouring province," John Trumbull of Connecticut complained in 1773, "ignorance wanders unmolested at our colleges, examinations are dwindled to meer form and ceremony, and after four years dozing there, no one is ever refused the honours of a degree, on account of dulness and insufficiency."

American colleges had already begun to put their money in impressive buildings, which they could ill afford, rather than in books or faculty endowments. During the twenty-five years before the Revolution five of the colonial colleges spent about £15,000 for the erection or remodeling of buildings. Such expenditures supposedly brought favorable publicity, and hence students. But at the College of Philadelphia and the College of Rhode Island, these heavy initial costs left the institutions bankrupt almost before they had begun to operate.

Despite the competition between colleges, higher education was still not cheap. In the mid-18th century, the combined cost of room, board, and tuition ranged from about £10 a year (at the College of New Jersey or of Rhode Island), to twice that sum (at King's College); a wealthy student might spend as much as £50. This was at a time when a carpenter's annual earnings would have been no more than £50, a college instructor's about £100, and a prosperous lawyer's only £500. Although an ambitious parent might secure a loan to educate his son, a college education obviously was not for the poor: there was not yet a regular or extensive system of scholarships and, except at Dartmouth, it was uncommon for students to work their way through college. Still, everything considered, the situation was a great deal better than in Eng-

land, where a higher education could not be secured for much less than
£ 100 a year.

* * *

One obvious effect of this dispersion and competition of colleges
was an increase in the number, though not in the quality, of college
degrees. About fourteen hundred men graduated from the three colonial
colleges in the thirty years before 1747; in the next thirty years the
colleges of British North America awarded more than twice that many
bachelor's degrees, about half the increase being due to the newly-founded
colleges. No American who could afford the fee of ten pounds a year
for four years could fail to secure, if he wanted it, the hallmark of a
"higher" education. American colleges were not simply distributing to
the many what in England was reserved for the privileged few; they were
issuing an inflated intellectual currency.

The early colonial dispersion established a pattern which was never
broken. From time to time after the Revolution, grandiose hopes were
expressed for a single great institution supported by Congress. It was
to be situated in the national capital, where students of republican sentiment could be drawn from abroad, where the intellectual resources of
the nation could be concentrated, and where local prejudices might
be dissolved. There was such talk even in the Federal Constitutional
Convention. Charles Pinckney's draft expressly gave the Federal legislature the power to establish a national university at the seat of government, and Madison seems to have favored such a power. In the
showdown the proposal was defeated, either because members believed
the power already had been given by implication or because they considered it undesirable. George Washington was attracted by the idea
of an institution at the nation's capital to "afford the students an opportunity of attending the debates in Congress, and thereby becoming more
liberally and better acquainted with the principles of law and government." But the Founding Fathers supported the local institutions which
had sprung up all over the country.

Until nearly the end of the 18th century, the typical American college
consisted of a president (usually a cleric, sometimes the pastor of a
neighboring church) and a few (seldom more than three) tutors who
were themselves usually young men studying for the clergy. There were
few "professors"—mature men with a full command of their subject.
Under these circumstances the curriculum of American colleges, as
distinct from their institutional framework, inevitably remained traditional. Despite a few notable exceptions and some influence of the

English dissenting academies and the Scottish universities, American colonial colleges stuck to the curriculum which the tutors had learned from their tutors and which ultimately could be traced back to the English universities and their medieval forebears. What distinguished the American college was not its corpus of knowledge, but how, when, where, and to whom it was communicated.

As colleges became more dispersed, developing their interdenominationalism and their links with their local communities, they also became less identified with any particular profession. During the 18th century a decreasing proportion of American college graduates entered the ministry. By the second half of the 17th century even Harvard, which had been founded with an ecclesiastical purpose, was drawing many sons of artisans, tradesmen, and farmers. By the end of the 18th century only about a quarter of the graduates of all American colleges were becoming clergymen. Meanwhile the lack of specialized legal and medical training affected those learned professions themselves, making them depend more on informal apprenticeship.

American colleges that aimed to make good citizens would only accidentally produce profound or adventuring scholars. The Marquis de Chastellux, traveling through the country in the 1780's, observed that here the philosopher needed less to promote educational institutions than to remove obstacles to their progress. "Leave owls and bats to flutter in the doubtful perspicuity of a feeble twilight;" he warned with an eye to the English vices, "the American eagle should fix her eyes upon the sun."

The peculiar promise of American academies lay in their numbers. From the beginning, American colleges, in contrast with those of England, were more anxious to spread than to deepen the higher learning. A community of two million inhabitants or less, dispersed over the long seacoast of a vast continent, would have had to concentrate its learned minds in some American Athens if they were most effectively to stimulate one another. But there was no American Athens, and Americans came to value the intellectual virtues which grew in diffusion: the sense of relevance, the free exchange between the community's experience and that of its teachers. If by ancient criteria Americans were less learned, they were shaping new tests of the value of learning. If they did not know their sacred texts so well, they were opening a thousand windows.

30

The Ideal of the
Undifferentiated Man

WHILE EUROPEAN CULTURE had developed elaborate ways of fragmenting, specializing, and monopolizing pieces of man's knowledge and functions, American culture from its very beginning allowed many of these to come together. American life promoted a new fluidity in man's thinking about his knowledge and about himself. It produced a novel, half-articulate educational ideal—the ideal of the undifferentiated man, fostered by facts deeply rooted in the provincial age.

The vagueness of American social classes. The ideals of medieval education, if they were nothing else, were at least precise. Long before the founding of the American colonies, the traditional "liberal" education had been defined as an induction into the seven (not six or eight) Liberal Arts. Such were the studies suitable for a free man—hence the "liberal" education. With equal precision, the "higher" university faculties included Theology, Law, and Medicine. Under American conditions, neither liberal nor professional education could retain its ancient precision. Where a man's status was as ambiguous and as shifting as it was in the New World, he could not know in advance which types of learning would be especially appropriate for him. In European culture the distinctions of social status had been represented in distinctions of subject-matter: the "liberal" arts, suitable for a "free" man, were labors of the mind; the "servile" arts required the handling of physical objects. That distinction long separated science from technology, and its breakdown was essential to progress. Similarly, the distinction between "philosophers" on the one hand and practical inventors—known variously and condescendingly as "mechanics," "projectors," or economic "adventurers"—on the other was sharp and divisive. Distinctions which had been hallowed by custom, law, and language in Europe came to seem vague and artificial in America.

Although colonial society was doubtless a good deal more aristocratic than we have been in the habit of imagining, many circumstances prevented a clear definition of this aristocracy—except perhaps in South Carolina, Virginia, and upstate New York. In colleges with small and transient faculties, the coverage of traditional subjects was necessarily crude and haphazard. The multiplication of college degrees—which came to stand for the most diverse subject-matters at all different levels— further confused the ancient European standards, and made it less clear what the authentic standard really ought to be.

The diffusion of roles. The traditional list of "liberal" arts, already beginning to break down in Europe, would no longer liberate man in America. Here men found it hard to prepare for any role, even that of a "liberally" educated man, simply because their roles had not yet been sharply defined. Similarly, in the professions, no traditional preparation could actually prepare a man for the novel tasks of clergyman, doctor, lawyer, or professor in America. Where the learned professions were loosely organized, where nearly everybody was doing some of the work of the doctor, the lawyer, or the teacher, the criteria of professional eminence became vague. A successful New England clergyman was also likely to be something of a physician, a politician, and a teacher, and perhaps to have other jobs as well.

A remarkable instance of all this was the new and more diversified role of women in American life. By the 18th century the rise of the middle classes and the spread of literacy had already begun to improve the education of European women. Although our knowledge is only fragmentary, evidence suggests that women in colonial America were more versatile, more active, more prominent, and on the whole more successful in activities outside the kitchen than were their English counterparts. The system of household manufactures, under which the husband's craft was practiced in or near the home, gave the wife or daughter an opportunity to learn. There was a surprisingly large number of women printers and newspaper publishers in the colonial period, and not all were widows carrying on the work of their husbands. Women were apothecaries and even general medical practitioners. Especially on a Southern plantation a man needed his wife's coöperation to carry on his business. William Byrd's secret diaries dramatically describe how important was the help of a competent and energetic wife. In New England, where seafaring husbands left their wives alone for months or years, women prospered as merchants and tradeswomen.

Everywhere the scarcity of labor tended to remove social prejudices. In early New England it was not unheard of, and apparently not frowned upon, for the daughter of a good family to go out to domestic service.

Judge Samuel Sewall noted that his sister planned to become a maid to a Boston family. At the death of William Sheaffe, deputy collector of customs at Boston in 1771, his wife, who was the daughter of a prominent citizen, was set up by her friends in the grocery business.

Great distances, social and geographic mobility, and the scarcity of schools for the rising classes broadened women's interests by imposing on them the responsibility for educating the family. Perhaps this made it less odd than it might seem today that Cotton Mather taught his daughter Katherine both Latin and Hebrew. George Wythe, one of the leading figures of Revolutionary Virginia under whom Jefferson had served his legal apprenticeship, was reputed to possess "a perfect knowledge of the Greek language, which was taught him by his mother in the back woods." Jefferson's own plan of reading for his daughter Patsy, he explained in 1783, needed to be "considerably different from what I think would be most proper for her sex in any other country than America. I am obliged in it to extend my views beyond herself, and consider her as possibly at the head of a little family of her own. The chance that in marriage she will draw a blockhead I calculate at about fourteen to one, and of course that the education of her family will probably rest on her own ideas and direction without assistance. With the best poets and prosewriters I shall therefore combine a certain extent of reading in the graver sciences."

Even such fragmentary evidence suggests that women in the colonies were successful in more different activities and were more prominent in professional and public life than they would be again until the 20th century. Colonial laws tended to assimilate the legal status of men and of women. The rights of married women and their powers to carry on business and to secure divorce were much enlarged; the law protected women in ways unprecedented in the English common law.

American men who, like American women, were generally less specialized than their European counterparts, had become versatile through the force of circumstances. They were not "universal men" but "jacks-of-all-trades." Their tasks and opportunities made their interests broad and fluid. The "businessman," not the virtuoso, was the prototype of American versatility, for the businessman took his clues from his opportunities. "All the people of New-England without an exception," Timothy Dwight observed in the early 19th century, "beside what is created by disease, or misfortune, are men of business. . . . The business of a Clergyman it is here believed, is to effectuate the salvation of his flock, rather than to replenish his own mind with that superiour information, which, however ornamental or useful in other respects, is certainly connected with this end in a very imperfect degree. . . . Clergymen, here, are rarely possessed of libraries, sufficiently extensive to make such attainments practicable." In the other learned professions, too, men were judged by how well they performed rather than by how much they knew of some subject matter. College faculties were viewed as instruments for education rather than as repositories of wisdom; they were primarily "teachers." Whenever women took their cues from their new tasks and opportunities, their emphasis was also crudely instrumental; they had several jobs to do. The traditional standards of feminine gentility would not serve.

Out of all the limitations and opportunities of colonial America grew an American ideal, which sprang from the conviction that knowledge, like the New World itself, was still only half-discovered. English handbooks, like Brathwait's *English Gentleman,* warned the would-be gentleman not to seem too proficient in any specialty (whether dancing, swordplay, reading, or writing) lest it seem that he had been forced by a lack of lordly acres to make his living as a mere craftsman. If in the earliest years some Virginia would-be gentlemen were deterred by this fear of appearing too proficient, it was not for long; gentlemanly ineptness went against the American grain. Here all proficiencies, except perhaps those of the pedant or the monopolist, were welcome.

America lacked enthusiasm for the man of profound, detached, and "pure" intelligence. A wholesome fear of the exotic and the hieratic, of the power of the mind to raise any man above men, inspired American faith in the "divine average," a faith which would not have grown without American opportunity. "He does not find, as in Europe," Crèvecoeur observed of the immigrant to America in 1782, "a crowded society, where every place is over-stocked; he does not feel that perpetual collision of parties, that difficulty of beginning, that contention which oversets so many. There is room for everybody in America; has he any particular talent, or industry? he exerts it in order to procure a livelihood, and it succeeds."

PART SEVEN
THE LEARNED LOSE
THEIR MONOPOLIES

"It was a Place free from those 3 great Scourges of Mankind, Priests, Lawyers, and Physicians . . . the People were yet too poor to maintain these Learned Gentlemen."

WILLIAM BYRD

31

The Fluidity of Professions

THE AMERICAN PROVINCIAL AGE, we have already seen, was not
an age of genius so much as an age of liberation. Its legacy was not great
individual thinkers but refreshed community thinking. Old categories
were shaken up, and new situations revealed unsuspected uses for old
knowledge.

Colonial America was not the first age or place where such breaking
of old molds had occurred. The Protestant Reformation in Europe had
opposed the distinction between priest and layman, between the holders
of the Keys to Heaven and the multitude who sought admission. But
what the Reformers could accomplish was limited by their institutional
inheritance. In England, for example, the ancient Universities of Oxford
and Cambridge, which were to exercise such a pervasive influence on
English high culture, were a legacy of the Universal Church of the
middle ages, when clergymen were a different species from laymen. The
mere persistence of those great Universities perpetuated many of the old
distinctions, especially those between the custodians of the sacred learning and the community at large. Provincial America was free from all
this; it was therefore freer to allow a new fluidity to life and thought.
The universal priesthood of all believers attained a fuller expression in
American ways of daily living.

By the 18th century in Europe the departments of thought had been

191

frozen into professional categories, into the private domains of different guilds, city companies, and associations of masters; and the professions separated the areas of thought. Every professional field of learning bore a "No Trespassing" sign duly erected by legal or customary authority. In the newer culture of America few such signs had been erected; from the sheer lack of organized monopolists, old monopolies could not be perpetuated. America broke down distinctions: where life was full of surprises, of unexplored wildernesses, and of unpredictable problems, its tasks could not be neatly divided for legal distribution. Any man who preferred the even tenor of his way, who wished to pursue his licensed trade without the competition of amateurs, intruders, or vagrants, or who was unwilling to do jobs for which he had not been legally certified was better off in England.

At least four decisive facts about colonial America promoted this new fluidity in man's thinking about himself and about the departments of his knowledge. These were the product of no man's foresight but of the circumstances of a New World.

Regression. When a man finds himself plunged back into the conditions of an earlier age, he inevitably discovers many things. He rediscovers forgotten uses of his tools, and learns to think about them in the cruder categories of a primitive age. The sharp stone which early man used for killing was hardly different from the one he used for cutting, but in more developed cultures there arose a distinction between "weapon" and "tool" as each of them became a more specialized implement. Thus, in 18th-century Europe, the firearm became primarily a weapon; but for the colonial American backwoodsman, who had to protect himself and his family from marauding savages and who often shot meat for his table, the distinction between *weapon* and *tool* once again had little meaning. What was true of implements was also true of institutions and occupations. Under primitive conditions, there seem to have been few distinctions among those who practiced the different modes of healing and curing—between the man who muttered the incantation, the man who inserted the knife, and the man who mixed the potion. But in 18th-century England all these tasks were distinguished: each had become the private preserve of a different group —the barber-surgeons, the doctors of physick, and the apothecaries. In America such distinctions would have been difficult to preserve; the healer (sometimes a lawyer or a governor or a clergyman) once again performed all these different tasks.

Versatility required by the unexpected. Where the round of daily life has been worn into a groove by many generations living in the same place, men can prepare simply for the tasks which their ancestors have faced before them. But not in a New World. Here the unexpected was usual, and men had to be ready for it. The layman had to be prepared to act the lawyer, the architect, and the physician, and to practice crafts which others (only to be found across the ocean) knew much better. Versatility was no longer merely a virtue; it was a necessity. The man who could not be a little bit of everything was not qualified to be an American.

The scarcity of institutions. Where institutions were scarce, they could not be sharply distinguished from each other. Even the priests of different religions gradually tended to become assimilated. Puritanism gradually became less puritanical; Episcopalianism became less bishoply and more congregational; and religions like Quakerism which would not compromise with the New World could not long govern in it. "Thus all sects are mixed as well as all nations;" remarked Crèvecoeur in 1782, "thus religious indifference is imperceptibly disseminated from one end of the continent to the other; which is at present one of the strongest characteristics of the Americans. Where this will reach no one can tell. . . ."

The last serious colonial effort to set up a guild in the medieval mold took place in Philadelphia in 1718. Next to the occupational guilds, the most important agencies for monopolizing knowledge in the Old World had been the ancient educational institutions. But those too were lacking in America, and the New World thawed the categories of thought.

Labor-scarcity and Land-plenty. Labor and skills were scarce in colonial America; men had to do many things for themselves simply because they could not hire others to do them. Inevitably they came to set a lower standard, for otherwise a task could not have been done at all. The carpenter had to be cooper, cabinetmaker, and cobbler. The printer became writer, paper-manufacturer, binder, ink-maker, postmaster, and public figure. Land-plenty meant that even as a farmer the American generally needed to be much less efficient in order to make a living. Where men could "use up" their land, where they took for granted large tracts in reserve for the future, they lacked an incentive which prodded 18th-century English agriculture to reforms. Where everything, including the old homestead, was for sale, men were less attached to any particular piece of land. Once it ceased to support them, they would move on. Land itself lost many of its ancient legal and social peculiarities. The making of a living here required less specialization. At least for free white colonials, there were many different ways of earning a living and it was easy to change one's trade or the place where one practiced it.

"Strangers are welcome," Franklin explained in his *Information to those who would remove to America* (1782), "because there is room enough for them all, and therefore the old Inhabitants are not jealous of them." Since land was cheap, any diligent young man could rise. "Hence there is a continual Demand for more Artisans of all the necessary and useful kinds, to supply those Cultivators of the Earth with Houses, and with Furniture and Utensils of the grosser sorts, which cannot so well be brought from Europe. Tolerably good Workmen in any of those mechanic Arts are sure to find Employ, and to be well paid for their Work, there being no Restraints preventing Strangers from exercising any Art they understand, nor any Permission necessary." In America, he observed, everyone might hope and expect to become a Master, for any industrious young man could secure an apprenticeship which might have been too expensive for him in Europe. "In America, the rapid Increase of Inhabitants takes away that Fear of Rivalship, and Artisans willingly receive Apprentices from the hope of Profit by their Labour, during the Remainder of the Time stipulated, after they shall be instructed. Hence it is easy for poor Families to get their Children instructed; for the Artisans are so desirous of Apprentices, that many of them will even give Money to the Parent, to have Boys from Ten to Fifteen Years of Age bound Apprentices to them till the Age of Twenty-one; and many poor Parents have, by the means, on their Arrival in the Country, raised Money enough to buy Land sufficient to establish themselves, and to subsist the rest of their Family by Agriculture."

*   *   *

A new and fruitful social vagueness thus came into being in America. The ancient, familiar, and respectable idea of a "calling" had been displaced by the idea of opportunity. Historians in recent years have written a great deal about the change which supposedly occurred in Europe at the time of the Protestant Reformation. In contrast to the medieval Catholic view, according to Max Weber, all Protestant denominations took a novel view of men's occupations. This new view, says R. H. Tawney, required a man to give thought to his "choice" of a calling. But, in fact, European life offered very little choice to most men; they had no freedom but to perform the tasks to which their own family station assigned them. In Europe to hallow a man's "calling" was simply to sanctify his efficiency in his traditional job.

Few American men dared look to their inherited stations to define their callings. They had to look to their opportunities, to the unforeseen openings of the American situation. Where a rapid-flowing life informed a man of his tasks, he would be lost if he anchored himself to any fixed role. No prudent man dared be too certain of exactly who he was or what he was about; everyone had to be prepared to become someone else. To be ready for such perilous transmigrations was to become an American.

32

The Unspecialized Lawyer

IN 1758 when young John Adams consulted the leader of the Boston bar about the proper education of an American lawyer, the reply was an inquiry about Adams' general education and his knowledge of rhetoric. "Then Mr. Gridley run a comparison between the business and studies of a lawyer, a gentleman of the bar in England and those of one here: a lawyer in this country must study common law, and civil law, and natural law, and admiralty law; and must do the duty of a counsellor, a lawyer, an attorney, a solicitor, and even of a scrivener; so that the difficulties of the profession are much greater here than in England." In 17th- and 18th-century England, as Adams' mentor knew, the legal profession was elaborately organized and stratified and these divisions reflected both English legal thinking and the prejudices of English society.

At the top stood the "barristers," the aristocracy of the legal profession. Organized in their ancient "Inns of Court" in London near the High Courts, they possessed a monopoly over the practice in these courts. The "benchers" of Lincoln's Inn, The Inner Temple, The Middle Temple, and Gray's Inn from about the fifteenth century had held the power to admit to the bar; that is, to confer the right to be heard in court as a pleader. The English Civil War of the 17th century had scattered members of the Inns and interrupted their formal educational activities. Before the end of the 18th century even the requirement of a period of apprentice-residence had become a mere fiction. Still the Inns retained their monopoly.

But these gentlemanly barristers of the Inns offered only a small segment of the legal services of the community. Daily legal needs were met by at least two other quite distinct occupations. "Attorneys" were not authorized to plead in court but it was their function to set the machinery of the court in motion on behalf of a client. They were admitted to their monopoly by the judges of the courts in which they practiced, each court acquiring its own limited number of attorneys, who were not necessarily authorized to practice elsewhere. Another branch of the profession (called "solicitors") were the private legal agents, who were neither authorized to plead in the High Courts nor to set lawsuits in motion, but who looked after routine legal matters for their clients. These solicitors were a varied lot: some were also attorneys, some were not; some flourished in the Courts of Chancery. They multiplied rapidly to serve the rising landed and commercial classes. One resentful barrister in the early 17th century complained that the solicitors "like the grasshoppers in Egypt, devour the whole land." There were also the notaries, in their Scriveners' Company, who prepared all legal documents which had to be authenticated by a seal, the patent agents, and still other minor specialists.

Basic was the social distinction which separated barristers or "counsellors"—who alone were gentlemen and thus members of a true "profession"—from all the others. "There ought always to be preserved," the English judges ordered in 1614, "a difference between a counsellor at law, which is the principal person next unto the serjeants and judges in administration of justice, and attorneys and solicitors which are but ministerial persons and of an inferior nature." Solicitors had begun as mere agents, servants, or stewards; and attorneys were akin to tradesmen, since they supported themselves on the fees of individual customers. But it was from the ranks of barristers that the judges were drawn. Unlike tradesmen or craftsmen they did not receive "fees," but rather "honoraria," which neither then nor today are collectible by legal process.

To move all these fine distinctions across the ocean defied the efforts of even the most devout admirer of English institutions. The American uncertainty as to what really made a man a "gentleman" had blurred all the lines between high-tone "professions" and other occupations. Since there was no single center of appellate litigation in America, there was no one place where ambitious young pleaders and cadet-judges could learn their lessons. The higher colonial courts were dispersed into thirteen different headquarters, each with its slightly different laws. There was no American London where lawyers could consolidate their monopoly. Most important perhaps was the fact that for a long time legal business was too scarce to support so many specialties.

Whatever the reasons, there was no developed legal profession in any of the colonies before the mid-18th century. The ancient English prejudice against lawyers secured new strength in America. Despite the occasional outbursts in England against lawyers (as early as Jack Cade's Rebellion in 1450 and as recently as the Civil War of the 17th century), they were not dislodged from power and privilege; the Inns of Court, the Scriveners' Company, and other ancient guilds remained their strongholds. America had no such citadels of monopoly to begin with. Here where courts were more loosely and more extemporaneously organized, and where even judges commonly lacked legal training, distrust of lawyers became an institution. By the later 18th century when American commerce required a more skilled legal profession, it had already been determined that men of legal learning would not acquire the upper-class monopolistic position they held in England.

The newly-shaped ruling group in each colony preferred to keep the privileges which an established legal profession might have taken from them. In Virginia, for example, the landed aristocracy did much of their own law work rather than create a new class of colonial lawyers. In Massachusetts Bay the clergy, supported by Puritan prejudice against lawyers, delayed the growth of a trained, self-conscious bar: the colony's earliest known provision affecting lawyers (Body of Liberties, Art. No. 26) prohibited any man from giving a reward to another to represent him in court. In New York, too, the merchants and large landowners were unwilling to hand over any of their powers to a legal aristocracy. In Pennsylvania, the Quakers tried to avoid legal process altogether by using laymen as "common peacemakers."

But while the colonies could live and even prosper without barristers, solicitors, or scriveners, they could not live without law. As they became more populous and wealthy and as their commercial life became more intricate, some men made the law their special business. Before the end of the colonial era each colony possessed something like a legal profession. Nobody had planned the result, but each colony had provided for its needs in its own way. Each by a separate path had arrived at a common New World destination, which was as remote intellectually as it was geographically from the port-scented halls of London's Inns of Court. The scarcity of professional apparatus together with the lack of licensing guilds in law encouraged an informal apprentice system of training. English solicitors and attorneys had long been trained in something like an apprentice system. An Act of Parliament in 1729 required five years of apprenticeship under formally-drawn "articles" before a solicitor or attorney could practice in any court. The gentlemanly barristers, however, remained autonomous. For those socially and financially qualified, admission to their particular monopoly was, one historian has observed, like the return of stolen goods "without any questions being asked." For them there was not even a general requirement of apprenticeship. In colonial America, however, an apprenticeship, usually less formal than that required for English attorneys and solicitors, was the door to all branches of the legal profession.

Diversity was the rule. In New England and in the middle colonies by the time of the Revolution there had grown up a haphazard, weakly organized legal profession, with little esprit. In larger colonies, admission to legal practice tended to be dispersed into the different courts, each of which admitted its practitioners on whatever criteria appealed to it. In the smaller colonies (Rhode Island, Connecticut, and Delaware, for example), where all the judges and practitioners were likely to know one another, a lawyer who had been admitted by any one of the courts was generally allowed to practice in all of them. In North Carolina, New York, and New Jersey, Royal Governors held the technical power to appoint all attorneys, but they generally appointed only on the recommendation of a judge or a court. The earliest American association of lawyers was probably that in New York, which was founded sometime before 1748 and disappeared soon after 1765; in Massachusetts a bar association did not come into being until 1761. In all these colonies in the 18th century, practicing lawyers were distinguished by a higher level of education than that of the general population, but their education was quite unspecialized and had usually been secured in colonial colleges.

In the South, especially in Virginia and South Carolina, cities were fewer and English institutions were more highly valued and more consciously imitated. There the highest courts, though sometimes indirectly, controlled the admission of all attorneys. The leading practitioners had attended the Inns of Court in London. This vogue of the Inns seems to have increased unaccountably after about 1750: of approximately 236 American-born members of the Inns of Court before 1815, over half were admitted between 1750 and 1775. Of the whole figure nearly one-third came from South Carolina, nearly one-quarter from Virginia, and more came from Maryland than from Pennsylvania, New York, or Massachusetts. All this fits with the legal conservatism of the Southern leaders of the American Revolution. Who knew better than they the ancient ways of English lawyers and the traditional rights of Englishmen?

In America, then, the variety of climate, economy, landscape, and local tradition produced a variety of standards for the legal profession. The lack of a single commercial or political capital expressed and re-enforced this variety; there was no metropolitan focus for monopoly. The

Southern aristocracy's effort to make the Inns of Court the headquarters of their legal profession failed: London was too far away.

There did grow up a simpler, less snobbish kind of distinction: not a *dividing* or specializing of the profession, but an informal *grading* of practitioners by their education and experience. In some places only the better educated and longer experienced lawyers were allowed to practice in the highest courts. The few serious efforts (in early Virginia statutes, for example) to transplant the English distinctions were short lived: young Southern barristers, returned from the Inns of Court, for a while seemed to dominate practice in colonial courts, but the Revolution interrupted the flow of students to the Inns and disintegrated this distinction before it was well established. Even in Virginia in 1810 the courts plainly declared that the functions of a barrister and of an attorney were "inseparably blended in the same person."

The erasing of boundaries between the petty domains of the barrister, the solicitor, and the attorney was less significant than the breakdown of the walls which in Old England kept legal knowledge from the common citizen. Where land was more a commodity than an heirloom, many more people became landowners and, of necessity, learned some law. As colonials acquired personal knowledge of the legal rights of Englishmen, they distrusted still more the licensed professional monopolist.

One of the reasons we know so little about American law in the colonial era is that so many of the judges were laymen. They seem to have paid little attention to English precedents, only a few of which were available in the colonies, or to American precedents, none of which were yet reported in print. Their own opinions usually went unreported. We know very little of the judges' notions of substantive law, for even when a decision was permanently recorded, the reasons were seldom given. In none of the American colonies before the end of the colonial era were the courts manned predominantly by professionally trained lawyers. Even in the highest court of Massachusetts Bay, which during the 18th century possessed a larger and better organized bar than any other colony, men learned in the law were rare. Of the nine Chief Justices of Massachusetts between 1692 and the Revolution, only three had specialized legal training, two at the Inns of Court and one in the colony; the rest were clergymen, physicians, merchants, or simply men of general education. Of the twenty-three Associate Judges during this period only three possessed any regular legal education, the rest being clergymen or laymen; two judges in the Court of Admiralty had been trained as English barristers. The judges of Massachusetts included no other professionally trained lawyers. The situation in the other colonies was not much different: if anything, trained lawyers on the Bench were still more rare; everywhere the lay judge was the rule.

Jefferson recalled that just after the mid-18th century, when he practiced at the bar of the General Court, Virginia Attorney General John Randolph owned three manuscript volumes of reports of cases decided in that court between 1730 and 1740. Although this was Virginia's highest court, its decisions on matters of English law (according to Jefferson) were "of little value, because the Judges of that court, consisting of the King's Privy Counsellors only, chosen from among the gentlemen of the country, for their wealth and standing, without any regard to legal knowledge, their decisions could never be quoted, either as adding to, or detracting from, the weight of those of the English courts, on the same point. Whereas, on our peculiar laws, their judgments, whether formed on correct principles of law, or not, were of conclusive authority."

Lawbooks were scarce by English standards. John Adams recorded in his autobiography that, seeking an American legal education, he had "suffered very much for want of books." Of about one hundred and fifty volumes of law reports which had been published in England before the American Revolution, only about a fifth were commonly used here; the proportion of treatises and textbooks was even smaller. The first volume of American law reports was not published until 1790.

Where laymen were judges, there was little incentive for advocates to be learned lawyers. In fact, technical legal learning might have been a disadvantage, for an advocate could hardly show his learning without revealing the ignorance of the judge and arousing the suspicion of the jury. During a controversy between the Governor and the legislature of Massachusetts, John Adams "quoted largely" from Moore's Reports, "a law authority which no man in Massachusetts had ever read." Thomas Hutchinson (who had been Chief Justice of Massachusetts for over a decade) was not professionally trained in the law, but still was a great deal better read in the law than most men who sat on his bench. Adams reported that even Hutchinson was unacquainted with the authority and so "wriggled to evade it. He found nothing better to say than that it was 'the artificial reasoning of Lord Coke.'"

A colonial spokesman of the extreme anti-professional spirit was Chief Justice Samuel Livermore, who presided over the courts of New Hampshire in the late 18th century. "Judge Livermore, having no law learning himself," complained one of the few technically trained lawyers of the day, "did not like to be pestered with it at his courts. When West attempted to read law books in a law argument, the Chief Justice asked him why he read them; 'if he thought that he and his brethren did not know as much as those musty old worm-eaten books?' " In the very age when English lawyers were enthroning the strict rule of precedent, Judge Livermore dismissed a reference to an earlier contrary decision of his own by observing that "every tub must stand on its own bottom." "It is our business," Associate Justice John Dudley (a farmer and trader by occupation, who sat on the same bench with Livermore) charged a jury, "to do justice between the parties not by any quirks of the law out of Coke or Blackstone—books that I never read and never will—but by common sense as between man and man." When the learned Jeremiah Mason filed a "demurrer," one of the best-known devices in English legal pleading, Judge Dudley ridiculed the alien technicality as "no doubt an invention of the Bar to prevent justice."

If the American lawyer sometimes possessed less legal learning than his English counterpart, the literate American layman possessed more of it. Some lay judges—like two Chief Justices of Massachusetts, William Stoughton (1692-1701) and Samuel Sewall (1718-28)—had read widely in law and compared not unfavorably with many contemporary English judges. "Generally in our colonies," observed Dr. William Douglass, "particularly in New-England, people are much addicted to quirks in the law; a very ordinary country man in New-England is almost qualified for a country-attorney in England."

In England, the 18th century was the era of professional systematizing on a grand scale: Matthew Bacon's "Abridgment" appeared in 1736; Charles Viner's famous legal encyclopaedia (in 23 volumes) in 1742-53; Comyns' "Digest" in 1762. The great success of Viner's work financed the first professorship of English Law at Oxford, held by Sir William Blackstone, who delivered there as lectures his famous "Commentaries." And Blackstone's *Commentaries on the Laws of England* (1765-69) was the most ambitious and most successful effort ever made to reduce the disorderly overgrowth of English law to an intelligible and learnable system. Needless to say, colonial America produced no great legal systems or encyclopaedias. What it did produce were the varied, dispersed, and miscellaneous efforts of hundreds of laymen, semi-lawyers, pseudo-lawyers, and of a few men of solid legal learning. Of all the known legal treatises (about sixty) published in the American colonies before 1788, not a single one was properly a treatise for professional lawyers. Instead, they were editions of *The Constables Pocket-Book* and similar handbooks to help laymen do the work of lawyers.

"In no country perhaps in the world is the law so general a study," observed Edmund Burke in a famous passage in his speech on conciliation with America, ". . . all who read, and most do read, endeavor to obtain some smattering in that science." He saw the broad significance in this American dissolution of the lawyers' monopoly: such a citizenry would not allow itself to be oppressed. The people of the colonies would be united by their common understanding, or misunderstanding, of their legal rights. Was it not a fact—Burke said he learned it from an eminent bookseller—that by 1775 Blackstone's *Commentaries* had sold nearly as many copies in America as in England?

While Blackstone had violated the spirit of the common law by confining it in a system, he had provided for the first time the means by which any literate person could grasp the large outlines of his legal tradition. The vogue of Blackstone, who went through numerous American editions in the late 18th and early 19th centuries, therefore proclaimed the popularity and the thinness of legal knowledge in America. Blackstone was to American law what Noah Webster's blue-back speller was to be to American literacy. With nothing more than the four volumes of the *Commentaries* at hand, anyone—however far from ancient professional centers, from courts or legislatures—could become an amateur lawyer. Blackstone was a godsend to the rising American, to the ambitious backwoodsman and the aspiring politician. One of the delightful ironies of American history is that a snobbish Tory barrister, who had polished his periods to suit the taste of young Oxford gentlemen, became the mentor of Abe Lincoln and thousands like him. By making legal ideas and legal jargon accessible in the backwoods, Blackstone did much to prepare self-made men for leadership in the New World.

33

The Fusion of Law
and Politics

DURING the whole colonial period, America probably did not produce a single lawyer who was deeply learned by the strict English standards. Americans tended to be smatterers and admirers of the law, never its high priests; few if any of them were thoroughly at home in the man-made jungle of conveyancing, bills in chancery, and real actions.

Still, even the scarcity of lawbooks and the meagerness of the technical apparatus of legal learning did have some advantages. The few books available, while sometimes overvalued and idolatrized, were often thoroughly mastered. Jefferson found his legal learning in a few classics like Bracton, Coke, and Blackstone (which, as his Commonplace Book shows, he reread and made his own). He was more likely to see the broad outlines than if he had wandered in a library overflowing with the disordered legal lore of all past ages. In Lord Coke, for example, Jefferson saw not merely a crabbed legalist, but the champion of a broad and still relevant position: "a sounder Whig never wrote, nor profounder learning in the orthodox doctrines of British liberties. Our lawyers were then all Whigs." Jefferson much preferred Coke to "the honeyed Mansfieldism of Blackstone" which he thought had bred a subtle Toryism, even among the younger American lawyers who called themselves Whigs. Jefferson's reverence for the pristine Anglo-Saxon form of English common law—however vaguely grounded in historical facts—provided him with a framework for a sensible legal simplicity and for refurbishing the rights of Englishmen.

More than one wise modern lawyer has noted how the lawyer-framers of the Federal Constitution were served by the fact that they had so few books. Justice Miller, one of the ablest men to sit on the Supreme Court in the late 19th century, described ignorance as a major shaping factor in the law of our Western states; the first judges, he is supposed to have observed, "did not know enough to do the wrong thing, so they did the right thing."

The New World abounded with legal problems for which English precedents either did not exist, or were not available on this side of the Atlantic. So American judges boldly extrapolated half-understood principles or ingeniously adapted half-irrelevant English legislation. These tendencies were reenforced in the last third of the 18th century by the convenient appearance of Blackstone's *Commentaries,* which also deprived colonial lawyers of the dangerous temptation of making their own code.

While American legal knowledge became simplified and popular, the very idea of law acquired a new flavor which would long influence American legal thinking and political institutions. Any system of common law looks at how things have been done to determine how they ought to be done: it respects the going machinery of society and looks primarily to its functioning rather than to sudden legislation or to a legal code. Strangely enough this tendency was reënforced in colonial America. The boundary between technical "law" (once the monopoly of a learned class) and every other kind of knowledge became less clear.

To Americans like Jefferson the laws seemed interfused with everything else in the community. The numerous letters which Jefferson wrote to aspiring law students advised them to acquire a good general education, to read widely, and not to neglect languages, mathematics, or natural philosophy. "This foundation being laid, you may enter regularly on the study of the laws, taking with it such of its kindred sciences as will contribute to eminence in its attainment. The principal of these are physics, ethics, religion, natural law, belles lettres, criticism, rhetoric and oratory. The carrying on several studies is attended with advantage. Variety relieves the mind as well as the eye."

Colleges introduced "legal" matter, not for professional reasons, but because it was closely connected with theological and "philosophical" studies. The first curriculum of King's College listed for the fourth year "the Chief Principles of Law and Government, together with History, Sacred and Profane" and soon established a professorship of natural law. Jefferson's own plans, both for the College of William & Mary and later for the University of Virginia, included a broad study of law in close relation to humanistic subjects. The wider context of American legal studies, which shows how far the American concept of the profession had drifted from its English guild backgrounds, was nowhere better expressed than in President Ezra Stiles's plan (1777) for a professorship of law at Yale:

> The Professorship of Law is equally important with that of Medicine; not indeed towards educating Lawyers or Barristers, but for forming Civilians [citizens]. Fewer than a quarter perhaps of the young gentlemen educated at College, enter into either of the learned professions of Divinity, Law or Physic: The greater part of them after finishing the academic Course return home, mix in with the body of the public, and enter upon Commerce or the cultivation of their Estates. And yet perhaps the most of them in the Course of their Lives are called forth by their Country into some or other of the various Branches of civil Improvement & the public offices in the State. Most certainly it is worthy of great attention, the Discipline and Education of these in that knowledge which shall qualify them to become useful Members of Society, as Selectmen, Justices of Peace, Members of the Legislature, Judges of Courts, & Delegates in Congress. How Happy for a community to abound with men well instituted in the knowledge of their Rights & Liberties? This Knowledge is catching, & insinuates [among those] not of liberal Education—to fit them for public service. It is greatly owing to the Seats of Learning among us that the arduous Conflict of

the present day has found America abundantly furnished with Men adequate to the great and momentous Work of constructing new Policies or forms of Government and conducting the public arrangements in the military, naval & political Departments & the whole public administration of the Republic of the United States, with that Wisdom & Magnanimity which already astonishes Europe and will honor us to late Posterity. . . . It is scarce possible to enslave a Republic of Civilians, well instructed in their Laws, Rights & Liberties.

In a later age, when the American legal profession was to become more self-conscious, it would boast of the decisive role of "lawyers" in founding the nation and its institutions. Of the fifty-six signers of the Declaration of Independence, twenty-five were "lawyers"; of the fifty-five members of the Constitutional Convention in Philadelphia, thirty-one were "lawyers"; in the first Congress, ten of the twenty-nine Senators and seventeen of the sixty-five Representatives were "lawyers." But, contrary to common belief, this does not show the importance of a specialized learned profession in the making of our nation. The American experience had not bred awe for the learned specialist in law or in anything else. The boundaries of all American professional privilege were hazy. What it does show is the pervasiveness of legal competence among American men of affairs and the vagueness of the boundary between legal and all other knowledge in a fluid America. How little does it tell us about Jefferson—a self-trained lawyer with a brief apprenticeship in George Wythe's office—to say that he was a "lawyer" by profession!

What it meant to be a lawyer in America was classically expressed in the career of Andrew Jackson, who at the age of twenty, after an apprenticeship of rollicking travels with an itinerant court and the tutelage of the convivial Colonel John Stokes, in 1787 was declared by the court to be "a person of unblemished moral character, and . . . competent . . . knowledge of the law."

This early breakdown of the walls around technical legal knowledge provides a clue to American political life for decades to come. Out of a distrust of lawyers grew a widening respect for law. The American Revolution could be framed in legal language because that language spoke for the literate community. The great issues of American politics through the Civil War in the 19th century and the New Deal in the 20th would be cast in legal language—the sacred test of "constitutionality"—precisely because Americans saw the revered legal framework as the skeleton on which the community had grown. In this use of a legal test for politics there was a kind of conserving narcissism not often found among nonprimitive nations. In the world of dreams-come-true the community had begun to make its actual image the mold of its desires.

PART EIGHT

NEW WORLD MEDICINE

"They have the Happiness to have very few Doctors, and those such as make use only of simple Remedies, of which their Woods afford great Plenty. And indeed, their Distempers are not many, and their Cures are so generally known, that there is not Mystery enough, to make a Trade of Physick there, as the Learned do in other Countries, to the great oppression of Mankind."

ROBERT BEVERLEY

34

Nature-Healing and
Simple Remedies

THE AMERICAN EXPERIENCE hardly encouraged great work in the physical sciences. Even in the biological sciences the colonial period was barren of theoretical advance. But, in some fields of science which had become overgrown with dogmatic learning in Europe, the simplicity of American life as well as American naïveté proved fruitful in their own way. Medicine—including materia medica, or what was later called pharmacy or pharmacology—was one such field.

Natural history (especially botany) and medicine were closely connected in the 18th century. In those days the most commonly used medicines were botanical, and the most important treatises on botany were "herbals"—catalogs of common medicinal plants, telling where and how they grew and what they were good for. Nothing was more natural than that European-trained physicians, finding themselves in a new land with many unfamiliar plants, should seize the opportunity for botanical discoveries. Even laymen studied American flora in the hope of adding to medical knowledge.

In 1610, during the unhappy early years of the Jamestown colony, the Governor and Council wrote to the London Company about widespread sickness ("strange fluxes and agues") and dwindling medical supplies. The company physician, Dr. Lawrence Bohun, looked for the possible medical uses of local plants. Among other things, he found in the gum of white poplar a balm which would "heale any green wound," and he experimented with sassafras, which was common around Jamestown. Tobacco, from its first discovery, was of interest to Europeans for its medicinal possibilities. Harriot's *Briefe and True Report of the New Found Land of Virginia* (1588) touted tobacco as a medicine which "purgeth superfluous fleame & other grosse humors, openeth all the pores & passages of the body: by which meanes the use thereof, not only preserveth the body from obstructions; but also if any be, so that they have not beene of too long continuance, in short time breaketh them: whereby their bodies are notably preserved in health, and know not many greevous diseases wherewithall wee in England are oftentimes afflicted." It was claimed that smoking tobacco would heal gout and ague, cure hangovers, and reduce fatigue and hunger. The "Jamestown Weed" (*datura stramonium*), which modern medicine has proved to be sedative and antispasmodic when taken in small doses, and narcotic and poisonous when taken in larger doses, was praised for its "cooling" effect.

Robert Beverley in 1705 observed "the Planters abhorring all Physick, except in desperate cases":

> The Planters . . . have several Roots natural to the Country, which in this case they cry up as Infallible. They have the Happiness to have very few Doctors, and those such as make use only of simple Remedies, of which their Woods afford great Plenty. And indeed, their Distempers are not many, and their Cures are so generally known, that there is not Mystery enough, to make a Trade of Physick there, as the Learned do in other Countries, to the great oppression of Mankind.

It was two eminent English physicians who persuaded Mark Catesby to undertake the travels in 1710-19 which produced his *Natural History of Carolina, Florida and the Bahama Islands.* He found many therapeutic plants, including the May-apple, snake-root, ginseng, and witch-hazel. Among the most useful was the so-called "Tooth-Ache tree" whose "leaves smell like those of Orange; which with the Seeds and Bark, is aromatic, very hot and astringent, and is used by the People inhabiting the Sea Coasts of Virginia and Carolina for the tooth-ach, which has given it its name." Even Dr. John Morgan, who was devoted to the ways of European medicine and hoped for the establishment in America of all the respectable rigidities of European medical training, could not overlook the peculiarly American opportunities:

We live on a wide extended continent of which but the smallest portion, even of the inhabited part, has yet been explored. The woods, the mountains, the rivers and bowels of the earth afford ample scope for the researches of the ingenious. In this respect an American student has some considerable advantages over those of Europe, viz. The most ample field lies before us for the improvement of natural history. The countries of Europe have been repeatedly traversed by numerous persons of the highest genius and learning, intent upon making the strictest search into everything which those countries afford; whence there is less hopes or chance for the students who come after them to make new discoveries. This part of the world may be looked upon as offering the richest mines of natural knowledge yet unriffled, sufficient to gratify the laudable thirst of glory in young inquirers into nature. The discovery must greatly enrich medical science. . . . How many plants are there, natives of this soil, possessed of peculiar virtues?

This natural-history emphasis among American doctors was encouraged not only by New World opportunities, but even by one of the ancient dogmas of European medicine, the doctrine of "signatures." This dogma, expressed in the motto *similia similibus* ("like by like"—a doctrine which was to be curiously confirmed by the use of inoculation) implied that there was a necessary providential coincidence between the place where a disease occurred and the place where its remedy would be found. By the end of the 18th century some scientists were beginning to doubt this generalization, but it was so widely held that Benjamin Smith Barton's *Collections for an Essay towards a Materia Medica* (1801-1804) described as "trite" the theory "that every country possesses remedies that are suited to the cure of its peculiar diseases . . . that the principal portion of indigenous remedies is to be found among the vegetables of the countries in which the diseases prevail." Thus it was widely believed that the remedy for rattlesnake bite would probably be found on the same American terrain where the rattlesnake was found. And, sure enough, *Polygala Senega* (rattlesnake root) proved to be just the thing! Well might the Rev. Nicholas Collin, rector of the Swedish Churches in Pennsylvania and something of an inventor and natural historian, exclaim: "The bountiful Creator discovers his marvels in proportion to our wants . . . every country has native remedies against its natural defects." Even when this ancient dogma was diluted into only a hypothesis or a suspicion, it still encouraged students of American diseases to take special interest in the plants the Creator had placed here.

In America trained physicians showed an impressive and fruitful interest in the American landscape, its climate, its peculiar plants and animals. In part this was, of course, only an effect of the close traditional association (not particularly fortunate on either side) of botany and medicine as European academic subjects. But in those days most scientists, other than mathematicians and astronomers, commonly began with medical training. Carl Linnaeus, the great Swedish botanist, had been trained in medicine, and Herman Boerhaave, the director of a botanic garden, dominated European medicine in the early 18th century from his professorship of botany and medicine at the University of Leyden. To his disciples a botanical garden was standard equipment for medical institutions. Even in the early 19th century, the College of Physicians and Surgeons in New York City still maintained a botanical garden for teaching purposes.

Many of the leading American naturalists in the provincial age had medical backgrounds. Some, like John Bartram and John Clayton, were self-educated, but Cadwallader Colden, for example, possessed a London medical education, and Benjamin Smith Barton, author of the first notable American treatise on botany (*Elements of Botany*, 1803), and professor of medicine at the University of Pennsylvania, had come to the subject through materia medica.

Especially in the South, where books and trained experts of any kind were scarce, the physicians—often the only persons of scientific training for miles around—became the leading botanical discoverers. The career of Dr. Alexander Garden, after whom the "Gardenia" was named, was a parable of the opportunities, temptations, and limitations of American life. During his thirty years as a physician in Charleston, South Carolina, he discovered many new species and genera and was perhaps the most accomplished American botanist of the age; but even he never produced a significant systematic work. His most important scientific writing was in his letters. Soon after arriving in Charleston in 1752 with a medical degree from Edinburgh, where his botanical interests had been stimulated in the University's botanical gardens, he took up a correspondence with European naturalists including Linnaeus, and became acquainted with Americans like Colden, Clayton, and John Bartram, with whom he exchanged observations. Although energetic and imaginative, Garden's diffuse interests tended to be focused mainly on the questions put to him by European scientists. "In Charleston we are a set of the busiest, most bustling, hurrying animals imaginable," he complained, "and yet we really do not do much, but we must appear to be doing. And this kind of important hurry appears among all ranks, unless among the gentlemen planters, who are absolutely above every occupation but eating, drinking, lolling, smoking and sleeping, which five modes of action constitute the essence of their life and existence." Linnaeus urged him to collect the fish, reptiles, and insects of Carolina, with the result that Garden's name appeared more often than that of any other American in the famous twelfth edition of Linnaeus' *Systema Naturae*. But Garden never became more than a devoted gatherer of the raw materials from which European scientists built their systems.

Dr. John Mitchell of Urbanna, Virginia, who had also been trained in Edinburgh, claimed twenty-five new genera of plants, which made him the rival of Garden as a botanical discoverer. He described to the Royal Society the life-cycle and reproductive mechanism of that peculiar American animal, the opossum, and he inquired into the environmental causes of differences of color in the human races. The first satisfactory map of British and French North America (1755), which was used at the Peace Conference of 1783 and was still standard at the end of the century, was his work.

The members of this far-flung circle of American physician-naturalists were held together by their collaboration and by their half-known and tantalizingly amorphous American subject-matter. The systematizing of their knowledge they left to their correspondents in England, France, Germany, Holland, and Sweden, while they threw their energy into collecting, describing, and interpreting the natural novelties of their New World.

*   *   *

Any student of European medical education during the 17th and 18th centuries cannot fail to see the significance of this concrete and practical focus of the energies of American physicians. European medical learning, especially in the great University centers, was still enveloped in dogma. "Vitalists," "iatrochemists," and "iatrophysicists" argued with one another over which of their single causes explained all human health. With few exceptions, every eminent professor of medicine offered his own simplistic explanation of all bodily functions; every illness was supposed somehow to be another maladjustment of the general "system" of the body. Some attributed all diseases to disorder in the "humors," others to disturbance of the bodily "tension," and still others to even cruder doctrinaire causes. American physicians, if academically trained at all, had been trained in such dogmas, but the absence of American medical schools until 1765 removed them from the arenas of such tempting but fruitless debate. Later, as American medical education "improved," more such medical dogmatists would be found on this side of the water. Perhaps the most famous of them was Benjamin Rush, who expounded a monistic theory of bodily tension and who had nearly unbounded faith in bleeding. The ultimate proof of his theory was that any patient who was bled long enough would eventually relax!

Even the most charitable historian cannot be impressed by the amount of useful knowledge at the disposal of those learned European Doctors of Physick in the 18th century. The rise of Newtonian physics, a grand new system, seemed to encourage doctors in their temptation to make a simple system of the body. It was not until the growth of pathological anatomy, stimulated by the work of Morgagni of Padua in 1761, that the classification, understanding, and successful remedying of specific diseases made significant progress in the European medical schools. Until well into the 19th century dogmas were so rigid, theories so doctrinaire, hands and instruments so germ-ridden, and "remedies" so enervating that the learned doctor often did less to cure than to kill the patient. If the American patient had no other advantage, he was lucky that so much learned error had not been brought to these shores.

The common medical treatments here did not cure any more effectively than those administered in the Old World, but they probably interfered less with the patient's recovery. While the European physician frequently relied on extreme measures, which carried his simplistic dogma to its logical—if sometimes fatal—conclusion, the American amateur was more likely to let nature take its course. Instead of relying on ruthless emetics, purges, and bleeding (what medical historians have called "heroic" remedies), the self-trained practitioner was inclined to more timid and less damaging treatments.

The ministers in early Massachusetts, who were probably most familiar with the diseases of their community, were inclined to prescribe such wholesome and harmless treatments as rest, fresh air, and massage. The first medical publication of British North America was not written by a trained physician. *A Brief Rule to Guide the Common-People of New-England How to Order Themselves and Theirs in the Small Pocks, or Measels*, by Thomas Thacher, minister of the Old South (Third) Church in Boston, was published in January 1678 at the height of a smallpox epidemic. This broadside contained nothing new. It was apparently cribbed from the great English physician Thomas Sydenham— himself a pioneer in opposing "heroic" treatments—who had urged allowing "Nature to do her own work, requiring nothing of the Physician, but to regulate her, when she is exorbitant, and to fortifie her, when she is too weak." The single sheet which Thacher composed was a simple list of thirty numbered items in lay language. "As soon as this disease therefore appears by its signs, let the sick abstein from Flesh and Wine, and open Air, let him use small Bear warmed with a Tost for his ordinary drink, and moderately when he desires it. For food use water-gruel, water-potage, and other things having no manifest hot quality, easy of digestion, boild Apples, and milk sometimes for change, but the coldness taken off." Thacher freely confessed himself "though no Physitian, yet a well wisher to the sick," but doctors even now agree that Thacher's *Brief Rule* gave an adequate description of smallpox in nearly modern terms and offered a sensible regimen for the patient. It was a useful guide, perhaps even more useful than one by a learned doctor would have been. It was reprinted during the epidemics of 1702, and again in 1721.

In America it was not only the layman who inclined toward simpler, more common-sense treatments. The therapeutics of Virginia physicians in the 17th century was much simpler than that of their English contemporaries. Drugs, especially the exotic imported ones, were extremely expensive, and apothecaries skilled in elaborate concoctions were rare on this side of the ocean. Master pharmacists in Virginia sent their apprentices into the woods to find native remedies; most of their medicines were therefore simple, home-made, and less likely to disturb the healing course of nature. We cannot appreciate this simplicity until we have seen the indigestible concoctions of learned European doctors, which included human excreta, urine, and nearly everything else, mixed by complicated formulae. American physicians, especially the more learned of them, were not always free from such well-established practices: Governor Winthrop, for example, used to prescribe a paste made from wood lice. Cotton Mather reported to the Royal Society in London in 1724 that Boston physicians advised the swallowing of "Leaden Bullets" for "that miserable Distemper which they called the Twisting of the Guts." On one occasion the prescription entered the lung of a patient; "from which . . . unhappy experiments, I think, I should endure abundant, before I tried such a remedy."

Even the eminent 19th-century physician Dr. Oliver Wendell Holmes (the Autocrat of the Breakfast Table) though hostile to the Puritans, had to admit that the remedies of their clergymen-physicians were less harmful than those of their European contemporaries.

> What has come down to us of the first century of medical practice, in the hands of Winthrop and Oliver, is comparatively simple and reasonable. I suspect that the conditions of rude, stern life, in which the colonists found themselves in the wilderness, took the nonsense out of them, as the exigencies of a campaign did out of our physicians and surgeons in the late [Civil] war. Good food and enough of it, pure air and water,

cleanliness, good attendance, an anaesthetic, an opiate, a stimulant, quinine, and two or three common drugs, proved to be the marrow of medical treatment; and the fopperies of the pharmacopoeia went the way of embroidered shirts and white kid gloves and malacca joints, in their time of need. 'Good wine is the best cordiall for her,' said Governor John Winthrop, Junior, to Samuel Symonds, speaking of that gentleman's wife,—just as Sydenham, instead of physic, once ordered a roast chicken and a pint of canary for his patient in male hysterics.

One of the best examples of the dangers of the overzealous physician was in the area of prenatal care. In the days before antisepsis, when the causes of childbed fever were still unknown, it was during prenatal examination that the physician was most likely to introduce infection. The crude statistics of deaths from puerperal sepsis in Virginia before 1860 show a much higher mortality rate among whites attended by doctors than among Negroes attended by midwives. Similarly, the amateur, personal, small-scale nursing of colonial Virginia seems to have been superior to that of the great English municipal hospitals, where the poor, the insane, and the sick were brought together and where the manners and morals of the nurses were proverbially corrupt.

The scarcity of professionals taught Virginians to do things for themselves. Crossing the back-country to a remote plantation or to survey their lands, they had to provide their own medical services: William Byrd, for example, had no physician on his expeditions. When traveling into the North Carolina borderlands in 1733, he was troubled by "an impertinent Tooth." "Tooth-Drawers we had none amongst us, nor any of the Instruments they make use of. However, Invention supply'd this want very happily, and I contriv'd to get rid of this troublesome Companion by cutting a Caper." Byrd simply tied a string from his tooth to a log, and capered about till the tooth came out.

On any large plantation there was almost daily need for the layman to act the doctor. The Virginia planter could no more afford to summon a doctor for the minor ailments of his slaves than a modern farmer can afford to call a carpenter every time his barn or his fences require minor repairs. Even on large plantations the owner commonly relied on himself, his wife, or the overseer for routine medical treatment and for more serious cases in an emergency. When William Byrd arrived at his plantation near Richmond in October, 1732 and learned of a fatal epidemic of dysentery raging in the neighborhood, he instructed his steward "to make use of the following Remedy, in case it shou'd come amongst my People. To let them Blood immediately about 8 Ounces; the next day to give them a Dose of Indian Physic, and to repeat the

Vomit again the Day following, unless the Symptoms abated. In the meantime, they shou'd eat nothing but Chicken Broth, and Poacht Eggs, and drink nothing but a Quarter of a Pint of Milk boil'd with a Quart of Water, and Medicated with a little Mullein Root, or that of the prickly Pear, to restore the Mucus of the Bowels, and heal the Excoriation. At the same time, I order'd him to communicate this Method to all the poor Neighbors, and especially to my Overseers, with Strict Orders to use it on the first appearance of that Distemper, because in that, and all other Sharp Diseases, Delays are very dangerous." George Washington commonly prescribed for the ills of his slaves, and in his own last illness it was his overseer, and not a doctor, who first treated him by bleeding. When Thomas Jefferson returned to Monticello from the White House one summer, he inoculated with his own hand seventy or eighty people on his plantations and he supervised his neighbors in the inoculation of another hundred-odd.

Much of the burden of doctoring fell upon the planter's wife, who might be called out of bed at any hour of the night to deliver a baby or to care for the violently ill in the slave-quarters. The nursery for the infants of slave working-mothers was in her charge. "She takes great care of her negroes," the Marquis de Chastellux wrote in 1781 of Mary Willing Byrd, widow of William Byrd III, "makes them as happy as their situation will admit, and serves them herself as a doctor in time of sickness. She has even made some interesting discoveries on the disorders incident to them, and discovered a very salutary method of treating a sort of putrid fever which carries them off commonly in a few days, and against which the physicians of the country have exerted themselves without success."

It is not surprising to find medical guides for laymen among the commonest books in Virginia libraries. *Every Man his own Doctor; or, the Poor Planter's Physician* (1734) attained vast popularity by prescribing "plain and easy means for persons to cure themselves of all, or most of the distempers, incident to the climate, and with very little charge, the medicines being chiefly of the growth and production of this country." Benjamin Franklin published three editions of this book in Philadelphia (1734, 1736, 1737). The first pharmacopoeia ever printed in British America was Dr. William Brown's thirty-two page pamphlet, which he put together in 1778, in the stringent days of the Revolution, to list the simplest, cheapest, and most available drugs.

The colonial situation, which sometimes bred a disrespect for learning, also encouraged distrust of the omniscient professional, who already was receiving his share of ridicule in Europe. The elder William Byrd distrusted doctors so much that he would not call one even in his last illness. His son, the famous William Byrd II, also preferred his own practical methods. And in Franklin's Philadelphia people were handing about a pointed epigram of "The Advantages of having two Phisicians":

> One prompt Phisician like a sculler plies,
> And all his Art, and skill applies;
> But two Phisicians, like a pair of Oars,
> Convey you soonest to the Stygian Shores.

Jefferson in 1807 was eloquent against the presumptuous dogmatism of the physicians:

> Having been so often a witness to the salutary efforts which nature makes to re-establish the disordered functions, he [the wise physician] should rather trust to their action, than hazard the interruption of that, and a greater derangement of the system, by conjectural experiments on a machine so complicated & so unknown as the human body, & a subject so sacred as human life. Or, if the appearance of doing something be necessary to keep alive the hope & spirits of the patient, it should be of the most innocent character. One of the most successful physicians I have ever known, has assured me, that he used more bread pills, drops of colored water, & powders of hickory ashes, than of all other medicines put together. It was certainly a pious fraud. But the adventurous physician goes on, & substitutes presumption for knoledge. From the scanty field of what is known, he launches into the boundless region of what is unknown. He establishes for his guide some fanciful theory of corpuscular attraction, of chemical agency, of mechanical powers, of stimuli, of irritability accumulated or exhausted, of depletion by the lancet & repletion by mercury, or some other ingenious dream, which lets him into all nature's secrets at short hand. On the principle which he thus assumes, he forms his table of nosology, arrays his diseases into families, and extends his curative treatment, by analogy, to all the cases he has thus arbitrarily marshalled together. I have lived myself to see the disciples of Hoffman, Boerhaave, Stahl, Cullen, Brown, succeed one another like the shifting figures of a magic lantern, & their fancies, like the dresses of the annual doll-babies from Paris, becoming, from their novelty, the vogue of the day, and yielding to the next novelty their ephemeral favor. The patient, treated on the fashionable theory, sometimes gets well in spite of the medicine.
>
> From this side of the Atlantic, that Europe, which has taught us so many other things, will at length be led into sound principles in this branch of science.

While Americans seemed somewhat less vulnerable to complicated forms of quackery, their circumstances tempted them in the direction of

nature-healing. The bookish cure-alls of the Doctors of Physick were
sometimes replaced by the environmental cure-alls sensationally advertised in promotional literature: the New England air, the Virginia water,
the Georgia climate. Where Nature was so generous, men easily expected too much of her.

The record of the age did not yet justify Dr. David Ramsay's prophecy
on the second anniversary of Independence that the arts and sciences
"require a fresh soil, and always flourish most in new countries." He was
closer to the truth when he boasted of the success of amateur doctors
whose common sense was accomplishing what academic learning had
found difficult or impossible. "The pride of science is sometimes humbled
on seeing and hearing the many cures that are wrought by these pupils
of experience, who, without theory or system, by observation and practice
acquire a dexterity in curing common diseases."

35

Focus on the Community

IT WAS PRECISELY in the area of common diseases—which now
obviously became problems in public health—that American experience
had most to offer. Some diseases which in Europe seemed part of the
inevitable round of life could be avoided here by prudent public measures. Ailments which were endemic, or continually prevalent, in England
tended to become epidemic—sudden and dramatic menaces to the community—in America.

Public concern over a disease depends less on the actual mortality than
on the dramatic intensity with which it is impressed on the public. Although smallpox probably caused fewer fatalities among white settlers in
America in proportion to the population than it had in England, it occurred here almost exclusively in the spectacular form of epidemics.
During the 17th and 18th centuries in England and on the European
continent, smallpox was a common disease of childhood. By the time a
person had grown up he had almost certainly been exposed to it and

had either proven himself immune or had acquired immunity by surviving the disease. Smallpox was therefore not an epidemic disease among adults in Europe. But in America, where the disease had not existed until it was introduced by Europeans, it was much less widespread. Many inhabitants lived through childhood without having been exposed.

During the 18th century, a common American objection to sending sons to England for a higher education was the mortal danger from smallpox. When a French visitor, Francis Louis Michel, visited William & Mary College in 1702, he was surprised to find as many as forty students there; he learned that wealthy parents who formerly had sent their sons to England now preferred the intellectual crudities of a colonial education to the perils of the English smallpox. The Rev. Hugh Jones, in 1724, observed that more Virginians would have been given an English education "were they not afraid of the Small-Pox, which most commonly proves fatal to them." The church of Virginia might not have developed its distinctive features and might not have been quite so autonomous, if parents had been readier to risk an English education for children wishing to enter the church.

Because smallpox had been unknown among the Indians, they proved especially vulnerable. In 1633, as Governor Thomas Hutchinson later recorded in his *History,* "the small pox made terrible havock among the Indians of Massachusets. . . . They were destitute of every thing proper for comfort and relief and died in greater proportion than is known among the English. John Sagamore of Winesimet and James of Lynn with almost all their people, died of the distemper." Even as late as the 19th century, certain Indian tribes which had until then escaped the disease were being wiped out; fatalities in some tribes exceeded 90 per cent. There can be little doubt that more Indians died from epidemics than from white men's muskets.

Among the white settlers, too, smallpox was primarily an epidemic disease. It swept through the colonies at intervals—sometimes a generation apart—and afflicted large numbers of adults. No longer one of the normal trials of childhood, it became a sudden and terrifying scourge that paralyzed the community and forced the regular activities of commerce and government to be suspended. Where communities were small and nearly all types of skill were scarce, losing the only carpenter or gunsmith put everyone in trouble. Even the very high proportion of fatalities due to disease is no adequate measure of the impact on the life of the community.

Perhaps the most dramatic example of the public-health emphasis in American medicine came from New England, where compact Boston and the Puritan concern with community set the stage. One of the most successful onslaughts against disease in all American history took place there in the 18th century. How to treat the smallpox was publicly debated by doctors, ministers, and journalists. The unlikely hero of the story was none other than Cotton Mather (1663-1728), on whom has been focused the ill-informed hatred of generations of liberal historians. But sober scholarship has lately begun to divest Mather of his Mephistophelian character, so that we can now see him as a vivid symbol of the potentialities as well as the limitations of early New-England science.

Cotton Mather had a strangely miscellaneous, observant, and practical mind. We can understand Mather better if we think of him as an early version of Benjamin Franklin (1706-1790), who in fact heard Mather preach on several occasions in Boston. He had read Mather's *Essays to Do Good* (Franklin's first pen name was "Silence Do-Good"), and in his *Autobiography* called it the book "which perhaps gave me a turn of thinking that had an influence on some of the principal future events of my life." In it he probably discovered the literary genre which he was to make famous in his *Poor Richard*. Even Franklin's "Junto"—both the general idea and the detailed procedure for its meetings—seems to have been borrowed from Mather's scheme of neighborhood benefit societies for Boston. Some of the most characteristic of Franklin's enterprises were thus directly suggested by Cotton Mather, but more important than any direct influence were their intellectual affinities.

It is misleading to separate Mather and Franklin by the academic antitheses between "Calvinism" and "The Enlightenment." The similarities in the interests and achievements of these two great men reveal distinctive features of American culture in the provincial age: an undiscriminating universality of interest surprisingly unconfined by a priori theories; a lack of originality; an intense practicality; an unsystematic and random approach to philosophy; and, above all, a willingness to be challenged by New World opportunities. In his own day, Cotton Mather's fame as an observer of American novelties reached British scientists, who awarded him an honorary degree from the University of Aberdeen (1710) and a coveted membership in the Royal Society (1713).

By the standards of his day Mather was an alert and accurate observer of nature. His scientific communications (which counted nearly 100 after 1712) to European friends and fellow-naturalists included notes on American plants and Indian cures; on American birds, including the wild turkey, the eagle and the vast flights of pigeons; on the rattlesnake; on the violence of thunder and lightning in America; on a triton; on an egg found within a hen's egg; on Indian divisions of time; and on dozens of similarly miscellaneous items. In a letter (July 24, 1716) which accompanied a shipment of six or seven plants peculiar to America, he gave the earliest known account of plant hybridization. His observation significantly concerned Indian corn, a plant which later geneticists also found peculiarly well-suited to their experiments. Mather was even open-minded enough to accept the hypothesis, then newly expounded by Nehemiah Grew, that flowering plants reproduced sexually.

From his early years Cotton Mather had been interested in medicine. He had once thought of making it his profession, but the lack of formal courses on the subject at Harvard had left him to his own devices, and largely to independent reading. In this respect, too, Mather's career has a later parallel in that of Franklin; for, like Franklin's discoveries in electricity, Mather's medical ideas could hardly have grown in the mind of a learned professional.

So far as we now know, the first general treatise on medicine written in the English colonies in America was the work which Cotton Mather completed in 1724. The title of his work, "The Angel of Bethesda," came from the name of the famous healing-pool mentioned in the Gospel according to John (5:2-4), but it seems to have been suggested to Mather by the writings of the eminent physicist Robert Boyle. While Mather and others published many fragmentary items on such topics as smallpox and measles, this general work, although widely known to exist in manuscript, was not published during the 18th century. Cotton's son, Samuel, for a dozen years after Cotton's death had tried hard to have it published.

Mather's interest in diseases was probably sharpened by his Puritan theology, with its emphasis on original sin and on the dark dualism of man's nature. In a devious way the Puritan emphasis on sin thus seemed to reënforce the empirical emphasis of American science; it may even have helped liberate American medical practice from the dogmatism of their learned European contemporaries. To Mather, at least, this connection of ideas seemed obvious enough; he explained at the beginning of his first chapter:

> Lett us look upon Sin as the Cause of Sickness. There are it may be Two Thousand Sicknesses: and indeed, any one of them able to crush us! But what is the Cause of all? Bear in Mind, That Sin was that which first brought Sickness upon a Sinful World, and which yett continues to sicken the World, with a World of Diseases.

Mather's work became a survey of diseases. One of the proposals for its printing called it "An Essay upon the Common Maladies of Mankind: offering, first, The Sentiments of Piety, whereto the Invalids are to be awakened in and from their bodily Maladies. And then, a rich Collection of plain but potent and approv'd Remedies for the Maladies."

The book made no claim to originality. "Nor, can it be Expected," Mather explained, "that while Colonies are yett so much in their Infancy as ours are, and have had so many Serpents also to crush while in their cradles as ours have had, they can be so circumstanced as to produce many acute mathematicians, or allow them the Leisure for extraordinary Inventions and Performances." But Mather did himself an injustice: by the very organization and emphasis of his volume he had put himself among the most progressive medical students of his day. The idea of the separateness of diseases had only begun to make headway abroad. Until the middle of the 16th century the dominating concern of European medical men had been "the general state of the system" of which all diseases were thought to be mere variants. Only with the work of Paracelsus in the Renaissance was there a serious revival of the idea that there were many different diseases, each with its own causes and cures. In the 17th century the English physician Sydenham insisted that particular diseases might be as different as particular plants and animals, and that therefore they must be examined and classified in detail. How little progress had been made by 1700 appears from the fact that there were then known only two specific drugs (cinchona bark yielding quinine against malaria; and mercury against syphilis); even these had probably come directly from folk-medicine.

Mather's "Angel of Bethesda" expressed an empirical view alien to many learned European doctors. He showed himself less interested in the "causes" than in the remedies of diseases; his pages abound in what he called "remarkable, and often experimented" cures. In a chapter on the "Uncertainties and Contradictions" of Physicians, he illustrated the vagaries of learned doctors by their contradictory prescriptions for the consumption. "And here," Mather explains, "we will not concern ourselves with the Differences among the Physicians, about the Cause of this Distemper; (whereupon, who can read the Collection made by Dolaeus, and not cry out, The Diviners are mad!) but only see, how they differ about the Cure of it."

His hope that there might be a way to save the New England community from the scourge of smallpox was aroused by an item he read in the *Transactions of the Royal Society of London* for 1714. This was a letter from a Turkish doctor describing how "inoculation," or the deliberate infection of a healthy person with matter from a person suffering from the smallpox, usually produced a light case of the disease from which the patient recovered, and to which he was thereafter immune. Mather then wrote to a doctor in London:

How does it come to pass, that no more is done to bring this operation, into experiment & into Fashion—in England? When there are so many Thousands of People, that would give many Thousands of Pounds, to have the Danger and Horror of this frightful Disease well over with them. I beseech you, syr, to move it, and save more Lives than Dr. Sydenham. For my own part, if I should live to see the Small-Pox again enter into our City, I would immediately procure a Consult of our Physicians, to Introduce a Practice, which may be of so very happy a Tendency. But could we hear, that you have done it before us, how much would That embolden us!

Mather found his opportunity in April 1721, when a ship from the West Indies brought a smallpox epidemic to Boston. The events of the next decades sharpened the contrast between the medical opportunities on the two sides of the Atlantic. During the unusual outbreak of smallpox in London in that year, the fashionable Lady Mary Wortley Montagu, who had brought the practice from Turkey, finally persuaded George I to permit the inoculation of his two granddaughters. Despite the royal example, only about twenty scattered inoculations were performed in London; and, when two deaths occurred, the popular opposition increased and was reënforced by the medical profession. Inoculations temporarily ceased in England. They were soon resumed in considerable numbers in different parts of the country, but not enough in any one community to justify conclusions about the technique as a measure of public health. London, a sprawling city where smallpox was always present, was not a favorable proving-ground. No substantial progress was made until a serious London epidemic in 1752 focused public attention on the problem; and by that time the American successes, widely advertised in England, were an old story.

American progress against smallpox began when Mather publicly appealed to the physicians of Boston in early June 1721 to try inoculation to protect the community. He set off a violent controversy. As a whole the learned doctors—led by the splenetic Dr. William Douglass, the only physician in the city with a medical degree—opposed the experiment. They were understandably annoyed that laymen should try to tell them how to practice their art, and should urge techniques borrowed from "the Mussel-men, & faithful people of the prophet Mahomet." They did have the solid objection that the practice, as then crudely conducted, actually tended to spread the disease. But they leaned heavily on theological objections: to inoculate, they said, would violate "the all-wise Providence of God Almighty" by "trusting more the extra groundless Machinations of Men than to our Preserver in the ordinary course of Nature." *The New England Courant*, just begun by James Franklin with the help of his younger brother Benjamin, true to the conservatism of the colonial press, opposed Mather's new-fangled practice. But many of the clergy joined Mather in demanding a fair trial for inoculation. Passions ran high. Heated pamphlets were exchanged, with Mather producing over half a dozen. Public opinion became literally explosive: in November a bomb was thrown into Mather's house.

Everybody agreed that the cure of smallpox was a public problem. Despite the opposition, despite prohibition by the town government, and despite threats of divine vengeance, Zabdiel Boylston, supported by Mather and his clerical cohorts, managed to perform a number of inoculations in Boston during the epidemic. These were sufficiently numerous to provide statistical evidence that the calculated risk of death from inoculation was smaller than the risk in cases naturally contracted. In March 1722, after the worst of the epidemic was over, Mather pointed out to the Secretary of the Royal Society in London that of nearly 300 inoculated in Boston only five or six had died (and perhaps these had already been naturally infected before their inoculation), while of the more than 5000 who caught the disease naturally, nearly 900 had died. This meant that there was about nine times as much chance of death if one caught the smallpox in the ordinary course of infection as compared with the danger from inoculation. The fact that about half the population of Boston had contracted smallpox during the epidemic showed that from the point of view of the community as a whole the risk of inoculation was very much worth taking.

The collection of these Boston statistics was a pioneer work in public health, one of the first cases of quantitative analysis of such a medical problem. They later proved significant, not only in establishing inoculation as a measure of preventive medicine, but as valuable raw material for the development of the "calculus of probabilities" by mathematicians —Europeans, of course!

More than any other single fact, Mather's practical success with inoculation established the idea that the smallpox might eventually be conquered, and this incidentally opened men's minds to the curability of other diseases. Dr. Douglass himself bore witness to the power of the American empirical atmosphere; by the time the next Boston smallpox epidemic was imported from Ireland in 1729-30, he and most of his fellow physicians had been persuaded of the advantages of inoculation when properly controlled and they actually inoculated their own patients. In 1755 Douglass declared that the risk from inoculation was only two to three per cent and could still further be reduced. "I am at a loss for the reasons, why inoculation hitherto is not much used in our mother country, Great-Britain; considering that it has with good success been practised in our colonies or plantations, particularly in Boston, New-York, Philadelphia, and Charles-town of South-Carolina."

The influence of the Boston experiments spread up and down the colonies. When, early in 1738, a ship from Africa brought a smallpox epidemic to South Carolina—a province having "more Lands than Inhabitants to spare"—which had not suffered such a seizure for nearly thirty years, Dr. James Kilpatrick and his fellow physicians at once used inoculation on a large scale. In Charleston, which then possessed a population of around five thousand, one physician estimated that he inoculated 450 with his own hands. Before the epidemic abated about a thousand had received inoculation. The mortality rate for inoculated persons, according to Dr. Kilpatrick's account, was somewhere around one per cent, a minute figure compared with the heavy mortality of those naturally infected. In establishing inoculation as an American institution, a strong, if crude, empirical strain, a carelessness of theory, and an insistence on results were decisive. The dubious logic of Kilpatrick's propaganda pamphlet was often repeated: "That Nothing but the real Success of this Method could ever have continued it to this Time." But there was good sense in his warning that learned physicians beware of the "natural Shallowness and acquired Obscurity" which tempted them to ignore obviously successful results. There was a conscious continuity in the American practice; Kilpatrick, for example, was careful to offer a statistical chart of the earlier successes in the Boston epidemic of 1721.

At the same time, common sense itself seemed to oppose the practice. "The Novelty of seeking Security from a Distemper, by rushing into the Embraces of it," Dr. Kilpatrick observed, "could naturally have very little Tendency to procure it a good Reception on its first Appearance." And when popular and professional fears were reënforced by the "better opinion" back home in England they were not easily overcome. Nearly every colony prohibited inoculation at some time or other, but such laws did not stick. By 1760 the colonies were coming to regulate rather than to prohibit the practice; and by 1775, in the Middle and Southern Colonies at least, the laws aimed only to provide reasonable safeguards against the spread of infection by inoculated persons. Even in New England, where some laws prohibited the practice generally, the laws were suspended to allow inoculation during epidemics. In September 1774, when the Continental Congress was meeting in Philadelphia, the physicians of the city agreed to inoculate no more during the sitting of the Congress, "as several of the Northern and Southern delegates are understood not to have had that disorder."

Early in the Revolution the army carried smallpox all over the colonies. General George Washington, on the advice of Dr. John Morgan, physician-in-chief of the American armies, ordered the inoculation of the whole army. This mass inoculation, in special hospitals set up for the purpose, was probably the most extensive experiment of its kind until that day. When smallpox came to Boston again in 1792, nearly half of its twenty thousand inhabitants were inoculated.

Before the end of the colonial era, the smallpox menace—which increased in England until nearly 1800—was well under control in America: epidemics were less frequent and stirred less terror. A larger consequence of the American practical success was that it helped prepare men's minds, on both sides of the ocean, for the next step in the battle against the disease. At the end of the 18th century when Edward Jenner made the epochal discovery of vaccination, fewer people were frightened by the theoretic paradox. Within a dozen years of Jenner's discoveries and Benjamin Waterhouse's communication of them to the American newspaper-reading public (March 12, 1799 in the *Columbian Sentinel*), vaccination was widespread in America. State governments began subsidizing it, and the Congress authorized a Federal Vaccine Agent to send the virus post-free anywhere in the United States.

36

The General Practitioner

IN ENGLAND during America's provincial age, a "profession" could be precisely defined as an occupation "fit for gentlemen." Common usage referred (in Joseph Addison's phrase) to "the three professions of divinity, law, and physic." If none of these was sure to make a man rich, any one would give him a comfortably high social position. People included physicians among the professions; but they did not include surgeons or apothecaries, however skilled or learned, for theirs were not considered suitable occupations for members of the upper classes. These English boundaries between occupations, and hence between departments of knowledge, embodied the social snobbery of a well-established aristocracy. Exclusiveness, selfishness, and slothfulness had produced rigid corporations and petrified bodies of learning; they resisted new knowledge and new ways of doing things.

Next to the clergy, and perhaps the law, medicine was the earliest and most elaborately subdivided of English learned vocations. Nowhere were guild distinctions more subtle, more intricate, or more firmly entrenched. By the 18th century, however, the powerful forces of the Industrial Revolution were breaking down the ancient monopolies of the craft and commercial guilds; government regulation was becoming ineffective. But in areas of advanced and specialized learning, particularly in medicine, the old monopolies remained, and in some cases had even become more sharply defined. These occupational compartments perpetuated the compartments of thought.

In the early middle ages the "Doctor of Physick" was commonly trained in a monastic school; by the 15th century he was a man who had been graduated in medicine and had received from the University a license to practice. Yet his field was much more limited than that of the modern medical doctor. Necessarily a master of the classical languages in which medical knowledge from the past had been preserved, he was also a man of general learning. Thus, when Henry VIII chartered the Royal College of Physicians in 1518, he intended to set up both a learned academy and an exclusive guild for these practitioners of "physick."

Surgery was quite another matter. It held a much lower status. It had not been studied in the medieval universities, partly because of the ban on shedding of blood by the clergy and partly because its manual character made it less dignified. The healing and curing of wounds and all surgery and tooth-drawing came within the province of the barbers, who had had a guild of their own from the early fourteenth century. After 1540, practitioners of these skills were organized as the Barber-Surgeons, but a distinction within the guild forbade the barber to act as surgeon (except for drawing teeth) and forbade the surgeon to shave anyone. A widening social gulf then separated medicine and surgery, the two great branches of medical practice which now seem to us so closely related.

Pharmacy was still another specialty. Apothecaries originally were a species of grocer and were members of the grocers' guild, but in 1617 apothecaries received their own chartered monopoly and grocers were forbidden to sell drugs. Midwifery was yet another vocation. At least until the end of the 17th century it was practiced almost exclusively by women licensed by their bishops and later sometimes licensed by the Barber-Surgeons.

During the 17th and 18th centuries in England some changes—mostly for the worse—were taking place in the organization of the numerous medical professions. Rigidity and complexity increased, and there was no substantial improvement in the quality of instruction or in professional standards. By the 18th century, the Royal College of Physicians selected its entrants largely on the basis of their social accomplishments and ceased to offer any instruction worthy of the name; neither Oxford nor Cambridge had any longer an active school of medicine. Somehow or other—due perhaps to a line of brilliant practitioners—the surgeons' branch of the Barber-Surgeons' Company seems to have avoided fossilization. But they had troubles of their own; the physicians continued to lord it over them. A great nuisance which continued into the early 18th century was the ancient requirement that, before a surgeon could perform an operation, he had to secure a license from a bishop. Not until 1745 did the surgeons manage to secede from the barbers and form their own company. Apothecaries, following a lengthy conflict with the physicians, obtained legal authority in the early 18th century to carry on a limited and inferior type of medical practice. To add to this prolific confusion, there were numerous regional distinctions. By the end of the 18th century Great Britain had eighteen medical licensing authorities, each limited both in function and territory. Historians of the subject now throw up their hands at any effort to make sense of these myriad overlapping monopolies and regulations.

This attic-full of institutions was not transported to the New World, partly because of the lack of specialists. "Besides the hopes of being Safe from Persecution in this Retreat," William Byrd wrote in 1728, "the New Proprietors [of New Jersey] inveigled many over by this tempting Account of the Country: that it was a Place free from those 3 great Scourges of Mankind, Priests, Lawyers, and Physicians. Nor did they tell a word of a Lye, for the People were yet too poor to maintain these Learned Gentlemen." Although Byrd had oversimplified the reasons, he was accurate in observing that Americans were freer of learned monopolists than were their contemporaries in England.

The professional organization of doctors which developed here, in contrast with that of England, was loose; the boundaries of specialties were vague or non-existent. In the American colonies, governmental control over medical practice virtually disappeared. The tradition of licensing was not dead, but colonial regulations were unclear and unenforceable. The first medical law of Massachusetts Bay (1649) simply required that no person should administer any medical remedy "without the advice and consent of such as are skillfull in the same Art, (if such may be had) or at least of some of the wisest and gravest then present." Most colonial legislation on the subject was concerned with fees rather than with professional standards. The Assembly of Virginia as early as 1639 responded to protests against "the imoderate and excessive rates and prices exacted by practitioners of physick & chyrurgery." The Virginia Act of 1662 explained:

> Whereas the excessive and immoderate prices exacted by diverse avaritious and gripeing practitioners in phisick and chirurgery hath caused several hardhearted masters swayed by profitable rather than charitable respects, rather to expose a sick servant to a hazard of recovery, than put themselves to the certaine charge of a rigorous though unskilfull phisician, whose demands for the most part exceed the purchase of the patient, many other poore people also being forced to give themselves over to a lingring disease. . . .

The better-trained American physicians knew well enough that the European professional tradition required them to define their specialty and stick to it. Colonial students at the medical school of Edinburgh University, the main training-center for Americans abroad, formed a "Virginia Club" with articles signed by its members. The third article in 1761 was a solemn undertaking "That every member of this club shall make it his endeavor, if possible, for the honor of his profession, not to degrade it by hereafter mingling the trade of an apothecary or surgeon with it." In America, however, where the very distinction of a gentleman (and hence what was "fit" for him) was blurred, it was not so easy to confine oneself to proper gentlemanly pursuits. In English and other European rural communities, the fine professional distinctions did, of course, sometimes break down or become unenforceable. But in colonial America disregard of them was widespread.

The professional subdivisions were in fact of little practical significance among American doctors. Advertisements and indentures tell us of many, like Dr. Gustavus Brown in Charles County, Maryland (1734-40), who were practicing "Physick, Surgery, and Pharmacy." To these three distinct English occupations some colonials even added that of midwife. The occasional colonial non-conformist, like Dr. James McClurg, who had been educated at Edinburgh and stuck to his notions of a distinctive profession of physick, found himself unable to support his family. "This however is partly owing to my not uniting the apothecary's and surgeon's business with the physicians' as is common in this country. . . . It is easier perhaps to succeed to a certain degree as a surgeon and apothecary in this country than in any other." "I make use of the English word doctor," wrote the Marquis de Chastellux on his travels through America in 1781, "because the distinction of surgeon and physician is as little known in the army of Washington as in that of Agamemnon. We read in Homer, that the physician Macaon himself dressed the wounds. . . . The Americans conform to the ancient custom and it answers very well."

How, indeed, could nice distinctions be perpetuated in an America which lacked learned doctors, professional associations, academies, and legal or customary regulation? And so in America a fluid situation rather than ancient institutions shaped medical practice.

To earliest colonial New England, medical learning was transferred not so much by trained physicians as by ministers. In late 16th- and early 17th-century England some dissenting clergymen had studied medicine as a precautionary profession in case of their expulsion from the country. The Pilgrim Elder William Brewster, Edward Winslow, and Samuel Fuller all seem to have had such knowledge. For nearly a century after Fuller's death in 1633, there was no prominent specializing physician in Massachusetts. The medical needs of the community were served by ministers (like Thomas Thacher, who wrote the layman's brochure on how to treat smallpox), by schoolmasters, and by a remarkable line of governor-physicians. Governor John Winthrop, the first leader of Massachusetts Bay, was probably its leading medical adviser, treating patients about as well as did the average physician in England. His son, who became Governor of Connecticut, carried on an extensive practice, offering remote New Englanders by correspondence the best medical advice he could garner from his English books and acquaintances. There was hardly a political or religious leader of the region who did not dispense medical knowledge: Winslow treated the Indian chief Massasoit; the Apostle John Eliot tried to instruct the Indians in modern medicine; in times of epidemic the governors or assistants themselves commonly decided on proper health measures. The two great experimenters with the smallpox inoculation, Cotton Mather and Zabdiel Boylston, both lacked medical degrees. While in Old England the clergy had sometimes confined and stultified the practice of physick, in New England a versatile clergy helped both to free medicine from its old monopolistic bonds and to refresh it by a more empirical spirit.

Medical practice was thus dispersed into many different vocations. Of the fifteen pamphlets on medical subjects published in Boston between 1721 and 1752 of which we know the authors, only four (those by Dr. William Douglass) were written by a person who would have been accepted as a properly qualified physician in England. Not until 1781 was there a Medical Department at Harvard College or a Massachusetts Medical Society. The Society began spasmodic publication in 1790, but the printing of that year was not followed by another until eighteen years later. Protecting public health was a duty of the wise governor and the competent clergyman. Not only had numerous English specialties become amalgamated into the work of a general practitioner; the general practitioner himself had become more closely assimilated into the still larger class of persons concerned with the political and religious welfare of the community.

In the Southern colonies a similar result was produced by somewhat different causes. The European professional distinctions had not been imported there either, and a native professional organization had not yet come into being. If there was any distinction, it was simply between the men of more and of less education rather than between practitioners of different traditional specialties. On remote and widely dispersed plantations, the planters found responsibilities as new and varied as those of the New England clergy. The few Southerners who made their living from medicine in the 17th century were commonly active also as politicians, farmers, and lawyers. Not until 1691 were Virginia's medical men—along with ferrymen and Negroes—specifically exempt from militia service.

Even in Philadelphia, where neither a dominant and versatile clergy nor the emergencies of plantation life were present to break down the European categories, there developed a wholesome vagueness of professional distinctions. During the 18th century that city boasted more respectable medical learning than could be found anywhere else in the colonies: of the seventeen "physicians" known to have practiced in Philadelphia between 1740 and 1775, all but three had received some training in Europe. In 1765 Philadelphia became the site of the first American medical school, which was the earliest concerted effort to import the academic institutions of European medicine. Here, if anywhere in America, one might have expected professional pride and professional distinctions, but the familiar European distinctions were not to be found. When Dr. Adam Thompson of Edinburgh went to Philadelphia in 1748 to "practice Physick, Chirurgery and Midwifery" but publicly advertised that he would not keep his own apothecary shop, he seems to have stirred the resentment of his colleagues. They considered this an implied criticism of their willingness to be jacks of all the medical trades, even including pharmacy.

37

Learning from Experience

"HE IS of the clinical class of physicians," the visiting Scottish physician Dr. Alexander Hamilton observed of Dr. William Douglass in 1744, "and laughs att all theory and practise founded upon it, looking upon empyricism or bare experience as the only firm basis upon which practise ought to be founded. He has got here about him a set of disciples who greedily draw in his doctrines and, being but half learned themselves, have not wit enough to discover the foibles and mistakes of their preceptor." This was the same Dr. Douglass who, on professional grounds, had opposed Mather's inoculation experiment. Perhaps he had been chastened by the epidemic of 1721, for his doctrinaire attitude on that occasion was not typical of his career. From the point of view of a European physician at the time, the work of Dr. Douglass and his fellow Americans already revealed a striking emphasis—an interest in practical ways of treating particular diseases.

American doctors had been encouraged to such an emphasis by a number of circumstances, and especially by their informal system of medical education. Until 1765 there was no medical school in British North America; since few Americans could afford to study in Edinburgh, London, or Leyden, the apprentice system became standard. In 18th-century Virginia, only about one doctor in nine had a medical degree, and this seems to have been about the general proportion throughout the colonies at the outbreak of the Revolution. Zabdiel Boylston, perhaps the most effective and independent physician of colonial New England, had been taught by his father. The Clark family in Boston, the most eminent medical family of the colonial period, felt little need for a medical school: six generations of Clarks received their medical training at home. Between the first John Clark (who may have held an English medical diploma and who came to New England about 1638) and the seventh (who secured an M.D. degree in 1802), not a single one of these successful doctors had been given formal medical instruction.

All up and down the colonies, apprenticeship was the usual, almost the exclusive, path to the profession. Indentures surviving from early 17th-century Virginia reveal that the established doctor would keep a young man in his household for seven years doing chores as nurse, janitor, coachman, messenger, prescription-maker, and assistant surgeon, while reading a few books and learning mostly by observing his master. Though even this method of training was seldom cheap—the best Virginia practitioners asked about one hundred pounds a year—there was always considerable competition to enter the household of the most reputable masters.

Many colonial physicians recognized the special value of learning medicine where one was going to practice. In 1766, Dr. Thomas Bond observed in his clinical lectures at the Pennsylvania Hospital:

> Every Climate produces Diseases peculiar to itself, which require experience to understand and cure. . . . No Country then can be so proper for the instruction of Youth in the knowledge of Physic, as that in which 'tis to be practised; where the precepts of never failing Experience are handed down from Father to Son, from Tutor to Pupil. That this is not a Speculative opinion, but real Matter of Fact, may be proven from the Savages of America, who without the assistance of Literature have been found possessed of Skill in the cure of Diseases incident to their climate, Superior to the Regular bred, and most learned Physicians, and that from their discoveries the present practice of Physic has been enrich'd with some of the most valuable Medicines now in use.

Others, however, including some leaders of the profession, complained that American training was crude and inadequate; they urged the requirement of a more formal medical education. John Morgan (1735-1789) of Philadelphia was prominent among these. After a typical American medical training (apprenticeship under Dr. John Redman and experience as military surgeon for an expedition to Fort Duquesne), Morgan went abroad for a medical Grand Tour which included Edinburgh, London, Paris, Parma, and Padua. On his return to Philadelphia, Morgan announced his determination to engage in medicine "without turning apothecary or practising surgery." He made no headway in persuading other American doctors to leave cutting to surgeons and the mixing of medicines to apothecaries, but he did help persuade the trustees of the College of Philadelphia to establish the first American medical school, and he was himself appointed Professor of the Theory and Practice of Medicine. His now famous *Discourse upon the Institution of Medical Schools in America,* delivered in May 1765, is one of the best contemporary descriptions of the American medical profession. Morgan bitterly attacked the informality and lack of sharp subdivisions, what he called "the levelling of all kind of practitioners." Although he had studied long and hard and traveled widely, he complained, "yet I have been told, that to expect to gain a support here by my medical advice and attendance only, without becoming a surgeon and apothecary too in order to help out, is to forget that I was born an American." He pleaded for the "separate and regular practice of physic, surgery and pharmacy" such as was found abroad. Plainly Morgan had not yet discovered the truth which Henry Adams preached to Americans in the late 19th century: that just as important as drawing on European experience was learning the ways in which "the experience of mankind was useless to them." Nowhere was this more important than in the American learned professions, for there, more than anywhere else, in Adams' phrase, "the weight of society stifled their thought."

No one can deny that the American situation had impoverished medicine in many ways: the colonies were barren of theoretic advances and of imaginative and fruitful laboratory investigations. Although there was some progress in medical practice—for example, in immunology and public health—there were no epoch-making advances in medical science. What 18th-century American medicine saw was simply the advance of a novel medical profession. The frontiers of speculative medicine remained in the European centers. Still, in what Dr. John Morgan disparagingly called "the infant state of the colonies," lay an American opportunity. By allowing crude, fluid experience to overflow the ancient walls between departments of medical knowledge, men might see relations in nature which had been obscured by guild monopolies and by the conceit of learned specialists.

American experience thus broke down the social as well as intellectual distinctions between different branches of medical science. In the 18th century a prosperous New England physician dressed well and drove in a coach to see his patients. His English counterpart would have worn a powdered wig, a coat of red satin or brocade, short breeches, stockings and buckled shoes, a three-cornered hat, and would have carried a gold-headed cane. The snobbery of the European physician was no mere personal peccadillo; it divided the body of medical science, separating theory from practice, medicine from surgery and midwifery, and all of them from pharmacy. Simply to reduce or to remove this snobbery, whether by design or by the force of American circumstances, was to rejoin sundered fragments of experience. Not until well into the 19th century had medicine and surgery in Europe become more or less equal in the social scale; only then could their practitioners collaborate freely. In America their equality, hastened by the apprentice training they shared, had existed from the beginning.

His apprentice training inducted the young American physician into what, in more sophisticated modern terms, we would call a "clinical" emphasis—that is, a tendency to be more interested in the observation and treatment of actual patients than in artificial laboratory experiments. "At a time when in Paris and most European universities, medicine was taught purely theoretically, without any concrete bedside illustration," Dr. Henry E. Sigerist remarks in his history of American medicine, "in America it was learned in daily practical contact with patients." This emphasis, though, was one which no one had designed or intended and which men of respectable learning were actually trying to prevent. Its most eloquent defense was to be made in the next century by Dr. Oliver Wendell Holmes (whose own work was a brilliant if unconscious product of the same emphasis), in his famous introductory lecture (1867) on "Scholastic and Bedside Teaching" delivered to medical students at Harvard:

> When I compare this direct transfer of the practical experience of a wise man into the mind of a student,—every fact one that he can use in the battle of life and death,—with the far off, unserviceable "scientific" truths that I and some others are in the habit of teaching, I cannot help asking myself whether, if we concede that our forefathers taught too little, there is not a possibility that we may sometimes attempt to teach too much. I almost blush when I think of myself as describing the eight several facets on two slender processes of the palate bone, or the seven little twigs that branch off from the minute tympanic nerve. . . .
>
> I can hear the voice of some rough iconoclast addressing the Anatomist and the Chemist in tones of contemptuous indignation: "What is this stuff with which you are cramming the brains of young men who are to hold the lives of the community in their hands? Here is a man fallen in a fit; you can tell me all about the eight surfaces of the two processes of the palate-bone; but you have not had the sense to loosen that man's neck-cloth, and the old women are all calling you a fool? Here is a fellow that has just swallowed poison. I want something to turn his stomach inside out at the shortest notice. Oh, you have forgotten the dose of the sulphate of zinc, but you remember the formula for the production of alloxan!"
>
> "Look you, Master Doctor,—if I go to a carpenter to come and stop a leak in my roof that is flooding the house, do you suppose I care whether he is a botanist or not? . . . If my horse casts a shoe, do you think I will not trust a blacksmith to shoe him until I have made sure that he is sound on the distinction between the sesquioxide and the protosesquioxide of iron?"
>
> —But my scientific labor is to lead to useful results by and by, in the next generation, or in some possible remote future.—
>
> "Diavolo!" as your Dr. Rabelais has it,—answers the iconoclast,—

"what is that to me and my colic, to me and my strangury? I pay the Captain of the Cunard steamship to carry me quickly and safely to Liverpool, not to make a chart of the Atlantic for after voyagers!"

The American apprentice system, with its early combination of theory and practice and its immediate transfer of the wisdom of the practitioner, seems to have made the American doctor a more successful healer in his daily rounds. In 1820, Dr. Nathaniel Chapman commented that, although European physicians were more learned and original, in no country was medicine better practiced than in America.

This was not all. The dissolving of ancient boundaries between theory and practice, between the "higher" and the "lower" medical services, provided a freer atmosphere in which American medicine made its distinctive advances. Although 18th-century America produced no great medical scientists, it produced competent practitioners whose clinical interests would eventually bear their own fruit. A few Americans, not always doctors by profession, were aware of this promise. Dr. Thomas Bond noted (in 1766) that "more is required of us in this late settled world, where new Diseases often occurr." He urged an open-eyed, empirical, piecemeal approach. Where else could the exchange of experiences be so important? Jefferson, four decades later, still hoped to see here "the first degree of value set on clinical observation, and the lowest on visionary theories."

One of the first fruits of the American emphasis was an improvement of hospitals and of nursing. In 17th- and 18th-century Europe, hospitals were too often social cesspools in which the poor, the insane, and the miscellaneous unfortunate festered in the accumulated vermin of generations. American hospitals were not built in any numbers until the 18th century, when the curable sick, the insane, and the contagious had begun to be separated. Even in 17th-century Virginia the patient was more frequently housed in the residence of his physician, where the mere absence of institutionalized filth was itself a great advantage.

The Pennsylvania Hospital, founded by Dr. Thomas Bond in 1751 with the energetic assistance of Benjamin Franklin, was extraordinarily successful by the standards of its day. Erected as "a means of increasing the Number of People, and preserving many useful Members to the Public from Ruin and Distress," the hospital admitted 8831 patients between its founding and 1773; among these the managers reported 4440 complete cures and only 852 deaths. Its mortality rate was half that of general hospitals abroad. Dr. Benjamin Rush boasted in 1774 that by comparison with the hospitals of Europe "the Pennsylvania Hospital is as perfect as the wisdom and benevolence of man can make it."

The few important American medical publications of the colonial age, some of which we have already noticed, had an unmistakably clinical flavor. In Boston, Dr. William Douglass' report on the scarlet fever epidemic of 1735-36 was the first adequate clinical description of the disease to appear in English. Dr. Thomas Cadwalader's *Essay on the West-India Dry-Gripes,* printed by Benjamin Franklin in 1745, demonstrated that many gentlemen were suffering from lead-poisoning because they had been drinking Jamaica rum that had been distilled through lead pipes. In Charleston, Dr. John Lining prepared an accurate account of the yellow fever epidemic of 1748. From Philadelphia in 1750 came Dr. John Kearsley's detailed observations on yellow fever. Numerous observers described the course of smallpox and the relative efficacy of different treatments.

American colonial medicine produced nothing notable in a theoretical way. Dr. Benjamin Rush, following the dogmas of Cullen's disciple John Brown, made the most strenuous effort at an all-embracing medical theory: his doctrine of "sthenia" and "asthenia" attributed all disorders to an improper state of "tension." Rush's theoretic effort showed the medical doctrinaire at his worst, but even he was not doctrinaire in all things. He promoted the more humane treatment of the insane; and he tried to improve public health in Philadelphia by such common-sense expedients as sewage disposal, pure water, and clean streets.

Even into the 19th century the conspicuous successes of American medicine confirmed its clinical approach; the American accomplishments were the work of an undifferentiated medical profession under the pressure of emergencies. Two heroic figures, proper patron saints of American medicine, were melodramatic symbols of the peculiar opportunities of the New World. The first was Ephraim McDowell (1771-1830), a backwoods doctor who had studied in Edinburgh for one year but had not taken a medical degree. He encountered a woman patient who appeared to have a large abdominal tumor, so large in fact that he had originally mistaken it for a pregnancy. Before McDowell's day the range of surgery had included amputations, removal of stones, mending of ruptures, and some other items, but never a serious abdominal operation. On December 13, 1809, McDowell, assisted only by an apprentice nephew, laid the patient on a table in his house in Danville, Kentucky and, within twenty-five minutes, while she recited psalms to keep up her courage, he opened the abdominal cavity and removed the cystic tumor of the ovary. When McDowell returned to visit his patient five days later she was making her own bed; she lived thirty-one years more. This was the first ovariotomy in medical history; it might not have been performed except for the stringency of backwoods life and the scarcity of learned specialists.

The second heroic figure, William Beaumont (1785-1853), was an army doctor whose whole training had been by the apprentice method. On June 6, 1822, while Beaumont was stationed at remote Fort Mackinac in northern Michigan, a French-Canadian employee of the American Fur Company received a load of buckshot in his left side. Despite all that Beaumont could do to make it heal, the hole in the victim's stomach (technically called a "gastric fistula") remained open. Beaumont had the inspiration to take advantage of this rare opportunity to observe through the unhealed opening what actually was going on in the stomach. He took the man under his own roof, where he carried on his observations with exemplary skill and imagination but without benefit of books or laboratories. He noted the operation of the gastric juices and the effects of different stimulants such as tea, coffee, and alcohol. The result was his *Experiments and Observations on the Gastric Juice and the Physiology of Digestion* (1833), which became a classic of clinical medicine; this unpretentious little book laid foundations for the physiology of digestion and the science of nutrition. Were the works of McDowell and of Beaumont primarily the fruits of genius or of provincial opportunity? It is impossible to say. But if either of them had been more learned or could have called in an appropriate specialist, would he have dared as he did?

The immediate future of American medicine seemed to be at the bedside or in the clinic rather than in the laboratory. Perhaps the most important medical innovation which America exported to Europe during the 19th century was surgical anesthesia, a definitely practical and clinical discovery. Preventive medicine, dentistry, public health, clinical research, and general medical practice were the areas of special American competence. They were also the areas where the American standard of living, the loosening of social and professional distinctions, and the varied experiences of a new continent counted most.

PART NINE
THE LIMITS OF
AMERICAN SCIENCE

"We want hands, my lord, more than heads. The most intimate acquaintance with the classics will not remove our oaks; nor a taste for the *Georgics* cultivate our lands."

WILLIAM LIVINGSTON
to the Bishop of Llandaff

"Go on making experiments entirely on your own initiative and thereby pursue a path entirely different from that of the Europeans, for then you shall certainly find many things which have been hidden to natural philosophers throughout the space of centuries."

PIETER VAN MUSSCHENBROEK
to Benjamin Franklin

38

Popular Science:
Astronomy for Everybody

THE NATURAL-HISTORY EMPHASIS with its preference for the simple lessons of everyday experience, and the clinical emphasis with its prejudice against learning and theory, were by no means unmixed blessings. True, they were decidedly democratic. They encouraged the appeal to self-evidence and the American bias against a thinking class. They were friendly to "popular science," the belief that the greatest works of science ought to be understood by everyone. They fitted well with the ideal of the self-made scientist.

But, in many fields, progress had to build on technical foundations and on the professional learning of the past. The physical sciences, especially astronomy and physics, had acquired this character by the 18th century. In these fundamental sciences, therefore, colonial Americans did not shine: their ideals and hopes led them to exaggeration and confusion. They sometimes lost any sense of what was fundamental, and they ignored distinctions between the basic accomplishments of the theoretical and the peripheral advances of applied science. They often denied or obscured their limitations and claimed the laurels of a Newton or Einstein for colonial Americans whose work at best showed the applied ingenuity of an Edison or Ford. Their limitations are nowhere more obvious than in the men and achievements of which they boasted most loudly.

"America has not yet produced one good poet, one able mathematician, one man of genius in a single art or a single science." This common charge, repeated by the French savant Abbé Raynal in 1774, annoyed the colonials, and when Jefferson replied in his *Notes on Virginia*, he spoke the mind of many Americans. Jefferson admitted the charge against American literature, simply noting that America had not yet had time to produce a Homer or a Shakespeare, but he proudly offered George Washington as a great political and military leader. It was the accusation against American science that especially irritated him. Significantly, he refuted it not by any reference to American achievements in natural history (where Jefferson himself and many others had attained some distinction), but by two examples from the physical sciences, where he was a novice but where presumably Europeans would be most impressed. "In physics," Jefferson reminded European detractors, "we have produced a Franklin, than whom no one of the present age has made more important discoveries, nor has enriched philosophy with more, or more ingenious solutions of the phaenomena of nature. We have supposed Mr. Rittenhouse second to no astronomer living: that in genius he must be the first, because he is self-taught."

By examining the accomplishments of these two paragons and of their nearest rivals we can discover the limits of American culture in the colonial age, and we can begin to see the price Americans were paying for their democratic way of thinking.

In 18th-century Europe, the "New Science" of astronomy and physics meant, of course, Newtonian science. When Voltaire visited England in the 1720's he noted that although few people read Newton, everybody talked about him and attributed to him, like Hercules in the fable, the exploits of all the other heroes. Most Englishmen—even those in the educated classes—who talked of Newton had acquired their knowledge from popular books or public lectures, like Benjamin Martin's *Plain and Familiar introduction to the Newtonian Philosophy . . . Designed for the use of such Gentlemen and Ladies as would acquire Knowledge of this Science without Mathematical Learning* (1751). This was generally even more true among Americans. Newton's *Principia* was first published in England in 1687 (although some of his discoveries were made considerably earlier), but the first copy to arrive in the colonies appears to have been that which James Logan acquired in 1708. Even later, copies were rare: Yale College received the second edition (1713) from Sir Isaac himself, and John Winthrop IV owned a copy of the third edition (1726). Most of the Americans who acquired a reputation for astronomical and physical learning—including Franklin and Rittenhouse—seem to have secured their acquaintance with Newton's works mainly at second-hand.

Perhaps the most important American colonial contribution to Newtonian science was no theoretic insight but rather the observations made through the three-and-one-half-foot telescope which John Winthrop, Jr. had given to Harvard College in 1672. Through that telescope, Thomas Brattle made observations of the Great Comet of 1680 which Newton himself used and acknowledged in his *Principia.*

After Brattle's death and during the first half of the 18th century, the most accomplished American astronomer was without doubt John Winthrop IV (1714-1779), descendant of the first Governor of Massachusetts Bay and of a long line of New England scholar-leaders. Winthrop never became a folk-hero and so was not enumerated by Jefferson, but he was a man of broad learning and vast energy and was generally conceded to be the best that America had yet offered in the Newtonian line. His lectures on Comets (1759) and on the Transit of Venus (1769) showed an extraordinary talent for explaining complicated and difficult matters. His notes on sunspots (1739) suggested a connection between them and the aurora borealis not developed by other astronomers for at least another century. His sensible remarks on the causes of earthquakes (1755) revealed him to be a careful, clear-eyed observer. But as a whole Winthrop's work was not strikingly original; although a brilliant teacher, he added little of his own. When Winthrop was appointed Hollis Professor of Mathematics and Natural Philosophy at Harvard in 1738 he had already offered observations on natural history together with specimens of plants, animals, and minerals to members of the Royal Society in London. Only after his appointment at Harvard did his attention focus sharply on mathematics and astronomy. Still his work continued to reveal the natural-history emphasis. His scientific writings remained descriptive, fragmentary, and topical. Almost without exception they arose from some particular and dramatic natural phenomenon or catastrophe—a lightning stroke, the tremor of an earthquake, the appearance of a comet, a lunar eclipse—which could be observed in America.

Winthrop did not write an epochal book, but he did organize an epoch-making expedition. A transit of Venus across the sun occurred twice during his lifetime; one had not occurred within the preceding century and a quarter, and would not again for over a century. The Newtonian system had described the distances between planets and their distances from the sun only in relative terms, that is, by comparison with the earth's hypothetical distance from the sun. But observations of the transit of Venus taken from remote points would for the first time make it possible to calculate in miles the actual distance of the earth and hence of the other planets from the sun. Not only would such results be useful for astronomy, but for navigation, surveying, and map-making. Winthrop therefore organized a Harvard expedition to Newfoundland—the first American astronomical expedition and the first scientific expedition sponsored by a college in America. "This Phenomenon, (which has been observed but once before since the Creation of the World)," Governor Francis Bernard explained to the Massachusetts assembly, "will, in all Probability, settle some Questions in Astronomy which may ultimately be very serviceable to Navigation: For which Purpose, those Powers that are interested in Navigation, have thought it their Business to send Mathematicians to different Parts of the World to make Observations." The Governor prevailed upon Massachusetts to send Winthrop and his two assistants in its Province Sloop to St. John's, where their observations attracted the attention of scientists throughout the world.

Although Winthrop was a more learned astronomer, the popular symbol of American astronomy in the provincial age was David Rittenhouse (1732-1796). Many Americans shared Jefferson's judgment that Rittenhouse was "second to no astronomer living," and in genius the first, because he was self-taught. Rittenhouse had almost no formal education. He began as a clock- and instrument-maker, and for much of his life he owed his living to his clocks. Like Franklin, to whom his contemporaries often compared him, he seemed the embodiment of the American ideal of the undifferentiated man. Troubleshooter of the Revolution, he was engineer to the Pennsylvania Committee of Safety, helped to fortify the shores of the Delaware, and devised ways of manufacturing cannon and ammunition. A member of the convention which drew Pennsylvania's first constitution, Rittenhouse was also first Treasurer of his State and the first Director of the United States Mint. His knowledge of metals and of mathematics aided Jefferson in simplifying the crude and complicated coinage of the new nation. Jefferson held so high an opinion of his scientific talent—"the world has but one Ryttenhouse"— that he regretted Rittenhouse's political activities, fearing the versatile astronomer might "throw away a Newton upon the occupations of a crown." His fellow-colonials had made Rittenhouse, as they did Franklin, one of their champions against the giants of Europe. Upon Franklin's death, Rittenhouse, to whom Franklin had appropriately willed his telescope, succeeded him as President of the American Philosophical Society; when Rittenhouse died only a few years later he was mourned as a national hero. Americans did not realize that by eulogizing Rittenhouse as the Great American Astronomer they were in fact emphasizing the narrowness of colonial science.

The peculiar justification for calling Rittenhouse the Great American Astronomer came from the fact that he was the leading surveyor of his day. To survey small town-lots and farm boundaries in long-settled Europe, arithmetic with a smattering of trigonometry sufficed, but America offered a whole continent to be measured. The property lines of extensive tracts in the wilderness could not be drawn from a large rock or the stump of a familiar tree; they had to be defined by the astronomical dimensions of latitude and longitude. Rittenhouse's most enduring work was of this especially American kind; for him astronomy was a surveyor's tool. Between 1764, when he received £6 for helping Mason and Dixon draw the boundary of Pennsylvania, Maryland, and Delaware, and 1787, when he helped mark the long-disputed line between New York and Massachusetts, he drew boundaries of more than half the original thirteen colonies.

But even such large-scale surveying was no match for the Newtonian flights of mathematical imagination. Rittenhouse did make a few modest, if not entirely successful, efforts to deal with solar space: the 1769 transit of Venus gave him a great opportunity to establish among Europeans the respectability of American science. It was an even more attractive opportunity than the 1761 transit for which Winthrop had organized his Newfoundland expedition. In 1761 the most useful observations could not be made within the settled areas; but the 1769 transit was expected to be visible, weather permitting, all over the American colonies. Arranging the points of observation, providing the apparatus, and coordinating the results were precisely the kind of challenge which American scientists seemed able to meet.

There was widespread, if not always well-informed, interest throughout the colonies. Winthrop himself wrote a lucid little pamphlet explaining to laymen the importance of the spectacle, how to make a smoked glass for watching it, and how to record the crucial time and duration of the transit. In Massachusetts, the principal observations were to be made by Winthrop at the Cambridge observatory. In Philadelphia, where the Rev. William Smith of the College of Philadelphia was the principal organizer, David Rittenhouse held the center of the scientific stage. The Pennsylvania legislature provided £100 for a telescope and another £100 for an observatory on State House Square; arrangements were made for several other observations in the vicinity. Up and down the coast every city prepared for its observations, and amateur astronomers on distant farms readied their home-made instruments. Perhaps never before or since have so many "scientific" calculations depended on such crude apparatus.

At the long-awaited hour on June 3, 1769, observers in the middle colonies had a serene sky, but the drama of the occasion itself produced unforeseen difficulties. To observe the climactic moment through the telescope at his newly-constructed Norriton observatory, Rittenhouse lay on his back with his head supported by assistants. The strain proved too much for him: at the zero hour when Venus touched the sun—the object of months of planning and the moment for which Rittenhouse had been readjusting his specially designed clock—Rittenhouse fainted away. On recovering his senses he could do no more than estimate how much time had elapsed.

Rittenhouse had the major responsibility for collecting and correlating the data from different observation-points. In collaboration with the Rev. William Smith, he made the principal American effort to use the observations for calculating the solar parallax; this was vitally important work because the hour of the transit had made it impossible to see the phenomenon over most of Europe. Figures gathered from the many American observers varied widely, and the crudeness of their observations made any average scientifically worthless. Nevertheless, the final figure produced by Smith and Rittenhouse happily turned out to be close to the presently accepted distance of the earth from the sun. The validity of their result was more the product of good luck than of good science, but America's and Rittenhouse's reputation profited none the less. Smith claimed that American observations of the transit "hath done a Credit to our Country which would have been cheaply purchased for twenty times the Sum!"

Whatever exaggeration there may have been in ranking Rittenhouse among the world's great astronomers, Jefferson told the sober truth when he declared that "as an artist he has exhibited as great a proof of mechanical genius as the world has ever produced. He has not indeed made a world; but he has by imitation approached nearer its Maker than any man who has lived from the creation to this day." Among the colonists Rittenhouse's principal claim to fame was his ingenious contraption to help teach the public about astronomy, a working model of the solar system, then called an "Orrery." His machine was not the first of its kind nor even the first one made in America, but it was probably the most intricate and accurate astronomical model that had yet been produced. This was doubly remarkable because of his lack of formal education and his remoteness from the centers of European learning. Though a man of impressive humility, Rittenhouse dared (in his own words) "boldly affirm, that he has not copied the general construction, nor the particular disposition of any of its essential parts, from any Orrery or description whatsoever. Neither has he made use of any number he found in books, for one single wheel, but was at the pains of getting them by calculation himself, having never met with any that were exact enough for his purposes." If Americans could not add to the theory of solar mechanics, they could at least construct the best working model of the solar system known in their time.

"I would have my Orrery really useful," Rittenhouse wrote on January 28, 1767, when he first conceived his plan, "by making it capable of informing us, truly, of the astronomical phaenomena for any particular point of time; which, I do not find that any Orrery yet made, can do." Within a few months he communicated to the American Philosophical Society at Philadelphia details which substantially corresponded to the finished product. An elegant upright cabinet would frame a large center panel flanked by two smaller ones. In the middle of the center panel on a four-foot-square vertical sheet of brass was to be displayed a gilded brass ball representing the sun; round this ball would move others of brass or ivory, representing the planets, which rotated in elliptical orbits "their motions to be sometimes swifter, and sometimes slower, as nearly according to the true law of an equable description of areas as is possible." One of the smaller panels, each of them four feet by about two feet, would exhibit "all the appearances of Jupiter and his Satellites—their eclipses, transits, and inclinations; likewise, all the appearances of Saturn, with his ring and satellites." The other small panel would show "all the phaenomena of the moon, particularly, the exact time, quantity, and duration of her eclipses—and those of the sun, occasioned by her interposition; with a most curious contrivance for exhibiting the appearance of a solar eclipse, at any particular place on the earth."

When the machine was set in motion by turning a crank, the planets would proceed in their proper revolutions, three dials indicating precisely the hour of the day, the day of the month, and the year at which the planets would appear in these positions—for a period of 5,000 years either forward or backward. Spectacular heavenly phenomena, such as a transit of Venus or an eclipse of the sun or moon, could thus be foretold.

A still more remarkable device was a tiny telescope which could be directed from the earth to any other planet—"then will both the longitude and latitude of that planet be pointed out (by an index and graduated circle) as seen from the earth." The machine was also to be equipped, according to an original plan, to play "music of the spheres" as God's handiwork was displayed. The Rev. William Smith, the aggressive provost of the College of Philadelphia who had worked with Rittenhouse during the Transit of Venus, became enthusiastic over the project. Both Smith and Rittenhouse seem to have taken for granted that the completed Orrery would be offered to the College of Philadelphia, where Smith expected it to be a featured attraction. But Dr. John Witherspoon, who had just recently arrived from Scotland to become president of The College of New Jersey (later called Princeton), hurried over to Rittenhouse's workshop in Norriton and persuaded him to sell his Orrery for £300 to the New Jersey institution. The ambitious Rev. Smith declared that he "never met with greater mortification" than when he read in *The Pennsylvania Gazette* of April 26, 1770, three days after Witherspoon's successful visit to Rittenhouse, that the mechanical masterpiece of the age was lost to his college at Philadelphia. And especially that Rittenhouse "should think so little of his noble invention, as to consent to let it go to a village"!

Rittenhouse sought to mollify Smith (who had already agreed to purchase the second Orrery) by arranging for the first demonstration of the Princeton machine to take place at Smith's College of Philadelphia. With a ready eye for public relations, Smith announced a series of fourteen lectures during March and April 1771, climaxing in a lecture-demonstration by Rittenhouse himself. The Provincial Assembly of Pennsylvania so warmly admired the machine that they appropriated £300 "as a Testimony of the high Sense which this House entertains of his Mathematical Genius and Mechanical Abilities in constructing the said Orrery," and appointed a committee to arrange for Rittenhouse to construct a third (and, of course, larger) one.

Many Americans welcomed the Orrery as reassuring evidence that the New World could now compete with the scientific progress of the Old. When the American Philosophical Society for Useful Knowledge published its first volume of Transactions in 1771, the first section was entitled "Mathematical and Astronomical Papers" and the first paper was Rittenhouse's plan for his Orrery. "As this is an American Production, and much more complete than any Thing of the Kind ever made in Europe," *The Pennsylvania Gazette* (April 26, 1770) said in the first public announcement of the Orrery, "it must give great Pleasure to every Lover of his Country, to see her rising to Fame in the sublimest Sciences, as well as every Improvement in the Arts." When Witherspoon prepared a brochure to attract students to Princeton from the West Indies, he took care to explain that students would be given their Astronomy lessons "upon the Orrery, lately invented and constructed by David Rittenhouse, Esq., which is reckoned by the best judges the most excellent in its kind of any ever yet produced." The newly designed seal of the University of Pennsylvania, adopted in 1782, was inscribed only with the date and the name of the institution and otherwise consisted entirely of a view of the Rittenhouse Orrery. Jefferson's bill for reforming the College of William & Mary in 1779 specifically provided that the college should purchase such a machine—"the mechanical representation, or model of the solar system, conceived and executed by that greatest of astronomers, David Ryttenhouse"—and that it "be called by the name of the Ryttenhouse." At his second meeting of the American Philosophical Society, Jefferson offered a motion which was unanimously agreed to, that the Society commission an Orrery to be presented to the King of France, not only to show American gratitude to an ally during the Revolution but also to refute the European detractors of American culture. The Rev. James Madison wrote to Jefferson enthusiastically endorsing "an excellent, as well as a very short Method of confuting those Flimsy Theorists, as you justly call them, by sending both Rittenhouse and his Orrery to Europe."

Neither Rittenhouse nor "the Rittenhouse" ever reached Europe, but many Americans and some friendly Europeans were now more hopeful for an American culture which could produce them.

39

Naïve Insights and Ingenious Devices: Electricity

ON A RARE OCCASION, an American could discover something, even in physics, simply because he was less learned than his European colleagues. Ignorance of the respectable paths of scientific thought might leave him freer to wander off wherever facts beckoned. Such was no foundation for a solid tradition of speculative science, but it was not absolutely impossible to advance physics under American conditions. To exploit naïveté in a subject as cumulative as physics required great genius, but at least one colonial American—Benjamin Franklin—was able to do so.

Franklin's concepts did of course grow in the context of Newtonian experimental science, but Franklin was not, and never pretended to be, well read in the Newtonian classics. The evidence even for his reading of Newton's *Optics* is only circumstantial; everything confirms our suspicion that Franklin lacked the mathematical knowledge to understand Newton's *Principia* or other works of similar difficulty. His theoretical equipment for advanced study in any of the physical sciences was meager.

Franklin's actual accomplishment was obscured by extravagant comparison here and abroad to the greatest mathematical and physical theorists. John Adams declared his reputation "more universal than that of Leibnitz or Newton, Frederick or Voltaire." Lord Chatham praised him in the House of Lords as "one whom all Europe held in high Estimation for his Knowledge and Wisdom, and rank'd with our Boyles and Newtons." The great chemist Joseph Priestley declared Franklin's discovery in his kite experiment "the greatest, perhaps since the time of Sir Isaac Newton." Franklin's special genius has been buried under the even less discriminating praise heaped on him since his death.

In fact his achievement illustrated the triumph of naïveté over learning. A clue to Franklin's peculiar success as a "physicist" is found in the explanation for Cadwallader Colden's failure. Colden, the New York official whose work as a naturalist we have already noted, aimed at greatness in the European mold. In his *Principles of Action in Matter* (1751), he professed to carry on the work of Newton, even to outdo Newton by providing a general theory of the "cause" of gravitation. Colden did not possess the specialized learning, the architectonic mind, nor the community with other learned physicists without which great works in mathematical physics have seldom been produced. Yet he pretended "to have discovered the true cause of the motion of the planets and comets, and from thence to deduce the reason of all the phaenomena, with that exactness as to agree with the most accurate observations." Happily, he explained, all this would be accomplished, "without any aid of the conic sections, or of any other knowledge, besides the common rules of arithmetic and trigonometry." Franklin, in contrast to Colden, had no illusion that he was at home in Newton's mathematical world; he merely set out to explain certain specific phenomena. Colden's work would probably have been of higher quality had he lived in Europe near the ancient seats of learning, but under such circumstances Franklin's work might not have been done at all.

Electricity was where Franklin earned his reputation as a physicist; only there did he make physical discoveries of lasting significance. Franklin's electrical discoveries were not embodied in treatises nor were they the minor premises of a large theory about the nature, origin, or causes of electricity, much less of all matter. His writings on electricity were diffuse and miscellaneous. His book, which became famous under the title *Experiments and Observations on Electricity, made at Philadelphia in America*, was actually a collection of letters, so loosely organized that some readers have doubted whether the items were intended for publication. They were not published as a book in America until 1941.

"He has endeavoured," said Sir Humphry Davy, "to remove all mystery and obscurity from the subject. He has written equally for the un-initiated and for the philosopher; and he has rendered his details amusing as well as perspicuous, elegant as well as simple." Even today the reader is amazed to find that so fundamental a work is so commonplace and non-mathematical in its language. This work, the basis of Franklin's scientific reputation, reads more like a book of kitchen-recipes or instructions for parlor-magic than like a treatise on physics. In explaining "the wonderful effect of pointed bodies, both in drawing off and throwing off the electrical fire," in one of his most important letters, he writes:

> Place an iron shot of three or four inches diameter on the mouth of a clean dry glass bottle. By a fine silken thread from the cieling, right over the mouth of the bottle, suspend a small cork-ball, about the bigness of a marble; the thread of such a length, as that the cork-ball may rest against the side of the shot. Electrify the shot and the ball will be repelled to the distance of four or five inches, more or less, according to the quantity of Electricity. — — — When in this state, if you present to the shot the point of a long, slender, sharp bodkin, at six or eight inches distance, the repellency is instantly destroyed, and the cork flies to the shot. A blunt body must be brought within an inch, and draw a spark to produce the same effect.

In Franklin's day it was possible to carry on important electrical experiments with kitchen equipment because the subject was still in its infancy, and had not yet begun to become mathematical. Of all the sciences which saw great advances in the 17th and 18th centuries electricity had had the least history. There was a great deal less to know, or to be ignorant of, in electricity than in astronomy or mathematical physics in general. Since it seemed to have no practical application at the time, there was full scope for the play of idle curiosity. Franklin's interest in electricity was, if anything, less "practical" than that of some of his contemporaries, for he doubted that electricity would ever be the medical cure-all that some were then predicting it would be. His amateur and non-academic frame of mind was his greatest advantage; like many another discovering American, he saw more because he knew much less of what he was supposed to see.

When Franklin first became interested in electricity, just after 1746, he knew very little of what had been done in Europe. Returning to Philadelphia after a trip to Boston, where he had happened to witness "electrical entertainments," Franklin was delighted to find that the Library Company had received some glass tubes from Peter Collinson. Three fellow-amateurs joined him in repeating the experiments he had seen. Most active was Ebenezer Kinnersley, an ordained Baptist minister who never had a pulpit—"an ingenious neighbor," according to Franklin, "who, being out of business, I encouraged to undertake showing the experiments for money." The other two were Philip Syng (1703-1789), a silversmith by trade, and Thomas Hopkinson (1709-1751), a lawyer and the father of the ingenious Francis Hopkinson. Both were to be among the founders of the American Philosophical Society. The precise role of each in the important early experiments is not easy to assign, partly because Franklin showed no excessive modesty in his accounts. But no one of the miscellaneous group was primarily a "natural philosopher"; none held a regular university degree nor could have been called learned by English standards.

The Philadelphia amateurs were quite out of touch with the work of European natural philosophers. They thought that Syng had accomplished something novel and important when he "invented" a simple electrical machine: a sphere of glass that turned on an iron axle producing friction which collected the electricity. This seemed a great improvement over the "fatiguing exercise" of rubbing a glass tube. But machines like Syng's had long before been used in England and were already popular among electrical experimenters on the continent.

It seems that Franklin's only knowledge of earlier European work on electricity was what he had gained from his London correspondent Peter Collinson. That was not a great deal. Franklin reported to Collinson that he and his three Philadelphia collaborators were observing "some particular phaenomena, that we look upon to be new." But he had no way of knowing whether these were really discoveries or had already been noticed by European scientists. Franklin's later letters to Collinson (which became the book on electricity) continued to have the tantalizing quality of a journal by an explorer who does not know whether anyone has seen his land before.

If Franklin had been better informed of what European scientists had accomplished, he might not have dared to make his boldly simple suggestion: that electricity was a single fluid, not varying with the material from which it was produced. This was Franklin's fundamental electrical discovery. The two forms of electricity he then described simply as "plus" and "minus," depending on what he conceived to be the direction of the flow.

Sophisticated European thinking on the subject had already "advanced" to Du Fay's more elaborate doctrine:

> There are two distinct Electricities, very different from one another; one of which I call vitreous Electricity and the other resinous Electricity. The first is that of Glass, Rock-Crystal, Precious Stones, Hair of Animals, Wool, and many other Bodies. The second is that of Amber, Copal, Gum-Lack, Silk, Thread, Paper, and a vast Number of other Substances.

Franklin seems to have known nothing of Du Fay's distinction. He proceeded directly from his own observations to his epochal assumption that all electricity was a single fluid. Even if Franklin had known the misleading distinction which European scientists had made, he might have offered his own simple explanation. But it would have required boldness of imagination from a man whose forte was not boldness but common sense. It is more likely that he would not have dared even to voice his revolutionary observation.

Fortunately for our understanding of Franklin's work, we know what happened to his thinking after he became better acquainted with the writings of his European contemporaries. From the standard European writings on electricity, many of which Peter Collinson sent to the Library Company of Philadelphia, Franklin learned the respectable ideas and the conventional vocabulary. His own insights lost their freshness. As early as 1748, he showed a tendency to learn from books rather than from observation; he began to see things as his European contemporaries saw them. A pamphlet published in London in 1751 with four of Franklin's letters on electricity offered nearly all his basic contribution to the subject. The more perceptive European scientists themselves feared that if Franklin acquired their learning he would soon see no more than they did. Pieter van Musschenbroek, discoverer of the principle of the condenser and an inventor of the Leyden jar, warned the American scientist. On receiving Franklin's request for books on electricity in 1759, he urged him to "go on making experiments entirely on your own initiative and thereby pursue a path entirely different from that of the Europeans, for then you shall certainly find many other things which have been hidden to natural philosophers throughout the space of centuries."

Unfortunately, by this time Franklin had already become "learned" in electricity and the damage was done.

Franklin's writings on electricity, then, were not exceptions to the descriptive, limited character of colonial science. With his usual good luck, Franklin had happened on a subject where his lack of mathematics was no disadvantage, where his lack of learning was in fact an advantage, and where the play of his idle curiosity could bear fruit. Here was hardly enough to justify Jefferson's boast that America was already producing great physicists to vie with those of the Old World. Least of all did it show that America was a fruitful soil for basic scientific discoveries of a theoretical character. If it suggested anything, it was the contrary. American barrenness of other discoveries in the physical sciences during the colonial period only emphasized the atypical and coincidental character of Franklin's discovery in this field.

The achievement by Franklin which most fired the popular imagination and which has been hallowed in American folklore, was even further from the rarefied world of Newtonian physics: his proof of the identity of lightning and electricity, and his invention of the lightning-rod thus made possible. Franklin's famous experiment of the electrical kite was not a basic theoretical discovery. It was a clever way of putting to practical use the "power of points" and the "single fluid" theory of electricity, both of which had already been developed in Franklin's letters. It was a combination of applied science and mechanical ingenuity. The identity of lightning and electricity had already been suspected by Europeans, but they had found no way to prove it. Franklin's contribution was a simple device that, as he said, "might have occurred to any electrician," but which somehow had not occurred to European physicists preoccupied with their "electrical machines," their laboratory experiments, and their theoretical arguments among themselves.

When Dr. John Lining of Charleston asked Franklin how he had come to think of the kite experiment to test the identity of lightning and electricity, Franklin replied by quoting from his scientific journal:

> Nov. 9, 1749. Electrical fluid agrees with lightning in these particulars: 1. Giving light. 2. Colour of the light. 3. Crooked direction. 4. Swift motion. 5. Being conducted by metals. 6. Crack or noise in exploding. 7. Subsisting in water or ice. 8. Rending bodies it passes through. 9. Destroying animals. 10. Melting metals. 11. Firing inflammable substances. 12. Sulphureous smell.—The electric fluid is attracted by points. —We do not know whether this property is in lightning.—But since they agree in all the particulars wherein we can already compare them, is it not probable they agree likewise in this? Let the experiment be made.

Once Franklin had proposed the obvious and only conclusive test of the hypothesis, several Europeans made the trial. They may even have pursued Franklin's suggestion before Franklin himself got around to it.

The Abbé Nollet, one of the most "advanced" and learned of the French physicists and a leading exponent of the two-fluid theory, rejected such a direct appeal to "mere" observation. Franklin recounted in his *Autobiography* that Nollet, already offended by Franklin's omission of his name from the *Experiments and Observations on Electricity,* "could not at first believe that such a work came from America and said it must have been fabricated by his enemies at Paris, to decry his system. Afterwards, having been assur'd that there really existed such a person as Franklin at Philadelphia, which he had doubted, he wrote and published a volume of letters, chiefly address'd to me, defending his theory, and denying the verity of my experiments, and of the positions deduc'd from them." Still Franklin would not be drawn into quibbling over questions that could be settled only by observation. "My writings contain'd a description of experiments which any one might repeat and verify, and if not to be verifi'd, could not be defended. . . . I concluded to let my papers shift for themselves, believing it was better to spend what time I could spare from public business in making new experiments, than in disputing about those already made."

So eager was Franklin for the application of his ideas, that in the very letter in which he proposed his experiment to test the identity of lightning and electricity (and even before the experiment had been made or his hypothesis had been confirmed), Franklin described the lightning-rod. "If these things are so," he wrote from Philadelphia in 1749, "may not the knowledge of this power of points be of use to mankind, in preserving houses, churches, ships, &c. from the stroke of lightning, by directing us to fix on the highest part of those edifices, upright rods of iron made sharp as a needle, and gilt to prevent rusting, and from the foot of those rods a wire down the outside of the building into the ground, or down round one of the shrouds of a ship, and down her side till it reaches the water?" In *Poor Richard's Almanack* for 1753, he published a simple description of a lightning-rod under the heading "How to secure Houses, &c. from Lightning."

The lightning-rod quickly took hold in America. Even though academic learning on electricity was scarce, what men did know about electricity was soon put to more widespread practical use than in the great centers of European learning. We do not have reliable statistics, but observers from both sides of the Atlantic noticed that lightning-rods were more widely used in America than in England. "No country has more certainly proved the efficacy of electrical rods, than this," the Rev. Andrew Burnaby noted as early as 1759 when he traveled through Virginia. Although buildings were sometimes struck by lightning, rods were so generally in use that it had become rare to hear of their being damaged. Burnaby hoped that this American example would inspire others to give up their religious prejudices against using scientific devices for human safety.

Even in America, however, the introduction of the lightning-rod had been delayed by religious prejudice and scientific conservatism. In 1755, soon after rods had first come into use, Boston was shaken by a severe earthquake, which the Rev. Thomas Prince explained in a new appendix to his sermon *Earthquakes, The Works of God and Tokens of His Just Displeasure.* "The more points of Iron are erected around the Earth, to draw the Electrical Substance out of the Air; the more the Earth must needs be charged with it. . . . In Boston are more erected than anywhere else in New England; and Boston seems to be more dreadfully shaken. O! there is no getting out of the mighty Hand of God! If we think to avoid it in the Air, we cannot in the Earth: Yes, it may grow more fatal." But the sensible Professor John Winthrop, who understood Franklin's points, read a lecture in the Harvard College Chapel to refute such wild imaginings; and the cases in which the rods had actually worked seemed in the popular mind to outweigh fancy theoretical objections. In London in 1772, Franklin found it curious that the English were only then beginning to use lightning-rods although in America rods had already been in common use for nearly 20 years and were found not only on public buildings, churches, and country mansions but even on small private houses.

The circumstances of life here had probably prodded the Americans. "Thunder Storms are much more frequent there [in America] than in Europe, . . ." Franklin wrote from London in 1772. "Here in England, the Practice [of using rods] has made a slower Progress, Damage by Lightning being less frequent, & People of course less apprehensive of Danger from it." Meteorologists tell us that, although the frequency of thunderstorms in southern Canada is about the same as in Europe (occurring on the average on about eleven days in the year), the frequency increases as one goes south until thunderstorms are nearly seven times as frequent in states bordering the Gulf of Mexico (occurring on the average on about 72 days in the year). All such figures are crude, and it is possible that the weather was different in the 18th century. But we do have enough information to make us suspect that lightning and thunder were more frequent here than in Europe. At any rate they must have seemed more threatening to colonial Americans dispersed over a half-known continent.

40

Backwoods Farming

THE ANONYMOUS AUTHOR of *American Husbandry,* the best surviving 18th-century survey of colonial agriculture, concluded in 1775 that "the American planters and farmers are in general the greatest slovens in christendom." He made this observation when Europe was in the full tide of an agricultural revolution, when England had been, for several decades, a center of new developments. There the accelerating "enclosure" movement—the fencing in of old common-lands and old pastures—which had long been going on, encouraged more efficient and more capitalistic methods. Jethro Tull invented a drill for planting seeds in rows, and in his *Horse-Hoeing Husbandry* (1733) he urged regular plowing to destroy weeds and to increase the nourishment of plant-roots. Lord "Turnip" Townshend, whose grandson was author of the Townshend Acts, following Tull's suggestions improved the rotation of crops. Before mid-century, Robert Bakewell made a science of stock-breeding; and by the end of the century Arthur Young was using his sharp powers of observation and his fluent pen to popularize these and other new techniques. Although the peasants and small farmers were slow to change their methods, agricultural experiment became a hobby for some wealthy landlords, and before the American Revolution it was a national fashion. Queen Caroline subscribed to Tull's book, and George II heard Tull's system explained at court. George III, "Farmer George," who could be seen carrying about the latest volume of Young's agricultural journal, said he owed more to Young than to any of his other subjects.

But in America, the colonial period was an age of stagnation in agricultural science. George Washington, who himself had been a pretty

conservative farmer, surveyed the American situation in a letter to
Arthur Young on December 5, 1791:

> An English farmer must entertain a contemptible opinion of our hus-
> bandry, or a horrid idea of our lands, when he shall be informed that
> not more than eight or ten bushels of wheat is the yield of an acre; but
> this low produce may be ascribed, and principally too, to a cause . . .
> that the aim of the farmers in this country, if they can be called farmers,
> is, not to make the most they can from the land, which is, or has been
> cheap, but the most of the labour, which is dear; the consequence of
> which has been, much ground has been scratched over and none culti-
> vated or improved as it ought to have been: whereas a farmer in Eng-
> land, where land is dear, and labour cheap, finds it his interest to
> improve and cultivate highly, that he may reap large crops from a small
> quantity of ground.

This was a fair summary. The proverbial ingenuity of the American
backwoodsman produced a few improvements—in the axe and the rifle,
for example. But most of what we know about colonial farmers suggests
a prevailing backwoods conservatism. The natural abundance, which
in later American history encouraged an experimental spirit, discouraged
it during the colonial years.

"Waste" is, of course, a relative term. To the American colonists
for whom labor was scarcer than land, it seemed more economical to
use up the land and move on than to spend precious hours in cultivating
and fertilizing. In their own way the colonists were very much interested
in economy. But they wanted "labor-saving" devices. And in these early
years the most obvious labor-saving device happened to be the wasteful
use of land. Most of the new agricultural techniques being developed
in England were aimed at making old land more productive—usually at
considerable expense of labor.

Since few farmers kept detailed records, we have a lot to learn about
the common farming methods of colonial America. But the European
travelers, who looked for something new over here, were unanimous
on the backwardness of American farming methods. "The Europeans
coming to America," the Swedish botanist Peter Kalm remarked of the
middle colonies in 1748-51, "found a rich, fine soil before them, lying
as loose between the trees as the best bed in a garden. They had nothing
to do but to cut down the wood, put it up in heaps, and to clear the dead
leaves away. They could then immediately proceed to plowing, which in
such loose ground is very easy; and having sown their grain, they got
a most plentiful harvest. This easy method of getting a rich crop has
spoiled the English and other European settlers, and induced them to

adopt the same method of agriculture as the Indians. . . . This is like-wise the reason why agriculture and its science is so imperfect here that one can travel several days and learn almost nothing about land . . . except that from their gross mistakes and carelessness of the future, one finds opportunities every day of making all sorts of observations, and of growing wise by their mistakes. In a word, the grain fields, the meadows, the forests, the cattle, etc. are treated with equal carelessness. . . . their eyes are fixed upon the present gain, and they are blind to the future." While Kalm probably exaggerated the natural fertility of the soil and the ease of its first cultivation, he did not exaggerate the widespread care-lessness of American farmers.

Many other observers noticed the broken fences and the stunted cattle running at large, unfed and unprotected. Their manure was put to no use. Artificial pasture long remained a rarity, and few farmers stored feed for the winter. In Virginia a French traveler of the late 17th century saw "poor beasts of a morning all covered with snow and trembling with the cold, but no forage was provided for them. They eat the bark of the trees because the grass was covered." Wild animals—wolves, bears, and savage dogs—attacked the helpless cattle, and made the raising of sheep difficult. The abundance of fish and game, while improving the colonial diet, was no incentive to better husbandry; yet the colonists of the English middle and lower classes were not skillful hunters. They had come from a country where the chase was an upper-class monopoly. English breeds deteriorated under American neglect. "Hogs swarm like Vermine upon the Earth, and are often accounted such," Robert Beverley reported; they were not even inventoried in estates. The early settler was always tempted to seize whatever nature offered, especially if it was food, and so free himself to enlarge his capital by clearing more land.

The plentifulness of land and game were not the only facts which had discouraged the improvement of American farming. The man who farmed in America was likely to be an amateur: "all sorts of people turn farmers . . . no mechanic or artizan—sailor—soldier—servant, &c. but what, if they get money, take land, and turn farmers." Although the English farmer may have looked advanced by colonial standards, his methods left a good deal to be desired when compared to those of his European contemporaries, German farmers, for example. The techniques exported to the colonies from Great Britain were seldom the best.

The arriving colonists used any method which would produce quick results, regardless of how it exhausted the land. Their first need was an assured supply of food, and they learned their first lessons in hus-bandry from the natives. Indian corn—Europeans called it "maize"—

remained the main bread-crop all over the colonies. Although the Indians had perfected a high-yielding strain, their techniques of cultivation were primitive; the colonists long followed their example. Moreover, uninterrupted crops of corn soon exhausted the soil. "The land, in their system, after it is done with corn," the author of *American Husbandry* observed, "is of no more value than the sky to them."

The recurrent colonial wars made planning difficult, increased the scarcity of manpower, and kept American farmers conservative. "We are all military Men, as well as Farmers," Jared Eliot complained in 1759, "our Circumstances being like that of the old Romans, from the Plow to the War, and from the War to the Plow again." In the preceding year alone, he figured, at least 5000 men had left their farms to fight the French or the Indians—"which, together with heavy Charges consequent upon it, renders it neither safe nor prudent, to leave the old beaten Paths, for new Inventions. . . . having neither Hands nor Money to spare, for the Prosecution for any New Schemes, or untry'd Methods."

The range of farming problems, from those of the unfamiliar heavy winters of the northern colonies to those of the equally unfamiliar heat of the Carolinas, was far wider than in little England. And there were as many different kinds of bad husbandry as there were soils and crops and climates. The snowy New England winters, covering the frozen land for several months, made it impossible to follow the advice of English theorists who told the frugal farmer to spend his winter dressing and plowing his fields; the New England farmer had to crowd his manuring, fencing, and harrowing into a short spring. This system was self-perpetuating, because low yields made the New Englander spend whatever time he could spare on clearing another acre which in its turn would soon be used up.

In the middle colonies, and especially in Pennsylvania, where farming methods may have been somewhat better, the temptations to overextend —"taking too much land for their money"—were especially corrupting. Draft animals were needed, but they were scarce, and the colonists did not know how to care for them. "They clear a field and have not strength of ploughs and cattle and men to crop more than that; they therefore stick to it as long as they can get any corn, and when the land will no longer bear it, they clear another piece and serve that in the same manner. . . . this must necessarily be the system while the settlers spend half their fortune in buying the land, that is, in paying the province fees for it: if a man has a hundred pounds in his pocket, and was able with it to cultivate properly forty or fifty acres, and he takes three or four hundred, which in patent fees costs him half his fortune, he then plainly lessens his ability to cultivate."

We have already seen how tobacco-culture in Virginia exhausted the soil, making plantation-owners into land-speculators, and how this was reflected in the government of the colony. Farther south, farming methods were even worse. The sparseness of population in North Carolina, which lacked a good seaport, increased incentives to use up land and move on. A wealth of pitch, tar, and turpentine could be taken from the wild growth. In South Carolina, the rice grown in swamps was a crop unfamiliar to Englishmen; its cultivation involved expensive irrigation and drainage problems which the colonial planters showed no special ingenuity in solving. Indigo, also strange to English farmers, quickly exhausted the soil.

This wide variety of climates, soils, and products was itself an obstacle to concerted efforts for improving American agriculture. Each region had to learn its own lessons. The difficulties of inland communication and the scarcity of useful books kept methods stagnant. Costly experiments in such things as silk and wine were repeated partly because later experimenters lacked reliable accounts of earlier failures. But nothing was more obstructive than the sheer novelty of American conditions which made useless much of the advice found in English books. It was remarkable that any progress had been made, Jared Eliot observed in 1748, "When we consider the small Number of the first Settlers, and coming from an old Cultivated Country, to thick Woods, rough unimproved Lands; where all their former Experience and Knowledge was now of very little service to them: They were destitute of Beasts of Burthen or Carriage; Unskill'd in every Part of Service to be done: It may be said, That in a Sort, they began the World a New."

What English agriculturalists meant by improvement in the colonies did not necessarily mean a better life for the colonial farmers. From the British imperial point of view, it was most desirable to encourage the production of staples like hemp, sugar, indigo, silk, and wine, which would not grow in the British Isles and for which British gold had to be sent abroad. We have already seen the effect in Georgia of this doctrinaire approach to colonial agriculture. In nearly every colony, costly and futile efforts were made to increase the production of exotic staple crops. "There is all the reason in the world to think that the nation's expectations of having hemp from the colonies will at last, after so many disappointments, be answered by the lands on the Ohio," the author of *American Husbandry* optimistically remarked. "This is precisely what has been so long wanted. . . . Neglect of this sort sometimes gives rise to ideas of incapacity in a country, when the fault is only in the cultivator ... they ought to have been bound to supply the navy with a given quantity of hemp, the growth of the colony, annually: this would have forced them to give a degree of attention to this important article."

More realistic, organized efforts to improve American agriculture came slowly. From New England in the mid-18th century, when land had ceased to seem so rich or plentiful and when wood shortage had become a problem, came the first important American treatise on agriculture. The Rev. Jared Eliot's six essays, first published between 1748 and 1759, were collected into a volume, *Essays upon Field Husbandry in New England, as it is or may be Ordered* (Boston, 1760). Eliot, a Connecticut clergyman and the grandson of the apostle John Eliot who had tried to convert the Natick Indians, was also the leading physician of his colony. Many Connecticut doctors served their apprenticeship under him. His long career as a clergyman-physician—"more than Thirty Years in a Business that required a great deal of Travel"—provided him, he said, with the information for his essays and his own experiments. "An Ounce of Experience is better than a Pound of Science," Eliot observed. His essays contributed little that was new to agricultural science but he did collect useful hints on drainage, crop-rotation, manuring, stock-breeding, and dozens of other subjects. He improved Jethro Tull's planting-drill and adapted Tull's method to American conditions. But even Eliot still hoped for a large silk-making industry in Connecticut, and he argued for small landholdings as the best means of defending the borders of empire.

It was several decades before many others joined Eliot in an effort to improve American agriculture. Local agricultural societies in Great Britain, even before mid-century, were pooling the experience of gentlemen-farmers and exchanging the results of experiments. But it was not until 1785 that an effective organization for agricultural improvement was founded in America. Earlier in the century the American Philosophical Society at Philadelphia had announced agricultural improvements among its objectives, but it accomplished very little. Jefferson's main contributions—for example, his famous mould-board plow (1798)—came only late in the century. Progress in American agriculture came during the years after the Revolution.

Of course, there were exceptions to this laggard character of colonial farming. The famous Narragansett pacers of Rhode Island—"some of them pace a Mile in little more than two Minutes, a good deal less than three"—showed that it was possible here to breed first-class stock for export. The German farmers who came in the early 18th century, arriving mostly at Philadelphia on their way westward to the rich farmlands of Pennsylvania and toward the Ohio Valley, showed a frugality which contrasted sharply with the slovenliness of other American farmers. They made their Conestoga Valley famous—not only by the "Conestoga Wagons," the heavy, broad-wheeled covered wagons which later symbolized the westward movement—but by the "Conestoga Horse" which they developed from English stock into the finest draft animal of the colonial age. Their methods, as Benjamin Rush surveyed them toward the end of the 18th century, were a catalogue of the omissions of other American farmers. "A German farm may be distinguished from the farm of the other citizens of the state, by the superior size of their barns; the plain, but compact form of their houses; the height of their inclosures; the extent of their orchards; the fertility of their fields; the luxuriance of their meadows, and a general appearance of plenty and neatness in everything that belongs to them." In their efficient farming methods the Germans were using the specialized skills they brought with them. They were simply being conservative after their fashion.

BOOK THREE

LANGUAGE AND
THE PRINTED WORD

"The people of one quarter of the world, will
be able to associate and converse together like
children of the same family."

NOAH WEBSTER

BRITISH COLONIALS were already beginning to talk like
Americans. In what they read and in what they printed, the New
World was having its way. We will see, in the following chapters, the
beginning of an American language and of an American style in
reading; and how American printing-presses came to serve American needs. Here the printed word ceased to be the property of a
literary class and began to belong to the public.

PART TEN
THE NEW
UNIFORMITY

"Those people spell best who do not know how to spell."

BENJAMIN FRANKLIN

41

An American Accent

WHILE Englishmen along the colonial seaboard tried to cling to the familiar local ways of the different parts of England from which they had come, they founded—without meaning to—a culture which was in many ways more homogeneous in vast America than it had been in little England. The settlers clung to their mother language, and in the course of moving about the New World and in moving up and down the social scale, they made it more uniform. A single spoken language soon echoed across the continent, overcoming space as the printed word overcomes time. The American language would fulfill the Elizabethan prophecy of Samuel Daniel written in 1599:

> And who, in time, knowes whither we may vent
> The treasure of our tongue, to what strange shores
> This gaine of our best glory shall be sent,
> T'inrich unknowing Nations with our stores?
> What worlds in th' yet unformed Occident
> May come refin'd with th' accents that are ours?

Only two centuries later when this dream had become a fact, Noah Webster foresaw that "North America will be Peopled with a hundred millions of men, *all speaking the same language*." Contrasted with Europe, America promised a "period when the people of one quarter of the

271

world, will be able to associate and converse together like children of the same family."

The American language has indeed shown a spectacular uniformity. Only after we have looked at polyglot nations like India, the Soviet Union, and China, or when we remind ourselves that Europe, with an area of less than four million square miles, possesses at least a dozen major languages, can we appreciate our advantage. The people of the United States, spread over three million square miles, speak only one language. There is more difference between the speech of Naples and Milan, or of Canterbury and Yorkshire, or of a Welsh coal-miner and an Oxford undergraduate, or of a Provençal peasant and a Paris lawyer than there is between the language of Maine and California, or between the speech of a factory-worker and a college president in the United States.

The linguistic uniformity of America is geographic (without barriers of regional dialect) and social (without barriers of caste and class). Both types of uniformity have had vast consequences for the national life; they have been both symptoms and causes of a striving for national unity. When we note what a large French-speaking population has meant in Canadian political life or how numerous languages have obstructed federation in India, we begin to realize how different our political life might have been without our language unity. Many other features of modern American culture—including the geographic mobility of the population, the public educational system, the mail-order catalogs, the networks of radio and television, the national mass-circulation magazines and "national advertising" (with all these have meant for the standard of living)—would have been more difficult in a nation of several languages. What would have happened to the Log-Cabin-to-the-White-House style of American politics if, as in England, a man who lacked the "proper" background betrayed himself in every word? Our common, classless language has provided the vernacular for equality in America.

The other "American" qualities of our language seem trivial beside this monumental uniformity, which can be traced back to the earliest age of English settlement. If the roots of this linguistic uniformity had not been strongly developed during the colonial period, before the numerous and motley immigrations of the 19th century, the United States might not today offer the world the paradoxical spectacle of a nation of many peoples who speak a single language. Almost from the first settlement there were pressures toward uniformity.

First, consider pronunciation. Men in areas as remote from each other as Massachusetts Bay and Virginia had brought with them the same language. They had come mostly from the same regions—London, the Midlands, and southern England—and they represented roughly the same social classes. Although the speech differences between New England and the South even today are not great enough to make them barriers to understanding, the most remote parts of the Atlantic colonies in 17th-century America probably did not show even these small differences. New Englanders and Southerners then spoke with something like what we now call a "Southern accent." Southern pronunciation today is thus in many respects a survival of older ways and the "English" characteristics of later New England speech are apparently innovations.

Once on American shores, English speech tended to become more uniform, because of some general colonial and some peculiarly American forces. "In consequence of the frequent removals of people from one part of our country to another," John Pickering in his vocabulary of Americanisms (1816) noted "greater uniformity of dialect throughout the United States . . . than is to be found throughout England." Even before the end of the 18th century, such students of language as the Rev. John Witherspoon, who had come from Scotland to become president of Princeton, noted this fact. "The vulgar in America speak much better than the vulgar in Great-Britain," he remarked in *The Druid* (1781), "for a very obvious reason, viz. that being much more unsettled, and moving frequently from place to place, they are not so liable to local peculiarities either in accent or phraseology. There is a greater difference in dialect between one county and another in Britain, than there is between one state and another in America." The once-isolated English regional dialects met and had to speak to one another. Recent linguistic scholars have noted this tendency toward uniformity to be a general characteristic of the speech of any colony compared to that of its mother country.

America, then, in the 18th century was a melting pot, although the distinctions among the ingredients were subtler in its earliest period. In the 19th and 20th centuries such diverse elements as Irish, German, Polish, Jewish, Italian, Mexican, and Chinese were to be compounded; in the 17th and 18th centuries the immigrants came from Yorkshire, Norfolk, Suffolk, Essex, London, Kent, Hampshire, and other English counties. Anyone who looks at a map of England marked to show the places of origin of traceable 17th-century immigrants to New England and Virginia cannot fail to be impressed with their dispersion over the face of the mother-country. Although, as we have already noted, there was some tendency to concentrate (those from the Midlands in Virginia; from London and East Anglia in New England), and immigration did not yet draw heavily from the peasantry, still the earliest American colonies included men from different social classes and from many parts of the homeland.

American life bred uniformity even within smaller areas, like New England itself. About seventy per cent of the traceable settlers of Plymouth, Watertown, Dedham, and Groton in Massachusetts during the 17th century seem to have come from London and the Eastern counties; the remainder were widely dispersed. Most important, the ruling group did not all speak a single dialect, so could not fix any particular dialect as the language of the community. The pronunciation revealed by the spelling of the semi-literate scribes of the New England towns, who had come from many parts of England, suggests a speech remarkably uniform and remarkably near the standard speech of England.

The same 18th-century travelers who noted the lack of dialects were impressed also by the proper and grammatical English spoken by Americans of all classes. In Virginia, the Rev. Hugh Jones observed in 1724, "the Planters, and even the Native Negroes generally talk good English without Idiom or Tone, and can discourse handsomly upon most common Subjects." Councillor Robert Carter preferred American-trained, rather than Scotch or English tutors for his children "on account of pronunciation in the English Language." The faculty of William & Mary College in the 18th century was especially concerned that the students learn proper pronunciation. In Philadelphia, the Scottish Lord Adam Gordon, traveling the colonies in 1764-65, found that "the propriety of Language here surprized me much, the English tongue being spoken by all ranks, in a degree of purity and perfection, surpassing any, but the polite part of London."

Some went so far as to say that the colonists "in general speak better English than the English do." Even critical observers agreed. The Rev. Jonathan Boucher (1737-1804)—who had lived in the South for about fifteen years, had taught Washington's stepson, John Parke Custis, and was a leading Loyalist in the Revolution—spent many years preparing a "Glossary of Archaic and Provincial Words." He felt that the absence of dialect in America had actually impoverished the tongue, but he still found it "extraordinary that, in North America, there prevails not only, I believe, the purest Pronunciation of the English Tongue that is anywhere to be met with, but a perfect Uniformity."

The state of American speech in the years just before the Revolution was summarized by William Eddis in his letter from America dated June 8, 1770:

> In England, almost every county is distinguished by a peculiar dialect; even different habits, and different modes of thinking, evidently dis-

criminate inhabitants, whose local situation is not far remote: but in
Maryland, and throughout adjacent provinces, it is worthy of observation, that a striking similarity of speech universally prevails; and it is
strictly true, that the pronunciation of the generality of the people has
an accuracy and elegance, that cannot fail of gratifying the most judicious ear.

The colonists are composed of adventurers, not only from every district of Great Britain and Ireland, but from almost every other European government, where the principles of liberty and commerce have
operated with spirit and efficacy. Is it not, therefore, reasonable to
suppose, that the English language must be greatly corrupted by such
a strange intermixture of various nations? The reverse is, however, true.
The language of the immediate descendants of such a promiscuous
ancestry is perfectly uniform, and unadulterated; nor has it borrowed
any provincial, or national accent, from its British or foreign parentage.

For my part, I confess myself totally at a loss to account for the
apparent difference, between the colonists and persons under equal
circumstances of education and fortune, resident in the mother country.
This uniformity of language prevails not only on the coast, where Europeans form a considerable mass of the people, but likewise in the interior parts, where population has made but slow advances; and
where opportunities seldom occur to derive any great advantages from
an intercourse with intelligent strangers.

The resistance of the American language during the colonial period
to borrowing and the invention of words shows the strength of the forces
toward a uniform English speech. Wholesale assimilation of foreign words
might have produced a semi-English patois, a pidgin English or a
papiamento, like those in the Caribbean or in parts of South East Asia.
But this never happened. The opportunities for the mixing of French and
German into English in the colonial period were so numerous that the
failure of English colonials to seize them is doubly remarkable. Few
words were borrowed from German before the Revolution, despite the
several German-speaking communities in Pennsylvania, in the Valley
of Virginia, in Georgia, and elsewhere. It was not until after the Louisiana
Purchase (1803), after the settlements across the Mississippi, and
especially during and after the Mexican War (1846-48), that many
words were taken from the Spanish. There were not many borrowings
from the French until after the Revolution, the Louisiana Purchase, and
the increasing contacts with the French along the Northwestern border;
although a few important words like *portage, chowder* and *caché* were
adopted very early, and *bureau* and *prairie* were adopted before the
Revolution. Some of the earliest borrowings were from the Dutch, for

example, *boss* and *Yankee,* but the whole intake of Dutch words was not large.

During the colonial period probably the largest number of additions to the English language in America were of two limited classes: borrowings of Indian words and new combinations of English words. The borrowed Indian words were mostly from place-names, especially for natural features, like *Massachusetts* Bay; or they were words having to do with Indian relations, Indian life, Indian crops, or objects in Indian use, such as *hominy, toboggan, pemmican, mackinaw, moccasin, papoose, sachem, powwow, tomahawk, wigwam, succotash,* and *squaw,* all of which were circulating by mid-18th century. America's novel plants and animals incited new combinations of familiar English words, such as *bullfrog, mudhen, catbird, catfish, muskrat, razorback, gartersnake,* and *groundhog,* and American life suggested *backwoods, backstreet, backlane, backlog, backcountry*, while a number of older English words—*bluff, cliff, neck, bottoms, pond,* and *creek* acquired novel meanings to fit the American landscape. Some of these new combinations already faintly smacked of that copious and spicy enrichment of the language which was to come in the early 19th century. But before the Revolution the only strikingly new character which the English language had acquired in America was its uniformity.

The very word "Americanism," meaning an expression formed or predominantly used in America, was not known until Witherspoon employed it in 1781. Before then there was surprisingly little need for it. That brashness and extravagance, the rip-snortin' (we owe the word to Davy Crockett) lingo of the frontier and the Wild West, the flowery spread-eagle bombast of 4th-of-July orators, which all seem so American, come not from the 18th but from the 19th century. The borrowings from French, Spanish, Italian, German, and Yiddish, and the free commercial invention of words (from *Kodak* to *Sanforized*), were also products of American life in the 19th and 20th centuries—of the vast immigrations, industrialization, mass production, the mixing of peoples in great cities, and the rise of advertising, national magazines, radio and television. The vocabulary did not become distinctively American until at least a half-century after the Declaration of Independence. The expansive, vibrant, motley, adventuring spirit of Elizabethan England was to find a latter-day counterpart in the spirit of 19th-century America; the enterprising spirit of both ages was expressed in a vitality, ingenuity, and experimentalism of language. "The Elizabethan quality in American English," Krapp has observed, "is not an inheritance but a development on American soil."

American speech remained conservative, clinging to an increasingly uniform standard, during the entire colonial period. Non-English-speaking peoples tended to become quickly assimilated. The French Huguenots who sought refuge in America after the Revocation of the Edict of Nantes in 1685 were, for example, soon absorbed. The numerous Germans who came here in the 17th century, occasionally as whole communities, and settled in Pennsylvania and the valley of Virginia, in some instances retained a modified German dialect for use among themselves, but their language exerted negligible influence upon American English. New immigrants expecting to rise into the higher social classes which were already speaking the American language felt every incentive to learn the common language of the community. By speaking "broken English" the parents expressed their own aspirations for the common language and the hope that their children might rise in the world.

42

Quest for a Standard

As soon as literary people in 18th-century America became conscious of their own language, they expressed an excessive enthusiasm for the standard language of England. Perhaps this was a characteristically colonial phenomenon—people still insecure in their new culture trying to reassure themselves by showing that they could be even more proper than the people back home. They were like the country cousin who overdresses when he comes to the big city. The colonial frame of mind bred an attitude toward language which still affects the life of every American schoolboy, and shapes the American accent to this day.

In this respect, as in many others, Benjamin Franklin was a spokesman for provincial America. It is symbolic of the tension within the colonial culture that although Franklin did not hesitate to do some superficial gadgeteering with the language, he clung to its ancient spirit. His unfinished *Scheme for a New Alphabet and Reformed Mode of Spelling* (1768), which would have abolished as unnecessary the letters *c, w, y,* and *j* and would have required the addition of six new characters, was as complicated as most systems of simplified spelling. He urged his scheme only in an affectionate letter to his "Diir frind" Mary Stevenson, but before long his good sense must have made him agree with Mary who could "si meni inkanviiniensis, az uel az difikyltis." However much Franklin might have been amused by tinkering with spelling, he never showed any desire to meddle with the approved English style of Addison in his own writing. He showed the same respect for the traditional English language that he showed for the traditional rights of Englishmen.

Franklin was to be the Father of Purism in American English. The 18th century has been called the Age of Pedants in the history of the English language, and it is at first surprising to find that Franklin, who was in so many other ways a champion of good sense and experiment, was in matters of language among the stodgiest. When Franklin sent David Hume, the English philosopher, a copy of his pamphlet on Canada and Guadeloupe, Hume replied with some criticisms of Franklin's language, to which Franklin readily acquiesced. Franklin (Sept. 27, 1760) accepted Hume's objection to his use of such new words as *pejorate, colonize,* and *unshakable:* "The introducing new words, where we are already possessed of old ones sufficiently expressive, I confess must be generally wrong, as it tends to change the language." Franklin did speculate that it would have been more convenient if English, like German, had allowed the novel combination of familiar words. "But I hope, with you," Franklin pledged, "that we shall always in America make the best English of this Island our standard, and I believe it will be so. I assure you it often gives me pleasure to reflect, how greatly the audience (if I may so term it) of a good English writer will, in another century or two, be increased by the increase of English people in our colonies."

From this quest for truly English English, Franklin never wavered. Nearly thirty years later (Dec. 26, 1789), in his famous letter to Noah Webster acknowledging the dedication of Webster's *Dissertations on the English Language,* Franklin, perhaps with a touch of irony, applauded Webster's "Zeal for preserving the Purity of our Language, both in its Expressions and Pronunciation, and in correcting the popular Errors several of our States are continually falling into with respect to both." He then called Webster's attention to certain "errors" in the hope that "in some future Publication of yours, you would set a discountenancing Mark upon them." The usages Franklin found particularly objectionable were *improved* (in the sense of "employed"), the making of verbs out of the nouns *notice* and *advocate,* and "the most awkward and abominable of the three," the use of *progress* as a verb! There was very little in this letter that could not have been written by Dr. Johnson himself; it breathed the spirit of the Age of Pedants.

We sometimes forget the power of Franklin's example in the direction of conformism and "purity" in language. One of the reasons for his high reputation among American writers, as John Pickering explained in 1816, was that "Franklin is one of the very few American writers whose style has satisfied the English critics." From Franklin's success the moral was generally drawn that to write the language well one had to stick to safe English models. Until well into the 19th century, as Henry Cabot Lodge shrewdly observed, "the first step of an American entering upon a literary career was to pretend to be an Englishman, in order that he might win the approval, not of Englishmen, but of his own countrymen."

In the later 18th century when Americans described the peculiarities of the American language, they did so, almost without exception, for the wholesome purpose (in Franklin's phrase) of putting "a discountenancing Mark" on them. The Rev. John Witherspoon in his *Druid* essays (1781), for example, showed a zeal for the "purity and perfection" of the language. According to him, the American pressures toward uniformity—toward a common speech for all classes—actually threatened the *purity* of the language, for the vulgarisms of one social class or one part of the country quickly contaminated the speech of everybody, even "scholars and public persons."

> The fourth class of improprieties consists of *local phrases* or *terms*. By these I mean such vulgarisms as prevail in one part of a country and not in another. There is a much greater variety of these in Britain than in America. From the complete population of the country, multitudes of common people never remove to any distance from where they were born and bred. Hence there are many characteristic distinctions, not only in phraseology, but in accent, dress, manners, &c. not only between one county and another, but between different cities of the same county. . . .

> But if there is a much greater number of local vulgarisms in Britain than America, there is also, for this very reason, much less danger of their being used by gentlemen or scholars. It is indeed implied in the very nature of the thing, that a local phrase will not be used by any but the inhabitants or natives of that part of the country where it prevails. However, I am of opinion, that even local vulgarisms find admission into the discourse of people of better rank more easily here than in Europe.

This search for a "purer" English, which in most instances meant simply a more English English, preoccupied writers on the subject even into the 19th century. Mencken estimated that from the beginning of the Revolution until 1800 more Americanisms came into the language than at any other time between the earliest colonial days and the rush to the West. Partly because of this wave of innovation, American purists intensified their efforts. "It has in so many instances departed from the English standard," John Pickering warned in 1816, "that our scholars should lose no time in endeavouring to restore it to its purity, and to prevent future corruption."

Among the leaders of the return to a purer English we find none other than the patron saint of American linguistic nationalism, Noah Webster. If any single purpose ran through Webster's writings it was to *purify* the American language; this he aimed to do by restoring it to the condition of the "best" language of the "best" period in England. When Webster was only thirty-one years of age, he published his *Dissertations on the English Language* (1789), which stated fully his ideas. He there expressed the theory (which he did not revise substantially until 1806) that every language at some epoch reached an apex.

> But when a language has arrived at a certain stage of improvement, it must be stationary or become retrograde; for improvements in science either cease, or become slow and too inconsiderable to affect materially the tone of a language. This stage of improvement is the period when a nation abounds with writers of the first class, both for abilities and taste. This period in England commenced with the age of Queen Elizabeth and ended with the reign of George II. It would have been fortunate for the language, had the stile of writing and the pronunciation of words been fixed, as they stood in the reign of Queen Ann and her successor. Few improvements have been made since that time; but innumerable corruptions in pronunciation have been introduced by Garrick, and in stile, by Johnson, Gibbon and their imitators.

Webster was not urging the superior advantage of a new *American* language, but the superior opportunity here to restore "the *English* language in its purity." The truly dangerous innovators, he argued, were the English writers of the later 18th century; Americans must not be corrupted by their example. The English critics who pointed out "corruptions" in the American language had simply revealed their own ignorance.

> On examining the language, and comparing the practice of speaking among the yeomanry of this country, with the stile of Shakespear and

Addison, I am constrained to declare that the people of America, in particular the English descendants, speak the most pure English now known in the world. There is hardly a foreign idiom in their language; by which I mean, a phrase that has not been used by the best English writers from the time of Chaucer. They retain a few obsolete words, which have been dropt by writers, probably from mere affectation, as those which are substituted are neither more melodious nor expressive. In many instances they retain correct phrases, instead of which the pretended refiners of the language have introduced those which are highly improper and absurd.

Webster was ready to justify even his spelling reforms in this conservative way. When he was charged with introducing novelties merely to secure simplicity, he stuck to his guns. "In the few instances in which I write words a little differently from the present usage," Webster wrote in 1809, "I do *not* innovate, but *reject innovation*. When I write *fether, lether,* and *mold* I do nothing more than reduce the words to their original orthography, no other being used in our earliest English books." He searched for the "primitive etymological orthography" which, along with a cleansing of style, would "call back the language to the purity of former times." The same went for pronunciation. "Your way of pronouncing *deaf* is *def*—ours, as if it were written deef," Webster told the visiting English naval officer, Captain Basil Hall, nearly twenty years later, "and as this is the correct mode from which you have departed, I shall adhere to the American way."

In his enthusiasm for the purity and uniformity of the American language Webster grossly underestimated the number of distinctively American words and American usages. He doubted, in his *Dissertations,* whether there were as many as a hundred English words in use in America "except such as are used in employments wholly local" which were not universally intelligible. Nearly forty years later, in 1828, the year of publication of his *American Dictionary of the English Language,* he boasted to Captain Hall that "there were not fifty words in all which were used in America and not in England." Webster's so-called *American Dictionary* drew copiously on the writings of Americans for examples, but, as Thomas Pyles has remarked, there was no other justification for calling it "American."

Yet Noah Webster was thoroughly American—and never more so than when he sought an external (and even an English) standard for the American language. His passion for linguistic legislation was, of course, to have its counterpart in an American passion for written constitutions and for almost every other kind of legislation. It expressed the cultural insecurity of a colonial people. After 1776 it began to express the quest for a national identity.

But how was a standard to be established? As early as 1724, the Rev. Hugh Jones, then professor of mathematics at William & Mary College, desired that a "Publick Standard were fix'd" to "direct Posterity, and prevent Irregularity, and confused Abuses and Corruptions in our writings and Expressions." In 1774, another writer, possibly John Adams, urged in the *Royal American Magazine* that where so many people over so wide an area spoke the same language, the opportunities for "perfecting" the English language should be seized by forming the *Fellows of the American Society of Language.* The Loyalist Governor of New Hampshire forwarded this proposal to the Secretary of State for the Colonies back in London. Only a few years later, after Independence, John Adams wrote to the president of Congress proposing that Congress set up an academy for "correcting, improving and ascertaining the English language." The fact that the English had never set up such an academy in England made it all the more important that there be one in America. "It will have a happy effect upon the union of States to have a public standard for all persons in every part of the continent to appeal to, both for the signification and pronunciation of the language." In 1806, a bill to establish such an academy was introduced in the Senate and reported favorably by a committee of which John Quincy Adams was a member; but when the title of the academy was amended to omit the word "National," the project died. On occasion Noah Webster also advocated legislation to fix the language and keep it pure, but for him the aid of Congress was almost superfluous. In his own realm Webster had become something of a dictator, and, like all dictators, he preferred to speak the law himself. These were only the first in a long series of zealous efforts reaching into our own century to use the legislature or the schoolmaster to keep our language pure and purely American.

By the end of the 18th century, observant Americans had begun to notice that, despite or perhaps because of the widespread uniformity of the language in the colonies, there had not yet arisen any class or locality on this side of the water which was the arbiter of linguistic propriety. "We are at a great distance from the island of Great-Britain, in which the standard of the language is as yet supposed to be found," Dr. Witherspoon remarked in 1781. "Every state is equal to and independent of every other; and, I believe, none of them will agree, at least immediately, to receive laws from another in discourse, any more than in action. Time and accident must determine what turn affairs will take in this respect in future, whether we shall continue to consider the language of Great-Britain as the pattern upon which we are to form ours: or whether, in this new empire, some centre of learning and politeness will not be found, which shall obtain influence and prescribe the rules of speech and writing to every other part." According to Dr. Johnson, this lack of a cultural capital, the wide dispersion of population, and the vast extent of America helped account for the barbarism of the American language. "A nation scattered in the boundless regions of America resembles rays diverging from a focus. All the rays remain but the heat is gone." What the pontifical Doctor disparaged as "the American dialect" simply showed the "corruption to which every language widely diffused must always be exposed."

In the early 17th century, when the American colonies were first settled, every man had spelled as he pleased. Orthography, like style or content, expressed the whim and personality of the writer or the printer. It was not until the early 18th century that the principal English authors all spelled pretty much alike; and not until Dr. Johnson's *Dictionary* (1755) that writers possessed a standard which nearly everybody accepted. It was handy for the rising middle classes to have a guide into the paths of linguistic elegance frequented by the upper classes. This was especially important in England, where language had long been (and till this day remains) an index of social class; the ability to speak and write the "standard" language of the ruling aristocracy was essential to an enjoyment of its other privileges. It is, then, not surprising that the late 18th and early 19th century saw an unprecedented number of dictionaries, grammars, and guides to correct speech. These "linguistic Emily Posts" enabled men to speak and write with unobtrusive propriety among their "betters."

It would have horrified Dr. Johnson and his Tory friends to discover that the dogma of "correctness" in language—the doctrine that to speak well one must speak by the book, and that to speak by the book is to speak well—would help men of low birth push their way up (grammar and dictionary in hand) into the best dining halls and salons. Before guides to correct usage existed, a man learned his speech as he learned his manners and his place in society, from his father and mother. There was probably no language more casual and relaxed than the aristocratic talk of the 17th- and 18th-century English drawing-rooms, from which such words as *ain't* and even *hain't* are relics. Before mid-18th century a man did not consciously learn, and did not need to be taught, the "proper" language for his social class, for he drank it in with his mother's milk. The very idea that there was a single "proper" speech which any literate person could learn from a recipe book was subversive of old ways and the old caste. It is easy to see why this way of looking at language would suit the New World.

43

Culture by the Book:
The Spelling Fetish

THE MOST INFLUENTIAL American writer on language was Noah Webster, Spelling-Master to America. The colossal popularity of his spellers—they had sold over sixty millions before the end of the 19th century—was both a symptom and a symbol of the mobility of American society. Webster's *American Spelling Book,* "containing an easy Standard of Pronunciation," appeared in 1789, but the demand it met, as Webster himself noted, had long been there.

In America there flourished a ritual or game which popularized the effort to make "proper" speech accessible to all. This was the spelling-bee; and the word "bee" in this sense was appropriately an Americanism. In this public ceremony contestants and audience bore witness that there was no secret about how to speak or write the most "correct" language of the community and hence that the linguistic upper class was open to all. The spelling-bee was already familiar, especially in New England, in the time of the Revolution. As early as 1750, Franklin had proposed a public competitive game of spelling; by the latter half of the 18th century spelling matches had become well-established in the schools. In rural communities and on the western frontier, where spelling was especially valued as a symbol of culture, the institution took on a new life in the 19th century, described, for example, in Bret Harte's "Spelling Bee at Angels." There we learn from Truthful James:

> Thar's a new game down in Frisco, that ez far ez I can see
> Beats euchre, poker, and van-toon, they calls the "Spellin' Bee."

At the particular bee which Bret Harte describes, all went peacefully— even through the spelling of *separate, parallel,* and *rhythm*—but the miners finally found it necessary to settle the spelling of *gneiss* by a fight with bowie knives.

Emphasis on "rules" of proper speaking and writing profoundly influenced the whole American attitude toward pronunciation. It explains what is still perhaps the most important distinction between English and American pronunciation, the American tendency toward "spelling-pronunciation." Very early, Americans began trying to discover how a word "ought" to be pronounced by seeing how it was spelled. This seemed to provide a ready standard of pronunciation in a land without a cultural capital or a ruling intellectual aristocracy.

We have become so accustomed to our own equation of spelling and pronunciation that we find it hard to imagine that a tendency to pronounce by custom rather than by spelling may have been an older and more "literary" tradition. Yet that seems to have been the case. The casual way of pronouncing which followed caste and custom and not the spelling-book had long prevailed in the English of England.

Our insistent spelling-pronunciation shows itself in our habit of preserving the full value of syllables. In long words like *secretary, explanatory, laboratory,* and *cemetery,* we preserve the full value of all, including the next-to-last syllable, while the English almost drop that syllable and say "secret'ry," "explanat'ry, "laborat'ry," and "cemet'ry." These are only a few examples of the American insistence on giving every spelled syllable its fully pronounced due. Some of these cases turn out to be historically complicated by the fact that the secondary accent we have preserved in the next-to-last syllable of a word like *secretary* seems also to have been characteristic of 17th- and 18th-century spoken English. But while in England these syllables have tended to become lost, in America they have been studiously preserved. This would not alter the argument but would simply show that American spelling-pronunciation, like much else in our speech, is conservative. Our deference to spelling as a guide to pronunciation has been so strong that we have kept alive here ways of speech which soon died in England. The ritual of the spelling-bee also tended to preserve the full pronounced values of syllables, and to promote literalness in pronunciation. In the early days, spelling was taught by reading a word aloud from the Speller letter by letter and syllable by syllable: "o, r—or; d, i—di; n, a—na; r, y—ry; ordinary." Students who had been taught the language in this fashion (often under the incentive of team competition) would be apt to remain careful, deliberate, and literal in pronunciation for the rest of their lives. Our weakness for spelling-pronunciation affected the pronunciation of proper names, and especially the names of places. In England these had a purely traditional and casual pronunciation, but Americans who hear *Worcester* pronounced *Wooster* are apt to spell it that way; and *Birmingham* is fully and carefully pronounced, never in the elided English manner.

The "Dictatorship of the Schoolmarm," often attacked by sophisticated

students, has dampened our ebullience and ingenuity. But the Schoolmarm, like her predecessor the Schoolmaster, by declaring teachable rules
of language has helped dissolve class distinctions and has kept one
more avenue open in a mobile society. Who could have predicted that a
free and equalitarian society would be promoted by a pedantically
precise standard of language?

H. L. Mencken has summed up the wider meaning of the special
precision of American speech:

> It may be described briefly as the influence of a class but lately risen
> in the social scale and hence a bit unsure of itself—a class intensely
> eager to avoid giving away its vulgar origin by its speech habits. . . .
> Precision in speech thus became the hall-mark of those who had but
> recently arrived. Obviously, the number of those who have but re-
> cently arrived has always been greater in the United States than in
> England, not only among the aristocracy of wealth and fashion but
> also among the *intelligentsia*. The average American schoolmarm, the
> chief guardian of linguistic niceness in the Republic, does not come
> from the class that has a tradition of culture behind it, but from the
> class of small farmers and city clerks and workmen. This is true, I
> believe, even of the average American college teacher. Such persons
> do not advocate and practise precision in speech on logical grounds
> alone; they are also moved, plainly enough, by the fact that it tends
> to conceal their own cultural insecurity. From them come most of the
> gratuitous rules and regulations that afflict schoolboys and harass the
> writers of the country. They are the chief discoverers and denouncers
> of 'bad English' in the books of such men as Whitman, Mark Twain
> and Howells. But it would be a mistake to think of their influence as
> wholly, or even as predominantly evil. They have thrown themselves
> valiantly against the rise of dialects among us, and with such success
> that nothing so grossly unpleasant to the ear as the cockney whine
> or so lunatic as the cockney manhandling of the *h* is now prevalent
> anywhere in the United States. And they have policed the general
> speech to such effect that even on its most pretentious levels it is
> virtually free from the silly affectations which still mark Standard
> English.

In this particular way, the American language has expressed both the
literate and the *non-literary* character of American culture. A printed
standard presupposes widespread literacy; the Dictatorship of the
Schoolmarm would never have been possible unless everybody in the
country had come under her jurisdiction through universal public education. Moreover, if America had had a powerful centralized literary aristocracy able to set up its casual practice as the criterion for the speech

of all cultivated men, textbook standards of precision would have been superfluous and impossible. Literacy displaces aristocracy. Students of language note that the tendency to make the spoken conform with the written form of a word "in general grows as the printed and written aspects of language become more prominent in the language consciousness of a people." While there has been some such tendency in England, it has been much stronger in America. "Each new group of American citizens," Krapp observes, "has entered into possession of the language not as a natural inheritance, not as a privilege, but as an acquisition, as something to be gained through intelligent application and study." Through learning to read, write, and speak the common language many peoples were amalgamated into a single nation.

The early New England settlers, middle-class and literate, champions of the common school, had a good deal to do with establishing uniformity in the first place. The Yankee schoolmaster, like the Yankee peddler, traveled widely, and both carried the spelling-book, the yardstick of linguistic respectability. In the early 19th century, a New England storekeeper could list for sale "Everything: whiskey, molasses, calicoes, spelling-books, and patent gridirons." Noah Webster profited handsomely from the fact that the uniformity of the American language depended on schooling and universal literacy. "Nothing but the establishment of schools and some uniformity in the use of books [preferably Webster's Speller!]," he argued in his *Dissertations on the English Language* (1789), "can annihilate differences in speaking and preserve the purity of the American tongue." But this would not have been possible without a high standard of living and of literacy:

> Let Englishmen take notice that when I speak of the American yeomanry, the latter are not to be compared to the illiterate peasantry of their own country. The yeomanry of this country consist of substantial independent freeholders, masters of their own persons and lords of their own soil. These men have considerable education. They not only learn to read, write and keep accounts; but a vast proportion of them read newspapers every week, and besides the Bible, which is found in all families, they read the best English sermons and treatises upon religion, ethics, geography and history; such as the works of Watts, Addison, Atterbury, Salmon, &c. In the eastern states, there are public schools sufficient to instruct every man's children, and most of the children are actually benefited by these institutions.

Webster obviously had great faith in a printed, external standard for language. Having made his fortune out of a spelling-book, he could hardly have been expected to believe otherwise. "To reform the abuses and corruption which, to an unhappy degree, tincture the conversation of the polite part of the Americans . . . and especially to render the pronunciation . . . accurate and uniform by demolishing those obvious distinctions of provincial dialects which are the subject of reciprocal ridicule in different states"—so read Webster's petition for copyright for his textbooks, and the introduction to his spellers.

At the same time that Webster legislated on language, he disclaimed the purpose of a legislator. All such legislation was superfluous, he said, because the real authority in matters of language was the American people. This was doubtless one of the things Webster meant when in the preface to his Dictionary he quoted Franklin: "Those people spell best who do not know how to spell." The trouble with most earlier (and especially English) writers on language, according to Webster, was that they tried to dictate, and "instead of examining to find what the English language *is*, they endeavor to show what it *ought to be* according to their rules." In contrast to this, Webster declared for himself, "The *general practice* of a nation is the rule of propriety, and this practice should at least be consulted in so important a matter, as that of making laws for speaking." His standards he found in "the rules of the language itself": or, in a phrase which he could not repeat often enough, in "the general practice of the nation."

A democratic respect for folkways was possible, Webster observed in his *Dissertations*, only in a country of social equality. In England, he explained, the appeal to general usage (the only true purifier and enlivener of language) was impossible for the simple reason that there a small isolated aristocracy, arrogant of its privileges, had elevated its own peculiarities.

> While all men are upon a footing and no singularities are accounted vulgar or ridiculous, every man enjoys perfect liberty. But when a particular set of men, in exalted stations, undertake to say, "we are the standards of propriety and elegance, and if all men do not conform to our practice, they shall be accounted vulgar and ignorant," they take a very great liberty with the rules of the language and the rights of civility.
>
> But an attempt to fix a standard on the practice of any particular class of people is highly absurd: As a friend of mine once observed, it is like fixing a light house on a floating island. It is an attempt to fix that which is in itself variable; at least it must be variable so long as it is supposed that a local practice has no standard but a local practice; that is, no standard but itself. . . .
>
> But this is not all. If the practice of a few men in the capital is to be the standard, a knowledge of this must be communicated to the whole

nation. Who shall do this? An able compiler perhaps attempts to give this practice in a dictionary; but it is probable that the pronunciation, even at court, or on the stage, is not uniform. The compiler therefore must follow his particular friends and patrons; in which case he is sure to be opposed and the authority of his standard called in question; or he must give two pronunciations as the standard, which leaves the student in the same uncertainty as it found him. Both these events have actually taken place in England, with respect to the most approved standards; and of course no one is universally followed.

The appeal to an aristocratic standard in language was thus only one example of the general error of elevating local practice into a general rule.

Variations in pronunciation over the American continent seemed to him no objection at all to making the "universal practice" of Americans the standard for the country. In his Speller he purported simply to give voice to this universal practice. "I have no system of my own to offer," he insisted. "General custom must be the rule of speaking, and every deviation from this must be wrong. The dialect of one State is as ridiculous as that of another; each is authorized by local custom; and neither is supported by any superior excellence." The standard for an American language would be distilled somehow from the very air of America.

Even before the Revolution, as the English editor of David Ramsay's *History of the American Revolution* (1791) noted, the American language had acquired a standard of its own. This dialectless language of the New World was to become more uniform and more universal than any yet known to Western man. Time would prove that Webster had spoken with the cryptic voice of prophecy when he urged that "we should adhere to our own practice and general customs." From these we would develop a standard American language, a language which, as Krapp says, "has grown, and is growing, in a thousand different places, by mixture, by compromise, by imitation, by adaptation, by all the devices by which a changing people in changing circumstances adapt themselves to each other and to their new conditions." Americans would show enthusiasm both for linguistic legislation and for linguistic folkways. Just as in their attitude to all other laws, Americans would combine a naïve faith in legislation with a profound reverence for ancient customs and the common law. This alchemy of opposites which gave vitality to our written Federal Constitution also gave vitality to our language.

Precisely because no part of our culture is more plainly borrowed, no other part could so well reveal the peculiarities of American life. James Fenimore Cooper summed up the development in his *Notions of the Americans* in 1828:

That the better company of London must set the fashion for the pronunciation of words in England, and indeed for the whole English empire, is quite plain; for, as this very company, comprises all those whose manners, birth, fortune, and political distinction, make them the objects of admiration, it becomes necessary to imitate their affectations, whether of speech or air, in order to create the impression that one belongs to their society. . . .

There exists a very different state of things in America. If we had a great capital, like London, where men of leisure, and fortune, and education periodically assembled to amuse themselves, I think we should establish a fashionable aristocracy, too, which should give the mode to the forms of speech as well as to that of dress and deportment. . . . we have no such capital, nor are we likely, for a long time to come, to have one of sufficient magnitude to produce any great effect on the language. . . . The habits of polite life, and even the pronunciation of Boston, of New York, of Baltimore, and of Philadelphia, vary in many things, and a practised ear may tell a native of either of these places, from a native of any one of the others, by some little peculiarity of speech. There is yet no predominating influence to induce the fashionables of these towns to wish to imitate the fashionables of any other. . . .

If the people of this country were like the people of any other country on earth, we should be speaking at this moment a great variety of nearly unintelligible patois; but, in point of fact, the people of the United States, with the exception of a few of German and French descent, speak, as a body, an incomparably better English than the people of the mother country. . . . In fine, we speak our language, as a nation, better than any other people speak their language. When one reflects on the immense surface of country that we occupy, the general accuracy, in pronunciation and in the use of words, is quite astonishing. This resemblance in speech can only be ascribed to the great diffusion of intelligence, and to the inexhaustible activity of the population, which, in a manner, destroys space.

Here, in place of the "King's English," there had developed a "People's English," peculiarly suited to a country without a capital, where everybody was privileged to speak like an aristocrat.

PART ELEVEN
CULTURE WITHOUT
A CAPITAL

"A nation scattered in the boundless regions
of America resembles rays diverging from a
focus. All the rays remain but the heat is gone."

SAMUEL JOHNSON

"Men who are philosophers or poets, without
other pursuits, had better end their days in an
old country."

BENJAMIN RUSH

44

"Rays Diverging
from a Focus"

THE POOR QUALITY of American literary works during the colonial period helped keep the market open to the imported product, and gave added significance to the ways of importing. Never before, surely, had so far-flung and so populous a civilization been so literate, nor had so literate a people produced less in the way of belles-lettres. Was there perhaps some connection between these two characteristics of American culture?—between the literacy of the whole community and the un-literary character of the ruling groups? In modern Western European culture the most honorific use of the printed word, except for sacred religious texts, has been in the ornamental literature of its privileged classes. Such cultures are judged by their dramas, poems, novels, and essays, which, like palaces and manor-houses, are the monuments of aristocratic cultures. But must we measure *our* culture by its ability to produce such monuments? Must we hope to induct an ever larger part of the American people into the mysteries of an aristocratic belles-lettres?

The printed word has had another destiny in America, a role less understandable by the traditional techniques of literary archeologists. The peculiarly American emphasis on relevance, utility, "reader-interest," and catholicity of appeal has made of printed matter a different institution. Not the litterateur but the journalist, not the essayist but the writer of how-to-do-it manuals, not the "artist" but the publicist is the characteristic American man of letters. His readers are found not in the salon but in the market place, not in the cloister or quadrangle but in the barbershop or by the fireplace of the average citizen. His kind of printed matter is "transparent": it calls attention to its object, not to itself. Placing less emphasis on form than on purpose, it has no tendency to create a class of professional "appreciators," a circle of the initiate who value the form for its own sake. Here, too, American life focuses on process rather than product: printed matter is treated less as "literature" than as communication. These tendencies reach deep into our past, and have flourished partly because in the colonial age our soil was not already overgrown with literary culture.

In Western Europe the literature of the dominant classes was first written in a dead and alien "classical" language; its inaccessibility added to its prestige and to the power and self-esteem of those who held the keys to the antique temples of learning. Among aristocratic cultures it is still generally assumed that the works of ancient Greece and Rome can never be equaled by mere moderns. The standard training for the English ruling class has long been the ancient classics—at Oxford they are significantly called simply "Greats"; it has been assumed that a prospective member of the governing groups should know an esoteric literature in Greek and Latin before coming to his own vernacular literature. In America much of this was to be reversed. Some of the most cultivated men would agitate against perpetuating "classical" standards in learning. Despite such romantic exceptions as George Sandys translating Ovid in Virginia in the 1620's, knowledge of an ancient language was never to acquire the widespread prestige in our culture that it had long possessed in England. We started with a vernacular literature which acquired its prestige from its utility.

Since books, unlike the spoken language, had to be carried in men's baggage, the kind of bookish culture to be found in colonial America (or in different parts of it) was, from one point of view, a product of the facilities for transportation. Because books are physical objects which are made in some particular place, they tend to remain near the place of manufacture, or at least near a few centers of distribution. To describe the books in colonial America, therefore, as if they were everywhere the same is especially misleading.

During the colonial period, the centers for the importing and selling of books and probably even for reading, were along the Atlantic seaboard.

It was easier to travel a thousand miles by water than a hundred by land, and it was infinitely less trouble to carry a dozen books in the hold of a ship for six weeks than to carry them inland for ten days. Bookish culture was substantially a foreign import. Many enduring features of American life were rooted in this simple fact and in the peculiar ways in which the importation was to be accomplished.

Books were an urban commodity, and there was no inland city of any significance before the era of the Revolution. Even as late as 1790, every one of the eight cities with a population of more than six thousand was on the seacoast. One consequence of the westward movement and the growth of inland towns was the rise of urban centers that were less accessible to the literary culture of Europe. But it was not until many decades after the first books were produced in America that they began to take the place of books brought in from England.

The mind of the American city looked across the water to London. "Because its outlook was eastward rather than westward," observes Carl Bridenbaugh, "it was more nearly a European society in an American setting." Moreover, almost without exception, the major paths for diffusing the American population started from some eastern seaboard city. The principal cities on the coast were so many separate funnels through which the bookish culture of Britain poured into the inland areas, to be dispersed throughout the countryside. The literary culture of colonial America thus remained for a long time city-filtered. The sole important exception was Virginia, where the numerous rivers and the tobacco economy had diffused distribution onto scores of private plantation-docks; but the cultural stream flowing through all Virginia had already been filtered in London.

No one of the five largest cities established an undisputed cultural dominance over colonial life as a whole. Despite similarities in their forms of government, in their taverns and sociable amusements, there were influential local differences important for the future of American culture. We are accustomed to think of Boston as dominating the culture of 17th-century America, yet as early as 1680 both New York (then still called New Amsterdam) and Newport had an urban life to rival Boston's. Though Boston was the most populous of the early colonial cities, by 1760 she had already fallen behind both New York and Philadelphia. During the 18th century, then, there was a race for leadership among the colonial cities: even in the early decades Philadelphia was neck-and-neck with Boston, and New York City was not far behind; Newport and Charleston were already large towns by English provincial standards. Numerous smaller cities gradually appeared: Portsmouth,

Salem, Hartford, New Haven, New London, and Albany, to mention a few. Such priority as ever did exist was frequently shifting. When Philadelphia became the most populous city, people could not forget that the position had not long before been held by Boston; and, by the end of the 18th century, New Yorkers were beginning to hope that they might in turn displace Philadelphia. But there was never an American London or Paris, a metropolis of undisputed historical, political, cultural, and commercial leadership.

One of the consequences was that American literary culture, even despite the arterial connection with London, began to acquire a varied responsiveness to local problems and to the manifold life of the continent. In the following centuries, too, this would characterize the bookish culture of the nation. The colonial period built this legacy from the variety of religious attitudes, from the numerous local ways of earning a living, and from a hundred other regional differences, all of which would make the hegemony of any one region difficult. The flourishing of an importing book-trade in the several colonial cities thus diffused the power to decide which books were worth the price.

45

Boston's "Devout and Useful Books"

THE MAJOR English libraries, those of the universities for example, had been accumulating for generations; in country houses volumes of recent publication were only a thin veneer on the ancestral treasure. Among books purchased for importation to the colonies, however, recent titles had a more prominent place. Of the approximately four hundred books John Harvard left in 1638 to the College that was to bear his name, more than a fourth were printed after 1630. There were, of course, a few instances of men bringing old family collections with them, but the proportion of recently published titles (accentuated by frequent colonial fires, like that which destroyed the Harvard Library in 1764) tended to grow as the 18th century wore on. This increased the importance of such patterns of selective importation as characterized, for example, Boston.

In early Boston, books were a surprisingly numerous and profitable commodity. In 1686, when the city was only a half-century old and with fewer than seven thousand people, it possessed a flourishing book-trade and over a half-dozen booksellers, at least one of whom made a substantial fortune in the business. Compare this with the book-trade in our own day in towns of about the same size to see the importance of books in the life of 17th-century Boston.

John Dunton, a London bookseller who visited Boston on business in 1686, left an account which, despite obvious exaggeration, reveals a prosperous and highly competitive booktrade. "I'm as welcome to 'em as Sowr Ale in Summer; they Look upon my Gain to be their Loss, and do make good the Truth of that old Proverb, That Interest will not lie." Dunton claimed that in less than five months he had collected five hundred pounds of old accounts due him for books, had sold the large stock he had brought with him, and had taken orders for many more which he would send back from England. Commerce in books continued to flourish; in 1719, Daniel Neal noted that the Exchange—on the site of the present State House—was "surrounded with booksellers shops" doing a thriving business.

The central commercial position of Boston gave it power over the literary taste and reading matter of its neighboring colonies. "The other governments of New-England," Governor Thomas Hutchinson remarked of the late 17th century, ". . . imported no English goods, or next to none, directly from England, they were supplied by the Massachusets trader." But the book-market of New England, while a great deal freer than the printing press, was also confined by its governing spirits.

"There is an old Hawker," Cotton Mather wrote in 1683, "who will fill this Countrey with devout and useful Books, if I will direct him; I will therefore direct Him, and assist him, as far as I can, in doing so." The energetic Mather and his fellow rulers of Boston exerted themselves to stimulate the flow of books and to be sure that those books were wholesome. When in 1713 the Massachusetts Assembly passed an act against "Hawkers, Pedlars, and Petty Chapman," whom the established merchants outside of Boston suspected of retailing stolen goods (as well as of interfering with their trade), Mather joined with the Boston booksellers "in addressing the Assembly, that their late Act against Pedlers, may not hinder their Hawkers from carrying Books of Piety about the Countrey."

When Mather wrote of "devout and useful Books" he accurately characterized the printed matter that the rulers of opinion and the book-buyers of Boston were importing for the city and its hinterland. So far as we can tell, the Boston market was dominated by books religious or didactic. There is interesting evidence of this in the invoices of John Usher, the Boston bookseller. In 1682 Usher received from London about 800 books, apparently selected for him by an English supplier. About half were religious, about one-fifth were romance and belles-lettres, about one-fifth were schoolbooks; the only other notable categories were navigation (60 volumes), history and travel (45 volumes), and medicine (12 volumes). This must have represented a London bookseller's estimate of New England tastes, but, judging from invoices three years later (when Usher made his own selection), Boston's didactic and unliterary flavor was even stronger than the London bookseller had guessed. Of the 800 books Usher himself ordered in that year, the volumes were almost equally divided between religious books and schoolbooks, with few of any other character—fifty on navigation, three dozen on law, and not over a half-dozen of romance or belles-lettres.

Other clues suggest that the religious emphasis of John Usher's stock of books was fairly typical of late 17th-century Boston, and would remain so for several decades. When Michael Perry, a Boston bookseller, died in 1700, the inventory of his estate showed that of approximately two hundred titles on hand two-thirds were religious.

The most important private libraries were, of course, owned by prominent divines. The largest and most impressive by far was that of Cotton Mather. "I do think," the enthusiastic John Dunton exclaimed in 1686, "he has one of the best (for a Private Library) that I ever saw: Nay, I may go farther, and affirm, That as the Famous Bodleian Library at Oxford is the Glory of that University, if not of all Europe, (for it exceeds the Vatican,) so I may say, That Mr. Mather's Library is the Glory of New-England, if not of all America. I am sure it was the best sight that I had in Boston." This library, of which we unfortunately possess no catalogue, Cotton's son Samuel described as "by far the most valuable Part of the family Property," running to "7000 or 8000 Volumes of the most curious and chosen Authors." There can be little doubt that the collection was heavily weighted on the religious side.

In those early years, Harvard College was still serving the purpose for which it had been founded, namely to provide a learned ministry for New England. Nearly three-quarters of the volumes John Harvard left to the college were theological; gifts made later in the century accentuated this theological flavor. Despite occasional complaints (beginning with President Henry Dunster in 1647) about the narrowness of the library, Boston did not have a respectable collection of non-theological books until the late 18th century.

Even in 1723, Joshua Gee's catalogue showed that two-thirds of the Harvard College collection consisted of theological and religious works. The most conspicuous weakness was in modern literature and belles-lettres. The library did have Shakespeare, Milton, and some lesser poets, but it left readers on their own to find Pope, *The Tatler,* or *The Spectator*. In many ways the Harvard College library was not much different from that of a small college library in the British Isles, but such biases and limitations were more influential in New England, where the College long dominated intellectual life. These limitations also expressed the sovereign literary tastes of the community, for it was primarily the ministers of New England who, in sermons and on a thousand other occasions, spread the knowledge of books.

While literary opportunities were surely more limited in New England than in London, they were hardly more limited than in remote places in the north or west of England. The literature of New England must not be compared with the whole of English literature in the 17th century, but only with that little segment which was the literature of the Puritans of the English provinces. Even so, it was narrow. In 17th-century Boston there was none of the residue of the earlier, more relaxed and adventuring ages of English culture. Books were brought to New England, with few exceptions, for a purpose. The cheap bookshops of London Bridge dared display items which would have brought a fine or the whipping post to a Boston bookseller. The miscellaneous frivolous, irreverent, obscene, and unorthodox books which seeped into the London market to titillate—and sometimes to stimulate and enlarge—the mind seldom found their way into Boston. Booksellers' invoices are depressingly barren even of the great imaginative works of the age.

Nothing was more "practical" in Puritan New England than religion. Their preoccupation with applied religion gave a point to religious books, but it also confined their vision. The circumstances which removed religious literature—if not all literature—from the realm of the ornamental, the aristocratic, and the speculative gave a crabbed, practical quality to their tastes. Paradoxically, that very interest in public education which was to make Massachusetts Bay one of the most literate and bookish communities of its age also helped confine the taste and concerns of the community during its earliest years. For literacy was considered primarily an aid to orthodoxy; only secondarily was it to be a means for acquiring other kinds of useful knowledge. "Devout and useful Books" were supposed to be the full stock of the literate mind. Works of "delight and amusement"—so much of the best of English literature—had no place in this scheme.

To be responsible for his own salvation, to see the Word of God through his own and not through a priest's eyes, a man had to be able to read. The General Court of Massachusetts Bay Colony (November 11, 1647) had explained:

> It being one chief project of that old deluder, Satan, to keep men from the knowledge of the Scriptures, as in former times by keeping them in an unknown tongue, so in these latter times by persuading from the use of tongues, that so at least the true sense and meaning of the original might be clouded by false glosses of saint-seeming deceivers, that learning may not be buried in the grave of our fathers in the church and commonwealth, the Lord assisting our endeavours.
>
> It is therefore ordered, that every township in this jurisdiction, after the Lord hath increased them to the number of fifty householders, shall then forthwith appoint one within their town to teach all such children as shall resort to him to write and read. . . .

The chief text of compulsory public education in Massachusetts was the *New England Primer*, which before the end of the 17th century had become the best-selling New England schoolbook. Within the next century and a half it was to sell upwards of three million copies. For New England, and even for other parts of the colonies, it was to be the instrument of literacy which Noah Webster's blue-backed Speller was later to be for the young nation. But while Webster's texts were designed to produce a universally literate people, speaking and spelling the same language, the *New England Primer* had a more dogmatic purpose. From the day he learned his alphabet and read the first syllable in his primer, the New England child was pressed to absorb the truths by which his community lived.

Some of the flavor changed after the Revolution, with the increasingly secular temper. In the 18th century the rhymed alphabet, instead of going from "Adam" to "Zaccheus," sometimes went from "Apple" to "Zany." In place of the earlier exhortation to learn to read in order to know the Bible and enter the Kingdom of Heaven, by the end of the 18th century some children were being warned:

> He who ne'er learns his A.B.C.
> Forever will a blockhead be.
> But he who learns his letters fair
> Shall have a coach to take the air.

Still these were minor changes; the hard core of religious matter—the Apostles' Creed, the Lord's Prayer, and some form of the Catechism—

remained well into the 19th century, when the Primer was finally engulfed by Noah Webster's spellers and readers.

As the decades of the 18th century passed, this strong practical and didactic flavor became diluted, even in New England. There, as elsewhere in the colonies, time produced an assimilation of tastes, for in most of the colonies the bookish culture was dominated by the wealthy men of the cities. These native aristocracies were commercial in origin, and, since commerce thrives on interchange, the culture of all American seaboard cities became more alike during the 18th century. By the second half of the century, the institutions for disseminating books—the booksellers, the private libraries, and the college library—were being supplemented: by "social libraries" (a kind of book club developed by Franklin in Philadelphia, whose members paid dues for the right to borrow books) and by commercial and public circulating libraries. These libraries were much less theological; they offered readers a selection of history, literature, travel, law, science, and fiction broad enough to satisfy city-dwellers anywhere in North America.

But the earlier characteristic of bookish Boston—the narrow practical spirit—long remained. If its literary culture had been more bland, less pungent of provincial puritanism, Boston might have begun a career as a cultural capital, which could conceivably have given a different turn to all American intellectual life.

46

Manuals for Plantation Living

ALTHOUGH VIRGINIA was governed by an aristocracy, its capital was not a city—a circumstance as decisive for Virginia's bookish culture as for her political institutions. In 1776 she was the most populous of the colonies, containing nearly twice as many people as Massachusetts, Pennsylvania, Maryland, or North Carolina, and one-fifth of all the inhabitants of the colonies. Yet while other colonies possessed metropolises (Philadelphia counted 40,000 and even Charleston had

12,000), the legal capital of Virginia, Williamsburg, had a year-round population of only 1500. Even though it was the seat of government, the home of the College of William & Mary, and a small center of literary life in the colony, Williamsburg remained for most of the year a sleepy village. Twice annually—at the so-called "Publick Times," when the General Court met or the Assembly convened—Williamsburg came quickly but briefly to life, and its population doubled. But like the fair towns of European medieval times, it remained a seasonal meeting-place.

During the colonial period, therefore, books that found their way into the libraries of Virginia plantations had not come through bookshops in nearby cities. Except for those which the settlers had brought on first coming, or on rare later trips to England, books were for the most part acquired from London on special orders. Each planter had to decide for himself—or more commonly let his London agent decide for him—what books should be sent. In 1722, Franklin later recalled in his *Autobiography,* there was "not a good bookseller's shop in any of the colonies southward of Boston." For the middle colonies this was something of an exaggeration, characteristically designed to magnify Franklin's own pioneering in libraries and bookshops. Yet his statement was true of Virginia, and would remain so for many years. There was probably not a bookstore in Williamsburg before 1736. Nearly a century later, Jefferson still complained to John Taylor (May 28, 1816) of "the difficulties of getting new works in our situation [Monticello], inland and without a single bookstore." But the lack of a prospering book trade showed the style of Virginia life rather than the absence of a demand for books.

The contents of their private libraries show that in books, as in other imports, Virginia gentlemen followed their English exemplars. By English canons they were permitted to be literate but dared not be bookish: pedantry and the squint of the specialist were to be avoided like the plague. They had to know enough of all things to act well and to satisfy their private questions, but, as Sir Thomas Peyton warned, "not to confound learned men and their books and friends with words newborn." In the training of a gentleman the emphasis was thoroughly practical. He was judged less by the furnishings of his mind, than by the furniture of his house, less by his intellect and learning, than by the charity and graciousness of his conduct.

There was little in the English model to inspire the Virginia emulator to become a man of letters or a collector of books. Near the bottom of the social scale there was little if any reading in 17th-century Virginia; most Virginians probably could not read. If we ask, not how many were literate, but how many were so illiterate they could not sign their names, we can find a rough answer. Philip Alexander Bruce, the social historian of colonial Virginia, examined 17th-century county records to see how many of the names were signed by a mark rather than by a proper signature. In 18,000 instances he examined, nearly half of the male white Virginians (including a few judges) were so illiterate they could not sign their names. Three-quarters of the white women were unable to sign their names. Even these figures probably exaggerate the literacy of Virginians, for we know that people who can sign their names sometimes can neither read nor write.

At the top of the social scale, a few planter-aristocrats, even in the 17th century, owned large libraries, but undue significance has been attached to such rare phenomena as the library of William Byrd, which by 1744 contained more than 3600 titles. Byrd was a prodigy: his collection, the largest in Virginia, elsewhere was rivaled only by Cotton Mather's and James Logan's. Other "first gentlemen of Virginia"—William Fitzhugh, the Lees, the Carters, and the Wormeleys—possessed considerable collections, but at no time were the leading men of colonial Virginia particularly bookish or widely-read. A study of about a hundred private libraries shows that these were, on the average, smaller than is commonly supposed; nearly half contained fewer than twenty-five titles. Before 1700 a library in Virginia containing more than one hundred volumes was a rarity; even in the 18th century it was not unusual in inventories of the estates of leading Virginians to find but a dozen books. More typical than the library of, say, Jefferson was Washington's handful of treatises for useful purposes or the estate of John Chilton, which, though valued at £1700, contained only "two small old Bibles and eighteen other books, mostly old."

The striking common characteristic of these collections is their practicality. The larger libraries contained a generous sprinkling of works in religion and general literature, including the ever-present Bible and Book of Common Prayer, but even such "religious" books were usually practical and devotional—like Bailey's *Practice of Piety* or *The Whole Duty of Man*—rather than theological or speculative. Their diversity, from orthodox Puritanism at one end to Deism at the other, attests the catholicity and tolerance of their owners.

In the 17th century, lawbooks often made up the biggest single group: not only in the large libraries of people like Robert Carter (whose library contained three hundred titles, of which one hundred were on law), but even in the small libraries. Col. Southey Littleton, a leading planter of Accomac County, on his death in 1680 left seventeen books, of which four were on law; Capt. Christopher Cocke of Princess Anne County in

1716 left a library of twenty-four titles, nine on law. The proportion of lawbooks seems to have increased during the 18th century; not alone among lawyers, but also among physicians, clergymen, and especially among the large planters. In this new country, where all fortunes rested on land and where legal claims were often disputed, lawyers were in short supply. As county justices, burgesses, and vestrymen, the leading Virginians faced all the legal problems of judge, legislator, and executive. They could not perform their simplest public duties without some knowledge of the English legal tradition which was the very cement of their community. It provided the institutions of Virginia and the framework for a new nation.

Especially in the smaller libraries, or in the collections of two dozen titles or less which ought not to be dignified as "libraries," one often found medical texts to help the planter or his wife treat the plantation sick. Their numerous handbooks on agriculture, building, horses, hunting, or fishing were not for the hobbyist; they were essential tools. Even the guide to horsemanship or gardening enabled the Virginian to etch in more minute detail his reproduction of English country life.

To Virginians, advice on how to lead the life of a Christian gentleman must have seemed hardly less practical than instructions on how to treat smallpox. Even the "classics" seem to have been valued less as ornaments of educated gentlemen than as handbooks for knowledge of men, of history, of nature, and of affairs. Plutarch, Aristotle, and Pliny were primarily sources of scientific information or political wisdom. The classical works increased into the 18th century but never appeared in large numbers. Virginians relied on translations. "They have few Scholars," the Rev. John Clayton wrote back to England from Jamestown in 1684, "so that every one studys to be halfe Physitian, halfe Lawyer, and with a naturale accutenesse would amuse thee for want of books they read men the more."

English visitors found it hard to believe that a prosperous ruling class would rather learn directly from experience than from books. Perhaps here was a new type of culture, where even gentlemen who could afford otherwise might choose to read men rather than books; and when they read their books, they might prefer to read them with a purpose. "Nevertheless," the Rev. Hugh Jones observed in 1724, "thro' their quick Apprehension, they have a Sufficiency of Knowledge, and Fluency of Tongue, tho' their Learning for the most Part be but superficial. They are more inclinable to read Men by Business and Conversation, than to dive into Books, and are for the most Part only desirous of learning what is absolutely necessary, in the shortest and best Method." Their outdoor life, their lack of leisure, the full-time demands of plantation management, and the loneliness of their remote mansions made conversation infinitely preferable to reading. George Washington was reputed to have stationed one of his slaves at a nearby crossroad to invite any casual passerby to enliven the dinner table with news of the outside world. More than one traveler wondered whether the proverbial "Southern hospitality" did not express loneliness as much as generosity.

The leading planters of Virginia, like the New England clergy, controlled the bookish culture of their part of the country. The roles of clergy and laity, however, were reversed, for many Anglican clergymen in Virginia (some were in fact chaplains to leading planters) relied on the libraries of the planter-aristocrats they served. Where else could the rector of Christ Church parish look for reading-matter if not to the books Robert Carter had collected at Corotoman? The manifold "religious" activities of a planter thus made him the supplier (and incidentally the censor) of books for the clergy of his parish. The lack of circulating libraries made him the librarian also for his poorer neighbors and parishioners. The Rev. Thomas Bray, Commissary of the Church of England for Maryland after 1696, thought the lack of books a menace to the competence and independence of the Southern clergy; and, partly to remedy this, The Society for the Propagation of Christian Knowledge was founded. Bray set up libraries in Maryland, New England, New York, New Jersey, Pennsylvania, and the Carolinas—but not in Virginia.

These conditions increased the influence of the planters' taste over that of the community at large. Their remoteness seems not to have led them to develop independence and variety in their literary tastes. Instead a surprising uniformity prevailed. The more remote the planters were, the more eager they were to cling to old English ways.

For Virginians books were in the main merely tools, the stock-in-trade of a plantation headquarters. And so they appear in the occasional orders planters sent their London agents. On August 27, 1768, William Nelson instructed the firm of John Norton & Sons:

> I have already by this Conveyance sent you a Bill of Loading for 6 hhds of my Crop of Tobo. & I am now to answer your Letter of the 23rd of May, I am obliged for your Endeavours to procure me some good red Herrings; but either they do not cure them so well as they did formerly; or, what is more probable, my Taste is alter'd; so you need not send any more; for I really don't like them; I shall however expect My Garden Seeds, Cheese, &ca. as soon as a new Crop comes in, with the Books I wrote for; & you will be pleased to add the following; vizt, Blackstone's *Commentary upon the English laws;* also one plain

Hat 6/—1 Laced Do. & 8 pr of strong Shoes & Pumps for a Boy of eight years old & the same Quantity of Hats & Shoes for two other Boys of 13 & 15 years old.

The practicality of Virginians had a different character from that of New Englanders. Virginians were unwilling, even if they had been geographically able, to accept cultural leadership from a New England capital. At the same time the taste of the planters was neither strong nor pungent enough to dominate that of other cólonies. A large variety of patterns was already producing the anti-literary and diffused character of American intellectual life. If the Virginia mind was less crabbed and less perverse than that of Puritan New England, it was equally hard-headed, legalistic, and unpoetic. Among Virginians there was no place for a literary class, a Grub Street, or a polite salon. They were not a cultivated élite; they were men of affairs trying to transplant and invigorate institutions.

47

The Way of the Marketplace: Philadelphia

THE BREADTH and liberality of the bookish culture of colonial Philadelphia gave it an alien flavor from the viewpoint of a New Englander or a Virginian. Its peculiarly Quaker tone also set it apart and, for most of the colonial period, further disqualified Philadelphia from being the capital of American culture. The account of the importing, buying, reading, and writing of books in the Friendly metropolis leads us into neither the drawing-rooms of patrons, the attics of Bohemia, nor the convivial meeting-places of literary circles. It takes us rather into the dispersed daily activities of physicians, businessmen, shopkeepers, and mechanics.

The difference between Samuel Johnson's circle in London and Benjamin Franklin's circle in Philadelphia is a measure of the difference between the place of books in the older and the newer culture. Dr. Johnson's famous letter to Lord Chesterfield, in which he expressed contempt for the arrogance of his patron, could never have been written in Philadelphia. Imagine Franklin seeking a patron, cooling his heels in the waiting room of a noble lord, and wasting his time writing letters to rebuke the discourtesies of a man who sought sycophants! Contrast Dr. Johnson's circle, frequented by James Boswell, Sir Joshua Reynolds, Edmund Burke, Oliver Goldsmith, David Garrick, and Edward Gibbon —all men of letters in the traditional sense of the word—with Benjamin Franklin's "Junto," its young, unknown membership including a glazier, a surveyor, a joiner, a cobbler, and several printers.

Curiously enough, the very doctrines of Philadelphia Quakerism—the inwardness, the distrust of dogma, the emphasis on the individual— which made Quakers uncompromising and ill-suited for governing a large community, also made them practical in their approach to knowledge. The ways of mysticism are unpredictable: for the very same reasons the Quakers refused to fight attacking Indians, they wished to fight pedantry. William Penn advised his children:

> Have but few Books, but let them be well chosen and well read, whether of Religious or Civil Subjects . . . reading many Books is but a taking off the Mind too much from Meditation. Reading your selves and Nature, in the Dealings and Conduct of Men, is the truest human wisdom. The Spirit of a Man knows the Things of Man, and more true Knowledge comes by Meditation and just Reflection than by Reading; for much Reading is an Oppression of the Mind, and extinguishes the natural Candle; which is the Reason of so many senseless Scholars in the World.

Within the ample frame of English puritanism, New England Puritans required that men attend to their books, but Pennsylvania Quakers with equal earnestness urged that men attend to experience. New England dogma might confine reading tastes to the practical purpose of building Zion, but Pennsylvania Quakers looked less into sacred texts than into their hearts and at the sins of their community. If their religion did not prod them to learning, it did not at least keep them from any kind of learning.

Unlike the Puritans, the Quakers were never adept at compromise. As the 18th century wore on they developed the only slightly inferior virtue of inconsistency, which never shone more clearly than in their attitude toward books. Despite his warnings, William Penn owned a considerable library and other leading Quakers possessed collections which served "for delight and profit." One of the three largest colonial libraries of the early 18th century (along with Cotton Mather's and William Byrd's) was owned by James Logan, the Quaker who was Penn's secretary, who later became leader of the conservative party, and who before he died had held almost every important office in the colony. Logan expected that the Hamburg merchant from whom he ordered works in Greek and Latin would be surprised "to find an American Bearskin Merchant troubling himself with such books." Yet he doted on his books and expected them to be the entertainment of his advancing years.

The intellectual life of Philadelphia offered a great deal of room in which active minds could range. Its citizens were less policed by orthodoxy than were those of New England, less confined by narrowly practical and political concerns than were those of Virginia, and less dominated by the tastes of a literary aristocracy than were those of London. These features disqualified Philadelphia from becoming the literary capital of all America, but they enriched an already heterogeneous colonial culture.

By the middle of the 18th century Philadelphia showed a wide variety of religious creeds and patterns of worship. An informal inventory of the buildings of the city made by the Rev. Andrew Burnaby in 1759-60 included "a good assembly-room belonging to the society of freemasons; and eight or ten places of religious worship; viz. two churches, three quaker meeting-houses, two presbyterian ditto, one Lutheran church, one Dutch Calvinist ditto, one Sweedish ditto, one Romish chapel, one anabaptist meeting-house, one Moravian ditto: there is also an academy or college, originally built for a tabernacle for Mr. Whitefield." This tolerant atmosphere in religion encouraged the interchange of books and ideas on many other subjects as well.

Philadelphia became a center of the book-trade, and its importance increased with each passing decade of the 18th century. In 1742 there were only five bookshops in the city; by 1760 fifty booksellers had opened shop; by 1776 the city had seventy-seven bookshops. While, at the end of the 17th century, Boston's book-trade had been second only to that of London in the English-speaking world, in the second half of the 18th century, the leadership had moved to Philadelphia.

Although the Philadelphia book-trade did not dominate colonial America, it grew and flourished. Its imports became more assorted. Some shops even found it profitable to specialize: James Chattin mainly in Quaker tracts; Sparhawk & Anderton in "a very great choice of books adapted for the instruction and amusement of all the little masters and misstresses in America"; William Woodhouse in rare books; Charles

Startin in classics and fine editions; Henry Miller in German books. By the 1770's a fifth of the city's booksellers carried books in the German language. The free and competitive atmosphere also invited books from France; in the latter part of the century there probably were more French books in the Philadelphia shops than could be found anywhere else in the thirteen colonies.

Competition among booksellers helped disseminate books and ideas. These were among the first American businesses to advertise extensively in newspapers and to use modern dramatic methods of merchandising. During the latter half of the 18th century, the newspapers were commonly filled with booksellers' ads (sometimes full pages). These reached into outlying towns, and, together with occasional broadsides and catalogues especially directed to the country trade, were the propaganda by which booksellers sold literacy to their fellow colonists.

The most enterprising of the early American merchandisers was Robert Bell, a Scot whose "doubtful" religion and morality—he fathered an illegitimate child and openly kept a mistress—seemed only to make him a more effective salesman. A pioneer in "national" advertising, he inserted ads in nearly all the colonial newspapers to announce the first American editions of Blackstone's *Commentaries* and other such works. He traveled over the continent to buy up choice collections to be brought to Philadelphia, where they were then sold or dispersed to other parts of the colonies. His most famous purchase was the library of William Byrd of Virginia, which he transported to Philadelphia in "perhaps as many as 40 waggon loads." To the rhythm of his auctioneer's hammer, he entertained Philadelphia audiences with his lively wit; he developed the book-auction into a major American institution. The book-auction had long been used on the continent of Europe, but it did not reach England until the end of the 17th century, nor Boston, despite its flourishing book-trade, until 1713. It was in flourishing, free-wheeling Philadelphia, with its motley audiences, that the vulgar commercial merchandising of reading-matter was most successful.

In 1744 Benjamin Franklin was advertising his own auction of choice books with the minimum price marked in each volume. His sessions were held daily at specified hours over a period of three weeks. The auction was by no means confined to second-hand books; publishers used this way of unloading their remainders directly on the reading public. Bell, advertising an auction in 1770, catalogued the retail price of his new books and announced that each would be offered for half-price. By such sales, a colonial printer explained, he could turn "dead stock into live cash, and may again attempt the work of some celebrated author whose writings will diffuse knowledge throughout America."

None could rival Bell, whose wit and antics were a staple Philadelphia entertainment. "Many, going to his auction for the merriment," a newspaper reported, "would buy a book from good humour. It was as good as a play to attend his sales. . . . There were few authors of whom he could not tell some anecdote, which would get the audience in a roar. He sometimes had a can of beer beside him, and would drink comical healths. His buffoonery was diversified and without limit." In mid-18th century, in this once-Quaker metropolis, books had become a mere commodity, a very profitable one. It would be hard to imagine a Boston clergyman or a Virginia planter taking part in such antics; for them books had both a narrower and a more vital purpose. But in pitching his sales-talk to the town "mechanick" and the passing customer, Bell showed himself a shrewd judge of the growing Philadelphia market, which was anything but highfalutin'.

The audience for imported books was widened and developed by another institution which had its first American success in Philadelphia, the so-called "social library," an early example of the American identification of learning with self-improvement. While not an American invention—such libraries were not uncommon in England in the 1720's—it held a special place in the life of this American city.

The "social library" was simply a club in which members paid an entrance fee plus annual dues for the privilege of using the group's collection of books. The earliest such institution known in the American colonies grew out of the "Junto" formed by Benjamin Franklin in 1727. This club of young artisans and tradesmen, established for "mutual improvement," was modeled after the earnest Cotton Mather's scheme for neighborhood benefit societies, to twenty of which he himself belonged. Its declared purpose was similar to that of later American "Service" clubs like Rotary and Kiwanis.

Franklin's group did not chat wittily about polite literature; it had topics for "debate." "Is it justifiable to put private men to death, for the sake of public safety or tranquillity, who have committed no crime? As, in the case of the plague, to stop infection; or as in the case of the Welshmen here executed?" "If the sovereign power attempts to deprive a subject of his right (or, which is the same thing, of what he thinks his right) is it justifiable to him to resist, if he is able?" "Whence comes the dew that stands on the outside of a tankard that has cold water in it in the summer time?"

When members of the Junto found themselves handicapped in debate by their lack of books, they did not ask a gift from a wealthy patron;

instead they pooled their small individual means. At first they simply collected the books owned by members onto shelves at one end of the clubroom, but this was not enough. In 1731 Franklin proposed his plan for the Library Company of Philadelphia "and, by the help of my friends in the Junto, procured fifty subscribers of forty shillings each to begin with, and ten shillings a year for fifty years, the term our company was to continue. We afterwards obtain'd a charter, the company being increased to one hundred." The Library Company of Philadelphia, during its long life—far longer than even the half-century Franklin had optimistically foreseen—encouraged that "purposeful reading" which was a common characteristic of American colonists north and south.

Like the members of later "Book Clubs," the members of Franklin's company did not rely on their own judgment, "and the Committee esteeming Mr. Logan to be a Gentleman of universal Learning, and the best Judge of Books in these Parts, ordered that Mr. Godfrey should wait on him and request him to favour them with a Catalogue of suitable Books." Logan's selections, costing forty-five pounds sterling, were ordered from London on March 31, 1732. There were forty-odd titles. The list included no work of theology—but dictionaries, grammars, an atlas, several multi-volume works of history, travel and biography, and a few books on politics and morals. About a third of the titles were on emphatically practical subjects: anatomy, biology, chemistry, geometry, mathematics, astronomy, agriculture—and Daniel Defoe's *Compleat English Tradesman*. Only a handful of ancient classics (and these the most obvious—the *Iliad*, the *Odyssey*, and Dryden's translation of Virgil) and the merest smattering of belles-lettres (*The Spectator*, *The Guardian*, *The Tatler*, and the works of Addison) showed any deference to the reading tastes of London literati. Although the library's scope widened, its character and appeal did not change much during the next half-century. "The librarian assured me," Jacob Duché reported in 1772, "that for one person of distinction and fortune, there were twenty tradesmen that frequented this library." Two years later, of its 8000 titles, barely 80 came under the classification "Fiction, Wit, and Humour."

This subscription library, and many others like it, flourished in Philadelphia and in the towns of New England, where fifty were founded in the next half-century. Within Philadelphia the Library Company tended to absorb other libraries; by the Revolution it had become a major institution in the cultural life of the city. To it was added the rich library of James Logan, given to the public at his death in 1751. Later Franklin boasted that his Library Company had been "the mother of all the North American subscription libraries now so numerous"; actually it had been only one expression of the diffused literacy of colonial America. He was not exaggerating, however, when he remarked that "these libraries have improved the general conversation of the Americans, made the common tradesmen and farmers as intelligent as most gentlemen from other countries, and perhaps have contributed in some degree to the stand so generally made throughout the colonies in defence of their privileges."

* * *

The variety of attitudes towards books described in these chapters was in fact even greater than appears here. In New York for most of the 18th century there was no impressive interest in books; before the Revolution it did not have as many bookstores as either Boston or Philadelphia, although its book-trade was comparable to that of such English provincial cities as Newcastle, Liverpool, or Bath. Practical commercial interests prevailed, and the confusing remnants of Dutch culture, together with competition among literary languages, stunted the book business. Charleston, South Carolina, which was the only large town south of Philadelphia before the rise of Baltimore in mid-18th century, showed an aristocratic character unique on the continent. Its upper class, newly-rich in rice, indigo, and slaves, enjoyed their exclusive private clubs and mimicked the ways of the London rich more successfully than did Americans anywhere else. With its busy round of concerts, dances, hunts, horse-races, cock-fights, and card-games, the city became famous also for its beautiful and well-dressed women. But the free-spending aristocracy did not spend much of its money on books; the first major bookshop in Charleston did not open until 1754, when Robert Wells offered an assortment of books "chiefly entertaining." This busy, gay, unbookish community had very much its own flavor, but certainly not one to qualify it as a cultural capital of the colonies.

48

Poetry Without Poets

THE SEABOARD CITIES, each for its own reasons, sifted the bookish culture of the mother country for a widely literate but not strikingly literary people. Uncannily, the tastes of distant parts converged toward the practical and the purposeful in the world of books. Almost wholly dependent on London for their books, the colonists could not avoid borrowing English ways of thinking about many things, but they did not borrow the institution of a literary class.

The rich variety and equal competition of town life in America deprived the colonies of the natural habitat of a literary class. That class usually cannot thrive unless it can sit at the center of things, and in America there was no center.

The cultural mountain top from which the English literary word was proclaimed was, of course, London. The simple fact that books in America were, for all the colonial era, primarily an imported English product held a vast significance: it helped make tolerable, or even desirable, to the minds of energetic Americans their own lack of a literary class. Actually, colonial America possessed a large stock of ready-made belles-lettres supplied from abroad and in its own language. The colonial situation thus provided Americans with the finest fruit of a great literature which they could in a sense call their own, yet without the institutions which had produced it. In short, the colonists could enjoy the best of poetry without having to put up with a class of poets; they could chuckle over the elegant trifles of Addison and Steele without having to support a class of essayists; they could amuse themselves with the products of Grub Street without having to build any such neighborhood. The colonists were able to reap the profit from several centuries of an aristocratic and leisured culture without having to accumulate for themselves the capital sum of social distinctions and intellectual and economic inequalities from which that culture had been produced.

Some observant colonists noted the opportunities and disadvantages of their situation. "Your Authors," Benjamin Franklin wrote to William Strahan, his bookseller friend in London (Feb. 12, 1744), "know but little of the Fame they have on this side of the Ocean. We are a kind of Posterity in respect to them." A posterity is in the comfortable position of being able to enjoy the most delightful fruits of a past society without having to endure its peculiar institutions: it can read Greek philosophers without experiencing the slavery on which the Greek community was based; it can relive Benvenuto Cellini's exploits without risking the murderous passageways of Renaissance Italy. A posterity can be eclectic; its detachment from the scenes and issues enables it to be more catholic in its taste. "I would not have you be too nice in the Choice of Pamphlets you send me," Franklin wrote to Strahan, "Let me have everything, good or bad, that makes a Noise and has a Run: For I have Friends here of different tastes to oblige with the sight of them." He explained his order for six sets of a new edition of Alexander Pope's works by saying that Americans had a broad interest in all the best English authors. "We read their Works with perfect impartiality, being at too great a distance to be byassed by the Factions, Parties and Prejudices that prevail among you. We know nothing of their Personal Failings; the Blemishes in their Charactre never reaches us, and therefore the bright and amiable part strikes us with its full Force. They have never offended us or any of our Friends, and we have no competitions with them, therefore we praise and admire them without Restraint. Whatever Thomson writes send me a dozen copies of. I had read no poetry for several years, and almost lost the Relish of it, till I met with his Seasons."

But American men of letters were not literati; they were clergymen, physicians, printers, lawyers, farmers. They were busy men; and the busier they were, the scantier the record which they left us. We have more ample literary accounts of American life during the earlier 18th century than of the turbulent years toward the end of the century. Perhaps no great event of modern times has left so poor an account of itself by participants as has the American Revolution.

In America this absence of a specifically literary class lasted into the 19th century. But it had not been much noted until writers like Washington Irving and James Fenimore Cooper actually began to found such a class. "We have no distinct class of literati in our country," Jefferson wrote in 1813, "Every man is engaged in some industrious pursuit, and science is but a secondary occupation, always subordinate to the main business of life. Few therefore of those who are qualified, have leisure to write." John Pickering agreed that here there was hardly such a thing as "authors by profession." "So great is the call for talents of all sorts in the active use of professional and other business in America," explained Justice Joseph Story (1819), "that few of our ablest men have leisure to devote exclusively to literature or the fine arts. . . . This obvious reason will explain why we have so few professional authors, and those not among our ablest men." President Timothy Dwight of Yale clearly described the consequences of being a nation with a borrowed literature:

> Books of almost every kind, on almost every subject, are already written to our hands. Our situation in this respect is singular. As we speak the same language with the people of Great Britain, and have usually been at peace with that country; our commerce with it brings to us, regularly not a small part of the books with which it is deluged. In every art, science, and path of literature, we obtain those, which to a great extent supply our wants. Hence book-making is a business, less necessary to us than to any nation in the world; and this is a reason, powerfully operative, why comparatively few books are written.

A few nostalgic, imitative spirits yearned for an American reincarnation of English letters. As late as 1769, a writer in the *Pennsylvania Chronicle* who called himself "Timothy Sobersides" warned that Philadelphians, while busily encouraging manufacture, should no longer ignore the Nine Muses: "It does not appear that any of those Lovely Personages migrated with our Ancestors in the early days of peopling this Continent from Europe." The critic hoped that "we shall no longer be so entirely beholden to the Mother Country, as we have hitherto been, for all the articles of Poetical Haberdashery; but that we may, at length, become able to furnish ourselves with a sufficiency of sing-song, the product of our own labour and Industry." Yet even in Philadelphia, where if anywhere on the continent there was a cosmopolitan atmosphere, efforts to produce a polite literature were stiff, self-conscious, and sterile. For example, the Rev. William Smith, provost of the College of Philadelphia, tried to gather a coterie of poets under the name of the Society of Gentlemen, but he found only poetasters. The best American utterance during the colonial age, as perhaps in later ages, was not confined in measured verse nor in the rounded essay. Instead it trickled out of a thousand miscellaneous places: statute-books, pamphlets of political controversy, projects, promotional brochures, sermons, speeches on the floors of legislatures, newspaper-columns, and the staccato proceedings of scientific societies. Such literature could never satisfy the men of letters of the Old World.

American printed matter thrived on the absence of a strong literary aristocracy. It was diffuse. Its center was everywhere because it was nowhere. Every man was close to what it talked about. Everyone could speak its language. It was the product and the producer of a busy, mobile, public society, which preferred relevant truths to empyrean

Truth and would always retain a wholesome suspicion of the private highfalutin' multilingual witticisms of the salon. In 1772 the Anglican Rev. Jacob Duché, one of the earliest of a long line of popular American pulpit orators, observed:

> The poorest labourer upon the shore of Delaware thinks himself intitled to deliver his sentiments in matters of religion or politics with as much freedom as the gentleman or the scholar. Indeed, there is less distinction among the citizens of Philadelphia, than among those of any civilized city in the world. Riches give none. For every man expects one day or another to be upon a footing with his wealthiest neighbour. . . . Such is the prevailing taste for books of every kind, that almost every man is a reader; and by pronouncing sentence, right or wrong, upon the various publications that come in his way, puts himself upon a level, in point of knowledge, with their several authors.

PART TWELVE

A CONSERVATIVE PRESS

"No American has within my knowledge been willing to inhabit a garret, for the sake of becoming an author."

TIMOTHY DWIGHT

49

The Decline of the Book

CONSIDERING the intellectual energy of colonial Americans, their output of books was strikingly small. Even the most literate of them—men like Franklin and Jefferson—did not express their most important ideas in books.

To say, as Franklin did in his circular letter of 1743 proposing an American Philosophical Society, that Americans did not write more books because they were too busy with other things and because American culture was still "immature" is misleading. The book did not flourish here, but other types of printed matter grew in profusion.

Everything dissuaded the colonial printer from undertaking the long volume. First, there was the scarcity of type. In England the supply had been limited as part of the control of the press; a Star Chamber Decree of 1637 allowed only four persons, each with a limited number of apprentices, to operate type-foundries at any one time. Not until the Revolution could American printers buy type of American manufacture. What made the situation in the American colonies even worse was that type brought here was likely to consist of fonts long used and already discarded by English printers. In 1779, when Franklin received copies of the Boston newspapers sent to him in France, he said the only thing he could see clearly in them was that American printers desperately needed new type. "If you should ever have any Secrets that you wish to be well kept, get them printed in those Papers."

In those days, long before linotype, the number of pages a printer could keep standing in type for any time depended directly on the amount of type he owned. The colonial printer with only a single font of a given size could not keep pages of type standing; he had to set a few sheets, print them, and then distribute the type before he could proceed. A rush order for job printing—for advertising brochures or for the legal and commercial forms which were the backbone of his business—might at any time require the use of his type. Under these circumstances, a prudent printer preferred small jobs which quickly repaid his investment rather than books, whose market was uncertain and on which the financial return might be postponed for a year or more.

The scarcity and the poor quality of paper was another deterrent to book printing. Although William Bradford, a Philadelphia printer, had established a paper mill near Germantown as early as 1690 and paper-production had increased during the colonial period, American printers still remained dependent on European supplies. One reason why the Stamp Act and the Townshend Acts were so irritating and helped set Revolutionary events in motion was that they included paper among the imported articles to be taxed. Even apart from any large issue of principle, the high price of paper itself gave colonial printers a reason to stir up American indignation. The crucial necessity of paper imports for colonial printers is shown by the fact that the cheaper grades of paper which were used for newspapers were excepted from some of the Revolutionary non-importation resolutions in 1769.

During the Revolution, George Washington had to write to his generals on odd scraps of paper because nothing better could be had; loose dispatches were sent to officers because paper was too precious to be used for envelopes. Correspondents wrote on fly-leaves torn from printed books and on the blank pages of old account-ledgers. Sometimes, for lack of paper, weekly issues of newspapers failed to appear, and often they were printed on whatever miscellaneous colors, sizes, and qualities of paper the printer could find.

The paper scarcity was acute during most of the colonial period because of both the scarcity of rags from which paper was made and the lack of skilled papermakers. When William Parks set up the first paper-mill in Virginia in 1744, he used the columns of his *Gazette* (July 26, 1744) to persuade citizens of Williamsburg to sell him their worn linen garments:

Tho' sage Philosophers have said,
　　Of nothing, can be nothing made;
Yet much thy Mill, O Parks brings forth
From what we reckon nothing worth. . . .
(And long that gen'rous Patriot live
Who for soft Rags, hard Cash will give!). . . .
　　Ye Fair, renown'd in Cupid's Field,
Who fain would tell what Hearts you've killed;
Each Shift decay'd, lay by with care;
Or Apron rubb'd to bits at—Pray'r,
One Shift ten Sonnets may contain,
To gild your Charms, and make you vain;
One Cap, a Billet-doux may shape,
As full of Whim, as when a Cap,
And modest 'Kerchiefs Sacred held
May sing the Breasts they once conceal'd.
　　Nice Delia's Smock, which, neat and whole,
No Man durst finger for his Soul;
Turn'd to Gazette, now all the Town,
May take it up, or smooth it down.
Whilst Delia may with it dispence,
And no Affront to Innocence.

New England printers used a more theological whimsy to promote their business. In the valuable paper-cargo of a captured Spanish ship which Thomas Fleet, Boston printer and stationer, bought in 1748, he found some bales of papal bulls or indulgences. On the backs of some he printed popular songs like "Black-Eyed Susan," "Handsome Harry," and "Teague's Ramble to the Camp," while others he advertised for sale: "the Bulls or Indulgences of the present Pope Urban VIII, either by the single Bull, Quire or Ream, at a much cheaper Rate than they can be purchased of the French or Spanish Priests, and yet will be warranted to be of the same Advantage to the Possessors."

Such paper as was made in the American colonies, then, while tolerable for newspapers, pamphlets, broadsides, almanacs and primers, was not fit for a book which had to last years. For books the colonial printer had to order from his London agent a supply of European (preferably Dutch) paper. It was difficult or impossible to secure enough paper of the same quality for a whole book; yet the printer could not afford to keep his small quantity of type standing until enough paper for the whole work had arrived. He therefore found it necessary to set only as much of the book as he had paper for; he then stored the printed sheets and distributed the type, until the arrival of more paper allowed him to go on.

Ink was also a problem. The leading printers' handbook (Moxon's *Mechanick Exercises* of 1683) advised that manufactured ink was inferior to that which printers might mix for themselves, but colonial printers lacked the lamp-black and varnish from which ink was made. They therefore continued to rely heavily on inferior ready-made ink imported from England. Printing presses, too, had to be imported; it was 1769 before Issac Doolittle of New Haven built the first American press as a commercial venture.

It is not surprising, then, that few books were printed in the American colonies and that the staple commodity of the American bookseller throughout the colonial period was the imported book. Revolutionary non-importation agreements in 1769 were careful to enumerate "printed books and pamphlets"—along with gunpowder and fishhooks—among the items that might still be brought from England. Not until the end of the 18th century did the importation of English books begin to be affected by the competition of American imprints.

It is remarkable, indeed, that the colonial printer succeeded in printing even those books he did—the solid volumes of statutes, the occasional works of recent history, or the religious tracts. Everything he printed bore the mark of his crude equipment and scarce materials. Economy of materials induced the printer to save paper by using a smaller type than was desirable. In some instances economy encouraged simplicity but the paper shortage generally discouraged the spacious design which would have pleased the eye.

Though Americans tried to import some of the English improvements, American printing lagged technically far behind that of England throughout the 18th century. During his stay in England after 1724, Benjamin Franklin—with his uncanny talent for being in the right place at the right time—happened to work for some of William Caslon's sponsors and was therefore in a position to know about Caslon's improved typefaces, which he imported to America in the 1740's. But not until 1790, after type-founding and paper-making were well-established American enterprises, did the first monumental work appear from an American press: the serial publication beginning in 1790 of the American issue of the *Encyclopaedia Britannica* which ran to 18 volumes and required seven years to print.

Since the beginning of his trade, the European printer had tried to protect his investment by securing in advance the support of a rich patron, who in return usually expected a flattering dedication. Gradually, as the book-market widened, printers sought many patrons instead of one for each publication; people agreed in advance to buy a particular book when it finally came off the press. When the market became still wider, as in 18th-century England, publishers began to risk their own funds. But the longer American books continued to be published with the patronage of public officials, governors, and legislative bodies. The sycophantic dedication to a Lordly patron, who had bought and paid for his compliments, is rarely found in volumes printed on this side of the ocean. During the 18th century the American printer, more than his English counterpart, tried to cover his investment by advance subscriptions.

When books had to be subscribed in advance, there was every reason for the printer to play safe, to be wary of the novel idea, the unknown author, the radical questioner. Whenever a printer ventured a book without subscription, he tried not to venture into the unknown. The publishing list of even the enterprising Benjamin Franklin was solidly conventional. Franklin published, as Carl Van Doren has pointed out, to make either money or friends; preferably both. His government printing, his almanacs, and such books as *Every Man His Own Doctor* (1734), *The Gentleman's Farrier* (1735), and his edition of *The New England Primer* brought in a tidy profit.

The output of American books increased during the 18th century, but few works of lasting significance appeared. The longer and more numerous items, especially in New England, tended to be religious works —sermons, tracts, practical guidebooks, and Biblical commentaries— though not necessarily works of theology. Leading the large sellers among American imprints were schoolbooks like *The New England Primer,* practical handbooks like John Tennent's *Every Man His Own Doctor,* business manuals like William Bradford's *Young Secretary's Guide,* ready reckoners, and books of tunes. In the South, religious works were outnumbered by legal books. Because the colonies possessed many legislatures, few trained lawyers, several systems of courts, and a largely lay judiciary, legal handbooks were everywhere in demand among laymen. There were, of course, a few oddments, like *The Bay Psalm Book* (1640), Jonathan Edwards' *Enquiry into the Freedom of the Will* (1754), and the Mennonite Book of Martyrs, *Der Blutige Schau-Platz* (1748), which with its 756 leaves had the distinction of being the largest (reputedly also the ugliest) book published in the colonies before the Revolution.

In the words of the observant author of *Bibliotheca Americana,* who wrote from London in 1789:

> North America may want some of the fopperies of literature. She boasts not those dignified literati, who in Europe obtain adulation from the learned parasite, and applause from the uninformed multitude, for

pursuits and discoveries that terminate in no addition to the real elegancies or conveniences of living. . . .

Whatever is useful, sells; but publications on subjects merely speculative, and rather curious than important, and generally such on the arts and sciences, as are voluminous and expensive, lie upon the bookseller's hands. They have no ready money to spare for any thing but what they want; and, in literary purchases, look for present, or future use.

50

The Rise of the Newspaper

THE AMERICAN PRINTER was the servant of literacy rather than of literature. While he produced few literary books, his presses turned out countless other items more urgently needed for business and government. In these he was at least the equal of his English contemporaries. His job was not the same as that which tradition and aristocracy had cut out for his fellow-craftsmen on the other side of the ocean.

The colonists, as we have seen, possessed a ready-made body of belles-lettres which they simply imported from the mother-country, and the leading books of English literature were probably just as available in the principal colonial cities as in the English provincial towns. If a printer could import and sell a book from London, why should he strain to produce an inferior and more expensive colonial edition? Colonial printers did not produce a complete Bible in English until 1782, but by 1663 they had already issued over a thousand copies of John Eliot's famous translation of the Bible "into the Indian tongue." Bibles in English could easily enough be procured from England, but the Indian translation essential to New England's mission could be had nowhere else. The American printer was left free to serve the special needs of his community. Jefferson, with some exaggeration, boasted that, while Americans were saved from the "swarm of nonsense" which issued from the European presses, they were far ahead of Europe in the production of useful scientific matter.

As we shall see, it was the needs of the colonial governments that supported printers in the beginning. Also, the dispersion of government into several colonial capitals very early diffused agencies of literacy and of public information. The printing press did not spread generally into English provincial towns until after 1693, when the last restriction acts finally expired; there were still no presses in such English towns as Liverpool, Birmingham, and Leeds. But, by the end of that year in the American colonies, presses had already appeared in Cambridge, Boston, St. Mary's City (in Maryland), Philadelphia, and New York. If each colony had had to wait for presses until the demand for books or for commercial printing produced an adequate income, many decades would have passed, but American presses were flourishing by the mid-18th century. Everywhere they owed their first establishment to government subsidy. In 1762 when Georgia, the last of the thirteen colonies to acquire a press, attracted James Johnston to Savannah as government printer, there were already about forty presses operating throughout the colonies.

In the earliest years the bulk of what issued from the presses was government work: statutes and the votes and proceedings of colonial assemblies. The first item printed in English America was not a poem or a sermon; it was a printed legal form, the Freeman's Oath of 1639. Legal and commercial forms were a staple commodity, for their demand did not fluctuate with the tides of literary taste. When Franklin opened his stationer's shop in about 1730, his first stock included many such blanks, which his *Autobiography* modestly describes as "the correctest that ever appear'd among us." The numerous colonial governments, each with its own regulations and its own system of courts and records, multiplied the number of forms required.

Poor Richard's fame has overshadowed the myriad other almanacs which served daily needs; every ambitious colonial printer issued his own. Almanacs offered an 18th-century American farmer the services now performed by agricultural extension, urban newspapers, magazines, radio, and television. The hours of the rising and setting of the sun, the cycles of the moon and the tide, and the prospects of weather were the time-table of his life—as necessary to him as the railroad schedule to a modern commuter. For many a farmer, the almanac was the most important printed matter he possessed other than the Bible. It told him the dates of court-sessions and the schedules of post-riders, coaches, and packet-boats. It combined features of *Better Homes and Gardens, Popular Mechanics,* and *The Reader's Digest.* It contained practical hints, like the recipe offered in Jonas Green's *Almanack for the Year 1760* "by which Meat, ever so stinking, may be made as sweet and wholesome, in a few Minutes, as any Meat at all." Few printers failed to offer sage, if shopworn, advice, and special thoughts for "the solitary dwellings of the poor and illiterate, where the studied ingenuity of the learned writer never comes." Old issues were preserved, to pass the long winter days, to amuse the overnight guest, or to use for notebooks and accounts. A thumbed-over accumulation of a dozen or more back numbers, with their ever-relevant snippets of advice, information, and literary gems, became the staple of remote readers. Almanacs spread up-to-date political information, opinion, and arguments in the years just before the Revolution.

While no printer could make his mark without publishing an almanac, the larger income and future lay with the newspaper. The account-books of Franklin's printing partnership (1748-1765) with David Hall show that income from the *Pennsylvania Gazette* in this period was much the largest single item (over sixty per cent) of their business; the remainder was about equally divided between public and job printing and miscellaneous publishing, including *Poor Richard's Almanack*. While the size of Franklin's business was unusual, its proportions were probably typical —a heavy emphasis on contemporary and topical works, a meager list of "literature." Before the end of the 18th century, an English observer who had made a survey of American printed matter could report:

> The newspapers of Massachusetts, Connecticut, Rhode Island, Pennsylvania, and Maryland, are unequalled, whether considered with respect to wit and humour, entertainment or instruction. Every capital town on the continent prints a weekly paper, and several of them have one or more daily papers.

In the early decades of the 18th century, when the first English provincial newspapers were being printed, newspapers had already become a familiar institution in the American colonial capitals. By 1730 seven newspapers were being published regularly in four colonies; by 1800 there were over 180. The *New York Gazette or Weekly Post Boy* boasted (April 16, 1770):

> 'Tis truth (with deference to the college)
> News-papers are the spring of knowledge,
> The general source throughout the nation,
> Of every modern conversation.
> What would this mighty people do,
> If there, alas! were nothing new?
> A news-paper is like a feast,
> Some dish there is for every guest;
> Some large, some small, some strong, some tender,
> For every stomach, stout or slender.

At the end of the 18th century, the Rev. Samuel Miller noted that although the population of the United States was but half that of Britain, the number of newspapers circulating here annually, estimated at over twelve million, was more than two-thirds the number circulated in the mother country. "The Reading Time of most People," Franklin wrote from Philadelphia in 1786, "is of late so taken up with News Papers and little periodical Pamphlets, that few now-a-days venture to attempt reading a Quarto Volume."

This precocious development of the American newspaper was in some ways merely a colonial expression of what was also taking place in England, but it was further stimulated by many local circumstances: the spread of literacy, the extent of the country, the existence of several capitals each with its own political news, and the competition among a number of seaboard cities. Much that Americans said about their reading habits was patriotic exaggeration, but there were plenty of facts to confirm the Rev. Samuel Miller's portrait of America about 1785:

> A spectacle never before displayed among man, and even yet without a parallel on earth. It is the spectacle, not of the learned and the wealthy only, but of the great body of the people; even a large portion of that class of the community which is destined to daily labor, having free and constant access to public prints, receiving regular information of every occurrence, attending to the course of political affairs, discussing public measures, and having thus presented to them constant excitements to the acquisition of knowledge, and continual means of obtaining it. Never, it may be safely asserted, was the number of political journals so great in proportion to the population of a country as at present in ours. Never were they, all things considered, so cheap, so universally diffused, and so easy of access.

The most appropriate literary expression of an American life so shifting, so full of novelty, motion, and variety was the kaleidoscopic, ephemeral, miscellaneous newspaper. A newspaper has to be useful and relevant, but it cannot require long study or concentration; it must be literate, but it cannot separate the artistic and expressive from the commercial and productive areas of living. It must mix public and private; it must take the community into account, but with a view to action and the specific event rather than to the universal principle. The newspapers were a symbol of how America broke down all distinctions. "They have become the means of conveying, to every class in society," a contemporary printer observed, "innumerable scraps of knowledge, which have at once increased the public intelligence, and extended the taste for perusing periodical publications."

In saving newspapers from becoming too "literary" nothing was more important than the advertisement, which tied it to daily commercial concerns. "The advertisements, moreover, which they daily contain, respecting new books, projects, inventions, discoveries and improvements," Isaiah Thomas, the colonial printer-historian explained, "are well calculated to enlarge and enlighten the public mind, and are worthy of being enumerated among the many methods of awakening and maintaining the popular attention, with which more modern times, beyond all preceding example, abound." Very early the American newspaper had to justify itself as a commodity rather than as a purveyor of orthodoxy. While in France Robespierre and Mirabeau each owned his own newspaper to address his constituents, this was not the American style. Jefferson indignantly denied any control over the press that defended his point of view. Only for an interlude of about a half-century after 1790 was the American press dominated by a bitterly partisan spirit. For most of the history of American journalism, the independence and high quality of the American press have been tied instead to the commercial spirit and the need to offer his money's worth to a purchaser in the open market.

While the earliest American magazines bore some mark of their locality, they were far less essential than the newspaper to the round of daily life. And so they were slower to flourish on the American scene. The magazine, like the book, is a "mixed" literary form, containing miscellaneous entertainment and instruction; it approaches the book in format, in permanence of interest, and in demands made on the printer. Its unprecedented success in America did not come for another century and a half, when it became a sign of the pervasively literate though emphatically non-literary character of our culture. In 18th-century England the magazine still bore the flavor of that small circle of literati for whom it was designed.

Not until 1741 did the first American magazine with a continuous history begin to appear. Until the era of the Revolution, American magazines were few, short-lived (the longest had lasted three years), and pallid. It was almost the end of the 18th century before a viable, widely-distributed, distinctively American magazine made its appearance. Most early American magazines frankly imitated the English *Gentleman's Magazine* and *London Magazine;* they were, as Frank Luther Mott says, little more than "British magazines published in the Colonies." Their lack of literary invention was impressive; they seem to have been composed primarily with the scissors rather than with the pen. American periodicals were in the habit of copying at least three-fourths of their content from other (mostly English) books, pamphlets, newspapers, and magazines—a means of composition easier in the days before copyright made plagiarism disrespectable.

51

Why Colonial Printed Matter Was Conservative

WHEN PRINTING PRESSES, type-fonts, paper, and ink had to be imported, when land transportation was crude and cities were few, no man could own or operate a printing press without the knowledge and assent of the government. Never was the press more effectively controlled than during the earliest years of the American colonies. One did not find in this vast unsettled country those "secret presses" which in England tantalized and enraged the authorities during the 17th century.

In none of the colonies was there anything that would today be recognized as "freedom of the press." By 1686 the English government was including in its regular instructions to provincial governors the following paragraph:

> And forasmuch as great inconvenience may arise by the liberty of printing within our said territory under your government you are to provide by all necessary orders that no person keep any printing-press for printing, nor that any book pamphlet or other matters whatsoever be printed without your especial leave and license first obtained.

This control remained among the legal duties of royal governors as long as there were royal governors in the thirteen colonies. Although difficult or imprudent to enforce, the power was in the background and must have deterred colonial printers.

Authorities were still impressed by the great power for irresponsible attack which a press could put in any man's hands. The European governing classes would no more have thought of leaving the manufacture of explosive printed matter unregulated than they would have permitted the unlicensed manufacture of gunpowder or the raising of private armies. In America control was exercised, sometimes in one way, sometimes in another, and the need to censor varied with the flow of events. But one fact is clear: the traditional European idea of monopolizing the press to cement the social order was successfully transplanted to American shores. American circumstances made that control even more effective than it had been in England.

Between 1639 and 1763, more than half the imprints of American presses came from New England, and all but a small number of these were printed in and around Boston. The Massachusetts press restrictions were therefore one of the largest single influences of the early age. For two decades after the establishment of the first printing-press in Massachusetts in 1638, there was no official board of censorship, but the meager output of the Cambridge press included not a single item that could have displeased the magistrates. Disputes within the community— such as the Anne Hutchinson affair or the demand for legal reform led by Dr. Robert Child—produced no printed matter in Massachusetts to support the discontented. The Cambridge press was supervised by the president of Harvard College. In 1662 the Massachusetts legislature, worried by "incendiaries of commonwealths," passed an Act "for prevention of irregularities & abuse to the authority of this country by the printing presse," and the law set up a board to censor all copy before it went to press. The story of printing in colonial Massachusetts, then, is simply a tale of different forms and degrees of control. Censorship was strictly enforced until about 1685, somewhat more laxly for the next forty years. After 1723, the colonial government did not exercise its control by censoring manuscripts before they went to press but by frequent threats of prosecution (and occasional actual prosecutions) under the extensive law of libel.

In England during these years, the increase of population, the multiplication of presses, and the rise of liberal ideas had made government control of the press harder to enforce. But government control of the press remained effective in Massachusetts. Because Massachusetts was a colonial government acting under its own laws, the lapses in the English law of censorship (as for a period after 1679) and even the expiration of all English censorship laws in 1695 did not have the same permissive effect on the American side. Censorship (that is, control *before* publication), though somewhat relaxed, continued in Massachusetts Bay for another quarter-century. Thus, when the *News-Letter*, the first regular newspaper in America, appeared in Boston on April 24, 1705, it carried the insignia of censorship already obsolete in England: the tell-tale phrase "published by authority." The Governor's Council continued to maintain an unquestioned right to suppress offensive printed matter.

Effective press control continued into the era of the Revolution. In 1770, during the early stages of the Revolutionary agitation in Massachusetts, the English Lords of the Council for Plantation Affairs complained that the colonial government had failed to punish "seditious and libellous publications." The Massachusetts Governor's Council replied that, within the constitutional limits, it had actually been more successful than the House of Lords had been in England. "Why is there not a charge against the House of Lords . . . that they do not suppress those seditious and libellous publications at home? If we have any amongst us, there are fifty in England to one here." Nevertheless, the Council tried to vindicate itself by starting libel prosecutions against offensive printers. By the time of the Revolution, suppression of opposition presses was an established practice; freedom of printing had acquired no general support, nor had it become fixed in the habits of the community. Therefore, as the Revolutionary spirit rose in Boston, the radical party used mob terror against writers and printers who dared defend King and Parliament. When Massachusetts drew up its new constitution in 1778, it included a declaration in favor of freedom of the press, but the declaration was rhetorical and ambiguous, probably because of widespread doubts of the wisdom of such a novel institution. During the War, when all publications unfavorable to the Revolutionary movement were suppressed, there was no effective freedom of the press. After peace came, political leaders in Massachusetts demanded, not a "free press," but return to a "well-regulated" press.

John Adams, for example, had long argued that "license of the press is no proof of liberty." As early as 1774, when a defender of the British cause argued that the Revolutionary accusations of tyranny were unfounded because the most diverse opinions were allowed to be published in Massachusetts, Adams complained of "the scandalous license of the tory presses." "There is nothing in the world so excellent that it may not be abused. . . . When a people are corrupted, the press may be made an engine to complete their ruin; and it is now notorious, that the ministry are daily employing it, to increase and establish corruption, and to pluck up virtue by the roots. . . . and the freedom of the press, instead of promoting the cause of liberty, will but hasten its destruction." It is not surprising that John Adams and his fellow Federalist leaders in Massachusetts favored the Alien and Sedition Acts of 1798; they were worried only that the laws might not be effective. "If there is ever to be an amelioration of the condition of mankind," Adams was still warning two decades later, "philosophers, theologians, legislators, politicians and moralists will find that the regulation of the press is the most difficult, dangerous, and important problem they have to resolve. Mankind cannot now be governed without it, nor at present with it."

In colonial Massachusetts, ruling clergymen, like the Mathers in their heyday, had found ways outside the law to enforce their standards. When Increase Mather wrote a book in 1700 attacking the practices of a church newly-established in the colony by the Rev. Benjamin Colman and his friends, the accused minister prepared a reply, but to secure its publication he had to send his manuscript to New York. "The Reader is desired to take Notice," Colman's pamphlet explained, "that the Press in Boston is so much under the aw of the Reverend Author, whom we answer, and his Friends, that we could not obtain of the Printer there to print the following Sheets, which is the only true Reason why we have sent the Copy so far for its Impression and where it [is] printed with some Difficulty." Bartholomew Green, the Boston printer, explained the good commercial reason behind his refusal: the last time he had done a printing job without advance government approval, he had been required to revise and reprint it before publication to meet official criticism.

Printing began under government sponsorship in all the colonies. The press was supposed to be a prop for existing institutions; where there was danger that it might serve another purpose, authorities preferred no press at all. "I thank God, we have not free schools nor printing," Sir William Berkeley, governor of Virginia for thirty-eight years, boasted in 1671, "and I hope we shall not have these hundred years. For learning has brought disobedience and heresy and sects into the world; and printing has divulged them and libels against the government. God keep us from both." Some Virginia leaders of the next century did not share Berkeley's enthusiasm for illiteracy, but for many years his modest ambitions for Virginia were fulfilled at least with regard to the press. In 1682, the government received its first scare from a press and printer imported by John Buckner, rich landowner and merchant of Gloucester County, whose offense was to print some of the colony's laws without authority. Buckner was called before the Governor and Council, was ordered to cease his subversive activities, and "for prevention of all troubles and inconveniences, that may be occasioned thorow the liberty of a presse" was required to post bond for his good behavior. In 1683 the King of England ordered that to prevent any such "troubles and inconvenience" in the future, the Governor of Virginia should "provide by all necessary orders and Directions that no person be permitted to use any press for printing upon any occasion whatsoever." Until 1730, when William Parks set up shop in Williamsburg, there was no printing press in Virginia. From then until 1766 Virginia had only a single press and that was the official organ of the government. "I do not know that the publication of newspapers was ever prohibited in Virginia," Jefferson recalled many years later. "Until the beginning of our revolutionary disputes, we had but one press, and that having the whole business of the government, and no competitor for public favor, nothing disagreeable to the governor could be got into it."

Outside of Boston, the two leading colonial printing centers were Philadelphia and New York City. In both places, the right of the authorities to control printed matter—if not by censorship, then by libel prosecutions and by legislative censure—continued to be recognized at least until the Revolution. In Philadelphia, William Bradford, who was Pennsylvania's first printer (first imprint: 1686), was in continual trouble with the government and the Society of Friends, usually for the most trivial indiscretions. Finally, in 1693, when he was prosecuted for publishing a tract on one side of an internal Quaker dispute, he left the colony in disgust and became the royal printer in New York. For the next half-dozen years, there was no press at all in Philadelphia. William Bradford's son, Andrew, who returned to Philadelphia and became the official "Printer to the Province" in 1719, was only slightly more successful than his father in satisfying the authorities. Libel trials and suppression of the opposition press were common there until the eve of the Revolution.

Much the same story is told of New York, which did not begin to rival Boston or Philadelphia as a source of printed matter until after 1760. The famous case of John Peter Zenger (1734-35), which affirmed the power of juries in libel cases to decide the law as well as the fact, is important in retrospect and as a landmark of legal doctrine. But it was not a turning point in the practices of the community; even after the Zenger case, the question in New York was not whether the press should be "well-regulated" but who should have the power of regulation. Zenger's reward for his vindication in the trial which made him a hero in later histories of freedom of the press, was his appointment to the monopoly of "Publick Printer" in 1737. Twenty years later another printer, Hugh Gaine, was brought to the bar of the Assembly and reprimanded; he "humbly asked their Pardon" but still was required to pay costs—all for the offense of printing part of the public proceedings of the representative body! James Parker, Printer to the General Assembly of New York, obeyed Governor Clinton's ban in 1747 on publishing the Assembly's remonstrance against the Governor; although the next year he dared to print it among the Assembly's votes. But within a decade, in 1756, the Assembly itself declared Parker "guilty of a high Misdemeanor and a Contempt of the Authority of this House" for printing an article critical of them in his newspaper. And so it went.

It was not only by government control, by censorship, and by threat of libel prosecution that the American colonial press was confined. The earliest American presses owed their very existence to the colonial governments, a fact which inevitably affected the character of printers and the output of their shops: government support meant government control. In these scattered colonial communities—where what little passion there was for literature could be satisfied with books imported from the mother country—the introduction of printing presses might have been delayed for decades if it had depended on the market for polite literature. But soon after the first settlements, each government needed a printing press to circulate proclamations and laws, to provide copies of debates, proceedings, decisions, and votes to the members of the governors' councils and representative assemblies, and to supply the legal forms needed every day. Even in the earliest years of each colony, when the market for commercial printing was small, the demand for locally printed books non-existent, and the market for newspapers and periodicals still undeveloped, the government could offer an annual contract with an assured income to anyone who promised to meet its needs.

The story of the introduction of printing into the American colonies is, in short, an account of how the thirteen different governments subsidized a public service. In Massachusetts the earliest press was, as might be expected, under the close surveillance of the leading clergymen and of Harvard College; it served church and state at the same time. Its scope and limits were symbolized in its first three products: the recently revised Freeman's Oath (1639); an almanac calculated for New England (1639); and the famous Bay Psalm Book (1640), a new and supposedly more literal translation of the Psalms by three New England divines. The staples of this earliest press in the English colonies were the enactments of the General Court.

Benjamin Franklin, being an enterprising businessman, valued his appointment as clerk of the Pennsylvania Assembly mainly as a way to secure the government printing business for his presses. Within less than a dozen years (1739-1750) Franklin received as clerk's fees and for printing statutes and paper currency the sum of £2,762 of Pennsylvania money. Franklin's *Modest Enquiry into the Nature and Necessity of a Paper Currency* (1729), which he had both written and printed, urged the printing of more provincial paper money secured by Pennsylvania's plentiful supply of land. "My friends there (in the House,) who conceiv'd I had been of some service, thought fit to reward me by employing me in printing the money; a very profitable jobb and a great help to me. This was another advantage gain'd by my being able to write." On another occasion, Franklin was even paid for destroying the colony's currency when it had become worn through use. About this time, too, the neighboring colony of Delaware gave Franklin its contract to print money, laws, and government proceedings.

William Parks, who in 1730 brought Virginia its first press in a half-century, had only a few years before set up shop in Annapolis as official printer to the province of Maryland, which had attracted him by a guaranteed annual fee for printing the debates, votes, and laws of its Assembly. Parks set up his press in Williamsburg only after the Virginia legislature had offered him their official printing and an increasing yearly sum which began at £120 and reached £280 before his death. Not all the colonies were so fortunate; some had to send their work to neighboring colonies or even abroad. Although the Assembly of South Carolina began offering a bounty as early as 1722 in order to attract a printer, it was nine years before one could be persuaded to settle there.

Under these circumstances, the colonial press could hardly be a nursery of novel, startling, or radical ideas. The printer had to be a "government man," acceptable to the ruling group in his colony. Only the government business made it at all possible for a man to live by his press in the colonies; therefore, government printing held the first claim on a prudent printer's time, as was evidenced by the many apologetic prefaces to privately-supported books that had been delayed or had to appear in abridged form. As the commerce and population of each colony grew, however, government printing gradually became a smaller proportion of the total printing business. Only then did it become financially possible for a dissident or unconventional printer to make his way.

52

"The Publick Printer"

FOR CENTURIES TO COME the influential American "gentlemen of the press" would not be "gentlemen" at all by European standards. The ancestors of the American newspaperman were not essayists, wits, and professional writers, but primarily *printers*—craftsmen dealing in useful public information. They were not literati, whose habitat was the drawing room, the coffee house, or the salon. On the contrary, they were servants of the general public: in 18th-century language, "Publick Printers." Their hands stained with printers' ink, they frequented the legislative assemblies and the marketplace to gather a salable commodity. Their print-shops became forums and post offices, centers for news and opinions. To make their living, they had to win the confidence of the government, to discover sources of news, and to find ways of distributing their commodity quickly. They were already beginning to develop the unprecedented network of public information which eventually would hold a vast nation together, stimulating as it satisfied the appetite for news.

Some special features of colonial life increased the influence of men who made a living from this kind of work. The most important single fact was the large number of separate governments—each with its own executive and legislature, each with its own acts, laws, debates, votes, proceedings, and orders to be printed. The mere existence of so many separate political units gave a focus and a practical public purpose to the earliest American printed matter, and so helped put the printing press in the service of the whole literate community.

By the time of the Revolution, each colonial government had a printer in its own capital to serve its own needs, and printers could be found in all the principal cities up and down the Atlantic seaboard. If one colonial government was displeased with its Public Printer, another would welcome him and set him up with its official business. Men qualified to become "Publick Printers" always remained in demand.

At the same time that printing presses were spreading out into the towns of America, they were also going out from London, Oxford, and Cambridge into the English provinces, but the American colonial printer had a dignity and influence (as well as several new functions) unknown to his English provincial counterpart. The "Publick Printer" was an American institution. William Parks, Benjamin Franklin, William and Andrew Bradford lived at the centers of government, where news was made. Their influence in public life foreshadowed the special American relation between politics and the press which has most recently found expression in the regular Presidential Press Conference. The English provincial printer was just another craftsman; only the King's Printer in London held an official position. But the Public Printer of each American colony held an important public post.

As printer of the colonial laws, the proceedings of the assembly, and the principal newspaper, the Public Printer was the chief local customer of the post office. Therefore, he always found it convenient, and often found it profitable, to become the local postmaster. Not only could he then use the post-riders to deliver his papers at public expense (Franklin did this for a while), but he profited from the postmastership in many indirect ways. The great distances, which sharpened the appetite for news, made the post office in each town a gathering place for men of affairs. Since all letters passed first through the postmaster's hands, he had the quickest and most confidential access to news. When towns-people came to get their mail, he could gather news items of local interest and at the same time sell books, magazines, cough medicine, sealing wax, chocolate, lemons, writing paper, pens, and fiddle strings. The printer's shop came to resemble the later General Store. In every community its owner was a person of influence.

The first regularly-published American newspaper, the *Boston News-Letter* (April 24, 1704), was "published by Authority" by John Campbell, Postmaster, "Publick Printer" to the colony. Succeeding Postmasters in Boston even came to think that such a publication was attached to their office. Ellis Huske's paper, founded in 1734, bore the significant name of *The Boston Weekly Post-Boy* and the imprint:

> Boston; Printed for Ellis Huske, Post-Master: Advertisements taken in at the Post-Office in King's-Street, over against the North-Door of the Town-House, where all Persons in Town or Country may be supplied with this Paper.

In Connecticut also the first newspaper was established by a printer who was postmaster of the colony. The advantages of being postmaster helped keep the press in the hands of respectable men who possessed the confidence of their government.

The earliest printers (and often the writers) of books and newspapers in the American colonies were thus intimately acquainted with the public taste and with the problems of selling and delivering printed matter to a wide public. One of the few occasions when Franklin violated his rule that one should "never ask, never refuse, nor ever resign" a public office, occurred in 1751 when he sought the job of Deputy Postmaster General for the American colonies and authorized his friends in England to pay up to £300 for it. "The Place has commonly been reputed to be worth about £150 a Year but would be otherways very suitable to me, particularly as it would enable me to execute a Scheme long since form'd of which I send you enclos'd a Copy, and which I hope would soon produce something agreeable to you and to all Lovers of Useful Knowledge for I have now a large Acquaintance among ingenious Men in America." This "scheme" was to lead to the formation of the American Philosophical Society, first conceived by Franklin as a kind of clearing house for useful knowledge. Correspondence was its primary purpose, for Franklin believed that progress would come from pooling casual information from men living in "different climates, having different soils, producing different plants, mines, and minerals, and capable of different improvements, manufactures, &c."

During his long association with the colonial postal service—first (after 1737) as Deputy Postmaster at Philadelphia and later (1753-1774) as Deputy Postmaster General for all the American colonies—Franklin did a great deal to speed up the postal service and to make it profitable to himself. By 1769 the office, which had barely repaid expenses before he took it over, netted Franklin a profit of £1,859. When Franklin had become Postmaster at Philadelphia in 1737, there was no legal provision for admitting newspapers to the mails nor any established rates for carrying them. As Postmaster he could simply hand his own papers to the postriders (and forbid them to carry competing papers). The other publishing advantages of his job were numerous: "it facilitated the correspondence that improv'd my newspaper, increas'd the number demanded, as well as the advertisements to be inserted, so that it came to afford me a considerable income. My old competitor's newspaper declin'd proportionably."

When Franklin became Deputy Postmaster General for all the colonies he widened the experiment he had tried in Philadelphia of allowing his competitors to use the mail. In 1758, he established for the first time fixed (and highly profitable) postal rates for newspapers. Even this reform was designed less to provide a free press than to strengthen and increase a conservative press. His aim, he explained, was "to remedy these Inconveniences and yet not to discourage the Spreading of Newspapers, which are on many Occasions useful to Government and advantageous to Commerce and to the Publick."

The control over newspaper distribution, and hence over printed opinion, by the colonial governments became more burdensome as the conflict of opinion sharpened. William Goddard (1740-1817) and his sister, Mary Katherine Goddard (1736-1816), earned places as patron saints of a free press in America by opposing the post-office monopoly. In many ways a prototype of the American businessman, Goddard was restless, humorless, and tactless, but he was remarkably endowed with aggressiveness, organizing ability, and a knack for making himself heard. The son of the physician-postmaster of New London, Connecticut, Goddard had learned the printer's trade as an apprentice to James Parker and John Holt, postmasters and newspaper publishers of New Haven. In 1762 Goddard set up a printing press in Providence, Rhode Island, founded a newspaper, and became the town's postmaster. Unable to secure the eight hundred subscriptions necessary to make his newspaper pay, he moved first to New York and then to Philadelphia to try his fortune in different publishing ventures. He finally established himself in Baltimore, where his *Maryland Journal and Baltimore Advertiser* (1773-1793) spoke out in the last years before independence.

As proprietor of "a very free press," he had been victimized by the government-controlled post office, which charged him one pound a week for delivering three hundred and fifty newspapers to places outside Philadelphia. Goddard reacted to such abuses by setting up his own postal system to make his publications independent of the government. Goddard's project grew and, on December 30, 1773, news of the Boston Tea Party was brought from New York to his office in Baltimore by his own postriders.

Desire for a freer, more "constitutional" postal service was in the main stream of Revolutionary sentiment. As early as 1711 the Virginia House of Burgesses had refused to appropriate money for the post office, which had been recently reorganized under an act of Parliament, on the ground that the rates established by the British Act amounted to taxation without consent. Not until later in the 18th century, after nine years of Franklin's absentee management of the post office, was there any effective competition for the old system. By then the rise of newspapers had enlarged the demand for postal service, and the courage, enterprise, and organizing ability of William Goddard had made a new system possible. "Having at all times acted consistently, and to the utmost of his power in support of the English Constitution and the rights and liberties of his countrymen . . . especially as a printer, regardless of his own personal safety or private advantage," explained John Holt, printer of New York, in May 1775, Goddard had "by this conduct, incurred the displeasure of many men in power, and been a very great sufferer (the greatest, he believes, in this Country) by the stoppage and obstruction given to the circulation of his newspapers by the Post-Office, which has long been an engine in the hand of the British Ministry to promote their schemes of enslaving the Colonies and destroying the English Constitution."

The needs of the Continental Congress, of the new American army, and of the rising colonial newspapers brought into being the first United States post office. When the publicly-owned American postal system was set up on July 26, 1775, it was not on the foundation of the British system but on that of Goddard's private enterprise which had aimed to free the post office from the domination of government. Yet, the new government expressed its conservatism when it named as first Postmaster of the United States, not Goddard who had conceived and organized it, but Franklin who had for many years run the British system. In one way or another the American post office—and especially the Postmaster General and the local postmasters—would continue to be involved in politics.

The colonial printer-journalist-postmaster was thus pursuing a new and distinctively American profession. He started in America as a craftsman and small businessman rather than as a man of letters, but he had an important function in government, which kept him in touch with public affairs. The dispersion of government into thirteen different centers, the urgent need for certain kinds of practical information, and the combination of the printshop with the post office interfused the currents of the printed word and the currents of the public mind.

BOOK FOUR

WARFARE AND DIPLOMACY

"Why forego the advantages of so peculiar a situation? Why quit our own to stand upon foreign ground?"

GEORGE WASHINGTON

AMERICAN experience in the colonial age shaped a particular view of peace and war which would long affect our attitude toward the objectives of war, the uses of diplomacy, and the place of the military in political life. War and peace are more than the presence or absence of sound, smell, destruction, pain, and bloodshed; they are institutions. What a nation means by war or peace is as characteristic of its experience and as intimately involved with all its other ways as are its laws or its religion. In the following chapters we will see how American ways of warfare and diplomacy began.

PART THIRTEEN
A NATION OF
MINUTE MEN

"They were soldiers when they chose to be so, and when they chose laid down their arms."

JOSEPH DODDRIDGE

53

Defensive Warfare and
Naïve Diplomacy

THE PERIOD during which the American colonies were founded is
generally described as the Age of Limited Warfare in Europe. From
about the time in the early 17th century when the Puritans settled
Massachusetts Bay until the French Revolutionary Wars near the end
of the 18th century, Europe showed notable restraint. After the bloodbath of the religious wars, the "Enlightened Age" offered Europe a relief,
less from the fighting itself than from its worst horrors. War was
moderated less through efforts to abolish it than through the growth of
formal rules of warfare and by the specialization of the military function.
Since the restraints which made wars less destructive also made them less
decisive, European history during the colonial period was a story
of continual indecisive warfare. "Now it is frequent," Daniel Defoe
remarked in 1697, as the War of the Dutch Alliance dribbled out, "to
have armies of fifty thousand men of a side stand at bay within view
of one another, and spend a whole campaign in dodging, or, as it is
genteelly called, observing one another, and then march off into winter
quarters. The difference is in the maxims of war, which now differ as
much from what they were formerly as long perukes do from piqued

beards, or as the habits of the people do now from what they then were. The present maxims of war are—

> Never fight without a manifest advantage,
> And always encamp so as not to be forced to it.

And if two opposite generals nicely observe both these rules, it is impossible they should ever come to fight."

Battles tended to take place on large open fields, where the customary rules and formations could be obeyed. At the opening of a battle, the opposing forces were set up like men on a chessboard; each side usually knew what forces the other possessed, and each part of an army was expected to perform only specific maneuvers. Sneak attacks, irregular warfare, and unexpected and unheralded tactics were generally frowned on as violations of the rules. "This way of making war," Defoe succinctly put it, "spends generally more money and less blood than former wars did." Though armies increased, casualties declined. In the year 1704, which witnessed decisive battles of the War of the Spanish Succession, only 2000 British soldiers and sailors died in action and no more than 3000 died of wounds, disease, or other causes connected with the war.

Such moderation would have been impossible if the waging of wars had not become a specialized occupation from which the mass of the people felt removed. War had become the task of warriors, whose functions were as separated from those of the common man as were the tasks of the learned barrister, the doctor of physick, or the cleric. Officers of opposing sides enjoyed the fraternity of all professionals and of the international European aristocracy: between engagements they wined and entertained one another with balls, concerts, and dinner parties. Usually aristocratic professionals, they were drawn from the nobility and the upper classes, for whom the duty of military service to their prince remained a relic of feudal days. Private soldiers, who had not yet acquired the kudos of "fighting for their country," were few by modern standards and tended more and more to be the dregs of society. Driven to recruit from the jails and taverns, the sovereign preferred, if he could afford it, to fill his ranks with such mercenary professionals as the Swiss or the Hessians.

War, then, was not an encounter fought by two fully mobilized communities and hallowed by patriotism. Military engagements occurred not in the rubble of factories and cities, but usually on a military playing field, a plain at some distance from the populace. There the "rules of warfare" were neatly and scrupulously followed, with the least possible interference to the peaceful round of household, farm, and fair. Commanders would no more have undertaken a battle in thick underbrush or woods, at night, or in bad weather, than a modern professional baseball team would consent to play in dense woods on a wet day. There were exceptions, but surprisingly few.

From the middle of the 17th until near the end of the 18th century, European war was merely an instrument of policy. It was not waged to exterminate another people or to change their ways of life or their political or economic institutions. Usually it was the effort of one ruling prince to extend his territory, to vindicate his honor, or to secure a commercial advantage from an opposing sovereign, who was likely to be his cousin. Objectives were much more limited than they had been during the religious wars of the 16th and early 17th centuries.

The pan-European character of the aristocratic literary culture provided the common ideas out of which grew a specialized literature defining the just occasions and proper limits of warfare. During most of this period, the leading handbook was Grotius' *De jure belli ac pacis* (On the Law of War and Peace), 1625-31, which set up authoritative "rules" for civilized nations; it was displaced in the later 18th century by Vattel's *Le droit des gens* (The Law of Nations), 1758, which made some changes but still assumed that civilized nations were bound in peace or war by certain natural regulations.

The American Indian who lay in wait for the earliest colonists had, unfortunately, not read Grotius or Vattel. He had no international aristocracy, nor was he persuaded of the advantages of limited warfare that was waged only during clear weather in open fields. He had his own weapons and his own ways, the ways of the forest. He was not accustomed to pitched battles nor to the trumpet-heralded attack. The Indian bow, unlike the matchlock, was silent, accurate, and capable of rapid fire even in wet weather; the tomahawk was a more versatile weapon than the fifteen-foot pike. When the Indian captured an enemy he did not obey Grotius' laws of war by taking prisoners and seeking to exchange them. On the contrary, massacre and torture were his rule; he thought nothing of flaying his enemy or bleeding him to death with jabs of pointed sticks. The Rev. Joseph Doddridge observed the savage attacks in Western Virginia in the later 18th century:

> The Indian kills indiscriminately. His object is the total extermination of his enemies. Children are victims of his vengeance, because, if males, they may hereafter become warriors, or if females, they may become mothers. Even the fetal state is criminal in his view. It is not enough that the fetus should perish with the murdered mothe , it is torn from her pregnant womb, and elevated on a stick or pole, as a

trophy of victory and an object of horror to the survivors of the slain. If the Indian takes prisoners, mercy has but little concern in the transaction. He spares the lives of those who fall into his hands, for the purpose of feasting the feelings of ferocious vengeance of himself and his comrades, by the torture of his captive.

This American scene created a new type of adventure literature—stories of Indian captivities—which recounted the suffering and heroism of ordinary settlers, their wives, and children.

The Indian was omnipresent; he struck without warning and was a nightly terror in the remote silence of backwoods cabins. The New England settlers, Cotton Mather recalled, felt themselves "assaulted by unknown numbers of devils in flesh on every side"; to them the Indians were "so many 'unkennell'd wolves.' " Every section of the seacoast colonies suffered massacres. The bloody toll of the Virginia settlements in 1622, and again in 1644, was never forgotten in the colony. In Virginia in 1676, Nathaniel Bacon's Rebellion expressed the demand of western settlers for more aid against the Indians. We have already seen how the Indian massacres of the mid-18th century sharpened the crisis of the Quaker government of Pennsylvania. Such nightmares shaped the military policy of settlers until nearly the end of the 18th century. The Indian menace, which haunted the fringes of settlement through the whole colonial era, remained a terror to the receding West well into the 19th century. Not until ten years after the massacre of Custer's force in 1876, when the few remaining Indians had been removed to Indian Territory or to reservations, did the Indian threat disappear.

The Indian was not the only menace. Parts of the English colonies suffered intermittent threats of invasion by European powers—the French, the Dutch, or the Spanish. While England remained relatively safe from foreign invasion from the time of the Armada (1588) at least until the time of Napoleon, the earliest settlers of Virginia were often in terror that the Spanish massacre of the Huguenots at Fort Caroline in Florida might be repeated in their own province. More than once the pioneer settlers of Jamestown raised the alarm that Spanish ships were coming up their rivers; they anxiously watched every approaching sail in fear that it might bring invaders. Boston was alarmed by the approach of La Tour in a French ship of 140 tons in 1643, and on numerous later occasions had reason to fear attack from some European force. Even the pacifism of Pennsylvania Quakers was strained by the appearance of Spanish ships in the very harbor of the city.

Such threats forced whole communities to huddle together in time of danger. The garrison house, built as a common dwelling and refuge during Indian raids, became a symbol of the unlimited nature of warfare in America. At the first alarm of Indian attack, neighboring inhabitants would collect their most valuable belongings and gather in the garrison. In New England, such garrisons increased during the alarms of King Philip's War in 1676, and a number continued to be maintained during the French and Indian Wars well into the 18th century. The same general scheme was followed up and down the colonies. Sometimes a particular private dwelling—suitably constructed with thick walls perforated by loopholes, with an overhanging second story, and possibly with flankers at the corners for lookout—was agreed upon as the customary refuge. Or, some towns—like Hadley, Northampton, and Hatfield in the Connecticut Valley—imitated the Indians by surrounding the town with a defensive stockade.

The crowded life of the garrison houses, as the Rev. Doddridge reminds us, was no picnic; it made settlers dread what they called the "Indian summer."

> A backwoodsman seldom hears this expression without feeling a chill of horror. . . . during the long continued Indian wars sustained by the first settlers of the west, they enjoyed no peace excepting in the winter season, when, owing to the severity of the weather, the Indians were unable to make their excursions into the settlements. The onset of winter was therefore hailed as a jubilee by the early inhabitants of the country, who, throughout the spring and the early part of the fall, had been cooped up in . . . uncomfortable forts, and subjected to all the distresses of the Indian war. At the approach of winter, therefore, all the farmers, excepting the owner of the fort, removed to their cabins on their farms, with the joyful feelings of a tenant of a prison recovering his release from confinement. All was bustle and hilarity in preparing for winter, by gathering in the corn, digging potatoes, fattening hogs, and repairing the cabins. To our forefathers the gloomy months of winter were more pleasant than the zephyrs and the flowers of May. It however sometimes happened, after the apparent onset of winter, the weather became warm; the smoky time commenced, and lasted for a considerable number of days. This was the Indian summer, because it afforded the Indians another opportunity of visiting the settlements with their destructive warfare. The melting of the snow saddened every countenance, and the genial warmth of the sun chilled every heart with horror. The apprehension of another visit from the Indians, and of being driven back to the detested fort, was painful in the highest degree, and the distressing apprehension was frequently realized.

In such colonial warfare all were soldiers because all lived on the battlefield. The bravery of women became a byword. In 1766 in Shenandoah county in the Valley of Virginia, two men were taking their wives and children in a wagon toward the safety of a fort when they were attacked by five Indians and both men were killed. "The women," Kercheval reported, "instead of swooning at the sight of their bleeding, expiring husbands, seized their axes, and with Amazonian firmness, and strength almost superhuman, defended themselves and children. One of the Indians had succeeded in getting hold of one of Mrs. Sheetz's children, and attempted to drag it out of the wagon; but with the quickness of lightning she caught her child in one hand, and with the other made a blow at the head of the fellow, which caused him to quit his hold to save his life. Several of the Indians received pretty sore wounds in this desperate conflict, and all at last ran off, leaving the two women with their children to pursue their way to the fort." Only a few years later, Mrs. Experience Bozarth, in whose house a number of neighbors had taken refuge, defended them all after their two men were severely injured, by skillfully handling an axe with which she brained two Indians and disembowelled a third. The backwoods was no place for the squeamish; anyone who waited for the arrival of "troops" did not last long.

The boys' pastimes early prepared them for defense. Shooting small game with a bow or a gun and throwing a tomahawk became life-saving skills when Indians attacked. By the time a boy reached the age for service in the militia he was already at home in the forest and knew the ways of the Indian. "A well grown boy," Doddridge noted of the Valley of Virginia in the 1760's, "at the age of twelve or thirteen years, was furnished with a small rifle and shot-pouch. He then became a fort soldier, and had his port-hole assigned him. Hunting squirrels, turkeys and raccoons, soon made him expert in the use of his gun."

Hunting, Indian-fighting, and skirmishes in the backwoods encouraged numerous American improvements in the rifle. By the mid-18th century, the "Pennsylvania" rifle, later to achieve fame as the "Kentucky" rifle, was already noticeably different from its Alpine prototype. It was longer and more slender; had a smaller bore (a calibre of about .50), used a ball weighing only about half an ounce, and was more accurate. In contrast, even as late as the American Revolution, the German rifle was still clumsy, heavy, and short-barrelled; it used a ball about twice the weight, was slower to fire, was heavier in recoil, and offered much less range and accuracy. Slow loading—with short iron rod, mallet, and ramrod— had not disqualified the rifle for backwoods use, but the American developed a quicker and less strenuous means of loading: the "patch," a small greased cloth encasing a lead ball (slightly smaller than the bore), which could be pushed smoothly down the barrel. By insuring a tight fit in the rifling, the patch also prevented waste of fire-power. The resulting weapon had unprecedented convenience, economy, and accuracy.

By the Revolution this weapon, still practically unknown in England

and found only among hunters in the mountain fastnesses of Europe, had become common in the American backwoods. "Rifles, infinitely better than those imported, are daily made in many places in Pennsylvania," an Anglican minister wrote from Maryland in 1775, "and all the gunsmiths everywhere constantly employed. In this country, my lord, the boys, as soon as they can discharge a gun, frequently exercise themselves therewith, some a fowling and others a hunting. The great quantities of game, the many kinds, and the great privileges of killing making the Americans the best marksmen in the world, and thousands support their families by the same, particularly riflemen on the frontiers, whose objects are deer and turkeys. In marching through woods one thousand of these riflemen would cut to pieces ten thousand of your best troops." Such reports as these made the English regulars expect every American to be a sharpshooter.

The myth of the omnipresent American marksman, clothed not in a military uniform but in a hunting shirt, became potent in psychological warfare. Dixon & Hunter's *Virginia Gazette* (Sept. 9, 1775) reported an exhibition by riflemen bound for Boston: while one man held between his knees a small board with a bull's-eye the size of a dollar, a rifleman at sixty yards put eight successive bullets through the bull's-eye. Washington arranged a similar exhibition on Cambridge Common in August 1775, hoping that spies would carry the frightening word back to the British troops. At this very time the British musket was so crude that the official army manual did not even contain the command "aim" for its musketeers. Early in the Revolution, General George Washington issued an order in which he "earnestly" encouraged "the use of Hunting Shirts, with long Breeches made of the same Cloth. . . . it is a dress justly supposed to carry no small terror to the enemy, who think every such person a complete Marksman." But the rifle, unlike the European musket, was not equipped with a bayonet and was a slower, more fragile weapon of special skill. Ill-suited to the European formal battle-array, it remained a highly individualistic weapon, admirable for skirmishing or for picking off an individual enemy. Such tactics unnerved a rigidly trained professional army; they would help convince British officers that subduing the American populace was a hopeless task.

In America war had become an institution for the citizenry as well as the warriors. The colonials were in the habit of defending themselves on neighboring ground instead of employing professionals on a distant battlefield. Just as everybody in America was somewhat literate but none was greatly literary, everybody here was a bit of a soldier, none completely so. War was conducted without a professional army, without generals, and even without "soldiers" in the strict European sense. The

Second Amendment to the Federal Constitution would provide: "A well regulated Militia, being necessary to the security of a free State, the right of the people to keep and bear Arms, shall not be infringed."

The distinctive American experience would, of course, make difficulties whenever Americans would be arrayed in war or diplomacy against Europeans, for in Europe the professional army with its aristocratic officer class had made war a sophisticated, attenuated activity. To that sophistication there were two aspects. On the one hand, specialization of the soldier's function had made possible the limitation of warfare. On the other hand, it made possible a sophisticated diplomacy by which sovereigns used professional armies to serve their trivial or devious purposes and under which an uninterested populace lightly allowed their "nation" (i.e., the professional soldiery) to be committed to battle. A professional army was casually sent wherever the sovereign wished for imperial, dynastic, or commercial strategy. European war by the 18th century was far removed from the naïve defense of the hearth: specialized fighters were trained to kill for reasons they did not understand and in distant lands for which they had no love. As the 18th century wore on, such wars of policy commanded more and more of the blood and treasure of Europe. But these wars were barely intelligible, much less defensible, among colonial Americans, to whom war was the urgent defense of the hearth by everybody against an omnipresent and merciless enemy. Americans would long find it hard to understand the military games played by kings, ministers, and generals who used uniformed pawns on distant battlefields, or the diplomatic games in which such wars were only interludes.

54

Colonial Militia and the Myth of Preparedness

"To TRUST ARMS in the hands of the people at large has, in Europe, been believed . . . to be an experiment fraught only with danger," wrote President Timothy Dwight of Yale in the early 19th century. "Here by a long trial it has been proved to be perfectly harmless. . . . If the government be equitable; if it be reasonable in its exactions; if proper attention be paid to the education of children in knowledge, and religion, few men will be disposed to use arms, unless for their amusement, and for the defence of themselves and their country. The difficulty, here, has been to persuade the citizens to keep arms; not to prevent them from being employed for violent purposes." The story of the military institutions of the American colonies is an account of efforts to keep as much of the free population as possible armed and prepared to fight on short notice.

In Europe, where rulers were reluctant to put the means of revolt into the hands of their subjects, the high cost of firearms had anyway kept such weapons beyond the reach of most of the populace. But in America the requirements for self-defense and food-gathering had put firearms in the hands of nearly everyone. Separated by an ocean, their European sovereign could not have enforced a prohibition even if he had tried, but he did not fear that their arms would shake his throne. From a very early date, however, English Governors complained (and Americans boasted) of this armed citizenry. "How miserable that man is," wailed Governor Sir William Berkeley of Virginia, who had to deal with Bacon's Rebellion in 1676, "that Governes a People wher six parts of seaven at least are Poore Endebted Discontented and Armed." Even a century later Crèvecoeur observed that among backwoodsmen "surrounding hostility immediately puts the gun into their hands."

An armed citizenry was a response not only to the omnipresent threat of war but to the skirmishing type of warfare common in the American woods. Because of the poor communications, the vast terrain, and the ways of Indian fighting, war could seldom be a centrally-directed operation; instead it was a mass of scattered encounters by small groups and individuals acting largely on their own. When Indians attacked, the wise defenders hid themselves behind rocks and tree-trunks. "In our first war with the Indians," the Apostle John Eliot wrote to Robert Boyle in 1677, "God pleased to show us the vanity of our military skill, in managing our arms, after the European mode. Now we are glad to learn the skulking way of war. And what God's end is, in teaching us such a way of discipline, I know not."

The mass drill, precision, and discipline of the professional soldier were of little use, and decentralization of command was inevitable. Virginia Governors, fearing that a nervous populace might foment Indian troubles by fighting without provocation, in the early years actually forbade the raising of the militia in any part of the colony until the Governor's approval had been secured. But such delay was fatal, and by 1680 the right to summon the militia was conferred on officers in different parts of the colony. The commander of a remote backwoods fort had to show an independence, which sometimes amounted to contempt for his superior officers. When Captain Cadwalader Jones, commander of a Virginia fort on the Rappahannock, received a command in September 1679 which did not please him, he assembled his garrison, read the communication aloud, and burned it in full view of his men, exclaiming that this showed what he thought of Major Robert Beverley and the Governor! Under such conditions, what use was elaborate strategy by a commander far from the scene of action?

The early Pilgrims organized their landing parties in loose, impromptu fashion. Although they fortunately had a veteran military leader in Captain Miles Standish, their armed unit was not the permanently organized military company but, as one historian has aptly put it, a "pick-up team," chosen for each particular occasion from the men most available at the time. Their first encounters showed features which would continue to mark colonial military life: fighting by a band of casually gathered, haphazardly armed civilians, over whom there was no effective central command. The earliest settlers at Plymouth found that defense could hardly be separated from all the other tasks of daily living—of cultivating the land, getting food, and building shelters. "They are constantly on their guard night and day," observed a visitor to the town in 1627; men went to church, musket in hand, and during the service "each sets his arms down near him." But as the settlements pushed back from the coast and dispersed, as the Indian menace became only intermittent, a more formal organization became necessary. New England developed a militia system which became the common pattern of colonial defense.

An armed citizenry was by no means an American invention. A prime example of American "regression," it was a revival of the medieval Assize of Arms (1181), from which the English had developed a *militia* consisting of every able-bodied freeman, each required to provide himself with arms, to train periodically under a local officer, and to be ready on sudden call. By the later 17th and early 18th century, as Europe's "limited" warfare left fighting to a small number of professionals, the English militia system had become something of a joke— mainly a device for parade and ostentation by the gentlemen lords-lieutenants. In America, however, the ancient militia system, with a number of striking New World modifications, was the pattern by which whole communities organized against their enemies.

The unit in this system was not the trained professional soldier armed and supplied from above; it was the self-armed citizen. The Court of Assistants of Massachusetts Bay, in March 1631, ordered that within two weeks every town should see that all men (including servants but excepting magistrates and ministers) were supplied with arms approved by their militia officers. Anyone who did not already own arms was required to purchase them; if he could not afford the price, the money would be advanced by the town to be repaid by the citizen as soon as possible. The next year the colony ordered that any single man who had not so armed himself should be hired out as a servant, and this law remained. In Plymouth the requirements were still more detailed: after January 1633 each man had to have a musket or other suitable gun, a cartridge belt, a sword, two pounds of powder, and ten pounds of bullets. A long series of Acts in Massachusetts and neighboring colonies established a militia system in which every able-bodied man was armed and each town had its own company of militia, holding periodic trainings and inspections of arms.

The militia was a most unmilitary outfit by European standards. It wore no uniform. Although colonial Governors had sometimes been chosen because of their military experience, only seldom was a colonial militia actually drilled or commanded by a professional soldier. A striking and troublesome feature of the colonial militia was its unprofessional practice of electing its own officers. The occasions for these elections, as we have already seen, were celebrated by a peculiar New England institution: the "artillery election sermon" delivered to the community of armed congregants. With minor variations and occasional exceptions, the officers of the local militia owed their positions to popular choice, usually ratified by the colonial legislature; the arrangement became tolerable only as the custom developed of electing officers for an indefinite term or of automatically reëlecting satisfactory officers. This system mitigated the brutal discipline of the European professional armies (service in which, especially in remote colonies, was a form of punishment for crime); but it produced an informality between officers and men which weakened the force in combat. It also reminded the soldiers that they were fighting for themselves and encouraged them to desert when service become inconvenient.

In the South after about 1700, the problem of defense for the white European population was complicated by fear of a slave uprising. In South Carolina, for example, the "patrol"—the group of white men temporarily recruited from the civilian population who went regular rounds to apprehend and punish vagrant Negroes—soon became part of the militia. Elsewhere, too, the militia system was adapted to a slaveholding society. How widespread was the actual fear of uprising and to what extent that fear fostered a militant spirit is debatable, but no one can deny that features of a slaveholding plantation society helped disperse the military function into the whole white community. Military leadership fell on the civilian leaders of the community, who would have been as jealous of a military class as they were of lawyers or of any other group of specialized professionals. In Virginia the institution of the "county-lieutenant" acquired a new life, and the proverbial "Kentucky Colonel" remains a vestige of the earliest American military institutions.

Allowing for some variations, there was an impressive uniformity in the way colonists organized (or failed to organize) their defense. Everywhere, Americans relied on an armed citizenry rather than on a professional army. The failure to distinguish between the "military man" and every other man was simply another example of the dissolving of the monopolies and distinctions of European life.

The militia system itself, with its axiom that every man was a trained and ready-armed soldier who would instantly spring to the defense of his country, encouraged the belief—which often proved a dangerous illusion—that the community was always prepared for its peril. In a country inhabited by "Minute Men" why keep a standing army? At the time of the first World War, William Jennings Bryan would boast that when the President called, a million freemen would spring to arms between sunrise and sunset. His belief was based on the obsolete assumption that the very conditions of American life produced men who were always ready to fight. The fear of a standing army, which by European hypothesis was the instrument of tyrants and the enslaver of peoples, reenforced opposition to a professional body of men-in-arms. Moreover, so long as the men-in-arms were merely civilians temporarily distracted from their regular peaceful occupations, so long as there was no professional group concerned for its own prestige, few American politicians dared urge the advantages of a professional army.

The long-standing American myth of a constantly prepared citizenry helps explain why Americans have always been so ready to demobilize their forces. Again and again, our popular army has laid down its arms with dizzying speed, only to disperse into a precarious peace. This rhythm of our life began in the earliest colonial period. The people sprang quickly to arms: for example, on the night of September 23, 1675, during King Philip's War, an alarm at a town thirty miles out of Boston brought twelve hundred militiamen under arms within an hour. As soon as an alarm was past, an expedition over, or a campaign ended, militiamen showed the same speed in disbanding.

In New England after each of the early Indian wars the militia quickly disintegrated. King Philip's War of 1675-76 had brought heavy massacres to the miserably prepared colonies. They relied on the myth that, because every individual man was required to be prepared, the community as a whole did not need to worry. Their militia system, organized only for peacetime, lacked communications suitable for war. There was, in fact, no central command nor was there a permanent commissariat which might have kept an army continuously supplied. Village after village suffered surprise attack and had no way of securing assistance. Yet, the obvious lesson was lost on the colonists—at least they did nothing about it. As soon as a battle was over, they allowed their forces to fall into decay. By 1683, there was so little interest in local defense and such difficulty in filling the quotas of commissioned officers that in Plymouth Colony, for example, the government itself threatened to appoint militia officers if the towns continued to neglect their duty. When Indians fell upon the colonists in 1689, they were again disastrously unprepared.

55

Home Rule and
Colonial "Isolationism"

THE MILITIA had arisen to defend farms, homes, and towns, not to serve as pawns in anyone's grand strategy. When threatened by unpredictable bands of marauding Indians, colonists saw no sense in sending men off to fight in some distant place, while leaving their own homes unprotected. Anyway, there was seldom a battlefront in Indian warfare. From the very beginning, therefore, Americans thought of military defense in the most direct and simple terms. They did not think of men marching off to battle, but of a man standing, gun in hand, beside his neighbors to fend off the enemy attacking his village. Settlers were ready enough to build a stockade, a garrison house, or a fort for their own town, but they were reluctant to maintain a fort at some distance —however strategic it might be for their own defense.

Some of the crucial defenses of the colonies were never built, simply because the nearby towns could not afford the expense of an adequate fortification and remote towns were not enough interested. For example, Castle Island commanded the channel by which vessels had to approach Boston, and a strong, continuously-maintained fort there would have protected the whole colony. But repeated efforts to persuade outlying towns to bear their share of the expense were unsuccessful; the Island fortification lacked a permanent garrison, was never fully manned, and periodically fell into decay. The burden of maintaining it, when it was maintained at all, was assumed by Boston and a few adjacent towns. The same story could be told of Virginia and the southern colonies, where the danger of coastal invasion by foreign powers and by pirates was constant. At Jamestown, for example, the fortification had so decayed by 1691 that it could not even be used as a depot for supplies. Because the coastal defenses of the colonies required the largest investment, the most cooperation and planning, and the greatest support from remote places, they proved to be the weakest link in the colonial military scheme. For such defense, colonists came to rely on guard-ships arriving fully manned from England.

Perhaps the dominant fact about the relationship of the colonies to each other was this reluctance of any one colony to send its militia to join in the defense of its neighbor. The "burgher guard," or local militia, of New Amsterdam, which had been first mustered during the Indian War of 1644, was unwilling even to go outside the city limits. When New York or South Carolina fought in their own defense, they automatically defended the other colonies, but this was the consequence of their more exposed geographic situation; it was not due to any cooperative or far-sighted spirit. Nevertheless, no colony hesitated to use its neighbors. For a long time Virginia regularly sent a messenger to New York and New England to bring back word on the movements of the hostile French and the northern Indians—never to see whether help was needed in the North, but simply to be forewarned against a possible attack on themselves. A large proportion of the intercolonial communications consisted of explanations, more or less diplomatic, of why each dared not, or could not afford, to send its militia outside its own borders.

For example, when Governor Henry Sloughter of New York, in mid-summer 1691, wrote the Governor of Massachusetts proposing a joint conquest of Canada in order to remove their common frontier menace at its source, the reply was a parcel of inconsistent excuses. Massachusetts, Governor Bradstreet explained, was already occupied with new Indian outbreaks on her borders; she was trying to finance two ships to cruise her own coast against a French privateer; and besides she had no money to spare. But none of this prevented the Massachusetts Governor from asking whether New York would possibly be interested in establishing a garrison at Pemaquid, where the Indians menaced Massachusetts from the northeast. When Virginia received a similar request from New York (supported by a requisition from England) in 1693, her Burgesses asked: How could the defense of far-off New York amount to a defense of their Virginia? Virginia had her own exposed seacoast; to reduce her military force by sending any of it to New York would simply increase her own peril. Virginia had always been her own best defense, and (the Burgesses were still arguing in 1695) she wished to keep it that way. Needless to say, no Virginia forces were sent; the money sent to help New York in the common cause was provided only after the Virginia Governor and Council overruled the Burgesses. When Massachusetts suffered a new wave of disastrous Indian raids in 1703, she appealed in vain to neighboring Connecticut and Rhode Island. The Council of Connecticut plausibly explained that the colony was barely strong enough to defend her own valley-frontier. They ignored the fact, already proved by the fall of Deerfield, that this frontier could not be effectively defended except in Massachusetts. The people of Connecticut even appealed to their charter: their defense could not extend beyond their own borders without a special Act of their General Court, which, of course, could not be obtained.

The great obstacle to British efforts to combine all the colonial troops against the French and Indian menace in the mid-18th century was this pervasive localism. Sir Charles Hardy, Governor of New York, wrote from Fort George on May 7, 1756:

> To consider the general Good ought to be the Attention of every honest Man, & no time ever more strongly called for an Exertion of the united Strength of this extensive Dominion to defend His Majesty's just rights, & remove a perfidious & vigilant Enemy from their Encroachments, an Enemy watching every Neglect, & improving every Advantage, & tho' small in Number, when compared to our numerous Inhabitants, still acting as one Body, under one Order of Controul, & united in that Order, put Us poor disunited Millions in Defiance, committing by the Means of their Indians, the most unheard of Barbarities, & laying waste our Lands without opposition.

> This, My Lord, is the State of unhappy divided America. Your Lordship is desirous that a strong Army may appear in the Field; the Provinces that were concerned last Year, are raising a great many Men, intended to be 10,000 & I believe will fall little short of that

Number; This may in appearance promise great Things, but I cannot flatter myself in much Success; Our Measures are slow; one Colony will not begin to raise their Men in an early time, doubting whether their Neighbours will not deceive them, in compleating their Levies so largely as they promised.

Everywhere colonists feared to put their young men into a regular army that might be sent to a distant place as part of a large strategy. That seemed the surest way of depriving their homes and closest borders of necessary defense.

The issue of home-defense soon became involved with constitutional issues. The English Civil War of the mid-17th century had been fought, in part at least, over the question of parliamentary control of the army. The liberties of Englishmen, freedom from oppressive taxation, and representative government itself—according to the Commonwealth men— depended on the power of a representative assembly to raise, discipline, and command its own forces. If the British government could raise an army of colonials at colonial expense, could keep it under remote command and strict discipline, and could send it wherever British interests dictated, what meaning was there to the constitution and the self-governing rights of free Englishmen?

The older English fear of a standing army combined with the newer American fear of a drained-off, remotely stationed army. The colonies temporized, offering bad prudential excuses and good legalistic reasons; these all added up to each colony's refusal to release its armed men from its own separate control. "The truth is," Lord Loudoun shrewdly wrote from New York on November 22, 1756, "Governors here are Cyphers; their Predecessors sold the whole of the Kings Prerogative, to get their Sallaries; and till you find a Fund, independent of the Province, to Pay the Governors, and new model the Government, you can do nothing with the Provinces. . . . if you delay it till a Peace, You will not have a force to Exert any Brittish Acts of Parliament here."

War was becoming a different institution for the Americans. The "isolationism" of the separate colonies and the New World experience of war from which that isolationism sprang helps explain many things about the American Revolution. The War for Independence was a clash between two concepts of how, when, and where men should fight. In America, the British government had found it necessary to wage old-style European wars, fought for some very large or very petty (but always half-hidden) purposes by a regular army moved about the continent at the will of its commander. Incidentally, the colonists were defended and they profited in many indirect ways from participation in the Empire.

But it would be hard to prove simple "self-defense" for any of Britain's colonial wars. Sometimes they required an offensive in remote places to serve the large strategy. The justification was always elaborate: What benefit would accrue to the Empire if its professional military force was used to this or that end? British military policy was never obvious in the sense in which self-defense against marauding Indians was obvious to the American settler. Even at the conclusion of the long, expensive, and "victorious" French and Indian War in 1763, it was by no means clearly desirable that the British should acquire Canada and so force the French from North America. As we have seen, some English plausibly feared that removal of the French menace might make the colonists less dependent on the mother country, and they doubted that much profit could come from the frigid Canadian wilderness. Such questions of empire policy seemed irrelevant to the remote American settler, for whom defense meant protection against sudden death. Even the Americans who were more safe on the seacoast hoped in the New World to escape European dynastic and military policy.

The major financial and manpower burden of the French and Indian War was, of course, borne by the British government itself. Whether the colonists (despite their protests) bore their fair share of the cost and the fighting can be argued, but it is plain that the Colonial Assemblies did their best to keep their contributions as small as possible. If the colonists had been more "far-sighted" and less "isolationist," they might have seen that their concept of a Fortress America was narrow and they might have foreseen the many long-range advantages in sharing the expenses of imperial wars. Had they voluntarily undertaken such expenses, the occasion might never have arisen for those changes in British policy after 1763 which aimed to make the colonies pay their way, which fomented the constitutional debate over taxation, and without which the colonies might not have been stirred to rebellion.

From their American experience the colonies had come to believe that defense began at home. The more they worried the problem, the more they believed that the British Constitution hallowed their assertion that treasury and army must be locally controlled. Parliament had tried to commit the colonists to fight—and to finance—wars of policy. But the strongly particularist feelings of each of the colonies, which prevented them from helping one another in the earlier colonial wars and which plagued Lord Loudoun during the French and Indian War, led them toward a "War of Separation." In that war, and later in the War of 1812, a similar short-sightedness—again reënforced by legal, constitutional, financial, and prudential arguments—would again produce near-disaster.

There is, then, no paradox in the fact that the colonies were willing to "revolt" and yet were unwilling to unite; on the contrary, the two facts explain each other. The intense separatism and the determination to keep local resources to defend homes and towns also caused the nearly overwhelming difficulties which afflicted the colonial armies during the Revolution. These, too, were the very reasons why, in the long run, it was impossible for the British regular army to subdue the Americans. And these were the reasons which would make American federalism difficult, necessary, and in the long run spectacularly successful.

Here also were roots of a latter-day American "isolationism." In place of the European concept of wars undertaken to serve the half-secret needs of dynasty, commerce, or empire, there had grown here a notion of war as the urgent and temporary defense of the homeland. In the words of Washington's Farewell Address:

> Europe has a set of primary interests which to us have none or a very remote relation. Hence she must be engaged in frequent controversies, the causes of which are essentially foreign to our concerns. Hence, therefore, it must be unwise in us to implicate ourselves by artificial ties in the ordinary vicissitudes of her politics or the ordinary combinations and collisions of her friendships or enmities.
>
> Our detached and distant situation invites and enables us to pursue a different course. If we remain one people, under an efficient government, the period is not far off when we may defy material injury from external annoyance; when we may take such an attitude as will cause the neutrality we may at any time resolve upon to be scrupulously respected; when belligerent nations, under the impossibility of making acquisitions upon us, will not lightly hazard the giving us provocation; when we may choose peace or war, as our interest, guided by justice, shall counsel.
>
> Why forego the advantages of so peculiar a situation? Why quit our own to stand upon foreign ground? Why, by interweaving our destiny with that of any part of Europe, entangle our peace and prosperity in the toils of European ambition, rivalship, interest, humor, or caprice?

Under the new Federal Constitution, declarations of war were possible only through a cumbersome and time-consuming legislative process, in full public view. The after-image of the early American vision remained. And the American people retained a strong and often disorganizing hand on their nation's foreign policy.

56

The Unprofessional Soldier

THE BELIEF that American wars would always be fought by "embattled farmers" was rooted in the earliest facts of American life. Military men were to be simply citizens in arms. The military caste, the Man-on-Horseback, the Palace Revolution, the Coup d'État, the tug of war between army and civil government—these recurring motifs in continental European political life did not appear on the American scene. Civilian control over the army, clearly asserted in the Federal Constitution, merely declared what was already one of the firmest institutions of colonial life.

The typical American view of the military appeared in Doddridge's description of the backwoodsmen who "formed the cordon along the Ohio river, on the frontiers of Pennsylvania, Virginia and Kentucky, which defended the country against the attacks of the Indians during the revolutionary war. They were the janizaries of the country, that is, they were soldiers when they chose to be so, and when they chose laid down their arms. Their military service was voluntary, and of course received no pay."

Long before the end of the colonial period, British politicians and professional soldiers had learned that they could not rely on Americans to fill the ranks of the regular army stationed in America. While the backwoodsman with his sharpshooting rifle was ready and able to defend his home, he was intractable within a European-type professional army. The armed civilians of the separate colonies, which in their intense localism refused to cooperate in any large strategy, were inadequate to the large tasks of colonial defense. If the British government hoped to protect the colonies by preventing the accumulation of offensive French military strength, they had to send in a professional army from the outside. The capture of Louisbourg by New Englanders in 1745 was the only instance in the colonial period of a successful large-scale military operation by provincial fighters—and even that was the product not of wise planning but of lucky coincidence.

When General Braddock made his preparations for the disastrous campaign of 1755, he put relatively small reliance on American troops. Even at that he was expecting too much. The nucleus of his army was soldiers of regular regiments of the British Army, supposed to be brought up to full strength by American recruits, to be supported by voluntary financial aid from the colonial assemblies, and to be partly provisioned by the colonies. But Braddock was disappointed: few recruits were raised, the assemblies refused substantial assistance, and wagons and supplies were offered only at exorbitant rates. Characteristically, the northern colonies voted instead to set up a wholly provincial army under a general of their own choosing. This foreshadowed the difficulties which Lord Loudoun would meet on a larger scale a few years later and which would dramatize the divergence of American from European ways of war.

Loudoun's activities comprised the greatest British effort before the Revolution to control and centralize American military activities. According to plans made in advance, he arrived in America in 1756 carrying a broad commission to organize a force against the French and Indians; he was supposed to command a regular army of nearly fourteen thousand men (two-thirds of the privates besides replacements to be colonials). During two years of recruitment, the British, using dubious methods, managed to enlist about 7500 Americans; during the same period the British Isles supplied only about 4500. The year 1757 showed a decided reversal of proportions: in that year only about 1200 men were recruited in the colonies, while 11,000 came from England. Loudoun, with the hoped-for acquiescence of the separate colonial governments, was supposed to be supreme commander of all local forces, including, of course, their militia. But the more Loudoun learned of colonial troops and colonial ways, the less he came to rely on them— whether as recruits for the ranks of his regular regiments or as supporting forces organized in their own militia. "The King must trust in this country to himself and those he sends," Lord Loudoun wrote back from America as early as September 1756, ". . . for this Country will not run when he calls."

Everything that Loudoun, with the experienced eye of a professional soldier, saw of the American provincial militias appalled him. Upon his arrival, there were about seven thousand militiamen occupying the colonies' northern forts. These men had been raised, and their officers commissioned, each by his separate province; for all practical purposes each group was responsible only to its own distinct government. When Loudoun and his subordinates inspected the camp commanded by General John Winslow (who had been commissioned by the Governors of Massachusetts, Connecticut, and New York), they were horrified by the absence of decent military order or even rudimentary sanitation. They saw a hundred graves dug in a day for men dead of disease. "The fort stinks enough to cause an infection," Loudoun heard from Fort William Henry, "they have all their sick in it. The camp nastier than anything I could conceive, their necessary houses, kitchens, graves and places for slaughtering cattle, all mixed through their encampment." Deserters were only mildly punished. Loudoun was shocked to see men firing their guns at random after drill, sleeping on post, and taking pot shots at game while they were on the march. But the elected officers would seldom risk unpopularity by punishing offenders.

No commander in his right mind would admit men with such a conception of an army into a regiment of well-disciplined regulars. And why, indeed, should any American put himself under the strict discipline of the British Army? Everything was better in the provincial militias: a Massachusetts private soldier received all of 10¼ d sterling a day while a British regular private received no more than 4d; in addition, the provincial soldier received an annual bounty for reënlistment. Supplies for the provincials looked like luxuries to the regulars. The militiaman not only received a greater staple allowance, but after one summer's service, he was allowed to keep his hatchet, blanket, and knapsack—and he soon established the profitable custom of taking his musket home with him. He could count on his sugar, ginger, rum, and molasses; and his marching allowance was three times that of a British regular.

This life of a provincial militiaman was free-and-easy compared to that of the regular, who might be punished with flogging, or be forced to enlist for life in the West Indies. It was so free-and-easy in fact that the commander of provincial troops never really knew how many men he had at his disposal. The militiaman preferred to stay close to home, so that he could return to his family in case of need. When the General Court of Massachusetts voted troops for the expedition to Crown Point in northeastern New York, they expressly provided that the men "shall not be compelled to march southward of Albany, or westward of Schenechtedy." "The Troops are constantly coming & going," an observer wrote of General Johnson's New York army, "ill arm'd, ill cloath'd & worse disciplined, some having served their time out, as they phrase it, and some commencing fresh men. Never to be sure was such a motly Herd, almost every man his own master & a General."

The "leveling spirit" of the Americans was notorious among British officers. "Our Militia is under no kind of discipline. . . ." complained

Cadwallader Colden to Lord Halifax in 1754. "The Inhabitants of the Northern Colonies are all so nearly on a level, and a licentiousness, undei the notion of liberty, so generally prevails, that they are impatient undei all kind of superiority and authority." "The Officers of the Army with very few Exceptions," a colonial observer noted of such provincial troops, "are utter Strangers to Military Life and most of them in no Respect superior to the Men they are put over, They are like the heads and indeed are the heads of a Mob." Such "officers" had long been snubbed by British regulars. In 1741 in the expedition against Cartagena in the Caribbean, officers from Virginia, including even the experienced and highly competent Governor Gooch, had been passed over for promotion and brazenly mistreated. George Washington himself had traveled alone half-way across the colonies to settle just such a question concerning his own military rank. The established policy repeated by the Duke of Cumberland in 1754 ordered "that all Troops serving by Commissions signed by Us, or by Our General Commanding in Chief in North America, shall take Rank before all Troops which may serve by Commission from any of the Governors or Councils of Our Provinces in North America: And It is Our further Pleasure, that the Generals and Field Officers of the Provincial Troops shall have no Rank with the Generals & Field Officers who serve by Commissions from Us." Loudoun brought with him to America a modified order allowing colonial officers more rank, but by then it was too late.

There was not a single problem that plagued Loudoun in the French and Indian War that did not also trouble Washington in the War of Independence. Washington, trying to raise a unified Continental Army from unmilitary Americans, now stood in the shoes of Lord Loudoun. Although the "cause" was different, the difficulties were the same. The Continental Army, like the British Regular Army twenty years earlier, had to compete for men against the separate state militias, and Washington had only slightly more success. Had the American cause been forced to depend on an American regular army, the outcome would have been even more doubtful and drawn-out. Washington, however, took wise advantage of his opportunity to fight the war seriatim—first in New England, then in the Middle Colonies, then in the South—rather than all-at-once, as the French and Indian Wars had been fought. This made the dispersed militia more useful and his smaller army more effective.

The unseemly disputes over rank and precedence, in which regular British officers had lorded it over mere militiamen, were reënacted with the officers of the Continental line now assuming the old airs of the regulars. The Congress and the States showed democratic prodigality;

they lavished military titles on mere able-bodied citizens, regardless of competence. "My blacksmith is a captain," De Kalb reported in amazement. To avoid offense, it was always safer to assume that anybody was entitled to be addressed as a high officer. "Not an hour passes," Washington wrote to the President of the Continental Congress (Aug. 3, 1778), "without new applications and new complaints about rank. . . . We can scarcely form a Court Martial or parade a detachment in any instance, without a warm discussion on the subject of precedence." When Colonel Crafts of the militia and Colonel Jackson of the Continental army arrived to act as pall-bearers at the funeral of a fellow-officer, Crafts as the older man claimed the right to walk first, but Jackson argued that as a Continental officer he was entitled to precedence. Neither gave in, and Crafts and his friends walked out on the funeral.

Even Washington's patience wore thin; but since local prides were not to be overcome, he learned to live with them and somehow to harness them in the common cause. "I have labored, ever since I have been in the service," Washington wrote at the end of 1776, "to discourage all kinds of local attachments and distinctions of country [i.e. of State], denominating the whole by the greater name of *American,* but I have found it impossible to overcome prejudices; and, under the new establishment, I conceive it best to stir up an emulation; in order to do which would it not be better for each State to furnish, though not to appoint, their own brigadiers?" In 1780, to the inquiries of the Congress about his problems of promotion and rank, he replied: "If in all cases ours was *one* army, or *thirteen* armies allied for the common defence, there would be no difficulty in solving your question; but we are occasionally both, and I should not be much out if I were to say, that we are sometimes *neither,* but a compound of *both."*

All the American armies were competing against each other for men, for officers, for rank, and for glory. Privates from New England were being offered higher pay than those from the Middle States. Massachusetts even offered to pay its men by lunar rather than calendar months in order to secure a competitive advantage. This particular trick Washington stigmatized as the "most fatal stab to the peace of this Army, that ever was given. . . . Lord North himself could not have devised a more effectual blow to the recruiting Service." Problems were compounded by the familiar "leveling" tendencies of the Americans; by their refusal to allow a sufficiently higher pay to officers, they stirred discontent and bred an unmilitary familiarity between officers and men.

The widespread fear of a permanent professional army increased the difficulties. John Adams declared it safer in the long run to put public faith in a temporary though less effective militia. "Although it may cost us more, and we may put now and then a battle to hazard by the method we are in, yet we shall be less in danger of corruption and violence from a standing army, and our militia will acquire courage, experience, discipline, and hardiness in actual service. I wish every man upon the continent was a soldier, and obliged, upon occasion, to fight and determined to conquer or to die. Flight was unknown to the Romans. I wish it was to Americans." Proposals to offer long-term pensions to officers, in order to attract better men and to raise their morale, were widely opposed. Elbridge Gerry listed the reasons (Jan. 13, 1778): "the infant state of the country, its aversion to placemen and pensioners, whereby Great Britain is likely to lose her liberty, the equality of the officers and soldiers of some States, before the war."

Short-term enlistments (sometimes for as little as three months) expressed both the widespread fear of a professional standing army and the assumption that an army would be superfluous the day after the war was won. Washington repeatedly complained that this was the core of his problem. For example, in a circular (Oct. 18, 1780) to the several States from his headquarters near Passaic, he said:

> I am religiously persuaded that the duration of the war, and the greatest part of the Misfortunes, and perplexities we have hitherto experienced, are chiefly to be attributed to temporary inlistments. . . . A moderate, compact force, on a permanent establishment capable of acquiring the discipline essential to military operations, would have been able to make head against the Enemy, without comparison better than the throngs of Militia, which have been at certain periods not in the feild, but on their way to, and from the feild: for from that want of perseverance which characterises all Militia, and of that coercion which cannot be exercised upon them it has always been found impracticable to detain the greatest part of them in service even for the term, for which they have been called out; and this has been commonly so short, that we have had a great proportion of the time, two sets of men to feed and pay, one coming to the Army, and the other going from it.

Men went home just as they were beginning to understand their duties, and it was often necessary to recruit a new army in the face of the enemy. More than one American military defeat can be explained by the transient character of the army. General Richard Montgomery rushed into his disastrous assault on Quebec in late December 1775 because the enlistments of all his New England troops would expire at midnight on December 31, and he was sure they would not stay with him a day longer.

The unreliability and lack of discipline of the American armed citizenry, which had been so hastily gathered into military ranks, haunted brave Revolutionary commanders from Washington down to lieutenants in the field, and made large-scale planning mere wishful thinking. Time after time militia fled the battlefield, spreading defeatism as they went. "America," warned Washington, "has been almost amused out of her Liberties" by the proponents of the militia. "I solemnly declare I never was witness to a single instance, that can countenance an opinion of Militia or raw Troops being fit for the real business of fighting. I have found them useful as light Parties to skirmish in the woods, but incapable of making or sustaining a serious attack. . . . The late battle of Camden is a melancholly comment upon this doctrine. The Militia fled at the first fire, and left the Continental Troops surrounded on every side, and overpowered by numbers to combat for safety instead of victory." "Great god," exclaimed Daniel Morgan on Feb. 1, 1781, only a few days after his victory over Tarleton, "what is the reason we cant Have more men in the field—so many men in the country Nearby idle for want of employment." At this critical moment in the War, when Greene was retreating before Cornwallis, Edward Stevens vainly appealed to his troops.

> After crossing the Yadkin we could not have Paraded a greater Force than Eight Hundred for Action if even that Including Militia and all and a great part of the number was the Militia under me whose times were out. I saw the greatest necessity of these men remaining a few days till the Troops from General Greens Camp could get up, and this the General requested of me to endeavour to bring about. I had them paraded and addressed them on the Subject. But to my great mortification and astonishment scarce a man would agree to it, And gave for answer he was a good Soldier that Served his time out. If the Salvation of the Country had depended on their staying Ten or Fifteen days, I dont believe they would have done it. Militia wont do. Their greatest Study is to Rub through their Tower [Tour] of Duty with whole Bones.

But many militiamen were not this scrupulous of their duty; they often went home before their term was up. Desertions were commonplace. It is hard to assess the military tactics of some battles because one can never be sure how many of the "losses" of the Revolutionary army were due to desertion rather than to death or capture. Within a few weeks before the Battle of Bennington on August 16, 1777, more than four hundred men deserted—or, more accurately, disappeared. At the siege of Newport, about the same time, five thousand militiamen deserted within a few days, so weakening Sullivan's forces that he had to abandon any idea of attack. On many occasions—for example, near Savannah in

March 1779, at Johnstown in October 1781, and at other places too numerous to mention—large numbers of militia fled in panic. Although the Americans had outnumbered the British by more than fifty per cent at Guilford Court House on March 15, 1781, the wholesale flight of the militia to the woods gave victory to the British. The experienced General Daniel Morgan had shrewdly foreseen just this when he warned General Nathanael Greene against the "great number of militia" and advised, "If they fight, you beat Cornwallis, if not, he will beat you." "Put the . . . militia in the centre, with some picked troops in their rear with orders to shoot down the first man that runs." Greene followed Morgan's advice, but the anxiety of the North Carolina and Virginia militia prevailed.

How could such an ill-assorted, ill-disciplined, and ill-supplied army succeed against the well-organized forces of one of the great military powers? How, indeed, can we account for the final victory? Many acts of heroism, courage, and sacrifice embellished the records of the fighting Americans. The unorthodox imagination of amateur American generals, in sharp contrast to the professional rigidity of the British command, gave the colonials an unexpected advantage. But it is still hard to explain why the British surrendered so quickly after Yorktown. Today the most persuasive answer is not that the Americans won but that the British lost—or perhaps that they simply gave up, having seen the long-run hopelessness of their cause. The American terrain (together with the colonial dispersion, which meant that there was no jugular vein to be cut by British force) led the British to realize that to subdue America was beyond their means. Within the first four years of the Revolution, every one of the most populous towns—Boston, New York, Philadelphia, and Charleston—had fallen to the British and had been occupied by their regular troops, but always without decisive effect. The American center was everywhere and nowhere—in each man himself. In addition, the French brought crucial aid to the American militia and irregulars, and the spectre of a permanent American alliance with France haunted the British Empire.

Perhaps the most typical and most ominous of the military events of the war was the abrupt disbanding of the army. In January, 1781—ten months before Cornwallis' surrender at Yorktown—mutiny shook the army in Pennsylvania; again, on the brink of peace in June 1783, mutinous soldiers, in control of the powder magazines and public offices at the seat of the Continental Congress in Philadelphia, threatened to use force to get their wages. It was in the shadow of such disorder that the Continental Army was hastily dispersed and that General Washington on December fourth bade a tearful farewell to his officers. Nothing was more American about the Revolution than this conclusion of it, when armed citizens impatiently dissolved themselves back into the populace. In this, as in later wars in American history, "the end of the war" and the end of the army were substantially, and disastrously, synonymous.

In American folklore it is fitting that the first call to arms, the rousing of "embattled farmers," the sudden appearance of Minute Men, together with Washington's Farewell and the last dispersion of the army, should remain the most permanent and the most moving symbols. The story of the actual administration of the Army is dismal and discreditable— almost unprecedented in the annals of war.

Yet the very weaknesses of the professional army had already fore-shadowed strengths in American institutions. Unmilitary Americans freely chose a general for their first President. Washington might become "first in war, first in peace, and first in the hearts of his countrymen," but the political power given to a military leader meant something very different here from what it might have meant elsewhere. The American military ideal was not Caesar but Cincinnatus, not the skilled general glorying in the tasks of warfare to which he gave his life, but the planter who had unwillingly left his tobacco fields.

When, near the end of the war, American officers tried to set up an organization to perpetuate their comradeship, their memories, and their tradition (and perhaps their political influence), they significantly chose to call themselves the Society of the Cincinnati. Washington assumed its leadership—though only with the greatest reluctance, for he was suspicious of the organization and hoped to see it soon dissolved. Among the people at large it aroused violent fears of a military caste; they saw in such a hereditary military society a dangerous center of aristocracy, a focus of monarchic conspiracy. The Society was so congenial to the monarchic spirit that King Louis XVI of France authorized his officers to form a branch chapter and to wear the Order of the Cincinnati as a military decoration.

Long after the Society of the Cincinnati had faded from the public memory, another American military institution reached into many American homes. This was the Purple Heart Badge of Military Merit, which Washington established by a general order of Aug. 7, 1782:

> The General ever desirous to cherish a virtuous ambition in his soldiers, as well as to foster and encourage every species of Military merit, directs that whenever any singularly meritorious action is performed, the author of it shall be permitted to wear on his facings over the left breast, the figure of a heart in purple cloth or silk, edged with narrow lace or binding. Not only instances of unusual gallantry, but also of extraordinary fidelity and essential Service in any way shall

meet with a due reward. . . . Men who have merited this last distinction to be suffered to pass all guards and sentinels which officers are permitted to do.

The road to glory in a patriot army and a free country is thus open to all—this order is also to have retrospect to the earliest stages of the war, and to be considered as a permanent one.

Even though the Federal Constitution later gave the power to wage war to the central government, the American army was never fully unified. State militias, under their later guise of the "national guard," remained important; they helped keep alive a spirit of local allegiance and a variety of practice and military standards which eventually created all kinds of problems. The peacetime regional nucleus of the militia or "national guard" stayed together through a Civil War and two World Wars, so that many men continued to fight beside their neighbors.

Starting with Washington himself, American history would offer again and again—especially after the decline of the Virginia Dynasty—examples of men whose fame on the battlefield eventually led them to the highest civil office. Even in Great Britain, where there was little fear of military coups d'état during the 18th and 19th centuries, military men rarely became prime ministers; turning military success into a political career was almost unheard of there. But in America this became common: the prominent examples—Jackson, William Henry Harrison, Taylor, Grant, Theodore Roosevelt, and Eisenhower—come quickly to mind. Some of these men had begun, not in the ranks of the regular army, but in the local militia. And their military exploits—far from seeming mere success in a specialized profession—actually attested their success as undifferentiated Americans. Precisely because there was no military caste, the citizen-soldier easily found a place in American political life.

ACKNOWLEDGMENTS

The University of Chicago for the last fourteen years has offered me the freedom and the stimulating environment to pursue the research which has gone into this book. Its Social Science Research Committee has supported the work over many years. To the friendly atmosphere of the Department of History—and especially to its chairman, Walter Johnson—I owe more than I can say.

To the Relm Foundation of Ann Arbor, Michigan, I am especially indebted for its generous grant. The Foundation, and its Secretary, Richard A. Ware, have given me an unrestricted freedom to do my work. Unlike many other foundations, they have shown a faith in the individual scholar which has itself been an inspiration in this collaborative age.

The staff of the University of Chicago Library, and particularly Mr. Robert Rosenthal, Head of the Department of Special Collections, and Miss Katherine M. Hall of the Inter-Library Loan Department have been continually helpful.

A number of my friends and colleagues at the University of Chicago have shared their ideas with me, have given me their suggestions, and have read all or part of the manuscript. For their acute comments, their frankness, and their generosity, it is a pleasure to thank all of them. They include: Edward C. Banfield, Laura Banfield, William T. Hutchinson, Robert L. McCaul, Raven I. McDavid, Jr., Mitford M. Mathews, Sidney E. Mead, Charles L. Mowat, Richard J. Storr, and Ilza Veith. The profound historical insight and the sensitive literary judgment of Avery O. Craven have been invaluable. Others who have offered specific suggestions helpful to the research or who have read all or part of the manuscript are: Professor Carl Bridenbaugh of the University of California, Professor I. Bernard Cohen of Harvard University, Professor John Duffy of Louisiana State University, Professor Donald Fleming of Brown University, Professor Edmund S. Morgan of Yale University, Dean Emeritus Frank Luther Mott of the School of Journalism, University of Missouri, Dr.

373

Stanley Pargellis of the Newberry Library, Professor Thomas Pyles of the University of Florida, Dr. Leo Rosten of Look Magazine, Professor Richard H. Shryock of the Johns Hopkins University, Professor Frederick B. Tolles of Swarthmore College, Professor Harry R. Warfel of the University of Florida, and Dr. Lawrence C. Wroth of the John Carter Brown Library. They have saved me from many errors; but I have sometimes differed from them on facts or on interpretations, so that I alone am responsible for the errors which remain.

I have been fortunate in receiving stimulus, suggestions, and criticisms from my students at the University of Chicago, and I have been particularly lucky in research assistants who could not only help gather raw materials but who have also taught me a great deal. These include Professor Archie H. Jones, now of Humboldt State College, Arcata, California, and Professor Brook Ballard of Principia College. I have been especially indebted to Mr. Keith B. Berwick for his independent intelligence and constant encouragement during the last two years of the research and writing. The book has benefited immeasurably from his scholarly precision and resourcefulness.

For the checking of the final manuscript and for research on many specific facts I wish to thank Miss Charline Clawson, Mrs. Alan M. Fern, Mrs. Ramonda Jo Karmatz, and Mr. Albert Romasco. For permission to quote from H. L. Mencken's *American Language,* I wish to thank Alfred A. Knopf, Inc. of New York.

Invaluable secretarial assistance has come from Miss N. Miyake of Kyoto, Japan and Mrs. Kenneth Finlayson of Homewood, Illinois. The preparation of the manuscript has been greatly facilitated by the intelligence, efficiency, and scrupulous care of Mrs. Ed Stack of Homewood, Illinois, who has seen it through from the first draft to the printer's copy.

For sympathetic and imaginative editing I owe Mr. Jess Stein of Random House a debt which few authors can honestly acknowledge to their publishers.

My wife, Ruth F. Boorstin, has shared this book from the first outlines to the last proof corrections. Without her cheerful help it would never have been written. Her feeling for the appropriate word and her constant editorial advice have given me a unique advantage.

Following is a list of works useful for studying the period covered in this volume. It is meant to help the reader who may wish to pursue further some of the topics I discuss, to suggest the kinds of material on which I have relied in my research, and to indicate my heavy debt to other scholars. But it is not a complete bibliography of any aspect of the subject, nor does it include all the works I have used. After a General section, the bibliography is arranged into thirteen Parts, corresponding with the grouping of topics in my chapters. In each Part, I have begun by mentioning works of general interest and easiest accessibility, and I have then proceeded toward the more "primary" and more esoteric materials.

GENERAL

The last thirty years have probably produced more useful books about the colonial period than were written in the preceding century-and-a-half. But, with few exceptions, recent scholarship has aimed at clarifying and amplifying details rather than at reinterpreting the sweep of colonial history, much less at discovering the special character of American civilization. The reader who wonders what it all adds up to will still have to return to George Bancroft's *History of the United States from the Discovery of the American Continent* (10 vols., 1834-75), to Francis Parkman's *France and England in North America* (9 vols., 1865-92) and *The Conspiracy of Pontiac* (2 vols., 1851), or to the works of one of the few great interpretive historians who wrote earlier in our century—Frederick Jackson Turner's *Frontier in American History* (1920), Charles A. and Mary R. Beard's *Rise of American Civilization* (4 vols., 1927-42), or Vernon L. Parrington's *Main Currents in American Thought* (3 vols., 1927-30).

For particular aspects of the colonial period there are monumental works. For example, Herbert L. Osgood's *American Colonies in the Seventeenth Century* (3 vols., 1904-7) and his sequel on the 18th century (4 vols., 1924) provide an admirably clear and readable survey of constitutional history; and Charles M. Andrews' *Colonial Period of Amer-*

ican History (4 vols., 1934-38) is a comprehensive, if dull, survey of political history, with an occasional look at the social history. For important surveys of the more traditional topics see: Moses Coit Tyler's pioneer *History of American Literature, 1607-1765* (2 vols., 1878; reprinted, 1949) and *The Literary History of the American Revolution* (1897); William P. Trent and others (eds.), *The Cambridge History of American Literature* (3 vols., 1917; several times reprinted), Vol. I; Robert E. Spiller and others (eds.), *Literary History of the United States* (2 vols. and a 3rd vol. of bibliography, 1946); Clinton Rossiter's comprehensive and readable survey of colonial political thought, *Seedtime of the Republic* (1953); Louis B. Wright, *The Cultural Life of the American Colonies* (1957); L. H. Gipson, *The British Empire before the American Revolution* (7 vols., 1936-49).

Despite the rise of the so-called "New History" with its emphasis on the life of the common man, we still have few comprehensive works on non-political and non-belles-lettres aspects of the colonial period. The first three volumes of *A History of American Life* (Arthur M. Schlesinger and Dixon Ryan Fox, eds.; 1927-48) make a systematic but not very imaginative effort to cover social history. There are a few important intensive studies of particular topics, for example: Carl Bridenbaugh's *Cities in the Wilderness: The First Century of Urban Life in America, 1625-1742* (2d. ed., 1955), *Cities in Revolt: Urban Life in America, 1743-1776* (1955), and *The Colonial Craftsman* (1950); Marcus L. Jernegan, *Laboring and Dependent Classes in Colonial America* (1931); Michael Kraus, *Intercolonial Aspects of American Culture* (1928); Richard B. Morris' pathbreaking *Government and Labor in*

Early America (1946); A. E. Smith, *Colonists in Bondage* (1947); Anthony N. B. Garvan, *Architecture and Town Planning in Colonial Connecticut* (1951); S. Fiske Kimball, *Domestic Architecture of the American Colonies* (1927); Percy W. Bidwell and John I. Falconer, *History of Agriculture in the Northern United States, 1620-1860* (1941); Lewis C. Gray, *History of Agriculture in the Southern United States to 1860* (2 vols., 1941); and A. W. Calhoun, *A Social History of the American Family* (3 vols., 1917-19).

Among the more important recent efforts at synthesis and interpretation are: the volumes in *A History of the South* (Wendell H. Stephenson and E. Merton Coulter, eds.), Wesley Frank Craven on the 17th Century (1949) and John Alden on the South in the Revolution (1957), to be supplemented by a volume by Clarence Ver Steeg on the 18th century; Michael Kraus, *The Atlantic Civilization: Eighteenth Century Origins* (1949); Leonard W. Labaree, *Conservatism in Early American History* (1948); Anson Phelps Stokes, *Church and State in the United States* (3 vols., 1950); William W. Sweet, *Religion in Colonial America* (1942). The best recent multivolume survey which aims to include all aspects of the period is Thomas J. Wertenbaker, *The Founding of American Civilization* (3 vols., 1938-47); an excellent brief survey is Curtis P. Nettels, *The Roots of American Civilization* (1938).

For a microcosm of the problems faced by a society there is no substitute for biography. And there are a number of monumental but readable ones which throw light on colonial life in general: Albert J. Beveridge, *Life of John Marshall* (4 vols., 1916-19); Douglas Southall Freeman, *George Washington* (6 vols., 1948-

54); David John Mays, *Edmund Pendleton* (2 vols., 1952); Dumas Malone, *Jefferson and His Time* (4 vols., 1948——); and Carl Van Doren, *Benjamin Franklin* (3 vols. in one; 1938). Unfortunately, there are few brief lives of these or other major figures. This lack is beginning to be repaired by the admirable *Library of American Biography* (Oscar Handlin, ed.), a collection of concise biographical essays, of which a few colonial volumes—for example, Frederick B. Tolles on James Logan (1957), Edmund S. Morgan on John Winthrop (1958), and Verner Crane on Benjamin Franklin (1956)—have already appeared, and are noted under particular topics below. A valuable reference tool, full of readable brief essays and deserving of wider use is the *Dictionary of American Biography* (Allen Johnson and Dumas Malone, eds., 22 vols., 1928-44 and supplements).

For the geography, Charles O. Paullin's *Atlas of the Historical Geography of the United States* (1932), though in need of amplification and revision, is invaluable. Also useful are chapters I-X of Ralph H. Brown's *Historical Geography of the United States* (1948) and his *Mirror for Americans* (1943). The best guide to population figures is Herman R. Friis, *A Series of Population Maps of the Colonies and the United States, 1625-1790* (American Geographical Society. Mimeographed Publication no. 3, New York, 1940), supplemented by Evarts B. Greene and Virginia D. Harrington, *American Population before the Federal Census of 1790* (1932) and Stella H. Sutherland, *Population Distribution in Colonial America* (1936).

Among the more readable and stimulating accounts of the European background in the age of settlement are George Kitson Clark's brilliant *The English Inheritance* (1950); Eli F.

Heckscher's classic *Mercantilism* (tr. Mendel Shapiro, 2 vols., 1935); Paul Hazard, *The European Mind: The Critical Years* (1953); Wallace Notestein, *The English People on the Eve of Colonization* (1954); Sir Leslie Stephen, *History of English Thought in the Eighteenth Century* (2 vols., 1876); George M. Trevelyan, *Illustrated English Social History* (4 vols., 1949-52); and Basil Willey, *The Seventeenth Century Background* (1934) and *The Eighteenth Century Background* (1940). The delightful illustrations in A. S. Turberville, *English Men and Manners in the Eighteenth Century* (2d. ed., 1929) and in Roger Ingpen's edition (Boston, 1925) of Boswell's *Life of Johnson* add much that does not show up in print.

There is no better way to discover the questions which trouble colonial historians nowadays and to glimpse what scholars consider the frontier of their subject, than by occasionally reading *The William and Mary Quarterly* (published jointly by William & Mary College and the Institute of Early American History & Culture at Williamsburg), which offers learned and readable articles. Valuable articles on the colonial age are found in *The New England Quarterly, The Mississippi Valley Historical Review,* and *The Southern Historical Review;* in the journals and other publications of local historical associations—for example, *The Pennsylvania Magazine of History and Biography, The Virginia Magazine of History and Biography,* the publications of the American Antiquarian Society, the Colonial Society of Massachusetts, and the Massachusetts Historical Society (with a recent invaluable index), among others. *American Heritage,* under the brilliant editorship of Bruce Catton, offers the general reader lively and attractively illustrated essays.

More and more primary sources are coming into print. But the colonial records, statutes, and legislative proceedings (printed mostly in the colonial period and early 19th century and specifically referred to below) are basic. The best brief selection of sources is edited by Merrill Jensen, *American Colonial Documents to 1776* ("English Historical Documents, IX," 1955). A more extensive collection is the series of 19 volumes (still in print) edited with introductions under the supervision of J. Franklin Jameson, entitled *Original Narratives of Early American History* (1906-1917; reprinted, 1952); each of these volumes collects documents for particular colonies or topics, such as witchcraft or the colonial rebellions. Justin Winsor's *Narrative and Critical History of America* (8 vols., 1889) collects representative documents with still-valuable discussions of the sources by many authors; it remains one of the best introductions to the primary materials. Peter Force earlier in the 19th century transcribed and reprinted —in *Tracts and Other Papers Relating Principally to the Colonies in North America* (4 vols., 1836-46; reprinted, 1947) and *American Archives* (9 vols., 1837-53)—many valuable pamphlets and public documents which, thanks to him, are now available in numerous libraries. Many of the state and local historical societies have reprinted important documents rare in the original. There are numerous collections of colonial documents on special subjects, for example the early volumes of John R. Commons (ed.), *A Documentary History of American Industrial Society* (11 Vols., 1910-11) and Edgar W. Knight (ed.), *A Documentary History of Education in the South Before 1860* (5 vols., 1949-53).

The writings of leading figures of the colonial age are every year be-coming more generally accessible in more complete and better-edited form. The model for these new editions is the magnificent *Papers of Thomas Jefferson* being published by the Princeton University Press (1950——) under the general editorship of Julian P. Boyd. The collection will eventually run to fifty-odd volumes; it includes a generous selection of letters to Jefferson, and is illuminated by copious but sensible notes. These volumes give the student who does not have access to manuscript collections an unprecedented opportunity to witness daily life in that age. Comparable editions are now in preparation of the writings of Benjamin Franklin, John Adams, Alexander Hamilton, James Madison, and other leaders. These editions, complementing one another, will render obsolete all earlier editions. The expansion of microfilm and microcard facilities, and especially the preparation in Readex Microprint by the American Antiquarian Society (Worcester, Mass. 1955-) of every item in Evans' bibliography and the American Culture Series of microfilms (University Microfilms, Ann Arbor, Mich., 1941——), puts many scarce items within reach of every good research library in the country.

The writings of travelers are of special value for the colonial period; but of course they must always be read with due regard to the prejudices and competence of the observer. Especially useful in this area is Thomas D. Clark, *Travels in the Old South, a bibliography,* (2 vols., 1956); and important reprints are R. G. Thwaites (ed.) *Jesuit Relations and Allied Documents, 1610-1791* (73 vols., 1896-1901) and *Early Western Travels, 1748-1846* (32 vols., 1904-07). Newton D. Mereness (ed.) *Travels in the American Colonies* (1916) and Allan Nevins (ed.), *America through*

British Eyes (1948) are useful selections. The travel-books of the greatest general interest for the period include: Andrew Burnaby, *Travels through the Middle Settlements in North America in the Years 1759 and 1760* (3d ed., 1798); Francois Jean de Chastellux, *Travels in North America in the Years 1780, 1781, and 1782* (2 vols., 1787); Jonathan Carver, *Travels through the Interior Parts of North America, 1766-68* (1778); Nicholas Cresswell, *The Journal of Nicholas Cresswell 1774-1777* (1924); M. G. St. Jean de Crèvecoeur, *Letters from an American Farmer* (1782; reprinted, Everyman Paperback, 1957); Durand, *Un Français en Virginie* (1687) [trans. and ed. by Fairfax Harrison, *A Frenchman in Virginia, Being the Memoirs of a Huguenot Refugee in 1686* (1923)]; Timothy Dwight, *Travels in New England and New York* (4 vols., 1821-22); William Eddis, *Letters from America . . . from 1769, to 1777* (1792); Christopher Gist, *Journal* (1750-53; ed. Wm. Darlington, 1893); the journals of Alexander Hamilton, a Scottish-trained physician who traveled in New England and New York in 1744 (ed. Carl Bridenbaugh as *Gentleman's Progress*, 1948); Hugh Jones, *The Present State of Virginia* (1724) (Sabin's Reprints, V, 1865; also ed. Richard L. Morton, 1956); *The America of 1750: Peter Kalm's Travels in North America* (1770) (ed. Adolph Benson, 2 vols., 1937); Sarah Knight, *Journal* of a trip from Boston to New York in 1704 (1824); Johann D. Schoepf, *Travels in the Confederation* (ed. and translated from the German ed. of 1788 by Alfred J. Morrison, 2 vols., 1911).

Important contemporary surveys which sum up tendencies and compare trends in different parts of the country are William Douglass, *A Summary . . . of the British Settlements in North America* (2 vols., 1747-52); Tench Coxe, *A View of the United States of America* (1795); and Samuel Miller, *A Brief Retrospect of the Eighteenth Century* (2 vols., 1803).

The basic bibliographic tools are the two monumental works: Joseph Sabin and others (eds.), *Dictionary of Books Relating to America from its Discovery to the Present Time* (29 vols., 1868-92; reprinted, 1928-36) and Charles Evans (ed.), *American Bibliography: a Chronological Dictionary of All Books, Pamphlets and Periodical Publications Printed in the United States . . . 1639-1820* (12 vols., 1903-34).

BOOK ONE

THE VISION

AND THE REALITY

PART ONE

A CITY UPON A HILL:

The Puritans of Massachusetts Bay

When Parrington published the first volume of his *Main Currents in American Thought* in 1927, he painted the Puritans as joyless people, unusually bigoted even by the standards of their age. The only humane and lively spirits, we were told, were the Anne Hutchinsons and the Roger Williamses, whom the Puritans harried into the wilderness. A special butt of his attack was Kenneth B. Murdock's life of Increase Mather, which Parrington called "a somewhat meticulous defense . . . unhappily conceived in the dark of the moon, a season congenial to strange quirks of fancy." In the thirty years since, the scholarly portrait has been radically revised. This revision has been most effectively accomplished by several scholars at the old Puritan stronghold, Harvard College. Their work has inspired a wider reëxamination of the Puritans—their mind, body, and soul. Samuel Eliot Morison has done more perhaps than anyone else to humanize the Puritans, to remind us that they liked colorful clothing, enjoyed good beer, and had passions much like those of the people of other ages. Any student can profitably start his study of the Puritans with Morison's *Builders of the Bay Colony* (1930), go on to *The Puritan Pronaos* (1936; reprinted as *The Intellectual Life of Colonial New England,* 1956), and his three sprightly volumes on Harvard College (the founding, 1935; the 17th century, 2 vols., 1936), supplemented for the 18th century by *Three Centuries of Harvard, 1636-1936* (1936). The monumental studies by Perry Miller—especially his *New England Mind: The Seventeenth Century* (1936; reprinted, 1954); his *New England Mind: From Colony to Province* (1953); *Orthodoxy in Massachusetts* (1933); and a valuable collection of his essays, *Errand into the Wilderness* (1956)— have given the subtleties of Puritan theology a serious examination by a mind worthy of them for the first time since Jonathan Edwards. No one who works through Miller's volumes, following his reconstruction and dissection of the more sophisticated American Puritans, can fail to respect them and to see a human plausibility in their thinking. The main peril of Miller's approach is that he may sometimes take their distinctions more seriously and more precisely than 17th-century Puritans saw them to be. He is more interested in the intricacy of their philosophy than in the social

consequences of their ways of thinking and he is not much concerned with the vagueness and fluidity which ideas seem to acquire when they touch the confusing world of action. Puritan literature has been reëxamined in several further works by Kenneth B. Murdock, especially in his *Literature and Theology in Colonial New England* (1949) and his admirably discriminating little volume, *Selections from Cotton Mather* (American Authors Series, 1926), which helps Mather tell us about himself with a cogency which Mather himself lacked.

A less sympathetic view of the Puritans is found in James Truslow Adams, *Founding of New England* (1921) and *Revolutionary New England* (1923); and in Brooks Adams' incisive and bitter *Emancipation of Massachusetts* (1887).

Considering the extent of the literature, there are surprisingly few readable and authentic biographies of leading Puritans; by reading Barrett Wendell's *Cotton Mather, The Puritan Priest* (1891; reprinted, 1926) we see some of the prejudices which have obstructed our understanding of the Puritans as living individuals. A brilliant recent exception is Edmund S. Morgan's sprightly and perceptive biographical essay, *The Puritan Dilemma: The Story of John Winthrop* (1958).

Many particular aspects of Puritan life have been treated in useful monographs. The best survey in its field remains William B. Weeden, *Economic and Social History of New England, 1620-1789* (2 vols., 1891), which needs correction in many details. The following are valuable on topics in social history: E. A. J. Johnson, *American Economic Thought in the Seventeenth Century* (1932); Joseph Dorfman, *The Economic Mind in American Civilization, 1606-1865* (2 vols., 1946), Volume I; Bernard Bailyn, *The New England Merchants in the Seventeenth Century* (1955); Edmund S. Morgan, *The Puritan Family* (1944); Noah Porter, *The New England Meeting House* (1933); and Babette Levy, *Preaching in the First Half-Century of New England History* (1945). On witchcraft, a subject which in my opinion has exaggerated significance in the popular image of New England, see Charles W. Upham, *Salem Witchcraft* (2 vols., 1867) and George Lyman Kittredge, *Witchcraft in Old and New England* (1929).

Despite the copious literature, many topics still need comprehensive treatment. One of these is the legal history which the general student now has to glean from miscellaneous monographs such as William DeLoss Love's *Fast and Thanksgiving Days of New England* (1895); Charles J. Hilkey's inadequate *Legal Development in Colonial Massachusetts, 1630-1686* (1910); from several excellent articles by Julius Goebel Jr., for example, "King's Law and Local Custom in Seventeenth Century New England," *Columbia Law Review,* XXXI (1931), pp. 416-448; Mark DeWolfe Howe and Louis F. Eaton Jr.'s valuable "The Supreme Judicial Power in . . . Massachusetts Bay," *N.E.Q.,* XX (1947), 291-316; and Richard B. Morris' pioneer monographs, *Studies in the History of American Law* (1930) and *Government and Labor in Early America* (1946). The best survey of the spirit and practice of the laws of Massachusetts Bay is found in Zechariah Chafee Jr.'s brilliant introduction to the Records of the Suffolk County Court, 1671-1680, in the Colonial Society of Massachusetts *Publications,* Vol. XXIX.

Regional and family pride have combined to produce a great deal of valuable local history (together with many less valuable antiquarian and genealogical studies) and to make it accessible by reprinting many of the more important early documents. These are found, among other places, in the publications of the American Antiquarian Society (Worcester, Mass.), The Colonial Society of Massachusetts (Boston), The Essex Institute (Salem), The Massachusetts Historical Society (Boston), The Narragansett Society (Providence), and The Prince Society (Boston).

English Puritanism is a much more extensive and complicated subject than American Puritanism. The English background can be glimpsed in William Haller, *The Rise of Puritanism . . . 1570-1643* (1938); M. M. Knappen, *Tudor Puritanism* (1939); Wallace Notestein, *The English People on the Eve of Colonization* (1954); and Alan Simpson, *Puritanism in Old & New England* (1955). The amateur in English history who wants to start with a sampling of documents on the English side would do well to read in the earlier volumes of the Winthrop Papers, reprinted by the Massachusetts Historical Society. Especially interesting for contrasts with New England Puritanism is A. S. P. Woodhouse's admirably edited *Puritanism and Liberty: Being the Army Debates (1647-49) from the Clarke Manuscripts* (1951).

Early New Englanders left remarkably full and eloquent records of themselves and of their age. For the casual student, Perry Miller has provided a discriminating brief selection in *The American Puritans* (Anchor Books, 1956); and for the more serious student (with Thomas H. Johnson), *The Puritans* (1938) which, in addition to brilliant introductions and notes, has what is still the best bibliography. Everyone interested in the Puritans should read in their entirety (nor can he resist if he once starts): William Bradford, *History of Plymouth Plantations* (most recent edition, by Samuel Eliot Morison, 1952; and many earlier editions); and John Winthrop, *Journal* (sometimes called *The History of New England from 1630 to 1649,* best read in ed. James Savage, 2 vols., 1853, also found in J. F. Jameson's "Original Narratives" series, and other editions). Too little read is Cotton Mather's magnificent *Magnalia Christi Americana* (2 vols., 1853) which, despite its pedantry, remains the greatest literary monument to the classic age of New England Puritanism. If the reader once becomes accustomed to Mather's conceits and ceases to try to translate the ornamental phrases of Greek, Latin, and Hebrew, he will find himself stirred by a characteristically American epic.

From the later 18th century, Governor Thomas Hutchinson left us a readable and surprisingly comprehensive account, *The History of the Colony and Province of Massachusetts Bay* (Vols. I-II covering 1628-1750, first pub. 1764-1767; Vol. III covering 1750-1774, first pub. 1828. New ed., by Lawrence S. Mayo, 3 vols., 1936), which has a peculiar value because of the destruction of many of the documents from which it was written in the burning of Hutchinson's mansion during the Stamp Act riots of 1765. Also valuable are *The Hutchinson Papers* (1769), Prince Society *Pub.,* Vols. II-III (1865).

The Puritans were inveterate diarists. The most vivid and detailed of these are Cotton Mather's (published in Mass. Hist. Soc., *Coll.,* 7th Series, Vols. VII-VIII; reprinted, 2 vols., 1957) and Samuel Sewall's (Mass. Hist. Soc., *Coll.,* 5th series, Vols. V-VII).

Among the more accessible and more interesting collections of documents on particular topics are: Charles Francis Adams (ed.), *Antinomianism in the Colony of Massachusetts Bay, 1636-1638;* George L. Burr (ed.), *Narratives of the Witchcraft Cases, 1648-1706* ("Original Narratives" series, 1914); Daniel Gookin, "Historical Collections of the Indians in New England," Mass. Hist. Soc., *Coll.,* I, 141-226, and "An Historical Account of the Doings and Sufferings of the Christian Indians in New England in . . . 1675, 1676, 1677," Am. Antiq. Soc., *Coll.,* II (Trans., 1836), 423-534; William Hubbard, "A General History of New-England from the Discovery to 1680," Mass. Hist. Soc., *Coll.,* 2d Series, V-VI; Edward Johnson, *Wonder-Working Providence of Sions Savior in New England,* 1628-1651 ("Original Narratives" Series, 1910); John Josselyn, "An Account of Two Voyages to New England" (1674), Mass. Hist. Soc., *Proc.,* 3d Series, III, 211-354, and "New-Englands Rarities Discovered: in Birds, Beasts, Fishes, Serpents, and Plants of that Country" (1672), Am. Antiq. Soc., *Coll.,* IV (Trans., 1860), 105-238; Increase Mather, *Remarkable Providences . . .* (1856); Nathaniel Morton, *New Englands Memoriall* (1669) (fac. reprod., ed. Howard J. Hall, 1937); Michael Wigglesworth, *The Day of Doom* (1662) (ed. Kenneth B. Murdock, 1929); "Winthrop Papers," Mass. Hist. Soc., *Coll.,* 3d Series, IX; 4th Series, VI, VII; 5th Series, I, II, IV, VIII; 6th Series, III, V; William Wood, *New Englands Prospect* (1634; University Microfilms, American Culture Series, No. 31, Roll 4).

The most available collection of basic documents in the history of congregationalism in New England including such items as the "Cambridge Platform" of 1648, is Williston Walker,

The Creeds and Platforms of Congregationalism (1893). Some of the works most useful for the Puritan theology and attitudes toward religion are: William Ames, *The Marrow of Sacred Divinity* (1638) and *Conscience with the Power and Cases thereof* (1639); *The Bay Psalm Book* (ed., Zoltan Haraszti, 2 vols., 1956); John Cotton, *A Briefe Exposition of the Whole Book of Canticles* (1648); Cotton Mather, *The Wonders of the Invisible World* (1693) and *The Christian Philosopher* (1721; University Microfilms, American Culture Series, No. 110, Roll 10); Increase Mather, *Cases of Conscience* (1693), *Remarkable Providences* (1684; reprinted, 1856), and *An Historical Discourse Concerning the Prevalency of Prayer* (1677); John Norton, *The Orthodox Evangelist* (1654), one of the most popular handbooks of theology; William Perkins, "The Art of Prophecying" (1592) in Perkins' *Works* (London, 1631), II, 643-673; Thomas Shepard, *Works* (3 vols., 1853); Nathaniel Ward, *The Simpler Cobler of Aggawam* (5th ed., London, 1647); Michael Wigglesworth, "God's Controversy with New England . . . ," Mass. Hist. Soc., *Proc.*, XII (1871-73), 83-93; John Wise, *A Vindication of the Government of New-England Churches* (1717; reprinted, 1772).

Among the more accessible and more useful legal records are: William Brigham (ed.), *The Compact; with the Charter and Laws of the Colony of New Plymouth* (Boston, 1836); Zechariah Chafee, Jr. (ed.), "Records of the Suffolk County Court, 1671-1680)," Col. Soc. Mass., *Pub.*, XXIX-XXX; George Francis Dow (ed.), *Records and Files of the Quarterly Courts of Essex County Massachusetts, 1636-1692* (8 vols., 1911-21); Max Farrand (ed.), *The Laws and Liberties of Massachusetts; Reprinted*

from the copy of the 1648 Edition in the . . . Huntington Library (1929); *The General Laws and Liberties of The Massachusetts Colony* (revised and reprinted, Cambridge, Mass., 1672; University Microfilms, American Culture Series, No. 70, roll 7); John Noble (ed.), *Records of the Court of Assistants of the Colony of the Massachusetts Bay, 1630-1692* (3 vols., 1901-28); *The Records of the Town of Cambridge (Formerly Newtowne) Massachusetts, 1630-1703* (1901); "The Royal Charter of the Governor and Company of the Massachusetts Bay in New England, March 4, 1628/29," Mass. Hist. Soc., *Proc.*, LXII (1928-29), 251-273; Nathaniel B. Shurtleff (ed.), *Records of the Governor and Company of the Massachusetts Bay in New England* (5 vols., 1853-54); Nathaniel Ward, *The Body of Liberties, 1641* (Old South Leaflets, General Series, Vol. 7; No. 164; Boston, 1905); William H. Whitmore (ed.), *The Colonial Laws of Massachusetts, Reprinted from the Edition of 1672, with the Supplements through 1686, together with the Body of Liberties of 1641 and the Records of the Court of Assistants, 1641-44* (1890). Thomas Lechford's contemporary comments on the working of the legal system are found in "Note-Book Kept in Boston, Massachusetts Bay, from June 27, 1638, to July 29, 1641," Am. Antiq. Soc. *Coll.*, VII, and "Plain Dealing: or Newes from New England . . ." (1642), Mass. Hist. Soc., *Coll.*, 3d Series, III, 55-128.

Basic bibliographical tools—worth looking at, if only for some notion of the scope and productivity of Puritans as authors—are Thomas J. Holmes' monumental Mather bibliographies: *Increase Mather, A Bibliography of his Works* (2 vols., 1931), and *Cotton Mather, A Bibliography of his Works* (3 vols., 1940).

Quaker historians have shown a remarkable ability to discover the shortcomings of their fellow-Quakers while holding firm to their own Friendly convictions. Rufus M. Jones, perhaps the leading American Quaker of this century, was effective in pleading for the humane treatment of Quaker (and other) conscientious objectors in the two World Wars, yet he was incisive in his description of the dangers of Quaker obstinacy in earlier American history. A good place to start is his sensible and simply-written *Quakers in the American Colonies* (1911); then to *The Later Periods of Quakerism* (2 vols., 1921). Today the leading historian of American Quakers (also a prominent Quaker) is Frederick B. Tolles, whose writings, more than those of Jones, relate the special culture of the Quakers to American civilization as a whole. Tolles's profound and suggestive essays are perhaps the best path into further reading on the problems of Part II: *The Atlantic Community of the Early Friends* (Friends' Historical Society, London, 1952); "The Transatlantic Quaker Community in the Seventeeth Century," *Huntington Library Quarterly,* XIV (May, 1951), 239-258; *Quakerism and Politics* (The Ward Lecture, 1956, published by Guilford College, N. C., 1956); and "The Culture of Early Pennsylvania," *Penn. Mag. Hist. Biog.,* LXXXI (1957), 119-37; from these one should go on to his *Meeting House and Counting House: The Quaker Merchants of Colonial Pennsylvania* (Chapel Hill, N. C., 1948); then to his attractive biographies of two of the most prominent (and most American) of the early

American Quakers: *James Logan and the Culture of Provincial America* (1957) and *George Logan of Philadelphia* (1953). Besides these, the most readable studies of the environment of early American Quakerism are Carl Van Doren's *Benjamin Franklin* (New York, 1938) and Carl and Jessica Bridenbaugh's *Rebels and Gentlemen: Philadelphia in the Age of Franklin* (New York, 1942).

For the trials of Quaker pacifism see Robert L. D. Davidson's *War Comes to Quaker Pennsylvania, 1682-1756* (1957), which did not come to my attention until these chapters were going to press. Davidson gives more decisive significance than I would to the conflict between mercantile interests and religious principles, and he is less inclined than I to see the Quaker withdrawal as the climax of a conflict between mystic absolutism and perfectionism on the one hand and the world of political and economic conflict on the other. Other valuable general studies are: James Bowden, *The History of the Society of Friends in America* (2 vols., 1850-54); Howard H. Brinton, *Friends for 300 Years* (1952); George S. Brookes, *Friend Anthony Benezet* (1937); William Charles Braithwaite, *The Second Period of Quakerism* (1919); Solon J. and Elizabeth Buck, *The Planting of Civilization in Western Pennsylvania* (1939); Maxwell S. Burt, *Philadelphia, Holy Experiment* (1945); Henry J. Cadbury, "Intercolonial Solidarity of American Quakerism," *Penn. Mag. Hist. & Biog.,* LX (1936), 362-74; Verner W. Crane, *Benjamin Franklin and a Rising People* (1956); Thomas F. Gordon, *The History of Pennsylvania from its Discovery by Europeans to . . . 1776* (1829); Guy F. Hershberger, "The Pennsylvania Quaker Experiment in Politics, 1682-1756," *Mennonite Quarterly Review,*

X (1936), 187-221, and "Pacifism and the State in Colonial Pennsylvania," *Church History*, VIII (1939), 54-74; Samuel M. Janney, *Life of William Penn* (1852); Rayner W. Kelsey, *Friends and the Indians, 1655-1917* (1917); Mrs. Ethyn Kirby, *George Keith (1638-1716)* (1942); Arnold Lloyd, *Quaker Social History, 1669-1738* (1950); Albert C. J. Myers, *Immigration of the Irish Quakers into Pennsylvania, 1682-1750* (1902); Samuel Parrish, *Some Chapters in the History of the Friendly Association for Regaining and Preserving Peace with the Indians by Pacific Measures* (1877); John P. Selsam, *The Pennsylvania Constitution of 1776* (1936); Isaac Sharpless, *Political Leaders of Provincial Pennsylvania* (1919), *A History of Quaker Government in Pennsylvania* (2 vols., 1899), *Quakerism and Politics* (1905), *A Quaker Experiment in Government* (1898); William T. Shore, *John Woolman* (1913); Charles J. Stillé, *The Life and Times of John Dickinson, 1732-1808* (1891), and (ed.) "The Attitude of the Quakers in the Provincial Wars," *Penn. Mag. Hist. & Biog.*, X (1886), 283-315; and Theodore Thayer, *Israel Pemberton, King of the Quakers* (1943).

The best introductions to the writings of the early Quakers are John Woolman, *Journal and Other Writings* (Everyman's Library, 1952), supplemented by *The Works of John Woolman* (1774), and *George Fox, An Autobiography* (an edition of what is more commonly called Fox's *Journal;* ed. Rufus M. Jones, 1919). A handy selection is Frederick B. Tolles and E. Gordon Alderfer, *The Witness of William Penn* (1957). Penn's more important works are found at length in *A Collection of the Works of William Penn* (ed. Joseph Besse, 2 vols., 1726), or William Penn, *The Rise and*

Progress of the People Called Quakers (1695; reprinted, 1886). A useful contemporary history of 18th-century Quakerism is Robert B. Proud, *History of Pennsylvania* (2 vols., 1797-98); and William Smith, *A Brief View of the Conduct of Pennsylvania for the Year 1755* (1756). Some valuable documents on particular topics are: Thomas Balch (ed.), *Letters and Papers Relating Chiefly to the Provincial History of Pennsylvania* (1855); Anthony Benezet, *The Mighty Destroyer Displayed, in . . . the Dreadful Havock Made by ... Spirituous Liquors* (1774), and *Serious Considerations on Several Important Subjects* (1778); William Bradford, *An Enquiry How Far the Punishment of Death is Necessary in Pennsylvania* (1793); Gerard Croese, *The General History of the Quakers* (1696); Albert C. Myers (ed.), *Narratives of Early Pennsylvania, West New Jersey and Delaware, 1630-1707* ("Original Narratives" series, 1912); and William Smith, *A Brief View of the Conduct of Pennsylvania for the Year 1755* (1756). A particularly valuable collection of early Quaker writings is Ezra Michener (ed.), *A Retrospect of Early Quakerism* (1860).

Benjamin Franklin's *Autobiography* with a selection of his other writings is available in a Modern Library edition (ed. Nathan G. Goodman, 1932). The best edition of his *Writings* (until the definitive edition being prepared at Yale under the editorship of Lyman Butterfield) is that by Albert H. Smyth (10 vols., 1907).

The acts of the early Quaker martyrs are recounted in George Bishop, *New-England Judged, by the Spirit of the Lord* (London, 1703), and Humphrey Norton, *New England's Ensigne* (London, 1659; University Microfilms, American Culture Series, No. 63, Roll 6). A useful introduction to contemporary documents on Quaker-Indian relations is *Indian Treaties Printed by Benjamin Franklin 1736-1762* (ed. Julian P. Boyd, intro. by Carl Van Doren, 1938), and Charles Thomas, *An Enquiry into the Cause of Alienation of the Indians* (1789; reprinted, 1867).

Among the more valuable reprinted documents bearing on Quaker politics are: "The Correspondence of James Logan and Thomas Story, 1724-41," *Bull. of Friends Historical Assn.*, XV (Autumn, 1926), 1-92; "James Logan on Defensive War, or Pennsylvania Politics in 1741," *Penn. Mag. Hist. & Biog.*, VI (1882), 402-411; and "Correspondence between William Penn and James Logan, Secretary of the Province of Pennsylvania, and Others, 1700-1750," Hist. Soc. Penn., *Memoirs*, IX-X.

Some of the more interesting accounts by itinerant Quaker missionaries are those by Samuel Bownas (1756), John Churchman (1779), Thomas Chalkley (2d ed., 1751), Samuel Fothergill (ed. George Crosfield, 1844), John Fothergill (1754), William Reckitt (1776), and Daniel Stanton (1799). See also the controversial George Keith's *Journal of Travels . . . on the Continent of North America* (1706; University Microfilms, American Culture Series, No. 101, Roll 9).

Important sources for the legal and legislative history are: "The Fundamental Constitutions of Pennsylvania," *Penn. Mag. Hist. & Biog.*, X (1896), 283-301; *Laws of the Commonwealth of Pennsylvania (1700-1810)* (4 vols., 1810); *Minutes of the Provincial Council of Pennsylvania*, especially, "Petition of Hugh Pugh . . ." Vol. III (1717-1736), pp. 40-43, and petitions of Quakers at Vol. VII (1756-1758), pp. 84-86, 311-312, 638-647; "Papers of the Governors," ed. G. E. Reed,

Pennsylvania Archives, 4th Series, I-XII; William Penn, *The Excellent Priviledge of Liberty and Property . . . a Reprint and Facsimile of the First American Edition of Magna Charta* (1797); *Records of the Colony of Rhode Island and Providence Plantations in New England, (1636-1792)*, ed. John R. Bartlett (10 vols., 1856-65); *The Statutes at Large of Pennsylvania from 1682 to 1801*, ed. James T. Mitchell and Henry Flanders (16 vols., 1896-1908); and "Votes and Proceedings of the House of Representatives of the Province of Pennsylvania, Dec. 4, 1682-Sept. 26, 1776," *Pennsylvania Archives*, 8th Series, Vols. I-VIII.

PART THREE

VICTIMS OF PHILANTHROPY: *The Settlers of Georgia*

Much of the popular historical writing about early Georgia has aimed to defend the colony against the slanderous traditional rumor that it was settled mostly by bankrupts and by refugees from the London jails. Albert B. Saye's readable *New Viewpoints in Georgia History* (1943) uses careful scholarship to scotch this rumor, and is the most suggestive starting point for reading in early Georgia history. The best recent history of the state is E. Merton Coulter, *Georgia, A Short History* (1947); for an older view see Charles C. Jones Jr., *The History of Georgia* (2 vols., 1883). Some of the most useful studies have centered around the biography of Oglethorpe, for example: Amos A. Ettinger's full and lively *James Edward Oglethorpe, Imperial Idealist* (1936) and Leslie F. Church's valuable *Oglethorpe: A Study of Philan-*

thropy in England and Georgia (London, 1932). See also Thaddeus M. Harris, *Biographical Memorials of . . . Oglethorpe* (Boston, 1841), which reprints some documents, and Robert Wright, *A Memoir of General James Oglethorpe*. Sidelights on Oglethorpe are found here and there in Boswell's *Life of Johnson* (1791).

Readable accounts of the English background are: Rosamond Payne-Powell, *Eighteenth Century London Life* (1938); Arthur S. Turberville, *English Men and Manners in the Eighteenth Century* (1929; reprinted, Galaxy Books, 1957), and (ed.) *Johnson's England* (2 vols., 1933).

Important studies of special topics include: James D. Butler, "British Convicts Shipped to American Colonies," *Am. Hist. Rev.,* II (1896), 12-33; John P. Corry, *Indian Affairs in Georgia, 1732-1756* (1936); E. Merton Coulter and Albert B. Saye (eds.), *A List of the Early Settlers of Georgia* (1949); Verner W. Crane, "The Promotion Literature of Georgia," in *Bibliographical Essays: A Tribute to Wilberforce Eames* (1924) and *The Southern Frontier, 1670-1732* (1929; reprinted, Ann Arbor Paperbacks no. 4, 1956); H. B. Fant, "The Labor Policy of the Trustees for Establishing the Colony of Georgia in America," *Georgia Historical Quarterly,* XVI (1932), 1-16; Wesley M. Gewehr, *The Great Awakening in Virginia, 1740-1790* (1930), incidentally touching Georgia; James R. McCain, *The Executive in Proprietary Georgia, 1732-1752* (1914) and *Georgia as a Proprietary Province* (1917); David M. Potter Jr., "The Rise of the Plantation System in Georgia," *Ga. Hist. Q.,* XVI (1932), 114-135; and Reba C. Strickland, *Religion and the State in Georgia in the Eighteenth Century* (1939).

There is no better first-hand introduction to the life of the upper classes in mid-18th-century London than John Percival Egmont, *Manuscripts of the Earl of Egmont. Diary of Viscount Percival afterwards first Earl of Egmont* (3 vols., 1920-23), which does for this period much of what Pepys' diary does for London a half-century earlier. Egmont lacks some of Pepys' amiable vices, but he has peccadillos of his own which are almost as interesting and no less salacious. For few enterprises in American history do we possess so full, so frank, and so affable an account as Egmont has left us of the Georgia project. Additional light comes from the correspondence between Egmont and Bishop Berkeley (the philosopher and promoter of a missionary college in Bermuda), edited by Benjamin Rand, *Berkeley and Percival . . . The Correspondence of George Berkeley, afterwards Bishop of Cloyne, and Sir John Percival, afterwards Earl of Egmont* (1914).

The full flavor of the Georgia controversy can be sensed only from contemporary pamphlets, for example: Francis Moore, "A Voyage to Georgia Begun in the Year 1735" (1744), Ga. Hist. Soc., *Coll.,* I, 79-152; Robert Montgomery, "A Discourse Concerning the Design'd Establishment of a New Colony to the South of Carolina" (1717), in Force, *Tracts,* Vol. I, No. 1; "Reasons for Establishing the Colony of Georgia, with Regard to the Trade of Great Britain" (1733), Ga. Hist. Soc., *Coll.,* I, 203-38; Thomas Stephens, *A Brief Account of the Causes that Have Retarded the Progress of the Colony of Georgia in America* (1743); Pat Tailfer and others, "A True and Historical Narrative of the Colony of Georgia in America" (1741), Ga. Hist. Soc., *Coll.,* II, 163-263. Many other valuable documents are reprinted in the Georgia Historical Society Collections, published since 1840 (except for 1917-

51). Another useful collection is George White (ed.), *Historical Collections of Georgia* (1854). The problems of one of the most famous Methodist missionaries to Georgia in 1738 are recounted in George Whitefield, *Journal of a Voyage from London to Savannah in Georgia* (1826) and in his *Works* (ed. J. Gillies, 6 vols., 1771-72).

Materials for the legal and administrative history are found in *The Colonial Records of the State of Georgia* (ed. Allen D. Candler; 26 vols., 1904-16).

PART FOUR

TRANSPLANTERS: *The Virginians*

For Virginia where, as in New England, regional, local, and family pride have been strong, we have a voluminous historical literature which is, on the whole, of high quality and of considerable general interest. But Virginia, unlike Massachusetts Bay, has not been the center of "revisionist" controversies. The New England Puritans have been blamed for nearly every kind of social crime—from "witch-burning" to Prohibition. They have had rough handling from their own disgruntled great-great-grandchildren, as well as from newcomers. The Virginians have been more gently treated, not only by local historians but by the American people generally. No offensive catch-phrase like "Puritanism" misleads us into thinking that we have grasped the complexity of their life. Nearly all the writing about the Virginians—with the trivial exception of an occasional "debunking" biography like W. E. Woodward's life of Washington—has been friendly, and almost none has been as antagonistic as Brooks Adams, James Truslow Adams, or V. L. Parrington were in their writing about "Puritanism."

Still the public mind has had difficulty in catching the flavor of early Virginia life. Here, too, a large "organizing" concept has been the enemy of our understanding, but for the Virginians the tag-idea has been a favorable one. While "Puritanism," with which we have tagged early New Englanders has dark overtones of provincialism, bigotry, persecution, and narrowness, the cliché for the Virginians has been "The Enlightenment" or "The Age of Reason"— expressions bright with eulogistic overtones. In both areas the clichés have concealed the real character of colonial life.

To begin to understand the ways of living and of thinking of these Virginians one must look to the minutiae of daily living in particular places. Fortunately, much of the writing about the Virginians took a local (or even antiquarian) point of view from the very beginning; we now possess a wealth of detail, skillfully interpreted. A masterpiece of such interpretation is Colonial Williamsburg, at Williamsburg, Virginia, which everyone interested in our past should visit. I have commented on its peculiarly American character as a kind of historical document in "Past and Present in America," *Commentary,* XXV (1958), pp. 1-7. But life in Williamsburg was only one aspect of life in colonial Virginia; a comparable model of a going plantation community would add still more to our understanding.

The foundations for our knowledge of the social history of early Virginia were laid by Philip A. Bruce (1856-1933); his *Economic History of Virginia in the Seventeenth Century* (2 vols., 1895; reprinted, 1935), *Institutional History of Virginia in the*

Seventeenth Century (2 vols., 1910), *Social Life of Virginia in the Seventeenth Century* (1907), and *The Virginia Plutarch* (1929) are still the best treatments of many topics. Bruce wrote with a fluent but not eloquent style, he was prodigiously industrious, and he had the imagination to let the facts lead him into many corners which might have seemed unimportant on a priori grounds. His work is, however, marred by patriotic bias: whenever the facts are ambiguous, he chooses the interpretation most "favorable" to the Virginians. But without his warm affection for the early Virginians, his work might not have been done at all.

The most important recent books on early Virginia history are in the Bruce tradition: they gather and organize the details of daily life, usually in a sympathetic spirit, but they excel Bruce in their literary flair and in interpretive penetration. A good starting point for the general reader is Louis B. Wright's urbane and sprightly *First Gentlemen of Virginia* (1940), to which I am deeply indebted. Also suggestive is his *Culture on the Moving Frontier* (1955), esp. Ch. 1. A different emphasis is found in Carl Bridenbaugh's stimulating *Myths and Realities: Societies of the Colonial South* (1952) and *Seat of Empire: The Political Role of Eighteenth Century Williamsburg* (1950), which underline the special characteristics of Virginia's rural life. Among the most valuable studies of the social history are Thomas J. Wertenbaker's *Patrician and Plebeian in Virginia* (1910), *The Planters of Colonial Virginia* (1922), and *Virginia under the Stuarts, 1607-1688* (1914), brought together in a single volume under the title, *The Shaping of Colonial Virginia* (1958). Wertenbaker's theses about the social origins of the early Virginia settlers

and the size of their landholdings have been challenged in detail but still seem to me substantially correct.

For particular topics in the social and economic history there are a number of valuable special studies: John S. Bassett, "The Relation between the Virginia Planter and the London Merchant," Am. Hist. Assn. *Annual Report* (1901), I, 551-575; Julian P. Boyd, *The Murder of George Wythe* (1949); Avery O. Craven, *Soil Exhaustion as a Factor in the Agricultural History of Virginia and Maryland, 1606-1860* (1926); Wesley F. Craven, *The Dissolution of the Virginia Company: The Failure of a Colonial Experiment* (1932); Rutherfoord Goodwin, *A Brief and True Report Concerning Williamsburg in Virginia* (3d. ed., 1940); Oscar and Mary Handlin, "Origins of the Southern Labor System," *Wm. & Mary Q.,* 3d Ser., VII (1950), 199-222; Fairfax Harrison, "Western Explorations in Virginia Between Lederer and Spotswood," *Va. Mag. Hist. & Biog.,* XXX (1922) 323-341; Chester Kirby, *The English Country Gentleman, a Study of Nineteenth Century Types* (1937); Arthur P. Middleton, *Tobacco Coast: A Maritime History of Chesapeake Bay in the Colonial Era* (1953); Edmund S. Morgan, *Virginians at Home: Family Life in the Eighteenth Century* (1952) and (with Helen M. Morgan) *The Stamp Act Crisis* (1953); Fernando Ortiz, *Cuban Counterpoint: Tobacco and Sugar* (1927) for an interesting comparison with a Caribbean economy; Joseph C. Robert, *The Story of Tobacco in America* (1949); Mary (Newton) Stanard, *Colonial Virginia, its People and Customs* (1917); and Lyon G. Tyler, *Williamsburg, The Old Colonial Capital* (1907).

An amusing and scholarly brief introduction to Virginia politics is Charles S. Sydnor's *Gentleman Free-*

holders (1952). Political, legislative, and legal history are explored also in: Julian C. Chandler, *The History of Suffrage in Virginia* (Johns Hopkins University Studies in History & Political Science, 19th Ser., VI-VII, 1901) and *Representation in Virginia* (J.H.U., Studies, 14th Ser., VI-VII, 1896); Oliver P. Chitwood, *Justice in Colonial Virginia* (J.H.U. Studies, 23rd Ser., VII-VIII, 1905); Percy S. Flippin, *The Financial Administration of the Colony of Virginia* (J.H.U. Studies, 33rd Ser., II, 1915) and *The Royal Government in Virginia, 1624-1775* (1919); Evarts B. Greene, *The Provincial Governor in the English Colonies of North America* (1898); Fairfax Harrison, *Virginia Land Grants: A Study of Conveyancing in Relation to Colonial Politics* (1925); Albert E. McKinley, *The Suffrage Franchise in the Thirteen English Colonies in America* (1905); Elmer I. Miller, *The Legislature of the Province of Virginia; Its Internal Development* (1907); William Z. Ripley, *The Financial History of Virginia, 1609-1776* (1893); Arthur P. Scott, *Criminal Law in Colonial Virginia* (1930); St. George L. Sioussat, "Virginia and the English Commercial System," Am. Hist. Assn., *Annual Report* (1906), I, 71-97; and Wilcomb E. Washburn, *The Governor and the Rebel: A History of Bacon's Rebellion in Virginia* (1957). Thomas J. Wertenbaker's *Give Me Liberty: The Struggle for Self-government in Virginia* (1958) came to my attention as this book was going to press.

On religion in Virginia, the leading work is George M. Brydon, *Virginia's Mother Church and the Political Conditions under Which it Grew* (2 vols., 1947-52), which despite its strong bias in favor of the Church, is the best picture on a broad canvas, and one of the most solid studies of any of Virginia's early institutions. Moreover,

it is a useful corrective to the popular caricature of religion in Virginia—usually drawn from crude notions of the American "Enlightenment." An essential monograph is Arthur L. Cross, *The Anglican Episcopate in the American Colonies* (Harvard Historical Studies, IX, 1902). Other important studies dealing with the Virginia church are: James S. Anderson, *The History of the Church of England in the Colonies* (3 vols., 1845-56); Simeon E. Baldwin, "The American Jurisdiction of the Bishop of London in Colonial Times," Am. Antiq. Soc. *Proc.*, New Series, XIII (1899-1900), 179-221; Elizabeth H. Davidson, *The Establishment of the English Church in Continental American Colonies* (1936); Hamilton J. Eckenrode, *Separation of Church and State in Virginia; A Study in the Development of the Revolution* (1910); Wesley M. Gewehr, *The Great Awakening in Virginia, 1740-1790* (1930); Edward L. Goodwin, *The Colonial Church in Virginia* (1927); Evarts B. Greene, "The Anglican Outlook on the American Colonies in the Eighteenth Century," *Am. Hist. Rev.*, XX (1914-15), 64-85; William Meade, *Old Churches, Ministers and Families of Virginia* (2 vols., 1857); Perry Miller, "The Religious Impulse in the Founding of Virginia: Religion and Society in the Early Literature," *Wm. & Mary Q.*, 3rd Series, V (1948), 492-522, and "Religion and Society in the Early Literature: The Religious Impulse in the Founding of Virginia," VI (1949), 24-41; Daniel E. Motley, *Life of Commissary James Blair . . .* (J.H.U. Studies, 19th Series, X, 1901); William S. Perry, *The History of the American Episcopal Church, 1587-1883* (2 vols., 1885); and William H. Seiler, "The Church of England as the Established Church in Seventeenth-

Century Virginia," *Journal of Southern History*, XV (1949), 478-508.

For a rounded picture of the planter and his problems we must look to biographies such as: Richmond C. Beatty, *William Byrd of Westover* (1932); Irving Brant, *James Madison* (3 vols., 1941-50); Leonidas Dodson, *Alexander Spotswood, Governor of Colonial Virginia, 1710-1722* (1932); Douglas Southall Freeman's monumental *George Washington* (6 vols., 1948-54; completed in Vol. 7 by John A. Carroll and Mary W. Ashworth, 1958); Marie Kimball, *Jefferson: The Road to Glory, 1743-1776* (1943), *Jefferson: War and Peace, 1776-1784* (1947), and *Jefferson: The Scene of Europe, 1784-1789* (1950); Dumas Malone's definitive *Jefferson and His Time* (4 vols., 1948———); David John Mays' searching *Edmund Pendleton, 1721-1803* (2 vols., 1952); Robert D. Meade, *Patrick Henry* (2 vols., 1957———); Louis Morton, *Robert Carter of Nomini Hall: A Virginia Tobacco Planter of the Eighteenth Century* (1941); and Kate Mason Rowland, *The Life of George Mason, 1725-1792* (2 vols., 1892). A useful reference work is Lyon G. Tyler (ed.), *Encyclopedia of Virginia Biography* (5 vols., 1915).

Many of the writings of colonial Virginia have been reprinted. Perhaps the most attractive and the most frank, witty, and informative of the early Virginia writers is William Byrd II (1674-1744), who is too little known. There is no easily available and fully representative selection of his works, nor even a satisfactory complete edition of his writings, although one is now in preparation by Louis B. Wright and Marion Tinling. The best collection remains *The Writings of Colonel William Byrd of Westover in Virginia* (ed. John S. Bassett, 1901), which includes his main works

in unabridged form. For a more intimate portrait of Byrd and his family life, see *The Secret Diary of William Byrd . . . 1709-1712* (ed. Louis B. Wright and Marion Tinling, 1941) and *Another Secret Diary of William Byrd . . . 1739-1741; with Letters and Literary Exercises, 1696-1726* (ed. Maude H. Woodfin and Marion Tinling, 1942), and especially *William Byrd of Virginia: The London Diary (1717-1721) and Other Writings* (ed. Louis B. Wright and Marion Tinling, 1958) with Wright's admirable brief biographical introduction. For Byrd as a natural historian, see *William Byrd's Natural History of Virginia: or The Newly Discovered Eden* (ed. R. C. Beatty and W. J. Mulloy, 1940). No historian has yet discovered a satisfactory record of the lives, thoughts, and feelings of the lower classes in colonial Virginia.

The lives and characters of other great Virginians can be best explored through their own writings, which every reader should sample. Besides the multivolume editions (see General section above) of the writings of Jefferson and Washington, there are handy briefer selections, such as *The Life and Selected Writings of Thomas Jefferson* (ed. Adrienne Koch and William Peden, Modern Library, 1944) and *Basic Writings of George Washington* (ed. Saxe Commins, 1948).

Contemporary surveys, histories, and chronicles by Virginians, ·while lacking the grandeur of the works of Bradford, Winthrop, and Cotton Mather, possess some more amiable virtues, including greater attention to the beauties of the landscape. Among the more valuable of these are: for the earliest settlements, *Travels and Works of Captain John Smith* (ed. Edward Arber, 2 vols., 1910); Robert Beverley, *The History and Present*

State of Virginia (1705; ed. Louis B. Wright, 1947); Joseph Doddridge, *Notes, on the Settlement and Indian Wars of the Western Parts of Virginia and of Pennsylvania from 1763 to 1783* (1824; reprinted with Kercheval [below], 1883; and 1912); Henry Hartwell, James Blair, and Edward Chilton, *The Present State of Virginia, and the College* (1727; ed. Hunter D. Farish, 1940); Devereux Jarratt, *A Brief Narrative of the Revival of Religion in Virginia* (1778); Thomas Jefferson, *Notes on the State of Virginia* (1788; ed. William Peden, 1955); Hugh Jones, *The Present State of Virginia* (1724; Sabin's Reprints, V, 1865; also ed. Richard L. Morton, 1956); William Keith, *The History of the British Plantations in America* (1738); Samuel Kercheval, *A History of the Valley of Virginia* (1833); and William Stith, *The History of the First Discovery and Settlement of Virginia* (1747; reprinted, N. Y., 1865). A collection of some of the contemporary accounts of Bacon's Rebellion is Charles M. Andrews (ed.), *Narratives of the Insurrections, 1675-1690* ("Original Narratives" series, 1915).

The best summary introduction to the contemporary travel-literature is Thomas D. Clark, *Travels in the Old South, a bibliography* (2 vols., 1956). Of the dozens of travel-books which touch on Virginia, the more useful include: Andrew Burnaby, *Travels through the Middle Settlements in North America in the Years 1759 and 1760* (3rd ed., 1798); Gilbert Chinard (ed.), *A Huguenot Exile in Virginia* (1687; reprinted, 1934); Francis Michel, "Report of the Journey of Francis Louis Michel from Berne, Switzerland to Virginia, October 2, 1701—December 1, 1702," trans. William J. Hunke, *Va. Mag. Hist. & Biog.*, XXIV (1916), 1-43,

113-141, 275-303; and Charles Woodmason, *The Carolina Backcountry on the Eve of the Revolution; The Journal and Other Writings of Charles Woodmason, Anglican Itinerant* (ed. Richard Hooker, 1953).

An invaluable guide into one of the most valuable sources, especially for social history, is Lester J. Cappon and Stella Duff, *Virginia Gazette Index, 1736-1780* (2 vols., Williamsburg, 1950), a prodigious and meticulous work helpful for finding items on any conceivable topic in *The Virginia Gazettes 1736-1780* (reproduced by photostat in the Massachusetts Historical Society, Boston, 1925). Some of the more accessible contemporary letters, diaries, and records of less well-known figures, which throw light on social history are: *Letters of Robert Carter, 1720-1727; the Commercial Interests of a Virginia Gentleman* (ed. Louis B. Wright, 1940); *Journal and Letters of Philip Vickers Fithian, 1773-1774: A Plantation Tutor of the Old Dominion* (ed. Hunter D. Farish, 1943); "Diary of John Harrower, 1773-1776," *Am. Hist. Rev.*, VI (1900-1901), 65-107; William Keith, *A Collection of Papers and other Tracts* (1740); and *John Norton and Sons, Merchants of London and Virginia, Being the Papers from their Counting House for the Years 1750 to 1795* (ed. Francis N. Mason, 1937).

Materials for the religious history are found in: Samuel Davies, *Sermons on Important Subjects* (3 vols., 1841); Francis L. Hawks, *Contributions to the Ecclesiastical History of the United States* (2 vols., 1836-39); Devereux Jarratt, *Sermons on Various and Important Subjects in Practical Divinity adapted to the Plainest Capacities and Suited to the Family and Closet* (1805); William S. Perry (ed.), *Historical Collections Relating to the American Colonial Church* (5 vols

1870-78); and "Virginia's Cure: or an Advisive Narrative Concerning Virginia, Discovering the True Ground of that Churches Unhappiness and the Only True Remedy" (1662), in Force, *Tracts*, Vol. III.

The basic collections of sources for the legal, legislative, and administrative history are: *Executive Journal of the Council of Colonial Virginia, 1680-1739* (ed. Henry R. McIlwaine, 1925-30); *Legislative Journals of the Council of Colonial Virginia* (ed. Henry R. McIlwaine, 3 vols., 1918-19); *Journals of the House of Burgesses, 1619-1776* (ed. Henry R. McIlwaine, 13 vols., 1905-15); *The Statutes at Large; being a Collection of All the Laws of Virginia from the First Session of the Legislature in the Year 1619* (ed. William W. Hening, 13 vols., 1810-23); and *Calendar of Virginia State Papers and Other Manuscripts Preserved in the Captiol at Richmond, 1652-1869* (ed. W. P. Palmer and others, 11 vols., 1875-93). See also Joseph H. Smith's monograph, *Appeals to the Privy Council from the American Plantations* (1950).

Items of special interest for legal and legislative topics include: Richard Starke, *The Office and Authority of a Justice of the Peace* (Williamsburg, 1774) and William W. Hening, *The New Virginia Justice* (Richmond, Va., 1799), examples of the widely-used guides for justices of the peace; *The Commonplace Book of Thomas Jefferson: A Repertory of His Ideas on Government* (ed. Gilbert Chinard, 1926), an intimate view of Jefferson's reading on legal subjects; *The Official Letters of Alexander Spotswood, Lieutenant Governor of the Colony of Virginia, 1710-1722* (1882-85); and *An Essay upon Government of the English Plantations . . . An Anonymous Virginian's Proposals for Liberty under the British Crown, with Two*

Memoranda by William Byrd (1701, ed. Louis B. Wright, 1945). For a glimpse of problems of a colonial governor, see "Instructions to Francis Nicholson," *Va. Mag. Hist. & Biog.*, IV (1896-97), 49-54; "Governor Nicholson to the Council of Trade and Plantations, December 2, 1701," *Great Britain, Calendar of State Papers. Colonial Series. America and the West Indies, 1701*, 640-655; and "Council of Trade and Plantations to Governor Nicholson, November 4, 1702," the same series, *1702*, 700-702.

BOOK TWO

VIEWPOINTS AND

INSTITUTIONS

PART FIVE

AN AMERICAN FRAME OF MIND

It is peculiarly inappropriate, and can even be misleading, to try to sum up American thinking—much less American culture—through great philosophic systems or the literary and philosophic works of great men. For an American tendency to fuse the "high" and the "low" cultures which have been traditionally polarized in Western Europe, and an ineptitude at systematic philosophy and at monumental works of belles-lettres, have been striking features of our culture. In my *Genius of American Politics* (1953; Phoenix paperback, 1958) I have explored the characteristic American lack of political theory. "The Place of Thought in American Life," *The American Scholar*, XXV (1956), 137-50, is a more general article.

Some of my ablest and most learned colleagues think my view of American culture perverse, and even dangerous.

For the most part, writers have assumed that the categories of European philosophy and literature, and the approach by way of "systems" ("Puritanism," "Rationalism," "Romanticism," "Transcendentalism," etc.) are adequate to the examination of American culture. Pioneer and highly readable work of this kind was done by I. Woodbridge Riley in his *American Philosophy; the Early Schools* (1907) and *American Thought from Puritanism to Pragmatism and Beyond* (1923). Among the more important recent works in the same tradition are Herbert W. Schneider, *A History of American Philosophy* (1946) and Stow Persons, *American Minds: A History of Ideas* (1958). Especially notable in this tradition are the writings of Perry Miller (see Part I, above).

Some influential historians, while sharing the traditional emphasis on dominant systems of thought (sometimes described as "Climates of Opinion") and on the works of great thinkers, are more inclined to trace these ideas into the popular literature, and to write (as Merle Curti has) "a social history of American thought." But these writers, too, tend to give the seminal significance to such abstract, systematized, and cosmopolitan notions as "The Enlightenment," "Natural Law," etc. See, for example, Carl Becker's attractive essays, *The Declaration of Independence* (1922; reprinted 1933; Vintage paperback, 1957) and *The Heavenly City of the Eighteenth-Century Philosophers* (1932); and Merle Curti's compact and comprehensive survey, *The Growth of American Thought* (1943).

For the context in European sophisticated thinking of some of the ideas discussed in Part V, see Alfred North Whitehead, *Science and the Modern World* (1925) and *Adventures of Ideas* (1933), and J. B. Bury, *The Idea of Progress: An Inquiry into its Origin and Growth* (1932; Beacon paperback, 1956). And for a set of revealing American reactions to some of the European ideas of progress, see Zoltan Haraszti, *John Adams and the Prophets of Progress* (1952), which collects and skillfully interprets Adams' marginalia on his personal copies of several writers of the European "Enlightenment." One can follow the revisions of the text of the Declaration of Independence in the facsimiles reproduced in Julian P. Boyd, *The Declaration of Independence, The Evolution of the Text* (1945).

The shortest way to the geographic ideas of the colonial period is to look at contemporary maps, some of which are conveniently reproduced in Charles O. Paullin's *Atlas of the Historical Geography of the United States* (1932); then one should examine Jedidiah Morse, *American Geography* (London, 1794) or *The American Universal Geography* (2 vols., Boston, 1793). Especially useful are the works of Ralph H. Brown, *Historical Geography of the United States* (1948); and *Mirror for Americans: Likeness of the Eastern Seaboard, 1810* (1943), which contains an excellent brief introduction on the state of the geographic knowledge of America in the later 18th century. Valuable special studies include: Thomas D. Cope, "Collecting Source Materials about Charles Mason and Jeremiah Dixon," Am. Philos. Soc., *Proc.*, XCII (1948), 111-114; and Fulmer Mood, "The English Geographers and the Anglo-American Frontier in the Seventeenth Century," *U. of Cal. Pub. in Geography*, VI, no. 9.

In distinguishing different approaches to science and in defining the natural-history emphasis, I have found Stephen E. Toulmin's *Philosophy of Science: An Introduction* (1953) helpful. An adequate full-length history of natural history in America remains to be written, although William H. and Mabel Smallwood, *Natural History and the American Mind* (1941) is a useful exploratory monograph. Several years ago I tried to describe common American attitudes to science in the colonial period in *The Lost World of Thomas Jefferson* (1948), but that volume has many crudities of definition and gives too systematic a character to the thinking of American scientists. Yet I am still impressed by a distinctively American—a "natural-history"—flavor in the scientific writing of the era. For a valuable collection of writings on the borderlands of philosophy, including some early items otherwise difficult to find, see Joseph L. Blau, *American Philosophic Addresses: 1700-1900* (1946).

The best monograph on a period of colonial science is Brooke Hindle, *The Pursuit of Science in Revolutionary America, 1735-1789* (1956), which gives particular attention to the social organization of scientific activity. Valuable special studies include: Ernest Earnest, *John and William Bartram, Botanists and Explorers 1699-1777, 1739-1823* (1940); George B. Goode, "The Beginnings of Natural History in America," Smithsonian Institution, *Annual Report* (1897), in *U. S. National Museum,* II (Washington, 1901), 357-407; Josephine Herbst, *New Green World* (1954); Brooke Hindle, "Cadwallader Colden's Extension of the Newtonian Principles," *Wm. & Mary Q.,* 3rd Series, XIII (1956), 459-475; and Conway Zirkle, *The Beginnings of Plant Hybridization* (1935).

Representative colonial writings on natural history, found either in correspondence, in works on special topics, or in regional histories and surveys (in addition to the writings by Josselyn, Wood, Cotton Mather, and others mentioned in Part I above; and those by William Byrd, Jefferson, and others in Part IV above) include: Benjamin S. Barton, "Memorandums of the Life and Writings of Mr. John Clayton, the Celebrated Botanist of Virginia," *The Philadelphia Medical and Physical Journal,* II (1806), 139-145; John Bartram, *Observations on the Inhabitants, Climate, Soil, Rivers, Productions, Animals and other Matters worthy of Notice. Made . . . in his travels from Pensilvania to Onandago, Oswego and Lake Ontario in Canada . . .* (1751); William Bartram, *Travels through North and South Carolina, Georgia, East and West Florida* (1791; abridged, ed., Carl Van Doren, 1940); Jeremy Belknap, "The Belknap Papers," Mass. Hist. Soc., *Coll.,* 5th Series, II-III, 6th Ser., IV, and *The History of New Hampshire* (3 vols., 1791-92); John Brickell, *The Natural History of North-Carolina* (1737; reprinted, 1911); Andrew Burnaby, *Travels . . . in the Years 1759 and 1760* (3rd ed., London, 1798); William Byrd, *Natural History of Virginia . . .* (1737; ed. R. C. Beatty and W. J. Mulloy, 1940); Mark Catesby, *The Natural History of Carolina, Florida, and the Bahama Islands* (2 vols., 1731-43); Francois Jean de Chastellux, *Travels in North America in the Years 1780, 1781, and 1782* (2 vols., Dublin, 1787); John Clayton's work, incorporated into Johannes F. Gronovius, *Flora Virginica* (Leyden, 1739-43; 1762); Cadwallader Colden, *The History of the Five Indian Nations of Canada* (1727; 2 vols., N.Y., 1902) and *The Principles of Action in Matter* (London, 1751), "The Colden Letter Books," N.Y. Hist. Soc., *Coll.,* IX-X (1876-77) and

"The Letters and Papers of Cadwallader Colden, 1711-1775," N. Y. Hist. Soc., *Coll.,* L-LVI (1917-1923), LXVII-LXVIII (1934-35); William Darlington, *Memorials of John Bartram and Humphrey Marshall with Notices of their Botanical Contemporaries* (1849); William Douglass, *A Summary, Historical and Political of the . . . British Settlements in North America* (2 vols., Boston, 1747-52); "Governor Thomas Dudley's Letter to the Countess of Lincoln, March 1631," in Force, *Tracts,* II, No. 4; John D. Godman, *American Natural History, Part 1, Mastology* (3 vols., 1826-28); Peter Kalm, *The America of 1750: Peter Kalm's Travels in North America* (1770; ed. Adolph B. Benson, 2 vols., 1937) and "The Passenger Pigeon . . . accounts by Pehr Kalm (1759) and John James Audubon (1831)," Smithsonian Inst., *Annual Report* (1911), 407-424; Turhand Kirtland, *Diary . . . from 1798-1800 While Surveying and Laying Out the Western Reserve for the Connecticut Land Company* (1903); James E. Smith (ed.), *A Selection of the Correspondence of Linnaeus and Other Naturalists, from the Original Manuscripts* (2 vols., 1821); Thomas Smith and Samuel Deane, *Journals . . .* (1849); Earl Gregg Swem (ed.), *Brothers of the Spade: Correspondence of Peter Collinson of London, and of John Custis, of Williamsburg, Virginia, 1734-1746* (1957); Samuel Williams, *The Natural and Civil History of Vermont* (2d ed., 2 vols., 1809); and Alexander Wilson, *American Ornithology* (9 vols., 1808-14).

PART SIX

EDUCATING THE COMMUNITY

Although education has lately become one of our most talked-about subjects, the history of American education has until recently been much neglected. More historical study has gone into minor works of American literature than into the development of the major educational institutions. We still lack an adequate general history of higher education in the colonial period—much less a general history of American education.

As might have been expected from the fact that the roots of American higher education are in regional loyalties, some of the best works have been stimulated by affection for a particular college or university. A readable, brief introduction to colonial higher education is contained in the first seven chapters of Samuel Eliot Morison's brilliant *Three Centuries of Harvard, 1636-1936* (1936). Morison's *Founding of Harvard College* (1935) offers a detailed study of the continental and English background of 17th-century Harvard and a comparison with earlier European institutions; his *Harvard College in the Seventeenth Century* (2 vols., 1936) adds valuable details of the curriculum and of student life. Thomas J. Wertenbaker's *Princeton, 1746-1896* (1946) is also very readable. A work which throws much light on the peculiar features of American higher education is Richard Hofstadter and Walter P. Metzger, *The Development of Academic Freedom in the United States* (1955); incidental to an acute treatment of its special subject it gives us a better general account of colonial institutions of higher education than any other book. See also George P. Schmidt, *The Liberal Arts College: A Chapter in American Cultural History* (1957), esp. Ch. v on "The Old-Time College President."

Valuable specialized studies and contemporary records of particular aspects of college-founding, of student life, and of the government of colonial colleges are: Herbert B. Adams, *The College of William and Mary* (1887); Sadie Bell, *The Church, The State, and Education in Virginia* (1930); Walter C. Bronson, *The History of Brown University, 1764-1914* (1914); Samuel W. Brown, *The Secularization of American Education* (1912); Bailey B. Burritt, *Professional Distribution of College and University Graduates* (1912); Lyman H. Butterfield (ed.), *John Witherspoon Comes to America* (1953); Frederick Chase, *A History of Dartmouth College* (2 vols., 1891-1913); E. P. Cheyney, *History of the University of Pennsylvania* (1940); Edwin Grant Dexter, *A History of Education in the United States* (1922); Franklin B. Dexter (ed.), *Documentary History of Yale University Under the Original Charter of the Collegiate School of Connecticut, 1701-1745* (1916) and *Sketch of the History of Yale University* (1887); Timothy Dwight, *Travels in New England and New York* (4 vols., 1821-22); Edward C. Elliot and M. M. Chambers (ed.), *Charters and Basic Laws of Selected American Universities and Colleges* (1932); Allen O. Hansen, *Liberalism and American Education in the Eighteenth Century* (1926); "Harvard College Records: Corporation Records, 1636-1750," Col. Soc. Mass., *Pub.* (Colls. 1925), XV-XVI: *A History of Columbia University, 1754-1904* (1904); John W. Hoyt, *Memorial in Regard to a National University* (1892); William L. Kingsley, *Yale College: A Sketch of its History* (2 vols., 1879); John E. Kirkpatrick, *The Rise of Non-Resident Government in Harvard University* (1925); Edgar W. Knight (ed.), *A Documentary History of Education in the South Before 1860* (5 vols., 1949-53); Beverly McAnear, "College Founding in the American Colonies,

1745-1775," *Mississippi Valley Hist. Rev.*, XLII (1955), 24-44, and "The Selection of an Alma Mater by Pre-Revolutionary Students," *Penn. Mag. Hist. & Biog.*, LXXIII (1949), 429-40; Robert L. McCaul, "Whitefield's Bethesda College Project and other major attempts to found Colonial Colleges," in two parts, to be published in *Ga. Hist. Q.* in 1959, and "Education in Georgia During the Period of Royal Control, 1752-1776: Financial Support of Schools and Schoolmasters," *Ga. Hist. Q.*, XL (1956), 103-12, 248-59; John MacLean, *History of the College of New Jersey* (2 vols., 1877); Thomas H. Montgomery, *A History of the University of Pennsylvania from its Foundation to A.D. 1770* (1900); Forrest Morgan (ed.), *Connecticut as a Colony and as a State* (4 vols., 1904); Samuel Eliot Morison, "Precedence at Harvard College in the Seventeenth Century," Am. Antiq. Soc., *Proc.*, N.S., XLII (1932), 371-431; *The Original Charter of Columbia College . . . with the Acts . . . Relating to the College* (1836); Edwin Oviatt, *Beginnings of Yale (1701-1726)* (1916); Elsie W. Parsons, *Educational Legislation and Administration of the Colonial Government* (1899); Leon B. Richardson, *History of Dartmouth College* (2 vols., 1932); Herbert and Carol Schneider (eds.), *Samuel Johnson, President of King's College* (4 vols., 1929); Louis Shores, *Origins of the American College Library, 1638-1800* (1934); Richard H. Shryock, "The Academic Profession in the United States," Am. Assn. of U. Profs., *Bull.*, XXXVIII (1952), 32-70; *The Literary Diary of Ezra Stiles* (ed. Franklin B. Dexter, 3 vols., 1901); *Extracts from the Itineraries and Other Miscellanies of Ezra Stiles* (ed. Franklin B. Dexter, 1916); Donald Tewksbury, *The Founding of

American Colleges and Universities Before the Civil War with Particular Reference to the Religious Influences Bearing Upon the College Movement (1932), an especially valuable monograph; Charles F. Thwing, *A History of Higher Education in America* (1906); Leonard J. Trinterud, *The Forming of An American Tradition: A Re-examination of Colonial Presbyterianism* (1954); Oscar M. Voorhees, *The History of Phi Beta Kappa* (1945); *The Works of John Witherspoon* (2d ed., 4 vols., 1802); George B. Wood, *Early History of the University of Pennsylvania* (3d ed., 1896); and Thomas Woody, *A History of Women's Education in the United States* (2 vols., 1929). An important reference work is J. L. Sibley's biographical dictionary, *Harvard Graduates* (continued by C. K. Shipton, 8 vols., 1873-1951).

To understand the peculiarities of American higher education one must grasp some of the large features of the great European institutions and traditions. A brilliant essay is Charles H. Haskins' little classic, *The Rise of Universities* (1923; reprinted, Gold Seal paperback, 1957); with ideas that can be pursued in the relevant chapters of H. O. Taylor, *The Medieval Mind* (2 vols., 1925-27). Hastings Rashdall, *The Universities of Europe in the Middle Ages* (2 vols., 1895) is a readable full-length study. A lively brief study which includes the more recent period is Sydney C. Roberts, *British Universities* (1947). George Kitson Clark, *The English Inheritance* (1950), explores the foundations of British culture, including those that were laid in the Universities. On special topics see: *The Government of Oxford* (1931); Herbert McLachlan, *English Education under the Test Acts: Being the History of the Nonconformist Academies, 1662-1820*

(1931); Charles E. Mallet, *A History of the University of Oxford* (3 vols., 1924-28); Albert Mansbridge, *The Older Universities of England: Oxford and Cambridge* (1923); John A. R. Marriott, *Oxford: Its Place in National History* (1933); James B. Mullinger, *A History of the University of Cambridge* (1888); Irene Parker, *Dissenting Academies in England* (1914); Denys A. Winstanley, *The University of Cambridge in the Eighteenth Century* (1922); and Christopher Wordsworth, *Scholae Academicae: Some Account of the Studies at the English Universities in the Eighteenth Century* (1877). Edward Gibbon's *Autobiography* gives an acid and unforgettable, but probably unfair, portrait of 18th-century Oxford.

Some of the peculiarities of the legal history of the corporation in the American colonies which affected the history of colleges and universities are discussed in: Joseph S. Davis, *Essays in the Earlier History of American Corporations* (2 vols., 1917); E. Merrick Dodd, *American Business Corporations until 1860* (1954); and Shaw Livermore, *Early American Land Companies: Their Influence on Corporate Development* (1939).

For the position of American women in colonial business, public, and private life, see Mary S. Benson, *Women in Eighteenth-Century America; A Study of Opinion and Social Usage* (1935); Clarence S. Brigham, *Journals and Journeymen: A Contribution to the History of Early American Newspapers* (1950); Elizabeth W. (Anthony) Dexter, *Colonial Women of Affairs; A Study of Women in Business and the Professions in America Before 1776* (1924); Alice (Morse) Earle, *Home Life in Colonial Days* (1898); Richard B. Morris, *Studies in the History of American*

Law: With Special Reference to the Seventeenth and Eighteenth Centuries (1930); and Julia C. Spruill, *Women's Life and Work in the Southern Colonies* (1938).

PART SEVEN

THE LEARNED LOSE THEIR MONOPOLIES

One of the most striking facts about the literature of American history is the scarcity of works on the development of American law. Although we live by a common-law system based on custom and history and although we have the most prosperous law schools and the most influential (and probably the most liberally educated) legal profession in the Western World, our legal history remains a Dark Continent. It is hard to explain why this is true: some say it is because the materials of our legal history are too scanty, others because they are too voluminous, but none can deny that we are ignoramuses about America's legal past. Moreover, there is little prospect that this will cease to be so within the next half-century; even the wealthiest and most "interdisciplinary" of our law schools pay little or no attention to American legal history. Only the history of the Supreme Court and of constitutional law have been treated extensively. Lawyers insist that mere historians are not qualified to chronicle their subject, and historians find other less technical subjects more rewarding.

Among the few important works on the history of American lawyers and of American private law which are competent both from a technical legal and a historical point of view are: Julius Goebel, Jr. and T. Raymond Naughton, *Law Enforcement in Colonial New York; A Study in Criminal Procedure (1664-1776)* (1944); *Readings in American Legal History* (ed. Mark deWolfe Howe, planograph, Harvard U. Press, 1949); Mark deWolfe Howe, and Louis F. Eaton, Jr., "The Supreme Judicial Power in the Colony of Massachusetts Bay," *N.E.Q.,* XX (1947), 291-316; James Willard Hurst, *The Growth of American Law: The Law Makers* (1950); Eldon R. James, "A List of Legal Treatises Printed in the British Colonies and the American States before 1801," in *Harvard Legal Essays* (1934); Frank H. Miller, "Legal Qualifications for Office in America, 1619-1899," Am. Hist. Assn., *Ann. Report* (1899), I, 87-153; Richard B. Morris, *Studies in the History of American Law: With Special Reference to the Seventeenth and Eighteenth Centuries* (1930) and "Legalism Versus Revolutionary Doctrine in New England," *N.E.Q.,* IV (1931), 195-215; Hubert Phillips, *Development of a Residential Qualification for Representatives in Colonial Legislatures* (1921); Roscoe Pound, *The Formative Era of American Law* (1938); Max Radin, *Handbook of Anglo-American Legal History* (1936); Paul S. Reinsch, *English Common Law in the Early American Colonies* (1899), also found in *Select Essays in Anglo-American Legal History* (ed. Assn. of Am. Law Schools; 3 vols., 1907); *Two Centuries' Growth of American Law, 1701-1901* (1902).

We have a larger, though still surprisingly small, number of useful books on the history of the legal profession and legal education. The only general guide is Charles Warren, *A History of the American Bar* (1912). For the colonial period the following are especially helpful: George Dexter (ed.), "Record Book of the Suffolk Bar, 1770-1805," Mass. Hist. Soc., *Proc.,* XIX (1881-82), 141-179; Samuel H. Fisher, *Litchfield Law School,*

1774-1833: Bibliographical Catalogue of Students (Yale Law Library, *Pub.* No. 11; 1946) and the collection of manuscript notebooks which early students of the Litchfield Law School made from the lectures of Judge Tapping Reeve, which now are in the Yale Law Library; Frank W. Grinnell, "The Bench and Bar in Colony and Province (1630-1776)," in Albert B. Hart (ed.), *Commonwealth History of Massachusetts* (1928), II, 156-191; Paul M. Hamlin, *Legal Education in Colonial New York* (1939); E. Alfred Jones, *American Members of the Inns of Court* (1924); "Lawyers of the Seventeenth Century," *Wm. & Mary Q.*, VIII (1899), 228-30; William Draper Lewis (ed.), *Great American Lawyers* (8 vols., 1907-09); Joel Parker, *The Law School of Harvard College* (1871); Josef Redlich, *The Common Law and the Case Method in American University Law Schools* (1914); Alfred Z. Reed, *Training for the Public Profession of the Law* (1921), an especially useful study for the origins of American professional standards (in this connection see also, Esther Lucile Brown, *Lawyers and the Promotion of Justice,* 1938); Charles Warren, *History of the Harvard Law School and of Early Legal Conditions in America* (3 vols., 1908); and Emory Washburn, *Sketches of the Judicial History of Massachusetts from 1630 to the Revolution in 1775* (1840).

Miscellaneous biographical materials, and the notebooks, correspondence, and other writings of early American lawyers help us piece together a picture of their daily work. For example, the papers of John Adams (ed. Charles F. Adams; 10 vols., 1850-56) and of Jefferson (ed. Julian P. Boyd) shed some light on the subject. To define Jefferson's view of the law, I have tried to make use of the materials in the *Jefferson Papers* in my reviews in *Wm. & Mary Q.*, 3rd Series VII (1950), 596-609, VIII (1951), 283-285, and X (1953), 126-130; see also H. Trevor Colbourn, "Thomas Jefferson's Use of the Past," *Wm. & Mary Q.*, 3rd Series, XV (1958), 35-56, and Marie Kimball, *Jefferson: The Road to Glory, 1743-1776* (1943). Most important of all is Jefferson's Commonplace Book, with his notes on his legal reading (ed. Gilbert Chinard, 1926); see also the *Literary Bible of Thomas Jefferson* (ed. Gilbert Chinard, 1928). Other valuable biographical material is found in Charles P. Smith, *James Wilson, Founding Father: 1742-1798* (1956); Robert D. Meade, *Patrick Henry: Patriot in the Making* (1957), esp. chs. v-x; David J. Mays, *Edmund Pendleton* (1952); Samuel G. Heiskell, *Andrew Jackson and Early Tennessee History* (1918); and Marquis James, *Andrew Jackson, The Border Captain* (1933). I have examined several sets of manuscript notebooks kept by lawyers and judges during the colonial period (now in the possession of the Harvard Law Library) in order to provide themselves with records of precedents for use in practice; some of these are included in my *Delaware Cases: 1792-1830* (3 Vols., 1943).

Some of the significance of Sir William Blackstone's *Commentaries on the Laws of England* (4 vols., 1765-1769), which was the Bible and the Correspondence School for generations of American lawyers, can be grasped by surveying the number and variety of American editions of his work; see Catherine S. Eller, *The William Blackstone Collection in the Yale Law Library* (Yale Law Lib., *Pub.* No. 6; 1938). For the drift of Blackstone's work and some of the features which made it especially appealing see my *Mysterious Science of the Law: An Essay on Blackstone's Commentaries* (1941; Beacon paperback, 1958).

A valuable general history of the learned occupations in England is A. M. Carr-Saunders and P. A. Wilson, *The Professions* (1933). There is yet no comparable work for the history of the professions in America. An indispensable reference work for English legal history (which tells us more than any other single work about the laws of the colonies) is Sir William Holdsworth's monumental *History of English Law* (12 vols., 1922-38). A lively history of English thinking about the sources of the common law is Sir Carleton K. Allen, *Law in the Making* (1930 and later editions). The Littleton-Griswold Fund of the Association of American Law Schools has supported the publication of several volumes of early American legal records, with valuable introductions; for example, *The Burlington Court Book: A Record of Quaker Jurisprudence in West New Jersey, 1680-1709* (ed. H. Clay Reed and George J. Miller, 1944).

PART EIGHT

NEW WORLD MEDICINE

The best starting point for studying the history of medicine in America is a good local history which avoids irrelevant abstractions. There is no better way to begin than through Dr. Wyndham S. Blanton's comprehensive, careful, and readable *Medicine in Virginia* (3 vols.: 17th century, 1930; 18th century, 1931; 19th century, 1933). At present there is no other local history of medicine of comparable quality, but John Duffy will soon publish his full-length history of medicine in Louisiana. On a less ambitious scale,

Henry R. Viets, *Brief History of Medicine in Massachusetts* (1930) is valuable. Until we have more local studies of the quality of the Blanton and Viets works it will be hard for anyone to write a comprehensive history of medicine in this country; regional differences of climate, public health, and disease have been great, and local problems have tended to dominate writing in the field. Dr. Henry E. Sigerist's *American Medicine* (1934) is a concise and highly readable pioneer essay—valuable for its insights and its hints for future research, but sketchy in its facts.

Dr. Richard H. Shryock has come closer than anyone else to comprehending this large and varied subject. His works are remarkable, not only for their ability to organize a mass of intractable detail, but even more for their success in pointing the way from this technical subject to other, and more familiar, problems of social history. See his *Development of Modern Medicine: An Interpretation of the Social and Scientific Factors Involved* (1947) and *American Medical Research Past and Present* (1947). Dr. Shryock's brief studies include: "Eighteenth Century Medicine in America," Am. Antiq. Soc., *Proc.* (Oct., 1949), 1-20; "Women in American Medicine," *Journal of Am. Women's Med. Assn.*, V (1950), 371-379; "The Interplay of Social and Internal Factors in the History of Modern Medicine," *Scientific Monthly*, LXXVI (1953), 221-230. Francis R. Packard, *History of Medicine in the United States* (2 vols., 1931), although disorganized and sometimes inaccurate, is occasionally helpful. An especially interesting collection of essays are the papers in the "Symposium on Colonial Medicine in Commemoration of the 350th Anniversary of the Settlement of Virginia," *Bull. Hist. Med.*, XXXI (Sept.-Oct.

1957), which came to my attention only after these chapters had gone to press.

Some valuable special studies on medicine, medical practice, and medical education are: Malcolm S. Beinfield, "The Early New England Doctor: An Adaptation to a Provincial Environment," *Yale Journal of Biology and Medicine*, XV (1942-43), 99-132; Carl Bridenbaugh (ed.), Dr. Thomas Bond's clinical lectures (1776) in *Journal of the History of Medicine*, II (1947), 12 ff., and (with Jessica Bridenbaugh) *Rebels and Gentlemen: Philadelphia in the Age of Franklin* (1942), on the profession in Philadelphia; A. M. Carr-Saunders and P. A. Wilson, *The Professions* (1933) for the English side; Joseph Carson, *History of the Medical Department of the University of Pennsylvania* (1869); R. Hingston Fox, *Dr. John Fothergill and His Friends* (1919); H. Fielding Garrison, *An Introduction to the History of Medicine* (1924); James E. Gibson, *Dr. Bodo Otto and the Medical Background of the American Revolution* (1937); Thomas F. Harrington, *The Harvard Medical School: A History* (3 vols., 1905); Claude E. Heaton, "Medicine in New York during the English Colonial Period," *Bull. Hist. Med.*, XVII (1945), No. 1; Frederick P. Henry, *Standard History of the Medical Profession of Philadelphia* (1897); Brooke Hindle, *The Pursuit of Science in Revolutionary America, 1735-1789* (1956); Oliver Wendell Holmes, *Medical Essays, 1842-1882* (1883); John B. Langstaff, *Doctor Bard of Hyde Park: The Famous Physician of Revolutionary Times* (1942); Henry F. Long, "The Physicians of Topsfield, with Some Account of Early Medical Practice," Essex Institute, *Hist. Coll.*, XLVII (1911), 197-229; William Macmichael, *The Gold-Headed Cane* (2d ed., 1828), for social aspects of the English medical professions; Albert Matthews, "Notes on Early Autopsies and Anatomical Lectures," Col. Soc. Mass., *Pub.*, XIX (Trans., 1916-17), 273-89; Thomas G. Morton and Frank Woodbury, *History of the Pennsylvania Hospital, 1751-1895* (1895); William F. Norwood, *Medical Education in the United States Before the Civil War* (1944); William Pepper, *The Medical Side of Benjamin Franklin* (1911); Eric Stone, *Medicine among the American Indians* (1932); Joseph Toner, *Contributions to the Annals of Medical Progress and Medical Education in the United States Before and During the War of Independence* (1874); James J. Walsh, *History of Medicine in New York* (5 vols., 1919); Edward Warren, *Life of John Warren, M. D., Surgeon-General During the War of the Revolution* (1874); William Welch, "English Influence on American Medicine in the Formative Period of American History," in *Contributions to Medical and Biological Research dedicated to Sir William Osler* (2 vols., 1919); and Stephen Wickes, *History of Medicine in New Jersey . . . from the Settlement . . . to . . . 1800* (1879).

Reprints of major writings in early American medical history with useful introductions are available in the *Bibliotheca Medica Americana* (Institute of the History of Medicine, Johns Hopkins University), which includes, for example, Dr. John Morgan's *Discourse Upon the Institution of Medical Schools in America* (1765; reprinted, 1937) and Daniel Drake's *Practical Essays on Medical Education and the Medical Profession in the United States* (1832; reprinted, 1952). A basic document for understanding early New England medicine is the abridged edition of Cotton Mather's manuscript, "The Angel of Bethesda," edited with an interesting introduction by Richard H. Shryock and Otho T. Beall in *Cotton Mather, First Significant Figure in American Medicine* (1954); but see the criticism of the editors' interpretations by Donald Fleming in his review, *Isis*, XLVI (1955), 374-76. Other important contemporary medical writings include: Benjamin Smith Barton, *Collections for an Essay Towards a Materia Medica of the United States* (1801-4); Benjamin Rush, *Medical Inquiries and Observations* (4th ed., 4 vols., 1815); Johann D. Schoepf, *The Climate and Diseases of America* (tr. from German by James R. Chadwick, 1875); James E. Smith (comp.), *A Selection of the Correspondence of Linnaeus and other Naturalists* (2 vols., 1821); John Tennent, *Every Man His Own Doctor: Or, The Poor Planter's Physician* (2d ed., Williamsburg, Va., 1734); James Thacher, *American Medical Biography* (1828); and Joseph B. Walker (ed.), "Diaries of the Rev. Timothy Walker . . . 1730 to . . . 1782," New Hampshire Hist. Soc., *Coll.*, IX (1889), 123-191.

A number of the more important travel-books and historical and geographical surveys of the 18th and early 19th century were written by physicians and therefore include medical information; for example: Dr. William Douglass' *Summary* (1749-51); Dr. Alexander Hamilton's *Itinerarium* (1744; ed. Carl Bridenbaugh, 1948); Dr. David Ramsay's *History of South Carolina* (2 vols., 1809) and *History of the Revolution in South Carolina* (2 vols., 1785). For lively comments on many aspects of medicine and society, see *The Letters of Benjamin Rush* (ed. Lyman Butterfield; 2 vols., Princeton, 1951).

On colonial epidemics (and especially on smallpox) there is a more extensive literature than on any other topic. The literature is still very controversial; some of the ablest recent scholars have continued the debate between Dr. Douglass and Cotton Mather mentioned in Ch. 35. Valuable general discussions of the relation of epidemics to the rise of civilization are: Percy M. Ashburn, *The Ranks of Death: A Medical History of the Conquest of America* (1947) and Henry Sigerist, *Civilization and Disease* (1943). The best introduction to colonial problems is John Duffy's scholarly and readable *Epidemics in Colonial America* (1953). The best technical study of a particular epidemic is Dr. Ernest Caulfield's brilliant examination of a diphtheria outbreak, *A True History of the Terrible Epidemic Vulgarly Called the Throat Distemper . . . in . . . New England Colonies Between . . . 1735 and 1740* (1939). Perry Miller discusses the New England smallpox controversy in *The New England Mind: from Colony to Province* (1953), ch. 21; his sympathy lies on the side of traditional learning championed by Dr. William Douglass. The more useful special studies include: John I. Barrett, "The Inoculation Controversy in Puritan New England," *Bull. Hist. Med.*, XII (1942), 169-190; H. D. Behnke, "Colonial theories concerning the cause of disease," *Medical Life*, XLI (1934), 59-74; John B. Blake, *Benjamin Waterhouse and the Introduction of Vaccination* (1957); Edgar M. Crookshank, *History and Pathology of Vaccination* (2 vols., 1889); Reginald H. Fitz, "Zabdiel Boylston, Inoculation, and the Epidemic of Smallpox in Boston in 1721," Johns Hopkins Hospital, *Bull.*, XXII (1911), 315-327; George Lyman Kittredge, "Cotton Mather's Election to the Royal Society," Col. Soc. Mass., *Pub.*, XIV (Trans., 1911-1913), 81-114, and

"Further Notes on Cotton Mather and the Royal Society," 281-292, also "Cotton Mather's Scientific Communications to the Royal Society," Am. Antiq. Soc., *Proc.*, N.S., XXVI (1916), 18-57, and "Some Lost Works of Cotton Mather," Mass. Hist. Soc., *Proc.*, XLV (1911-12), 418-479; Arnold C. Klebs, "The Historic Evolution of Variolation," J. H. Hospital, *Bull.*, XXIV (1913), 69-83; Morris C. Leikind, "Variolation in Europe and America," *Ciba Symposia*, III (1941-1942), 1090-1101, 1124, "Vaccination in Europe," 1102-1113, "The Introduction of Vaccination into the United States," 1114-1124; Genevieve Miller, "Smallpox Inoculation in England and America: A Reappraisal," *Wm. & Mary Q.*, 3rd Ser., XIII (1956), 476-92, and *The Adoption of Inoculation for Smallpox in England and France* (1957); Hugh Thursfield, "Smallpox in the American War of Independence," *Annals of Med. Hist.*, 3rd Ser., II (1940), 312-318; and Joseph Waring, "James Killpatrick and Smallpox Inoculation in Charlestown," *Annals of Med. Hist.*, N.S., X (1938), 301-308.

A facsimile reproduction of Thomas Thacher's broadside, *A Brief Rule to Guide the Common-People of New England . . . in the Small Pocks or Measles* (1677-78) is found in *Bibliotheca Medica Americana* (Inst. Hist. Med., J.H.U., No. 1, 1937). The communication about inoculation that started the controversy between Mather and Douglass was Emanuel Timonius, "An Account, or History of the Procuring the Small Pox by Incision, or Inoculation; as it has for some time been Practiced at Constantinople," Royal Soc., *Phil. Trans.*, XXIX (1714-16), 72-82. Some of the more interesting contemporary writings on colonial diseases and epidemics are: William Currie, *An Historical*

Account of the Climates and Diseases of the United States (1792), *Memoirs of the Yellow Fever* (1798), *A View of the Diseases Most Prevalent in the United States . . . at Different Seasons of the Year* (1811), and (with Isaac Cathrall) *Facts and Observations Relative to the Origins, Progress, and Nature of the Fever . . . in . . . Philadelphia* (1802); William Douglass, *A Practical Essay Concerning the Small Pox* (Boston, 1730), *The Practical History of a New Epidemical Eruptive Miliary Fever . . . in the Years 1735 and 1736* (Boston, 1736); Dr. Fancher, "Progress of Vaccination in America," Mass. Hist. Soc., *Coll.*, 2d Ser., IV (1816), 97; Benjamin Gale, "Historical Memoirs, Relating to the Practice of Inoculation for the Small Pox in the American Provinces, Particularly in New England," Royal Soc., *Phil. Trans.*, LV (1765), 193-204; James Kirkpatrick, *A Full and Clear Reply to Doct. Thomas Dale Wherein the Real Impropriety of Blistering with Catharides in the . . . Small Pox is Plainly Demonstrated* (Charleston, 1739), *The Analysis of Inoculation* (2d ed., London, 1761), *An Essay on Inoculation, Occasioned by the Smallpox being Brought into South Carolina in the Year 1738* (London, 1743); "Extracts of two Letters from Dr. John Lining, Physician at Charles-Town in South Carolina . . . Giving an Account of Statical Experiments Made Several Times in a Day Upon Himself, for One Whole Year," Royal Soc., *Phil. Trans.*, XLII (1742-43), 491-509; "An Extract of Several Letters from Cotton Mather D.D. to John Woodward, M.D. . . ." Royal Soc., *Phil. Trans.*, XXIX (1714-16), 61-72; Increase Mather, *Several Reasons Proving the Inoculating or Transplanting the Small Pox is a Lawful Practice and that it has been Blessed by God for the Saving of Many a*

Life, with Cotton Mather, *Sentiments on the Small Pox Inoculated* (1721; reprinted with intro. by George Lyman Kittredge, 1921); Richard Mead, *A Discourse on the Small Pox and Measles* (1747); "Account of the Yellow Fever which Prevailed in Virginia in the Years 1737, 1741 and 1742, in a Letter to the Late Cadwallader Colden, esq. of New York, from the Late John Mitchell, M.D., F.R.S., of Virginia," *American Medical and Philosophical Register*, IV (1814; on microfilm in Amer. Periodical Series, Ser. 2.); Henry Newman, "The Way of Proceeding in the Small Pox Inoculated in New England," Royal Soc., *Phil. Trans.*, XXXII (1722-23), 33-35; Thomas Nettleton, "A letter from Dr. Nettleton, Physician at Halifax in Yorkshire, to Dr. Whitaker, Concerning the Inoculation of the Small Pox," Royal Soc., *Phil. Trans.*, XXXII (1722-23), 35-48, and another letter at 49-52; Noah Webster, *A Collection of Papers on the Subject of Bilious Fevers, Prevalent in the United States for a Few Years Past* (1796) and *A Brief History of Epidemic and Pestilential Diseases* (2 vols., 1799).

PART NINE

THE LIMITS OF AMERICAN SCIENCE

We do not yet possess a comprehensive history of science or technology in colonial America, or for any other era of our history. The closest approach to it is Brooke Hindle's *Pursuit of Science in Revolutionary America, 1735-1789* (1956). Donald Fleming will soon publish his three-volume history of American science and technology which should provide a much needed general guide. An admirable survey of the present state of the subject, with references to the most important printed works and to promising areas of research, is Whitfield J. Bell, Jr., *Early American Science: Needs and Opportunities for Study* (1955), the first of a valuable series of prospectuses published by the Institute of Early American History and Culture, Williamsburg, Va.

One must rely heavily on periodical literature: especially on the publications of the American Philosophical Society and of the Royal Society of London; on *Isis: International Review Devoted to the History of Science and its Cultural Influences* (Cambridge, Mass., 1913 to date), the beneficiary of the masterful editing of George Sarton, and now of I. Bernard Cohen; on *Osiris: Studies on the History and Philosophy of Science and on the History of Learning and Culture* (Bruges, 1936 to date); and on the professional and historical journals of different scientific specialties.

Among the more valuable items which touch on colonial science in general are: Whitfield J. Bell, Jr., "The Scientific Environment of Philadelphia, 1775-1790," A.P.S., *Proc.*, XCII (1948), 6-14; Frederick E. Brasch, "The Newtonian Epoch in the American Colonies (1680-1783)," Am. Antiq. Soc., *Proc.*, N.S., XLIX (1939), 314-32, and "The Royal Society of London and its Influence upon Scientific Thought in the American Colonies," *Scientific Monthly*, XXXIII (1931), 336-55, 448-69; C. A. Browne, "Scientific Notes from the Books and Letters of John Winthrop, Jr.," *Isis*, XI (1928), 325-42; Roger Burlingame, *March of the Iron Men: A Social History of Union Through Invention* (1949); I. Bernard Cohen, *Some Early Tools of American Science* (1950); Margaret Denny, "The Royal Society and American Scholars," *Scientific Monthly*, LXV (1947), 415-

27; Courtney R. Hall, *A Scientist in the Early Republic; Samuel Latham Mitchell, 1764-1831* (1934); Henry E. Huntington Library and Art Gallery, San Marino, Cal., *Science and the New World: an Exhibition to Illustrate the Scientific Contributions of the New World and the Spread of Scientific Ideas in America* (1937); Brooke Hindle, "The Quaker Background and Science in Colonial Philadelphia," *Isis,* XLVI (1955), 243-50; Theodore Hornberger, "The Scientific Ideas of John Mitchell," *Huntington Lib. Q.,* X (1946-47), 277-296, "Samuel Lee (1625-1691), A Clerical Channel for the Flow of New Ideas to Seventeenth-Century New England," *Osiris,* I (1936), 341-55, "The Science of Thomas Prince," *N.E.Q.,* IX (1936), 26-42, *Scientific Thought in the American Colleges, 1638-1800* (1948); Hornberger's edition of Charles Morton's *Compendium Physicae* (1687) (Col. Soc. Mass., *Pub.,* XXXIII) which, with an introduction by Samuel Eliot Morison, is invaluable for its glimpse of what Harvard students were learning at the end of the 17th century; Frederick G. Kilgour, "Rise of Scientific Thought in Colonial New England," *Yale Journal of Biology and Medicine,* XXII (1949), 123-130; Flora Masson, *Robert Boyle* (1914); Robert H. Murray, *Dublin University and the New World* (1921); John W. Oliver, *History of American Technology* (1956); Richard H. Shryock, "The Need for Studies in the History of American Science," *Isis,* XXXV (1944), 10-13; Raymond P. Stearns, "Colonial Fellows of the Royal Society of London, 1661-1778," *Osiris,* VIII (1948), 73-121; Dirk J. Struik, *Yankee Science in the Making* (1948), an elementary interpretation of the history of technology from a Marxist point of view; "Symposium on the Early History of Science and Learning in America," A.P.S., *Proc.,* LXXXVI (1942), 1-204; Charles O. Thompson, "Robert Boyle: A Study in Biography," Am. Antiq. Soc., *Proc.,* N.S., II (1882-83), 54-79; Lyon G. Tyler, "Virginia's Contribution to Science," Am. Antiq. Soc., *Proc.,* N.S., XXV (1915), 358-374; Charles R. Weld, *A History of the Royal Society* (2 vols., 1848); A. Wolf's two-volume reference work on the history of science, technology, and philosophy (16th and 17th centuries, 1935; 18th century, 1939).

Lacking a good general history of colonial astronomy, our best approach is through the work of one of the leading colonial astronomers like John Winthrop IV (1714-1779) or David Rittenhouse (1732-1796). On Winthrop see Frederick E. Brasch, "John Winthrop (1714-1779), America's First Astronomer, and the Science of His Period," Astronomical Society of the Pacific, *Pub.,* XXVIII (1916), 153-170, and "Newton's First Critical Disciple in the American Colonies— John Winthrop," in *Sir Isaac Newton, 1727-1927. A Bicentenary Evaluation* (1928), 301-338; Frederick G. Kilgour, "Professor John Winthrop's Notes on Sun Spot Observations (1739)," *Isis,* XXIX (1938), 355-361. Winthrop's own writings are scarce, but the more available are: *Two Lectures on Comets* (reprinted, Boston, 1811; in John Crerar Library, Chicago); *A Lecture on Earthquakes* (Boston, 1750; U. of Ill. microfilm); *Relation of a Voyage from Boston to Newfoundland, for the Observation of the Transit of Venus, June 6, 1761* (Boston, 1761; in Brown U. Library); *Two Lectures on the Parallax and Distance of the Sun as Deducible from the Transit of Venus* (Boston, 1769; in John Crerar Library, Chicago); "Extract of a Letter from John Winthrop . . . to B. Franklin . . ."

Royal Soc., *Phil. Trans.*, LX (1770), 358-362, and the correspondence between Winthrop and John Adams, Mass. Hist. Soc., *Coll.*, 5th Series, IV (1878), 289-313.

The best introduction to Rittenhouse is through Howard C. Rice Jr., *The Rittenhouse Orrery: Princeton's Eighteenth-Century Planetarium, 1767. 1954; A Commentary on an Exhibition held in the Princeton University Library* (Princeton U. Library, 1954), which offers a great deal more than its limited title would suggest. William Barton, *Memoirs of the Life of David Rittenhouse* (1813), is still the best biographical source, and reprints items by Rittenhouse. See also: Maurice J. Babb, "David Rittenhouse," *Penn. Mag. Hist. & Biog.*, LVI (1932), 193-224; Thomas D. Cope, "David Rittenhouse—Physicist," *Journal of the Franklin Institute*, CCXV (1933), 287-297; Edward Ford, *David Rittenhouse: Astronomer Patriot, 1732-1796* (1946). Brooke Hindle is writing a full-length biography of Rittenhouse. The history of American surveying in which Rittenhouse played a leading role also needs treatment. For some interesting suggestions, see: Lloyd A. Brown, *The Story of Maps* (1949); Thomas D. Cope, "Collecting Source Material about Charles Mason and Jeremiah Dixon," A.P.S., *Proc.*, XCII (1948), 111-114; William D. Pattison, *Beginnings of the American Rectangular Land Survey System, 1784-1800* (Research Paper, No. 50, Dept. of Geography, University of Chicago, 1958).

Colonial writings on astronomy and mathematics which are of special interest include: Cadwallader Colden, *The Principles of Action in Matter, the Gravitation of Bodies, and the Motion of the Planets, Explained from those Principles* (London, 1751); Samuel Danforth, *An Astronomical Description of the Late Comet or Blazing Star as it Appeared in New England in . . . 1664* (Cambridge, Mass., 1665); Increase Mather, *Kometographia, or A Discourse Concerning Comets* (Boston, 1683; Univ. Microfilms, Am. Culture Series, No. 83, Roll 8); and the valuable collection, "Mathematical and Astronomical Papers," American Philosophical Society, *Trans.*, I (1771), 1-180. A good source for popular astronomy is the colonial almanac (see Part XII, below). For a suggestive essay on one aspect of this history see Andrew D. White, *A History of the Doctrine of Comets* (1887).

For our knowledge of colonial physics, electricity, and the place of Franklin in the history of physical science, we owe most to the scholarly and readable works of I. Bernard Cohen. The basic book for this subject is Cohen's edition (with an introduction) of Benjamin Franklin's *Experiments and Observations on Electricity* (1941). Cohen offers books for any taste: a brief anthology and commentary for the general reader, *Benjamin Franklin: His Contribution to the American Tradition* (1953) or a massive monograph, *Franklin and Newton: An Inquiry into Speculative Newtonian Experimental Science and Franklin's Work in Electricity as an Example Thereof* (in *Memoirs of the American Philosophical Society*, Vol. XLIII, 1956). I incline toward the emphasis found in Cohen's earlier rather than in his later works. Although Cohen seems to draw other morals from the voluminous data collected in his latest study (1956), in my opinion he does not succeed in disproving his earlier suggestions that Franklin's important contributions owed much to his independent naiveté. In Cohen's six-hundred-odd pages of fascinating detail, the reader still finds strikingly little evidence of any direct influence of Newton's writings on Franklin—much less of Franklin's understanding of the subtleties of Newton's theories. From it all, I still have the picture of Franklin as a brilliant amateur.

On Franklin's knowledge of science, on electricity, lightning-rods, and the history of their introduction, the following are valuable: I. Bernard Cohen, "How Practical was Benjamin Franklin's Science?" *Penn. Mag. Hist. & Biog.*, LXIX (1945), 284-93, and "Prejudice against the Introduction of Lightning Rods," Franklin Inst., *Journal*, CCLIII (1952), 393-440; Austin K. Gray, *Benjamin Franklin's Library* (1936); Zoltan Haraszti, "Young John Adams on Franklin's Iron Points," *Isis*, XLI (1950), 11-14; Basil F. J. Schonland, *The Flight of Thunderbolts* (1950); Eleanor M. Tilton, "Lightning Rods and the Earthquake of 1755," *N.E.Q.*, XIII (1940), 85-97; Carl Van Doren, *Benjamin Franklin* (1938). For a sidelight on the lightning-rod controversy, see Thomas Prince, *Earthquakes, The Works of God* (Boston, 1755).

For colonial agriculture, useful surveys are found in the works by Bidwell and Falconer, and by Gray listed in the General section above. Many little-known facts and some stimulating generalizations are in Lyman Carrier, *The Beginnings of Agriculture in America* (1923). A still very suggestive pioneer monograph on the relation between agricultural technology and social history is Avery O. Craven, *Soil Exhaustion as a Factor in the Agricultural History of Virginia and Maryland, 1606-1860* (1926). In the Columbia University Studies in the History of American Agriculture we have excellent reprint editions with valuable introductions of basic works of the colonial era: Jared Eliot, *Essays Upon Field Husbandry in New Eng-*

land, And Other Papers, 1748-1762 (ed. Harry J. Carman and Rexford G. Tugwell, 1935); and *American Husbandry* (1775), the most comprehensive and detailed 18th-century survey (ed. Harry J. Carman, 1939). These are surprisingly readable works, which even the non-specialist can enjoy. An especially valuable description of the problems of one part of the country is Robert R. Walcott, "Husbandry in Colonial New England," *N.E.Q.*, IX (1936), 218-252.

Some items which give glimpses of different sides of this varied and complex subject are: E. Alexander Bergstrom, "English Game Laws and Colonial Food Shortages," *N.E.Q.*, XII (1939), 681-690; Beverly W. Bond, *The Quit-Rent System in the American Colonies* (1919); Thomas S. Brewer, "Agricultural Conditions in Colonial Pennsylvania" (unpublished Master's Thesis, Dept. of History, University of Chicago, 1915); Kathleen Bruce, "Materials for Virginia Agricultural History," *Agricultural History*, IV (1930), 10-14; S. J. and E. H. Buck, *The Planting of Civilization in Western Pennsylvania* (1939); *Jesse Buel: Agricultural Reformer; Selections from his Writings* (ed. Harry J. Carman, 1947); David Doar, *Rice and Rice Planting in the South Carolina Low Country* (1936); Everett E. Edwards (ed.) *Jefferson and Agriculture* (U. S. Dept. of Agric., 1943); Amelia Clewley Ford, *Colonial Precedents of our National Land System* (1910); W. Neil Franklin, "Agriculture in Colonial North Carolina," *No. Car. Hist. Rev.*, III (1926), 539-47; Norman S. B. Gras, *History of Agriculture in Europe and America* (1940); Ulysses P. Hedrick, *A History of Agriculture in the State of New York* (1933); Duncan C. Heyward, *Seed from Madagascar* (1937), a discussion of the origins of rice-culture in South Carolina; Arthur H. Hirsch, "French Influence on American Agriculture in the Colonial Period . . . ," *Agric. Hist.*, IV (1930), 1-9; Edward H. Jenkins, *Connecticut Agriculture* (1926); W. A. Low, "The Farmer in Post Revolutionary Virginia, 1783-1789," *Agric. Hist.*, XXV (1951), 122-27; Thomas Mairs, *Some Pennsylvania Pioneers in Agricultural Science* (1928); Deane Phillips, *Horse Raising in Colonial New England* (1922); U. B. Phillips, *American Negro Slavery* (1918); Aaron M. Sakolski, *Land Tenure and Land Taxation in America* (1957); Carl O. Sauer, "The Settlement of the Humid East," *Climate and Man* (U.S. Dept. Agric., *Yearbook, 1941*), 157-166; Joseph Schafer, *The Social History of American Agriculture* (1936); Richard H. Shryock, "British Versus German Traditions in Colonial Agriculture," *Mississippi Valley Hist. Rev.*, XXVI (1939-40), 39-54; Carl R. Woodward, *Ploughs and Politicks: Charles Read of New Jersey and His Notes on Agriculture, 1715-1774* (1941), *The Development of Agriculture in New Jersey, 1640-1880* (1927), and "Agricultural Legislation in Colonial New Jersey," *Agric. Hist.*, III (1929), 15-28; Harry A. Wright, "The Technique of Seventeenth Century Indian-Land Purchasers," *Essex Inst., Hist. Coll.*, LXXVII (1941), 185-97.

Especially valuable early American writings on agriculture include: John Beale Bordley, *Essays and Notes on Husbandry and Rural Affairs* (2d ed., Phila., 1801), *Sketches on Rotations of Crops and Other Rural Matters* (Phila., 1796); Samuel Deane, *The New England Farmer* (2d ed. Worcester, Mass., 1797); J. D. B. De Bow, "Indian Corn," *De Bow's Review*, I (1846), 465-497; William Erving, "Premiums Offered by the Committee of the American Academy of Arts and Sciences, Appointed for Promoting Agriculture," *American Museum*, II (1787), 355-56; Joseph Greenleaf, "Experiments for Raising Indian Corn in Poor Land," *Am. Mus.*, I (1787), 39-40; Thomas Nairn, *Letter from South Carolina* (2d ed., London, 1732); Benjamin Rush, "An Account of the Manners of the German Inhabitants of Pennsylvania" (ed. Theodore E. Schmauk, in Penn.-German Soc., *Proc.*, XIX, 1908); James Tilton, "Queries on the Present State of Husbandry and Agriculture in the State of Delaware," *Am. Mus.*, V (1789), 375-82; J. Warren, "Observations on Agriculture—its Advantages —and the Causes that have in America Prevented Improvements in Husbandry," *Am. Mus.*, II (1787), 344-348; and the revealing *Letters on Agriculture from . . . George Washington . . . to Arthur Young . . . and Sir John Sinclair*, ed. Franklin Knight (1847).

BOOK THREE

LANGUAGE AND THE

PRINTED WORD

PART TEN

THE NEW UNIFORMITY

Although our language, like our law, is one of the most characteristic developments of American culture, its history also has been neglected by general students of American history. But the history of the American language has been the object of comprehensive and intensive recent study by specialists, who have been among the wittiest and most literate of our social historians. The absence of any adequate contemporary system of phonetics for recording the actual sounds as spoken in the early days has left this field open for speculation.

The starting-point is a work of national piety, likely to be the most durable—and ironical—literary remain of H. L. Mencken: *The American Language* (1937), *The American Language: Supplement One* (1945; chs. 1-6), *The American Language: Supplement Two* (1948; chs. 7-11). A new combined edition of these volumes is in preparation by Raven I. McDavid, Jr. Another basic work is George Philip Krapp, *The English Language in America* (2 vols., 1925), less witty than Mencken, but still highly readable. He is less inclined than Mencken to note novelties in the American language. But he, too, is at home in the history of our culture, and his vision is sometimes broader than Mencken's. An indispensable reference work is Mitford M. Mathews' prodigious *Dictionary of Americanisms on Historical Principles* (2 vols., 1951; one-volume edition, 1956) which should be on the desk of every serious student of American history, and which is now available in a moderately priced one-volume edition. Mathews' work, which aims to trace the history of all words or expressions originating in the United States, builds on Sir William A. Craigie and J. R. Hulbert, *Dictionary of American English on Historical Principles* (4 vols., 1938-44).

Two delightful, suggestive, and brief recent surveys, admirably suited for the non-specialist are Thomas Pyles, *Words and Ways of American English* (1952) and Albert Marckwardt, *American English* (1958). A stimulating application of a developmental approach to language is Donald J. Lloyd and Harry R. Warfel, *American English in its Cultural Setting* (1956), a college textbook.

Here too, anyone seriously interested must get into the periodical literature, especially into such journals as *American Speech*, *Dialect Notes*, and *Publications of the Modern Language Association*. Some of the best articles for the non-specialist have been written by Allen Walker Read: "The Spelling Bee: A Linguistic Institution of the American Folk," *P.M.L.A.*, LVI (1941), 495-512, "British Recognition of American Speech in the Eighteenth Century," *Dialect Notes*, VI (1928-39), 313-334, and "Dunglison's Glossary, 1829-1830," *Dialect Notes*, V (1918-1927), 422-32. Some other valuable articles of interest to the non-specialist are: Henry Alexander, "The Language of the Salem Witchcraft Trials," *American Speech*, III (1927-1928), 390-400; Frank E. Bryant, "On the Conservatism of Language in a New Country," *P.M.L.A.*, XXII (1907), 277-90; J. H. Combs, "Old, Early, and Elizabethan English in the Southern Mountains," *Dialect Notes*, IV (1913-1917), 283-97; "Colonial and Early Pioneer Words," *Dialect Notes*, IV, 375-385; A. R. Dunlap, " 'Vicious' Pronunciations in Eighteenth-Century English," *Am. Speech*, XV (1940), 364-67; C. H. Grandgent, "From Franklin to Lowell: A Century of New England Pronunciation," *P.M.L.A.*, XIV (1899), 207-39; Leon Howard, "A Historical Note on American English," *Am. Speech*, II (1926-1927), 497-99, and "Toward a Historical Aspect of American Speech Consciousness," *Am. Speech*, V (1929-1930), 301-5; George H. Mc-Knight, "Conservatism in American Speech," *Am. Speech*, I (1925-1926), 1-17; Albert Mathews, "The Term State-House," *Dialect Notes*, II (1900-1904), 199-224; Louise Pound, "Research in American English," *Am. Speech*, V (1929-1930), 359-65; Evan T. Sage, "Classical Place-Names in America," *Am. Speech*, IV (1928-1929), 261-71; Charles W. Townsend,

"Concerning Briticisms," *Am. Speech,* VII (1931-1932), 219-222; Harold Whitehall, "The Quality of the Front Reduction Vowel in Early American English," *Am. Speech,* XV (1940), 136-43, and "An Elusive Development of 'Short O' in Early American English," *Am. Speech,* XVI (1941), 192-203; William H. Whitmore, "Origin of the Names of Towns in Massachusetts," Mass. Hist. Soc., *Proc.,* XII (1871-1873), 393-419.

Monographs of particular interest include: Richard M. Dorson, *Jonathan Draws the Long Bow* (1946), on early New England folklore; Gordon V. Carey, *American into English: A Handbook for Translators* (London, 1953); Henry Cabot Lodge, "The Decline of Colonialism," in *Studies in History* (1884); Mitford M. Mathews, *Some Sources of Southernisms* (1948) and (ed.) *The Beginnings of American English: Essays and Comments* (1931); Anders Orbeck, *Early New England Pronunciation, as Reflected in Some Seventeenth Century Town Records of Eastern Massachusetts* (1927), which ingeniously uses the naive spellings of early scribes to help discover their pronunciation; Robert E. Spiller, *Fenimore Cooper, Critic of His Time* (1931); G. R. Stewart, *Names on the Land* (1945), a popular study of place-names; Richard H. Thornton, *An American Glossary* (3 vols., 1912-1939); Jacob H. Wild, *Glimpses of the American Language and Civilization* (Bern, Switzerland, 1945). See Carl Van Doren, *Benjamin Franklin* (1938), for Franklin's attitude toward style and for his efforts at spelling-reform.

In one sense, of course, every work written in America illustrates the history of the American language. Some of the writings which explicitly discuss the early condition of the language include: James Fenimore Cooper, "Home as Found," in *Com-plete Works* (N.Y., 1893, Vol. XIV) and *Notions of the Americans* (2 vols., 1828); Nicholas Cresswell, *Journal, 1774-1777* (reprinted, 1924); Jacob Duché, *Caspipina's Letters* (1774), sometimes known as *Observations; Journal and Letters of Philip Vickers Fithian,* 1773-1774 (ed. Hunter D. Farish, 1943); Benjamin Franklin, *Autobiography* (Modern Library ed., 1932); Bret Harte, "The Spelling Bee at Angels," in *Writings* (1910), XII, 183-188; Hugh Jones, *An Accidence to the English Tongue . . . Considering the True Manner of Reading, Writing and Talking Proper English* (London, 1724) and *The Present State of Virginia* (1724; ed. Richard L. Morton, 1956); James Kirke Paulding, "A Sketch of Old New England, by a New England Man," in Richard Phillips (ed.), *New Voyages and Travels* (9 vols., 1820-1823, Vol. VIII) and *The Bulls and Jonathans* (1867, reprinting two earlier works comparing Englishmen and Americans); John Pickering, *A Vocabulary . . . of Words and Phrases . . . Peculiar to the United States* (Boston, 1816); John Witherspoon, *Works* (2d ed., 4 vols., 1802), which includes the important *Druid* papers.

The comments of English and other travelers and essayists are of varying reliability on the actual state of the language, but they are expressed with an almost uniform dogmatism. Some of the more interesting of these which touch on the American language are: Samuel Taylor Coleridge, *Essays on His Own Times, forming a Second Series of The Friend* (3 vols., 1850); William Eddis, *Letters from America . . . from 1769 to 1777* (London, 1792); Basil Hall, *Travels in North America in . . . 1827 and 1828* (3 vols., Edinburgh, 1829); Alexis de Tocqueville, *Democracy in America* (2 vols., ed. Phillips Bradley, 1945).

The best introduction to Noah

Webster is his own introduction to his *American Dictionary of the English Language* (2 vols., N.Y., 1828); then one should read his *Dissertations on the English Language* (1789; facsimile with intro. by Harry R. Warfel, 1951). Other important works by Webster are: *A Grammatical Institute, of the English Language* (3 vols., Hartford, Conn., 1783-1785), the first part of which became his famous blueback speller; *Compendious Dictionary of the English Language* (1806), the earlier form of his more famous *American Dictionary*; *An American Selection of Lessons in Reading and Speaking* (Phila., 1807); and his *Letters* (ed. Harry R. Warfel, 1953). The best biographies are Harry R. Warfel, *Noah Webster, Schoolmaster to America* (1936) and Ervin C. Shoemaker, *Noah Webster, Pioneer of Learning* (1936).

An interesting analogy to American linguistic conservatism, and an opportunity to compare the problems in a field where difficulties of transportation were more important, is the story of the log-cabin in America. On the Atlantic seaboard, despite the greater cost and inferior durability of the clapboard house, the early settlers clung to the English-type dwellings. The story is delightfully told and copiously illustrated in Harold R. Shurtleff, *The Log Cabin Myth* (1939), which every student of the emergence of American (or other colonial) culture should read.

PART ELEVEN

CULTURE WITHOUT A CAPITAL

The student of the history of reading habits will soon discover how little we know about what people actually read in the past. Literary historians have devoted themselves mostly to chronicling what was *written,* or rather what has been *printed.* Intellectual historians tend to be preoccupied with the mere presence of a book in a certain place. Social historians have given some attention to the composition of libraries and to the books sold or bought. But what people actually read is a fact almost as private and inaccessible as what they thought. We do not have even an approximate record of the actual reading—as contrasted with the book-buying, or book-ownership—of any major figure in our past. We might be astonished at the meagreness of a full and accurate list of the reading, say of Washington. In a few instances—such as the Commonplace Books (edited by Gilbert Chinard, 1926, 1928) in which Jefferson transcribed passages and made notes of some of his reading for certain years; or John Adams' library marginalia (edited and interpreted by Zoltan Haraszti, under the title *John Adams and the Prophets of Progress,* 1952)—we have first-hand evidence of actual reading habits. Occasionally accidents and odd facts help us. For example, the fire which destroyed the collection of the Library Company of Providence, R. I., on Christmas Eve, 1758, but which left unharmed the Register Book and the books actually in the hands of borrowers, gives us a tantalizing glimpse of the pattern of library-circulation—although not necessarily of reading. See Jesse H. Shera, *Foundations of the Public Library* (1949), 117 ff.

Historians have tended to be satisfied with mere circumstantial evidence. But everyone knows from his personal experience that the purchase of a book is sometimes a substitute for the reading of it; we would all be flattered to think that the contents of our libraries had got into our heads. Many volumes from the 17th and 18th centuries survive with uncut pages or in mint condition. While seldom admitting it, we have been inclined to study the literary furnishings of past houses as if they were the furnishings of past minds. Partly because of the special difficulties of the subject, and partly because of the bias of our literary scholars, I, too, have in Part XI come at reading habits indirectly—mainly through the contents of libraries and the character of the book-trade.

The most important evidence of everyday reading habits sometimes is self-destroying. Hornbooks, primers, and newspapers tend to be used up, and the items best preserved (and hence often most prominent in scholars' lists) are often preserved because they were not much used.

For general social history, for urban life, and for the differences between different parts of the colonies, many of the most valuable items will be found in the bibliographical notes above, especially the General section, and Parts I-IV. For the paths from social history to the history of reading habits, the writings of Carl Bridenbaugh, Louis B. Wright, and Lawrence C. Wroth are especially valuable. All Bridenbaugh's works throw light on the context of the literary culture: for urban life in general his work is definitive; for the South, see his *Myths and Realities: Societies of the Colonial South*; for Philadelphia (with Jessica Bridenbaugh) his *Rebels and Gentlemen* (1942); and see his "The Press and Book in Eighteenth Century Philadelphia," *Penn. Mag. Hist. & Biog.*, LXV (1941), 1-30. Wright's *First Gentlemen of Virginia: Intellectual Qualities of the Early Colonial Ruling Class* (1940) is indispensable for its wealth of detail and its judicious generalizations; see also his important article, "The Purposeful Reading of Our Colonial Ancestors," *ELH: A Journal of English Literary History*,

IV (1937), 85-111, "The Classical Tradition in Colonial Virginia," Bibliographical Society of America, *Papers*, XXXIII (1939), 85-97, and "The 'Gentleman's Library' in Early Virginia," *Huntington Lib. Q.*, I (1937-1938), 3-61. Lawrence C. Wroth, *An American Bookshelf, 1755* (1934), is an urbane, ingenious, and scholarly reconstruction of the "typical" library of a hypothetical mid-18th-century gentleman, and Thomas G. Wright, *Literary Culture in Early New England, 1620-1730* (1920), is the most thorough monograph for any region. See also the relevant parts of several of Frederick B. Tolles' books (Part II, above), and Frederick P. Bowes, *The Culture of Early Charleston* (1942). For minutiae of books in Virginia see the writings of Philip A. Bruce (Part IV, above).

On colonial libraries, especially valuable are: George M. Abbott, *A Short History of the Library Company of Philadelphia* (1913); Clarence S. Brigham, "Harvard College Library Duplicates, 1682," Col. Soc. Mass., *Pub.*, XVIII (Trans. 1915-1916), 407-17; Austin K. Gray, *Benjamin Franklin's Library* (1936); J. Katherine Jackson, *Outlines of the Literary History of Colonial Pennsylvania* (1906); E. V. Lamberton, "Colonial Libraries of Philadelphia," *Penn. Mag. Hist. & Biog.*, XLII (1918), 193-234; Samuel Eliot Morison's volumes on Harvard College describe its library (see Part I, above); James W. Phillips, "The Sources of the Original Dickinson College Library," *Penn. History*, XIV (1947), 108-117; A. S. W. Rosenbach, *Early American Children's Books* (1933); Jesse H. Shera, *Foundations of the Public Library: The Origins of the Public Library Movement in New England, 1629-1855* (1949); Louis Shores, *Origins of the American College Library, 1638-1800* (1934); William Sloane, *Children's Books in England and America in the Seventeenth Century: A History and Checklist* (1955); George K. Smart, "Private Libraries in Colonial Virginia," *American Literature*, X (1938-39), 24-52, a particularly helpful interpretation with many useful statistics; E. Millicent Sowerby (ed.), *Catalog of the Library of Thomas Jefferson* (1952——); Mary Mann Page Stanard, *Colonial Virginia, Its People and Customs* (1917); Frederick B. Tolles, "A Literary Quaker: John Smith of Burlington and Philadelphia," *Penn. Mag. Hist. & Biog.*, LXV (1941), 300-333; Andrew W. Tuer, *History of the Horn Book* (2 vols., 1896); Carl Van Doren, *Benjamin Franklin* (1938) for Franklin's library-founding activities; Stephen B. Weeks, "Libraries and Literature in North Carolina in the Eighteenth Century," Am. Hist. Assn., *Ann. Report* (1895), 171-267; J. T. Wheeler, "Reading Interests in Colonial Maryland," *Md. Hist. Mag.*, XXXVI (1941), 281-2, XXXVII (1942), 26-7, 291, XXXVIII (1943), 37-8, 167-8, 273-4; Lawrence C. Wroth, *The First Century of the John Carter Brown Library* (1946); and *A Catalogue of Books Belonging to the Library Company of Philadelphia: A Facsimile of the Edition of 1741 Printed by Benjamin Franklin* (1956; intro. by Edwin Wolf 2nd).

For the history of colonial book-buying and book-selling we have two admirable works of general interest: Frank Luther Mott, *Golden Multitudes: The Story of Best Sellers in the United States* (1947) and James D. Hart, *The Popular Book: A History of America's Literary Taste* (1950). Useful specialized studies include: Henry W. Boynton, *Annals of American Bookselling, 1636-1850* (1932); Carl L. Cannon, *American Book Collectors and Collecting From Colonial Times to the Present* (1941); Paul L. Ford (ed.), *The New-England Primer; a History of its Origin and Development; with a reprint of the Unique copy of the Earliest Known Edition* (1897); Worthington C. Ford, *The Boston Book Market, 1679-1700* (1917); Howard Mumford Jones, "The Importation of French Books in Philadelphia, 1750-1800," *Modern Philology*, XXXII (1934-1935), 157-177 with much valuable detail, and *America and French Culture, 1750-1848* (1927); Michael Kraus, *Intercolonial Aspects of American Culture* (1928); George E. Littlefield, *Early Boston Booksellers 1642-1711* (1900) and *Early Schools and School-Books of New England* (1904); George L. McKay, *American Book Auction Catalogues, 1713-1934; A Union List* (1937) and "Early American Book Auctions," *Colophon* (1939), pp. 71-78.

Contemporary items of special interest include: *Bibliotheca Americana; or A Chronological Catalogue of the most curious and interesting books, pamphlets, state papers, etc. upon the subject of North and South America, from the earliest period to the Present, in Print and Manuscript* (London, 1789), sometimes listed as by Arthur or Henry Homer, but for another view of the authorship, see S. C. Sherman, "L. T. Rede," *Wm. & Mary Q.*, 3d Series, IV (1947), 340; Jacob Duché, *Caspipina's Letters or Observations* (Phila., 1774); John Dunton, *Letters from New England, 1686*, in Prince Soc., *Pub.*, IV (1867), and see Chester N. Greenough, "John Dunton's Letters from New England," Col. Soc. Mass., *Pub.*, XIV (Trans. 1911-13), 213-57 and "John Dunton Again," XXI (Trans., 1919), 232-51; Timothy Dwight, *Travels in New England and New York* (4 vols., New

Haven, Conn., 1821-22); Benjamin Franklin, *Writings,* ed. Albert H. Smyth (10 vols., 1907), and *Autobiography* (Modern Lib. ed., 1932); Sarah (Kemble) Knight, *The Journal of Madam Knight* (1704; reprinted, 1935); *John Norton and Sons, Merchants of London and Virginia . . . Papers from their Counting House . . . 1750 to 1795* (ed. Frances N. Mason, 1937).

PART TWELVE

A CONSERVATIVE PRESS

The tendency to deal with the history of the printed word in America in the categories of European belles-lettres (lyric poem, epic, essay, etc.) has been misleading and has made difficult the discovery of some obvious features of our culture. It is in our special ways of using the printing press more than in our ways of producing works in the traditional European literary genres that characteristics of American civilization are revealed.

For the history of printing in the colonial years, the leading work is Lawrence C. Wroth, *The Colonial Printer* (1938), which includes many helpful illustrations. Other works by Wroth also lead from the details of printing into the largest questions of social history: *Typographic Heritage, Selected Essays* (1949) on the background of American typography, typefounding, and book-design; *A History of Printing in Colonial Maryland, 1686-1776* (1922), the best regional monograph for this period, valuable for its copious details concerning the publication of statutes and for its light on the relation of the "Publick Printer" to the newspaper and to the postal services; and *William Parks, Printer and Journalist of England and*

Colonial America (1926). A valuable modern survey which includes the colonial period is Douglas C. McMurtrie, *The History of Printing in the United States* (1929).

Through the life and works of Isaiah Thomas (1749-1831), a printer of Worcester, Mass., who has never been given the prominence he deserves in our history, we can glimpse the versatility of many American printers; their fame has been overshadowed by that of Benjamin Franklin, who was only the most famous of numerous printer-statesmen. If for no other reason, Thomas should be known as a historian. His readable *History of Printing in America with a Biography of Printers, and an Account of Newspapers* (2 vols., 1810; 2d ed., Am. Antiq. Soc., *Trans.,* V-VI, 1874), is one of the earliest and most satisfactory works of American social and cultural history. But Thomas was also an editor, publisher, and pamphleteer. In his day he was widely known for almanacs, hymnals, Bibles, and magazines, and for his violently pro-Revolutionary newspaper, *Massachusetts Spy,* which carried the motto "Open to all Parties, but Influenced by None" (1770-1904, Boston and Worcester). He founded the American Antiquarian Society in 1812. Thomas deserves a full-length biography to bring to life the long and active career of a self-educated boy who became one of the nation's leading shapers of opinion. For an amplification of his history, see "William McCulloch's Additions to Thomas's History of Printing," Am. Antiq. Soc., *Proc.,* N.S., XXXI (1921), 89-247.

Other valuable items for special topics in the history of printing include: W. H. Allnutt, "English Provincial Presses," *Bibliographica, Papers on Books, Their History and Art,* II, 23-46, 150-80, 276-308, and

III, 481-3; Arthur B. Berthold, "American Colonial Printing as Determined by Contemporary Cultural Forces, 1693-1763" (unpublished M.A. thesis, University of Chicago, 1934); Earl L. Bradsher, *Mathew Carey, Editor, Author and Publisher: A Study in American Literary Development* (1912); Paul L. Ford (ed.) *The New England Primer* (1897); Worthington C. Ford, "Broadsides, Ballads, Etc. Printed in Massachusetts, 1639-1800," Mass. Hist. Soc., *Coll.*, LXXV (1922) and "The Isaiah Thomas Collection of Ballads," Am. Antiq. Soc., *Proc.*, N.S., XXXIII (1923), 34-112; Zoltan Haraszti, *The Enigma of the Bay Psalm Book* (1956; companion volume to a facsimile reprint of the *Bay Psalm Book*, University of Chicago Press, 1956); Charles S. R. Hildeburn, *A Century of Printing, The Issues of the Press in Pennsylvania, 1685-1784* (2 vols., 1885) and *Sketches of Printers and Printing in Colonial New York* (1895); Eldon R. James, "A List of Legal Treatises Printed in the British Colonies and the American States before 1801," in *Harvard Legal Essays* (1934); Helmut Lehmann-Haupt, *The Book in America* (2d ed., 1951), including a valuable brief survey of the early period by Lawrence C. Wroth, and *Bookbinding in America* (1941); William E. Lingelbach, "B. Franklin, Printer —New Source Materials," Am. Philos. Soc., *Proc.*, XCII (1948), 79-100; George E. Littlefield, *The Early Massachusetts Press, 1638-1711* (2 vols., 1907); Douglas C. McMurtrie, *Beginnings of Printing in Virginia* (1935) and "The Beginnings of Printing in New Hampshire," *The Library*, 4th Ser., XV (1935), 340-63; James Bennett Nolan, *Printer Strahan's Book Account: A Colonial Controversy* (1939); John C. Oswald, *Benjamin Franklin, Printer* (1917); Robert A. Peddie, *Printing: A Short History of the Art* (1927), including an excellent brief survey of American printing by Lawrence C. Wroth; John H. Powell, *Books of a New Nation: U. S. Government Publications, 1774-1814* (1957); Robert Roden, *The Cambridge Press, 1638-1692* (1905); A. S. Salley, Jr., "The First Presses of South Carolina," Bibl. Soc. Am., *Proc.*, II (1907-08), 28-69; Margaret B. Stillwell, *Incunabula and Americana, 1450-1800: A Key to Bibliographical Study* (1931); Lyman H. Weeks, *A History of Paper-Manufacturing in the United States, 1640-1916* (1916); Stephen B. Weeks, *The Press of North Carolina in the Eighteenth Century* (1891); George P. Winship, *The Cambridge Press, 1638-1692* (1945); John T. Winterich, *Early American Books & Printing* (1935); Richardson L. Wright, *Hawkers and Walkers in Early America* (1927). The writings of Franklin contain many valuable items: a guide to the relevant passages is Carl Van Doren, *Benjamin Franklin* (1938); see also, "Letters from James Parker to Benjamin Franklin," Mass. Hist. Soc., *Proc.*, 2d Series, XVI (1902), 186-232. An important early survey which includes printing, among other aspects of American culture, is Samuel Miller, *A Brief Retrospect of the Eighteenth Century* (N.Y., 1803).

For an introduction to the history of American newspapers and magazines, we are fortunate to have the up-to-date, readable, and reliable books by Frank Luther Mott: his *American Journalism . . . 1690-1940* (1941) is less detailed than his monumental *History of American Magazines* (4 vols., 1930-57) which covers the early period in Vol. I; both these works should be on the shelves of any serious student of American civilization. A basic tool for the early period is Clarence S. Brigham, *History and Bibliography of American News-*

papers, 1690-1820 (2 vols., 1947); see also his suggestive *Journals and Journeymen: A Contribution to the History of Early American Newspapers* (1950). A pioneer monograph, full of fascinating detail on the development of the American newspaper and its relation to politics is Arthur M. Schlesinger, *Prelude to Independence: The Newspaper War on Britain, 1764-1776* (1958), which came to my attention only after my chapters had gone to press.

For other aspects of the early history of American newspapers and magazines, see: Willard G. Bleyer, *Main Currents in the History of American Journalism* (1927); Hennig Cohen, *The South Carolina Gazette, 1732-1775* (1953); Bernard Fay, *L'Esprit Revolutionnaire en France et Aux États-Unis à la Fin du XVIIIe Siècle* (1925) and *Notes on the American Press at the End of the Eighteenth Century* (1927); Sidney Kobre, *The Development of the Colonial Newspaper* (1944); James R. Sutherland, "The Circulation of Newspapers and Literary Periodicals, 1700-30," *The Library*, 4th Ser., XV (1935), 110-124; Reuben G. Thwaites, *The Ohio Valley Press Before the War of 1812-15* (1909); *Virginia Gazette* (see Part IV, above); J. B. Williams, "The Beginnings of English Journalism," in *Camb. Hist. Eng. Lit.* Vol. VII (1932), and *A History of English Journalism to the Foundation of the Gazette* (1908).

The best introduction to the almanacs is George Lyman Kittredge, *The Old Farmer and His Almanack* (1904), although he deals mostly with a later period. The almanacs themselves are now quite rare, but the American Antiquarian Society at Worcester, Mass. possesses an excellent collection; photostats of those for 1647-1700 are in The Newberry Library, Chicago. See also Charles L. Nichols,

"Notes on the Almanacs of Massachusetts," Am. Antiq. Soc., *Proc.,* N.S., XXII (1912), 15-134, and Chester N. Greenough, "New England Almanacs, 1776-1775, and the American Revolution," *ibid.*, XLV (1935), 288-316.

On the little-understood subject of the freedom of the press, for which we still need a good general history, see: Zechariah Chafee, Jr., *Free Speech in the United States* (1941), the leading work in its area, but emphasizing legal aspects; Clyde A. Duniway, *The Development of Freedom of the Press in Massachusetts* (1906); Giles J. Patterson, *Free Speech and a Free Press* (1939); and Livingston R. Schuyler, *Liberty of the Press in the American Colonies before the Revolutionary War with Particular Reference to . . . New York* (1905); *The Trial of John Peter Zenger* (1752; 1765 ed., reprinted Cal. State Library, 1940).

The best work on the early history of the post office is Wesley E. Rich, *The History of the United States Post Office to the Year 1829* (1924). See also Ruth L. Butler, *Doctor Franklin, Postmaster General* (1928); Victor H. Paltsits, "John Holt, Printer and Postmaster . . . ," N.Y. Pub. Lib., *Bull.,* XXIV (1920), 483-99; William Smith, "The Colonial Post-Office," *Am. Hist. Rev.*, XXI (1915-16), 258-75.

BOOK FOUR

WARFARE AND DIPLOMACY

PART THIRTEEN

A NATION OF MINUTE MEN

Much of the writing of our military history has centered on battles and other dramatic episodes, and on the lives of military commanders. Although our military institutions and our attitudes toward war have been decisively shaped in times of peace, relatively little has been done to describe these developments. We have no general military history of the colonial wars, but a great deal has been written about the Revolution itself.

The best recent history of the relation between our military ways and our civilization as a whole is Walter Millis' brilliant *Arms and Men: A Study of American Military History* (1956), which begins with the colonial period and is an admirable book for the non-specialist. Other useful works of a general nature are: Arthur A. Ekirch, Jr., *The Civilian and the Military: A History of the American Antimilitarist Tradition* (1956); Samuel P. Huntington, *The Soldier and the State: The Theory and Politics of Civil-Military Relations* (1957); John U. Nef, *War and Human Progress* (1950); Robert Osgood, *Limited War* (1957); Lynn Montross, *War Through the Ages* (1944), a popular survey; and Quincy Wright's monumental *Study of War* (2 vols., 1942).

One of the best places to savor the military experience of the colonial era and to see some of its wider significance for American life is in the vivid pages of Francis Parkman, *France and England in North America* (9 vols., 1865-92) supplemented by *The Conspiracy of Pontiac* (2 vols., 1851), where the military conflict between the British and French becomes the connecting thread of a broad, spectacular narrative. Another dramatic introduction to the colonial wars is found in Douglas Freeman's brilliant chapters on Washington's activities as aide to General Braddock, on the defeat at the Battle of the Monongahela (July, 1755) and the aftermath for Washington's military career; see his *George Washington*, Vol. II (1948), chs. i-xv.

The most important special studies of colonial warfare are the readable and definitive works by Stanley Pargellis, *Lord Loudoun in North America* (1933), *Military Affairs in North America, 1748-1765: Selected Documents from the Cumberland Papers in Windsor Castle* (1936), and "The Four Independent Companies of New York," in *Essays in Colonial History* (1931); these are models of their kind. Other valuable items touching colonial military life are: Arthur A. Buffinton, "The Puritan View of War," Col. Soc. Mass., *Pub.,* XXVIII (Trans. 1930-33), 67-86; David Cole, *An Outline of British Military History, 1660-1936* (1936); John W. Fortescue, *A History of the British Army* (13 vols., 1899-1930) and *The County Lieutenancies and the Army, 1803-1814* (1909); John Hope Franklin, *The Militant South, 1800-1861* (1956), esp. ch. 1; Wilbur R. Jacobs, *Diplomacy and Indian Gifts: Anglo-French Rivalry along the Ohio and Northwest Frontiers, 1748-1763* (1950); Douglas E. Leach, *Flintlock and Tomahawk: New England in King Philip's War* (1958), and "The Military System of Plymouth Colony," *N.E.Q.,* XXIV (1951), 342-64, an especially valuable article; William C. MacLeod, *The American Indian Frontier* (1928); Samuel E. Morison, "Harvard in the Colonial Wars, 1675-1743," *Harvard Graduates' Mag.* XXVI (1917-18), 554-74; Louis Morton, "The End of Formalized Warfare," *Am. Heritage,* VI (1955), 12-19, 95; R. W. G. Vail, *The Voice of the Old Frontier* (1949), a full bibliography of frontier literature; and Wilcomb E. Washburn, *The Governor and the Rebel: A History of Bacon's*

Rebellion in Virginia (1957), an important new interpretation.

On the history of weapons in colonial America there is a considerable literature, though much of it is antiquarian or designed for the gun-collector. The development of the American rifle is an especially suggestive topic on which much of the best writing has been done. The most useful works of general interest are Harold L. Peterson, *Arms and Armor in Colonial America: 1526-1783* (1956), copiously illustrated, reliable, and up-to-date in its scholarship, and Capt. John G. W. Dillin, *The Kentucky Rifle: A Study of the origin and development of a purely American type of firearm* (1924), with many valuable details, but imperfectly documented; and Roger Burlingame, *March of the Iron Men* (1938), which places the history of firearms in the context of social history. Other valuable items are: Ezekiel Baker, *Remarks on Rifle Guns . . .* (11th ed., London, 1835); W. Y. Carmen, *A History of Firearms from Earliest Times to 1914* (1955); Carl W. Drepperd, *Pioneer America, Its First Three Centuries* (1949), valuable for its history of folk-technology; Charles Ffoulkes, *Arms and Armament: An Historical Survey of the British Army* (1945); William W. Greener, *The Gun and its Development* (1885); George Hanger, *To All Sportsmen, and Particularly to Farmers, and Gamekeepers* (London, 1814); H. J. Kauffman, *Early American Gunsmiths, 1650-1850* (1942); Horace Kephart, "The Rifle in Colonial Times," *Mag. of Am. Hist.*, XXIV (1890), 179-191, an extremely suggestive article; Felix Reichmann, "The Pennsylvania Rifle: A Social Interpretation of Changing Military Techniques," *Penn. Mag. Hist. & Biog.*, LXIX (1945), 3-14; Q. D. Satterlee and Arcadi Gluckman,

American Gun Makers (1940); Charles W. Sawyer, *Firearms in American History: 1600 to 1800* (1910) and *Our Rifles* (1946); Philip B. Sharpe, *The Rifle in America* (1938); E. C. Wilford, *Three Lectures upon the Rifle* (2d ed., London, 1860), an apology for the late (1857) introduction of the (Enfield, Whitworth) rifle as the standard infantry weapon of the British army; Major Townsend Whelen, *The American Rifle* (1918); John W. Wright, "The Rifle in the American Revolution," *Am. Hist. Rev.*, XXIV (1924), 293-99.

The military history of the American Revolution has recently been the subject of many volumes which should appeal to the general reader. Two compact, up-to-date works giving the context for the military events are: John R. Alden, *The American Revolution, 1775-1783* (1954) and Edmund S. Morgan, *The Birth of the Republic, 1763-89* (1956). The best brief treatments of the military history are Howard H. Peckham, *The War for Independence, A Military History* (1958) and Willard M. Wallace, *Appeal to Arms* (1951). More detailed narratives attractive to the non-specialist include: Lynn Montross, *The Reluctant Rebels: The Story of the Continental Congress, 1774-1789* (1950) and *Rag, Tag and Bobtail: The Story of the Continental Army, 1775-1783* (1952); and George F. Sheer and Hugh F. Rankin (eds.), *Rebels and Redcoats* (1957), a discriminating selection of eyewitness accounts and other original records, with lively introductions.

A still more detailed account, for the armchair strategist or specialist in military history, is Christopher Ward, *The War of the Revolution* (ed. John R. Alden, 2 vols., 1952). Eric Robson's *The American Revolution in its Political and Military Aspects: 1763-*

1783 (1955) is a strikingly original study, suggesting intriguing connections between military and non-military affairs. On the problems of the revolutionary army, Louis C. Hatch, *The Administration of the American Revolutionary Army* (1904) is still basic.

Of the vast literature on the Revolution in general, the following are especially relevant to Part XIII: Thomas P. Abernethy, *Western Lands and the American Revolution* (1937); John R. Alden, *The South in the Revolution, 1763-1789* (1957) and *General Gage in America* (1948); Keith B. Berwick, "Prudence and Patriotism: The Backgrounds of Allegiance in Revolutionary Virginia" (unpublished M.A. thesis, University of Chicago, 1957); Charles K. Bolton, *The Private Soldier Under Washington* (1902); Robert E. Brown, *Middle-Class Democracy and the Revolution in Massachusetts, 1691-1780* (1955); Edmund C. Burnett, *The Continental Congress* (1941); Edward E. Curtis, *The Organization of the British Army in the American Revolution* (1926); Philip Davidson, *Propaganda and the American Revolution, 1763-1783* (1941); Wallace E. Davies, "The Society of the Cincinnati in New England, 1783-1800," *Wm. & Mary Q.*, 3rd Ser., V (1948), 3-25; Elisha P. Douglass, *Rebels and Democrats: The Struggle for Equal Rights and Majority Rule During the American Revolution* (1955); Louis C. Duncan, *Medical Men in the American Revolution, 1775-1783* (1931); Max von Eelking, *The German Allied Troops in the North American War of Independence, 1776-1783* (1893); John C. Fitzpatrick, *The Spirit of the Revolution* (1924), including some valuable essays on the common soldier and other military topics; Evarts B. Greene, *The Revolutionary Genera-tion* ("History of American Life" series, 1943) and "Some Educational Values of the American Revolution," *Am. Philos. Soc., Proc.,* LXVIII (1929), 185-194; Freeman H. Hart, *The Valley of Virginia in the American Revolution, 1763-1789* (1942); Brooke Hindle, "American Culture and the Migrations of the Revolutionary Era," in *"John and Mary's College"* (1956); J. Franklin Jameson, *The American Revolution Considered as a Social Movement* (1925; reprinted, 1956); Merrill Jensen, *The Articles of Confederation* (1948) and *The New Nation, 1781-1789* (1950); Edward McCrady, *The History of South Carolina in the Revolution, 1775-1780* (1901) and *. . . 1780-1783* (1902); Richard B. Morris (ed.), *The Era of the American Revolution* (1939); David Schenck, *North Carolina, 1780-81* (1889); Arthur M. Schlesinger, *The Colonial Merchants and the American Revolution, 1763-1776* (1917; reprinted, 1957); Frederick C. Stoll, "George Washington and the Society of the Cincinnati" (unpublished M.A. thesis, Dept. of History, University of Chicago, 1949); William W. Sweet, "The Role of the Anglicans in the American Revolution," *Hunt. Lib. Q.,* XI (1947-48), 51-70; Clarence L. Ver Steeg, "The American Revolution considered as an Economic Movement," *Hunt. Lib. Q.,* XX (1957), 361-372, and *Robert Morris: Revolutionary Financier* (1954); Winslow Warren, *The Society of the Cincinnati: A History* (1929); and William B. Willcox, "British Strategy in America, 1778," *Journal of Mod. Hist.,* XIX (1947), 97-121.

Many of the most valuable contemporary records are to be found in the collected writings of Franklin, Washington, Jefferson, Adams, and other military and political leaders of the age (mentioned in various notes above). Of special interest for their relevance to the topics of Part XIII are: *Warren-Adams Letters . . . a correspondence among John Adams, Samuel Adams, and James Warren,* Mass. Hist. Soc., *Coll.,* LXXII (1917) and LXXIII (1925); *Familiar Letters of John Adams and his Wife Abigail Adams during the Revolution* (ed. Charles F. Adams, 1875); Charles M. Andrews (ed.), *Narratives of the Insurrections, 1675-1690* ("Original Narratives" series, 1915); E. C. Burnett (ed.), *Letters of Members of the Continental Congress* (8 vols., 1921-38); Sir Henry Clinton, *The American Rebellion* (ed. William B. Willcox, 1954), the British commander-in-chief's own narrative of his campaigns, 1775-1782; Cadwallader Colden, *The History of the Five Indian Nations of Canada* (reprinted, 2 vols., 1902), for a colonial view of Indian warfare; Hector St. John de Crèvecoeur, *Letters from an American Farmer* (Everyman Lib., 1940), with many incidental comments on colonial warfare; Daniel Defoe, "An Essay upon Projects" (1697), in Henry Morley (ed.), *Earlier Life and the Chief Earlier Works of Daniel Defoe* (1889), for a cogent characterization of the European style of warfare at the end of the 17th century; Joseph Doddridge, *Notes on the Settlement and Indian Wars of the Western Parts of Virginia and Pennsylvania,* in Samuel Kercheval, *A History of the Valley of Virginia* (Winchester, Va., 1833; and later eds.); Timothy Dwight, *Travels in New England and New York* (4 vols., 1821-22);

Memoirs of the Life and Character of Rev. John Eliot, Apostle of the North American Indians (ed. Martin Moore, Boston, 1822), for some of the problems of praying with (and fighting against) the Indians in early New England; William Gordon, *History of the . . . Establishment of the Independence of the United States* (4 vols., London, 1788); William Hubbard, *A Narrative of the Indian Wars in New-England from . . . 1607, to the Year 1677* (Boston, 1677; reprinted, 1801); J. Franklin Jameson (ed.), *Narratives of New Netherlands, 1609-1664* ("Original Narratives" series: 1909); Hugh Jones, *Present State of Virginia* (1724), for valuable sidelights on the military as well as other institutions; *Diary of Frederick Mackenzie: Giving a Daily Narrative of his Military Service as an Officer of the Regiment of Royal Welch Fusiliers During the Years 1775-1781 in Massachusetts, Rhode Island, and New York* (2 vols., 1930); Cotton Mather, *Magnalia Christi Americana* (2 vols., 1702; reprinted, 1853), esp. Vol. II, Bk. VII, "The Wars of the Lord"; Dr. David Ramsay, *The History of the American Revolution* (2 vols., Phila., 1789) and *The History of South Carolina from . . . 1670 to 1808* (2 vols., 1809); James Thacher, *A Military Journal During the American Revolutionary War, from 1775 to 1783* (Boston, 1823); Mercy (Otis) Warren, *History of the Rise, Progress, and Termination of the American Revolution* (3 vols., Boston, 1805), one of the few important contemporary histories of the Revolution.

INDEX